MANAGING
EMOTIONS
IN THE
WORKPLACE

WITHDRAWN

Neal M. Ashkanasy
Wilfred J. Zerbe
Charmine E.J. Härtel
Editors

M.E. Sharpe
Armonk, New York
London, England

Library of Congress Cataloging-in-Publication Data

Managing emotions in the workplace / Neal M. Ashkanasy, Wilfred J. Zerbe, and
Charmine E.J. Härtel, editors.
    p. cm.
    With the exception of 2 chapters, the book is a selection of the best papers from the
2000 conference—Preface.
    Includes bibliographical references and index.
    ISBN 0-7656-0937-1 (alk. paper) — ISBN 0-7656-0938-X (pbk: alk. paper)
    1. Work—Psychological aspects—Congresses. 2. Emotions—Social aspects—
Congresses. I. Ashkanasy, Neal M., 1945– II. Zerbe, W.J. III. Härtel, Charmine E.J.,
1959–

HF5548.8.M359 2002
158.7—dc21   2001057686

Printed in the United States of America

The paper used in this publication meets the minimum requirements of
American National Standard for Information Sciences
Permanence of Paper for Printed Library Materials,
ANSI Z 39.48-1984.

∞

BM (c) 10 9 8 7 6 5 4 3 2 1
BM (p) 10 9 8 7 6 5 4 3 2 1

CONTENTS

LIST OF FIGURES AND TABLES

Figures

Tables

FOREWORD

Anat Rafaeli

When I started teaching organizational behavior classes, I had a bitter
sense that I was disappointing my students. I was loyal to my training
and taught what the main textbooks and journals in the field lauded as
"the latest findings." But in talking to students I found that they expected organizational behavior classes—the one class in their business
education that presumably will talk about *people* rather than numbers or
products—to *really* talk about what is different about and important to
people. To help them understand and relate to people in organizations.
To talk about the life in and of organizations. And it didn't. Students
could easily complete a comprehensive organizational behavior class
without talking about smiles and whether they mean happiness, anger
and how it relates to frustration, and influence and how it relates to leaders' or followers' feelings. This experience has dramatically shaped my
own research, although it has not made teaching any easier.

Talking and teaching about emotions of employees, emotions of managers, emotions of customers, and emotions of the organization as a
whole is messy and confusing, especially since until quite recently we
were completely lacking any scientific discourse of such issues. So for
many years our teaching and writing focused on concepts, models, and
variables that could be defined, measured, and correlated. We were like
the person looking for a lost key under the lamppost because that is
where there is enough light to see clearly. We could not accurately
describe—to ourselves, not to mention our students—what happens when
emotions are considered, so we either did not talk about them at all in
our classes, or we informed students that introducing emotional considerations into managerial contexts is wrong. One of the underlying

messages of this book is that it is not clear which of these two alternatives is worse. We cannot and should not completely ignore emotion, but we also cannot say that emotion is irrelevent to what happens in organization.

The bottom line is that people *are* emotions. Thus their behaviors, thoughts, and actions are inevitably wound up with what they feel. So one key thing that people bring to organizations is emotion. We now know that if we really claim to be studying people, then we must recognize that emotions are also a critical factor. And we must develop a deeper understanding of the role and interplay between emotion and organization. What the editors and authors of this volume do, and what many of them have been doing for several years now, is precisely that. They bring us ideas, theories, and findings about emotion in organizations. They help us talk about emotion in organizations. And in so doing they bring us a tad closer to being able to bring people, real people, and the emotions with which they are imbued, into our understanding of organizations and how they operate. This is a commendable accomplishment.

Of course, we are not there yet. We still don't know precisely how to conceptualize, measure, or predict employees' emotion, or precisely what impact various emotions may have on other organizational processes. What does this mean for the practice and research of organizational behavior? That there is still a long way to go. But then that should not be that surprising—as Einstein said long ago, "If we knew precisely what we were doing, it would not be called research."

We frequently see William James cited as posing the question of "What is an emotion?" The answer is yet to be found, especially when it comes to *organizational emotion:* Organizational? Or emotional? How do the two *really* go together? Am I a feeling person or am I an organizational actor? I venture to say that it is precisely the link between the individual emotion and the collective organization that makes up both who we are as individuals and what qualifies as "an organization," be it IBM, Phillips, or Insead. I have long had a sense that what makes up people's membership in an organization is inherently emotional—membership and organization cannot be aptly captured in any other way. Emotion is, if you will, the "organizational glue," that which pulls together the different people comprising an organization, be they employees, managers, customers, or consultants. Those who feel a belongingness coalesce into what is construed as an organization. This only serves to complicate things, because now it is not clear whose emotion we should be studying.

But such complication is useful because it is crucial to realize that we are still at the very beginning. Managing emotions in workplace settings . . . this is the title of this volume, but can we really manage emotions? Do we want to manage other people's emotions? Everyone's emotions? Will it still be emotion once it is managed? Is that ethical? These are moral, philosophical, as well as practical debates. Many who see this volume will raise these and similar dilemmas. And they are right. Some may choose to therefore dismiss some of the ideas presented. They should be reminded of the alternative—of completely ignoring the fact that there are emotions in the workplace, simply because there are difficulties and inaccuracies in studying them, discussing them, teaching them. Can we really get away with such escapism?

I hope that this volume allows us to bring emotion back into our teaching, writing, and conversing about organizations. And I hope that readers (of one chapter, or of the whole book), students, or faculty, junior or senior, will see in the chapters not only dry reports of academic research, but rather an inspiration to embrace organizations as contexts in which emotion is alive and very much influential, for better or worse. Let us not hide this from our students any longer, and let us allow the chapters of this volume to inform ourselves and our students a bit about how organizations *do* emotions and how emotions *do* organizations.

Dealing with emotions *is* messy and confusing, but that does not mean we can or should ignore them because people don't check their emotions at the door of their organization. This is precisely what the chapters of this book tell us—that when time cards are punched, emotions remain active players. Emotion is there at times of change such as mergers or downsizing, in interpersonal activities and in teamwork, and in decision making and in leadership. The chapters bring up theoretical issues that may not be helpful to undergraduate or even MBA students. To this I can humbly cite Mark Twain, who said, "To be good is noble, but to teach others how to be good is nobler—and less trouble." Assuming research is a form of teaching, many if not most of us know that it is really less trouble to teach and write about emotion than to practice what we preach. But the efforts invested by the authors of this book will help the world of management recognize that emotions *are* an inherent part of the everyday life of organizations. Emotion is what sets people and organizations in motion. So let's give it the attention it deserves.

PREFACE

Neal M. Ashkanasy, Wilfred J. Zerbe, and Charmine E.J. Härtel

Managing Emotions in the Workplace is the second book produced under the auspices of the Emonet group. Established in January 1997, the Emonet e-mail discussion list now serves more than 300 scholars and practitioners from around the world who are interested in emotions in organizational settings. Establishment of the list followed a symposium on this topic organized by Ashkanasy, and conducted at the 1996 Academy of Management meeting in Cincinnati. Subsequent activities at the annual meetings of the Academy of Management have included "caucuses" conducted in 1997, 1999, and 2001.

More significant in respect of this book, however, has been the biannual conferences organized through the Emonet group. These conferences, titled *Emotions and Organizational Life,* and chaired by the editors of this book, have been held to date in North America: San Diego, August 1998; and Toronto, August 2000. Future conferences are scheduled for July 2002 in Australia, and 2004 in Europe. The networks formed and the information disseminated at these conferences have proved to be important catalysts for cross-cultural research collaborations and rapid and strategic development of the literature on emotions in organizational life.

With the exception of Chapters 7 and 11, the substantive chapters in this book represent a selection of the best papers from the 2000 conference that were suitable for inclusion in a book on the subject of *managing* emotions. In this respect, we acknowledge the contributions of administrative assistants Carl Sinclair and Donovan Lawrence, and of conference local organizer Ian Sakinofski. Also, we would like to express our deep appreciation to the thirty-two conference paper reviewers who returned excellent and constructive reviews of the thirty-seven papers that were submitted to the conference:

Blake Ashforth	Suzy Fox	Stefan Meisiek
Sigal Barsade	Jill Francis	Michael O'Shea
John Basch	Theresa Glomb	Marjukka Ollilainen
Maree Boyle	Alicia Grandey	Jan Patterson
Rob Briner	Bob Jones	Nora Reilly
Celeste Brotheridge	Peter Jordan	Anne Rosch
Ronda Callister	Veronika Kisfalvi	Angelo Soares
Yochi Cohen-Charash	Susan Kruml	Lea Waters
Lorna Doucet	Dianne Layden	Helen Williams-Lawson
CynD Fisher	Kristi Lewis	Julie Wolfram-Cox
Julie Fitness	Ross Mecham III	

This book is a further reflection of an upsurge in interest in the study of emotions by organizational scholars that began in the mid-1990s. It is one of a number of books on emotions in organizational settings that have appeared in press over the years since the establishment of the Emonet group in 1997. Also, this period has seen several special issues of major journals in our field dedicated to the topic of emotions in organizational settings, and edited by members of the Emonet group. These include the *Journal of Organizational Behavior* (ed. Ashkanasy and Cynthia Fisher; published in March 2000), *Organizational Behavior and Human Decision Processes* (ed. Art Brief and Howard Weiss, published in October 2001), *Motivation and Emotion* (ed. Howard Weiss; forthcoming, 2002), and *Human Resource Management Review* (ed. Suzy Fox and Paul Spector; forthcoming, 2002). While most of the books and scholarly journals to date have focused on the foundations, antecedents, and immediate effects of emotions in workplace settings, this book moves the emphasis one step further, to the *management* of emotions in organizations. As such, we believe that this book marks an exciting new watershed in this field.

The interest in the study of emotions in organizations is also reflected in the programs of major conferences in the United States and Europe. The annual meetings of the Academy of Management, the Society for

Industrial and Organizational Society in the United States, in particular, where papers on this topic were once a rarity, now feature multiple sessions on this topic that regularly attract great interest and are frequently organized by members of the Emonet group. We believe that the activities of the Emonet group have been instrumental in this rise in interest in the field. In particular, we express our gratitude to Emonet Webmasters Jacob Eisenberg and Marc Dasborough, who both played a central role in helping us promulgate the activities of the Emonet group across the globe.

Finally, we would like to express appreciation to the contributors to this book, to Louise Earnshaw and Heidi Sturk, whose administrative excellence was invaluable to the production and editing of this book, and to Ann Philpott for producing the index. Last, but not least, we thank executive editor Harry Briggs and the staff of M.E. Sharpe for their work in bringing this exciting new book to print.

MANAGING
EMOTIONS
IN THE
WORKPLACE

1 MANAGING EMOTIONS IN A CHANGING WORKPLACE

Neal M. Ashkanasy, Wilfred J. Zerbe, and Charmine E.J. Härtel

Introduction

The modern workplace is often thought of as cold and rational, as no place for the experience and expression of emotions. Yet it is no more emotionless than any other aspect of social life (Ashforth and Humphrey 1995; Ashkanasy, Härtel, and Zerbe 2000b; Fisher and Ashkanasy 2000). Individuals bring their affective states and traits and emotional "buttons" to work; leaders try to engender in followers feelings of passion and enthusiasm for the organization and its well-being; groups speak of esprit de corps; and organizational consultants seek to increase job satisfaction, commitment, trust, and loyalty. Organizational members seldom carry out their work in an objective fashion based on cold, cognitive calculation. Instead, as Weiss and Cropanzano (1996) argue, workplace experiences comprise a succession of work events that can be pleasing and invigorating, or stressful and frustrating. Without a doubt, emotions are an inherent part of the workplace.

In recent years, we have witnessed a rise in the organized study of emotions in the workplace. The editors of this book have been at the forefront of this rise, including the publication of *Emotions in the Workplace: Theory, Research, and Practice* (Ashkanasy, Härtel, and Zerbe 2000a), the forerunner to the present volume. Ashkanasy was also guest editor (with Cynthia Fisher) of a Special Issue of the *Journal of Organizational Behavior* on this topic. Other books that are contributing to this

3

rise are by Fineman (2000); Ciarrochi, Forgas, and Mayer (2001); Lord, Klimoski, and Kanfer (2001); and Payne and Cooper (2001); and special editions of *Organizational Behaviour and Human Decision Processes* (Weiss 2001) and *Leadership Quarterly* (Humphrey, planned for 2002). An additional book is in preparation by Weiss, Cropanzano, and Ashkanasy (in press). Finally, the renewed interest is evident in the strong support of the biannual *Conferences on Emotions and Organizational Life*, chaired by the editors of the present volume. Collectively, these publications and activities are advancing our understanding of the causes and effects of emotions at work.

In this volume, we focus on extending theory about emotions in the workplace to consider specifically the implications for the management of emotions in today's changing workplace. We ask: What are the practical issues that are raised when we acknowledge organizations as places where emotions are aroused and suppressed, displayed and contained, used to achieve organizational goals and avoided in the hope of preventing discomfort or harm? We also explore in this book the debate on how organizations and individuals ought to manage emotions in the modern workplace.

Although the workplace emotions literature is growing, it is still a young area of study. As such it is characterized by diversity in theoretical orientation and topical focus. It also enjoys diversity of methodological practice, which some literatures experience only as they mature. It is difficult, therefore, to specify an all-encompassing yet parsimonious system that categorizes work in the field. At the same time, four domains capture a good deal of the area: (1) *Affective Events Theory* (Weiss and Cropanzano 1996), which is premised on the idea that everyday hassles and uplifts determine emotional states at work, has been proposed as an overarching model of emotions in organizations; (2) *Emotional Labor* deals with the question of why and how employees may display particular emotions, including emotions that differ from how they feel, and the effects of such labor (see Hochschild 1979); (3) *Mood Theory* examines the idea that positive and negative mood states can determine organizational members' attitudes and behaviors (e.g., George and Brief 1996a); and (4) *Emotional Intelligence* refers to the ability to read emotions in one's self and others and to be able to use this information to guide decision making (see Goleman 1998b; Mayer and Salovey 1993; 1995; 1997; Salovey and Mayer 1990). We will discuss recent developments in each of these areas in turn, as a means to set the scene for the chapters that follow. Following this background, we will briefly summarize the chapters in each of the four sections of this book.

Affective Events Theory

While there is yet to be an all-encompassing theory of emotions in workplace settings, affective events theory (AET) comes closest. Indeed, until Weiss and Cropanzano published their seminal paper on this topic in 1996, there was little in the organizational science literature that enabled scholars to appreciate properly the role of emotions. In AET, Weiss and Cropanzano argue that aspects of the work environment, including environmental conditions, roles, and job design, initiate emotions in organizational settings. These aspects of work thus constitute the "affective events," described colloquially as "hassles and uplifts" (Basch and Fisher 2000), that act systematically to determine affective states. These states, in turn, lead to attitudinal and behavioral outcomes. Emotions can also directly lead to behavioral outcomes such as productive work (see Wright, Bonett, and Sweeney 1993; Wright and Cropanzano 1998), pro- or antisocial actions (Organ 1990), or turnover behavior. AET also incorporates trait affectivity, a personal disposition that conditions the formation of positive and negative emotions. AET is illustrated in Figure 1.1.

From the perspective of the current volume, which deals with managing emotions in workplace settings, AET is of critical significance. It tells us that organizational characteristics and managerial policies can affect the emotional states of organizational members, and that these, in turn, can affect members' attitudes and performance. Although Weiss and Cropanzano (1996) initially presented their model as an untested theory, and research is still in early stages, results to date have been strongly supportive of the core ideas in the theory. Examples of studies to date include Fisher (2000); O'Shea, Ashkanasy, Gallois, and Härtel (1999; 2000a, b); Fisher and Noble (2000); and Weiss, Nicholas, and Daus (1999). These studies have all supported the idea that emotional states mediate the effect of work events on outcomes. In particular, they have shown that including measures of emotional states brings once elusive relationships between work events and work outcomes into focus. These emotional states encompass both mood, the rather generalized feelings of happiness or sadness that we all experience from time to time; and more specific emotional states, such as joy, pride, fear, anger,

Figure 1.1   **Affective Events Theory**

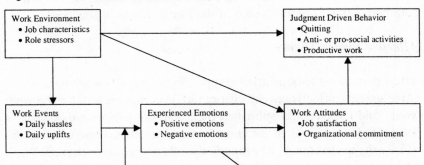

or disgust, that result from specific occurrences in our environment (see Russell and Feldman-Barrett 1999).

One of the more important outcomes of AET research is a new understanding of job satisfaction. For many years, researchers have been stumped by consistent findings that whether work performance is high or low, it bears no relation to workers' feelings of satisfaction (see Wright and Staw 1999, for discussion). These findings, however, seem to fly in the face of what managers see every day—that, by and large, satisfied workers are productive workers. In AET, however, attitudes and affective states relating to job satisfaction are viewed as separable (Fisher 2000). Accordingly, researchers today (e.g., Brief and Roberson 1989; Fisher 2000; Weiss, Nicholas, and Daus 1999) have argued that job satisfaction constitutes a set of attitudes toward work that do not necessarily include affective feelings. Indeed, in our previous volume we argued that whereas attitudes are evaluations about objects, such as one's job, emotions are evaluations of oneself; they are appraisals of one's own well-being (Zerbe, Härtel and Ashkanasy 2000; see also Cropanzano, Weiss, Suckow, and Grandey 2000). Further, AET makes it clear that many emotions are transient states rather than aspects of work life that remain constant for long periods of time. Employees at work can be overjoyed with a successful outcome one moment and be disappointed and perhaps even angry in the next moment when their boss does not appear to share their enthusiasm. In a recent study, Fisher and Noble (2000) demonstrated for the first time that satisfaction and performance are, indeed, strongly related on a moment-to-moment basis in employees' work lives, although they still appear to be unrelated when looked at over a longer period of time. Fisher and Noble argue that researchers have been looking in the wrong place for the satisfaction-performance link that managers report; instead of looking "between-people," researchers need to study "within-person" effects.

In effect, AET and the empirical findings that have been obtained so far are revolutionizing our view of behavior in organizations. We now know that behavior and performance of employees at work are not defined by job satisfaction as was traditionally thought. Instead, employees' behaviors and attitudes are constantly changing as they encounter everyday hassles and uplifts in their workplace (see Fisher 2000; Fisher and Noble 2000; Hodges and Wilson 1993).

In summary, AET has alerted researchers and managers alike to the importance of emotional states in organizational settings. In particular, the emotions that employees experience as a result of the everyday events that happen to them are now seen to be a central aspect of understanding employee attitudes and behavior. Further, Fisher (1998, 2000; see also Fisher and Noble 2000) has argued that it is the little things that can add up to determine how employees think and behave. In effect, it is the *frequency* with which these events occur, and the *accumulation* of events, rather than the *intensity* of particular events that determine the ultimate outcomes. Thus, while employees may be able to deal with one or two major events, they have more difficulty when adverse events unremittingly affect the way that they work, even if the events appear to be relatively minor. Importantly, however, the results also suggest that uplifting events, such as a complementary comment by a superior, or a friendly and supportive act by a colleague following a negative occurrence, such as a lost sale, can reverse the negative consequences that would normally be expected to flow from the event (see Grzywacz and Marks 2000).

Emotional Labor

The second topic we address is emotional labor. Emotional labor occurs when employees are required to display particular emotional states as a part of their job. Beginning with Hochschild (1983), emotional labor research has been the traditional flag bearer of research into emotions in organizations. According to Hoschchild (see also Rafaeli and Sutton

1987, 1989), employees in service industries, such as airline cabin crews, shop assistants, funeral directors, and even debt collectors, are required by their jobs to maintain particular displays of emotions. Flight attendants, for example, are supposed to smile at their customers, while funeral directors and police officers and debt collectors need to maintain the appropriate displays of negative emotion. More recently, the concept of emotional labor has been extended to include emotional displays by employees within the organization. For example, norms exist as to how employees relate to each other in work and social situations (see Humphrey 2000; Kruml and Geddes 2000).

One of the more powerful effects of emotional labor concerns what happens when there is a discrepancy between the emotions felt and those that a job requires a worker to display to conform to role expectations. Service workers, in particular, often find themselves in this predicament. Hochschild (1983) coined the term *emotional dissonance* to characterize this situation. She describes some typical incidents in her analysis of flight attendants, where the attendants were even found to engage in acts of retribution against customers because of the buildup of repressed emotions. Mann (1999) argues that this sort of repressed emotional energy has negative consequences for employees in general. Indeed, Ashkanasy, Fisher, and Härtel (1998) point out that such instances of emotional dissonance constitute affective events, and thus trigger an AET train of reactions, leading eventually to performance outcomes for employees. In this respect, there has been a good deal of attention paid to emotional labor and its effects on employee well-being and its consequences for organizational performance (see Schaubroeck and Jones 2000; Tews and Glomb 2000; Wharton and Erickson 1995).

From the perspective of the present volume, the implications of emotional labor for managing emotions in organizations are clear. This is especially so in the instance of so-called service encounters—where organizational members are providing service directly to the organization's clients or customers. In some of the seminal studies of emotional labor, Rafaeli and Sutton (1987, 1989; see also Sutton and Rafaeli 1988) showed that service employees' displays of positive emotion (e.g., smiling) were directly related to positive customer reactions and, hence, to sales and organizational effectiveness. This pattern, however, was not always found. In one study, for example, Sutton and Rafaeli (1988) found an inverse relationship between sales and smiling. They determined that clerks had more time to socialize with customers in shops with low sales whereas, in the high sales shops, there was no time for such niceties. Sutton and Rafaeli coined the term *Manhattan Effect* to describe the resulting (unexpected) negative relationship between sales volume and smiling.

In fact, it is in customer service quality that emotional labor has the strongest ramifications. Schneider and Bowen (1985), for example, argue that employees' attitudes and the attendant perceptions of service by customers are critical for maintenance of both individual and organizational performance. For example, in recent research that looked at emotional labor by bank clerks, Pugh (2001), found a positive relationship between positive displays of emotion and ratings of service quality. Pugh found, in particular, that the attitudes expressed by employees and evident in employees' faces can create favorable or unfavorable impressions in customers' minds, and negative attitudes could similarly engender unfavorable impressions (see also Härtel, Gough, and Härtel in press; Schneider, Parkington, and Buxton 1980). Other authors have argued that emotional intelligence may be a critical determinant of service providers' ability to produce positive attitudes, intentions, and behaviors in consumers (Härtel, Barker, and Baker 1999). Another aspect of emotional expression in service settings is *emotional contagion* (Hatfield, Cacioppo, and Rapson 1994), which is the tendency of observers to become "infected" with the emotional state expressed by actors. Verbeke (1997), for example, showed that customers in service settings tended to mimic the emotional tone of the service employees. From a manager's perspective, the imperative to ensure that employees in service jobs present the appropriate emotional expressions to customers is clear. In this regard, service employees have a special duty to ensure customer retention and satisfaction thorough appropriate emotion management. At the same time, managers need to ensure that the stress of emotional labor is not detrimental to employee performance (see Mann 1999).

Even as emotional labor can create economic benefits for organizations, it can have negative consequences on both the physical and the mental health of employees (see Mann 1999). The types of pent-up emotional outbursts described by Hochschild (1983), for example, result from a constant demand to manage emotions, and also to monitor the degree of felt emotional states. In the end, the strain of emotional labor can even lead to employee burnout (Kruml and Geddes 2000; Grandey 1998), and even physical symptoms (Parker and Wall 1998). Grandey (2000) and Schaubroeck and Jones (2000), for example, show that emotional strain leads to a weakened immune system and can result in fatigue, and, farther down the line, life-threatening diseases such as hypertension and cancer.

Faced with a discrepancy between felt emotions and those they "must" express, one way employees can choose to reduce this discrepancy is by displaying emotions closer to their feelings, even if this represents deviance from organizational norms. Alternatively they can seek to change their felt mood states. Tews and Glomb (2000) and Grandey (2000) argue that, if the dissonance can be reduced in this manner, then the resulting effect can even be positive, rather than negative. Hochschild, however, would argue that the long-term effect of such emotion management is alienation from the self. The implication for managers is that workplaces should be designed so that the feelings they create match those that employees are expected to express.

Emotional contagion may play a role in creating positive emotional environments. Research by Barsade (in press) and Bartel and Saavedra (2000) has found that even one member's positive emotional display can initiate positive emotions among work group members, leading to greater group cooperativeness, less group conflict, and positive perceptions of individual task performance (see also Härtel, Gough, and Härtel in press). Barsade concluded from her study that managers have a special role to play in this respect, namely, themselves displaying positive affect that carries through to socialization processes and the group's culture. Ashkanasy and Tse (2000) also stress the importance of managers' displays and management of positive emotion in engendering higher levels of group effectiveness and productivity.

In summary, although there is still scope for further research into the antecedents and consequences of emotional labor, the indications to date, beginning with Hochschild's (1983) research, are that emotional labor is a critical component of employee effectiveness. Recent research has extended the early findings in service settings to encompass everyday interactions at work. In this sense, emotional labor becomes another source of affective events that need to be managed if the full potential of individual and organizational work outcomes is to be realized.

Mood Effects in Organizations

The third topic we address in this introduction is mood in organizational settings. Moods differ from emotions in that they are more diffuse and longer lasting. Consistent with AET, recent research has demonstrated that both positive and negative moods affect the way employees think and behave at work (see George and Brief 1996a; Isen 1999). Research into mood in organizations began in the early 1990s (e.g., George and Brief 1992; Isen and Baron 1991), at around the same time as mood researchers in social psychology were beginning to have an impact (e.g., see Forgas 1995). Results of these studies have consistently highlighted the pervasive effects of mood. This research has also traditionally separated negative mood (e.g., George and Brief 1996b) from positive mood (Isen and Baron 1991). This distinction is particularly important from a manager's perspective because it implies that emotion management strategies in each instance are different. In the discussion that follows, therefore, we will treat positive and negative moods separately.

We begin with negative mood. The naïve view is simply that bad mood is intrinsically antithetical to employee productivity. Indeed, as George and Brief (1996a) show, employees who are in negative moods are less satisfied with their jobs and are prone to higher rates of withdrawal and turnover. In addition, managers in bad moods are more negative in their evaluations of others. They tend to see the negative side of employee performance in performance appraisal and even give lower ratings in employment interviews. The news on negative mood, however, is not all bad. Several authors have demonstrated that, compared to people in a positive mood, people in negative moods process cognitive information more accurately and make finer distinctions among choices (Alloy and Abramson 1979, 1982; Schwarz and Bohner 1996; Sinclair and Mark 1992). Further, researchers such as Rusting and DeHart (2000) report that people in negative moods can actively engage in positive thoughts and behaviors as a means to get rid of their bad moods. Strategies to do this can include working harder to take their mind off their problems or doing positive things to try to lift their bad mood. In this instance, people in bad moods may even be motivated to engage in helping behavior. They thus can feel better about themselves and, hopefully, lessen the negativity of their mood. The implication of this discussion is consistent with what we have noted earlier. It is naïve to simply assume that "happy workers are productive workers."

The effects of both negative and positive mood are postulated to result from a "mood congruence" process (see Bless et al. 1996). Specifically, the mood state of an individual is argued to result in thoughts congruent with that mood state being more readily accessible in memory and other mental processes. Thus, negative moods are accompanied by more negative evaluations. Positive mood, perhaps because it facilitates optimism, generally results in more positive outcomes (Isen and Baron 1991) such as increased job satisfaction (Connolly and Viswesvaran 2000), less turnover (Deery and Shaw 1999), and organizational prosocial or helping behaviors (Connolly and Viswesvaran 2000; Williams and Shiaw 1999). Kraiger, Billings, and Isen (1989) have shown further that positive mood leads to more positive evaluations in interviews, performance appraisals, and negotiations. Based on results such as these, it might appear as if positive mood states would be universally desired in an organization. But the evidence in respect to employee performance is not, in fact, all positive. George and Brief (1996a), for example, note that the effect of mood varies depending on the nature of the task. For some tasks, positive mood facilitates performance, while it seems to inhibit performance on other tasks. Again, the fit between the demands of the task and the mental consequences of positive or negative mood may be key. Where positive mood engenders associations that facilitate performance on a given task, it will be of benefit. A central example is tasks that require creativity. Here positive mood is an asset and negative mood a liability (see Estrada, Isen, and Young 1994), perhaps because of the criticism and self-censoring that comes more readily to individuals in negative mood states. In high-pressure jobs, on the other hand, employees may be striving to meet challenging goals (Locke and Latham 1990). In this situation, the press for high performance may be more consistent with the characteristics of a negative mood state. Similarly, for tasks that require a high degree of discrimination among choices, negative mood may be an asset. As we pointed out above, negative mood is associated with greater accuracy and may represent an antidote to the optimistic biases that come with positive mood.

In summary, while it is clear that the effects of mood are task contingent, it is also evident that there is much that we do not know. For managers who might be tempted to align mood with task demands, the research evidence on which to base such decisions is sparse and spotty. Tasks rarely are unidimensional. Further, seeking to influence employee mood through managerial action is surely a risky venture. The mood literature is vague with respect to its situational determinants. The literature on trait affectivity shows clearly that individuals can vary in their tendency to see the world positively or negatively. And, as we shall see in the next section, the emotional intelligence literature argues that individuals vary in their ability to manage their own feelings and the feelings of others.

Emotional Intelligence

Emotional intelligence is a relatively recent concept that has become both popular and controversial (see Fisher and Ashkanasy 2000). As we alluded to above, however, emotional intelligence has the potential to be important for the management of employees in organizations, from both an academic and a practitioner point of view. From a practitioner's perspective (e.g., see Cooper and Sawaf 1997; Goleman 1998b), emotional intelligence involves the identification, selection, and training of critical competencies involving emotional abilities. From a researcher's perspective, questions about the nature of emotional intelligence and its relationship with work outcomes remain to be answered (e.g., see Jordan, Ashkanasy, and Härtel 2000). These perspective differences have been attested to in the plethora of books, consulting agencies, workshops, journal articles, conference papers/symposia, and organized networks of individuals that are now available (see, e.g., Goleman 1998b; Cooper and Sawaf 1997).

Unfortunately, as things stand today, emotional intelligence has yet to be defined clearly. Agreement has yet to be reached even on its measurement (Davies, Stankov, and Roberts 1998), or about the specific nature of the competences that constitute emotional intelligence (Ciarrochi, Chan, and Caputi 2000; Davies, Stankov, and Roberts 1998). Mayer, Caruso, and Salovey (1999), the originators of the construct of emotional intelligence, for example, see emotional intelligence as a set of abilities dealing specifically with emotion. In this view, emotional intelligence is defined as the perception, identification, understanding, and management of emotion (see also Mayer and Salovey 1995). To Goleman (1995), Bar-On (1997), and Cooper and Sawaf (1997), on the other hand, emotional intelligence comprises a broad set of social skills, including such aspects as empathy, time management, decision making, and teamwork. Advocates of the latter view make heroic claims for the impact of emotional intelligence, even as others argue that there is little scientific evidence for such claims.

This state of affairs is the result of the twin solitudes of the academic and practitioner emphases. The academic, scientific point of view disallows claims about what something does until it is known what it is. The practitioner point of view, in contrast, argues that if something works, then precise definition and measurement is unnecessary. Clearly it would be beneficial to both camps to venture into the other side.

Still, at this point, there are enough data accumulated to suggest that emotional intelligence constitutes an individual difference variable that comprises a distinct set of abilities that develop over a person's lifetime and can be enhanced through appropriate training. Further, emotional intelligence is not the repackaging of previously identified social skills. Instead, it involves ability directly related to emotions and their role in determining attitudes and behavior. In particular, emotional intelligence encompasses an ability to identify and to perceive emotion in self and others, and then to assimilate and to use this information to manage emotions successfully (Mayer and Salovey 1997).

Four areas where emotional intelligence has been shown to be applicable in organizational settings are leadership, team effectiveness, interviews, and as a moderator of job insecurity. In the following paragraphs, we briefly review the evidence in each of these three areas and draw conclusions for the management of emotions in the workplace.

In respect to leadership, the dominant theory today is transformational leadership (see Bass and Avolio 1994). In this model, leaders inspire and motivate their followers through projecting a clearly articulated vision of future goals (Wilson-Evered, Härtel, and Neal 2001). Accompanying this inspiration are aspects of intellectual stimulation and individual consideration (Bass 1998; Bass and Avolio 1990).

The idea that emotional intelligence and transformational leadership are somehow linked is relatively new (see George 2000). Bass (1998), for example, identified emotional awareness of self and others as a central tenet of transformational leadership. Likewise, Bass (1998) notes that transformational leaders must be sensitive and empathetic to followers' emotional needs. Ashkanasy and Tse (2000), for example, describe how transformational leaders respond to the emotional needs of followers appropriately, and develop positive and constructive relationships with them. As such, emotionally intelligent transformational leaders develop trust in their followers and establish cooperation and enthusiasm for positive outcomes. Leaders also need to understand how their followers feel following disappointments and when they are under pressure (Bass 1998). These examples demonstrate that it is the leaders' emotional skills and abilities that lie at the core of transformational leadership.

It should be noted, as Conger (1990) has pointed out, that transformational leadership is not necessarily positive. He refers to a "dark side" of transformational leadership, where the vision is directed to evil ends. Leaders such as Charles Manson and Jim Jones, for example, are particularly powerful when followers are receptive to exploitation (Weierter 1997).

A corollary of emotional intelligence as a catalyst of transformational leadership is the role of emotional intelligence in teams. The idea of emotional contagion that we introduced earlier in this chapter, for example, implies that emotional states can be communicated among the members of teams. In this respect, the question arises as to the role of emotional intelligence in fostering more effective team performance. Indeed, one wonders if there exists an "emotionally intelligent team" as a counterpart to the idea of emotional intelligence as an individual characteristic.

Like the concept of emotional intelligence itself, however, the concept of the emotionally intelligent team is still vague and undefined. Druskat and Wolff (2001), in a recent case-based article, argue that emotionally intelligent groups are at the heart of team success in organizations. To Druskat and Wolff, however, emotionally intelligent teams exhibit the sort of team skills that are associated with good team interactions and goal focus (e.g., see Locke and Latham 1990). Jordan et al. (in press), on the other hand, see emotionally intelligent teams in terms of the emotion-based definitions of emotional intelligence (e.g., as per Mayer and Salovey 1997). Their conclusions, based on a team simulation study where undergraduate students participated in five- to seven-person "semi-autonomous learning teams," were quite different from Druskat and Wolff's. In Jordan et al.'s (in press) study, participants completed tasks using student-centered learning principles, and were coached over a nine-week period in goal-setting, interpersonal communication skills, and emotional understanding (Engel 1993). "Team emotional intelligence" was calculated by aggregating the emotional intelligence of team members, based on a measure administered at the end of the study period. Jordan and his colleagues expected to find that high emotional intelligence teams would perform better than low emotional intelligence teams. They found instead that, while the low emotional intelligence teams initially performed worse than the high emotional intelligence teams, both high and low emotionally intelligent teams were performing equally at the end of the study period. The implication of these results is that emotional intelligence in the context of teams is quite distinct from team skills, as advocated by Druskat and Wolff. Instead, the Jordan et al. (in press) results suggest that emotional intelligence in teams comes about as an aggregate of the emotional intelligence of team members, is relatively stable, and is not just a set of team interaction and goal-focus skills. An important corollary of their study is that training in team development can be targeted at teams whose members are low in emotional intelligence.

While the Jordan et al. (in press) findings are based on a student sample and must be regarded as preliminary, it does raise again the lack of understanding of emotional intelligence. Is this construct just a set of broad social skills, or is it a unique phenomenon, directly based in the idea that perception, assimilation, and management of emotion lie at the heart of effective behavior and functioning? This question remains to be resolved, but if the answer is that emotions do lie at the core of effective behavior, then the implications for managers are profound.

The elements of emotional intelligence concerning perception, understanding, and management appear to be critical factors in interview settings. For both the interviewer and interviewee, the interview process can be highly emotionally charged. Indeed, Baron (1993b) has described the interview as a process that is fraught with emotion, and where emotions are likely to affect the interview outcomes profoundly. Interviewees, for example, are striving to present an image of professionalism that has long-term consequences for their career. An interviewee who cannot handle the pressure of the interview, and who breaks down emotionally, is unlikely to be seen as a stable and reliable hire.

On the other side of the interview table, interviewers need to be able to read the intellectual and emotional qualities of the candidate, often based on immediate first impressions. The interviewer also has to maintain consistency in his or her own mood states so that the candidate will feel relaxed, while at the same time perceiving the interviewer and the environment to be appropriately professional. In this respect, emotional competencies are the key for the ultimate success or otherwise of the interview. Recent research by Fox and Spector (2000) reinforces this view. Their studies show that success in interviews is maximized when interviewees project positive affect and empathy. Their results also show that interviewers are susceptible to the emotional states of interviewees, and that the outcome of interviews can be biased by the interviewer's mood states (see also Baron 1993b).

The dynamics underlying the performance of less emotionally intelligent individuals in interview settings may be similar to those of employees with high levels of job insecurity. In the context of today's changing workplace, job insecurity is a pervasive and intractable problem for many employees (see Ashford, Lee, and Bobko 1989; O'Driscoll and Cooper 1996). In a recent theoretical review, Jordan, Ashkanasy, and Härtel (2000) set out a model of job insecurity effects where emotional intelligence plays a key moderator role. Jordan and his associates argue that emotional intelligence, defined in terms of the Mayer and Salovey (1997) model, is the key to the question of whether job insecurity acts as a motivator or disincentive for productivity. In the model, the emotionally intelligent employee is able to "ride" the emotional pressures created by job insecurity and can improve his or her performance in an insecure job. Employees whose emotional intelligence is low, on the other hand, succumb to the emotional pressures and the sort of stress and burnout detailed in O'Driscoll and Cooper (1996).

In summary, the four topics that we have discussed in this overview highlight the broad and pervasive role that emotions can play in organizational settings. Affective events, emotional labor, mood effects, and emotional intelligence cover distinct but overlapping areas of organizational functioning. Emotional intelligence, in particular, has the potential to be the "glue" that brings the field together. Unfortunately, and as is evident in our discussion of this topic, emotional intelligence remains a controversial and undeveloped field. We feel strongly, however, that the *emotional* focus of emotional intelligence is the key, rather than the broad view of emotional intelligence as a set of broad social skills (cf. Cooper and Sawaf 1997; Goleman 1998b). In this instance, emotional intelligence may indeed be a key topic for managers in today's workplace where, as we have argued, emotions are only now being recognized as a central topic.

Overview of Chapters

This opening chapter is intended to orient readers to the field of emotions at work, to update those who are more familiar, and to provide a foundation for those to whom this is new. The remaining chapters in this part of the book consider the role of emotions during change in organizations, specifically during two common contemporary experiences, organizational downsizing and firm mergers.

Part I: Change

In Chapter 2, Jan Paterson and Charmine Härtel consider how the effects of organizational downsizing can be improved, from both individual and firm perspectives, by considering the role of emotions. Specifically, they contrast two explanations for the proscription that organizations increase communication and employee participation when downsizing. On the one hand is the cognitive explanation that resistance is reduced when the perceived fairness of a change is increased. On the other is the emotion-based explanation that anxiety about a change is reduced by communication. Paterson and Härtel integrate these two perspectives into a model that explains the effect of change program characteristics on employees' responses to large-scale change.

Tina Kiefer adds to this perspective by considering how emotions have traditionally been viewed within organizational change. In a review of past approaches, she shows that emotions have been assumed to be negative reactions to change, to be irrational barriers to change, and as reactions to be minimized and "managed away." In contrast to these perspectives, she forwards the view that emotions are a key aspect of the social construction of a change experience, which provides valuable information about the perspectives of different stakeholders to the change initiative. This alternative way of thinking is applied to the analysis of interviews of managers currently experiencing a merger. Kiefer shows that emotions aroused by mergers are not merely negative and that, consistent with Paterson and Härtel's chapter, negative reactions often result from procedural elements. Further, Kiefer shows that negative emotions as well as positive emotions are created in merger situations and that both can contribute to positive outcomes.

In the concluding chapter in Part I, the editors apply and extend the work of Kiefer and Paterson and Härtel to a consideration of how to manage change and how to manage emotions in the change process.

Part II: Conflict/Interpersonal

Conflict within groups can be categorized into that which is related to the task facing the team, or to that arising from the nature of the social relationships among members. The latter is often referred to as emotional conflict and is typically associated with negative group outcomes (Jehn 1997). In Chapter 5, Oluremi Ayoko and Charmine Härtel discuss the role of emotion and emotion management in both destructive and productive conflict within culturally heterogeneous work groups. Diversity among team members in tendencies to experience and display positive affect has been linked to team performance (Barsade et al. 2000). Ayoko and Härtel extend this work to a study of culturally diverse teams, examining the emotions experienced with conflict and the ways in which group members and leaders respond to conflict-related emotions. Their findings have direct implications for those leading teams that are culturally diverse, as well as those that are not.

Jones and Rittman's work, in Chapter 6, probes beneath the surface of interpersonal effects to discern why they occur. They posit that the emotions that individuals display in interpersonal situations signal their motives and readiness to pursue particular outcomes. The accuracy of this signaling process depends, in turn, on the situation in which participants find themselves, and the abilities of the participants themselves. Display is also guided by social rules about its appropriateness. These and other propositions form a motivation, experience, and display of emotion model (MEDE) that describes the nature and outcomes of interpersonal encounters. This model has broad application to team interaction as well as to understanding service encounters.

Stéphane Côté and Debbie Moskowitz consider the role of emotion in another realm of interpersonal interaction—superior-subordinate relationships. They use this realm to test their proposition that workplace moods result from the balance of resources and demands that individuals carry at a particular time. Relational status affects this balance and creates differences in moods that have consequent effects for the individual and the organization. In three laboratory and field studies, Côté and Moskowitz show support for their argument and draw implications for how both superiors and subordinates should manage interactions and moods.

In the concluding chapter in this section, the editors again integrate and synthesize the preceding chapters, drawing on the broader literature and expanding on the implications of this work for future research and practicing managers.

Part III: Decision Making

Emotional intelligence, although often loosely defined and applied in writings, concerns individuals' awareness of the realm of emotions and how they decide to translate that awareness into action. This section contains four chapters that consider the nature of emotional intelligence, the role of emotions in decision making, and the interaction of power and emotion in mobilizing behavior.

In Chapter 9, Marta Sinclair, Neal Ashkanasy, Prithviraj Chattopadhyay, and Maree Boyle propose a model of managerial intuitive decision making in which affect moderates the relationship between the use of intuition and characteristics of the person and situation. Specifically, they propose that intuition, as opposed to a more analytic decision process, will be used when individuals have greater awareness of their feelings, when they are experiencing moderate positive affect, and when they receive affective confirmation for the use of intuition. When a decision maker is experiencing high-intensity positive or negative affect, the use of intuition depends on whether the decision maker focuses on the affect itself or on the decision outcome. Sinclair and her colleagues show how their model can be used to improve the speed, accuracy, and quality of decisions.

The complementarity of intuitive and analytic decision-making approaches, which Chapter 9 advocates, is consistent with the views of Aaron Ben-Ze'ev. In Chapter 10, he describes how the psychological mechanisms underlying emotion and intellect, together, are an integral part of human intelligence. Ben Ze'ev argues that "intelligence in its broad sense, which includes both intellectual and emotional intelligence, is the ability to use in an optimal manner both types of intelligence" and that "the optimal integration of the two systems expresses emotional intelligence." Practical effectiveness means understanding the tendencies and interests of each and applying this understanding to the regulation of our behavior.

In Chapter 11, Gibson and Schroeder consider how the power held by an agent affects his or her use of emotional display as an influence strategy. They present a model that integrates the interpersonal power and influence tactics literature with the management of emotions literature. Explicit in their model is the argument that emotional display is the result of a conscious decision-making process that stems from attributes of the agent and characteristics of the influence situation.

This section concludes with a chapter summarizing the implications for decision-making of the results and propositions raised in the preceding chapters. Again, work from other areas is integrated, notably the existing literature on the role of mood and emotion in decision making.

Part IV: Emotional Labor

The first chapter in this section, by Jamie Callahan and Eric McCollum, sets the stage for the following studies of emotional labor by clarifying and extending our understanding of what we mean by the term and its relationship to emotion work and the broader concept of emotion management. Callahan and McCollum center the distinction between emotion work and emotional labor on the distinction between use value and exchange value. Use value is the inherent and natural worth of something, whereas exchange value is its ability to be traded for something else of value. Emotion work has use value—it helps smooth interpersonal relationships with an indirect influence on organizational outcomes. Emotion labor has exchange value—it is performed in exchange for the rewards that result from effective job performance. The authors outline the implications of this distinction for selecting the most effective workplace interventions.

Lyndall Strazdins uses the concept of emotional contagion to provide one answer to the question of why and when emotional labor has effects on the well-being of those who perform it. Emotional contagion refers to the process by which participants in an interaction come to be experiencing similar emotional states. Strazdins shows, in a study of health care workers, that emotions are contagious and that the well-being of workers is influenced by the nature of the emotions they encounter. Emotional labor that involves dealing with negative emotions, such as distress and conflict, increases psychological distress, goal loss, and intention to leave the job. Emotional labor that involves improving positive emotions, in contrast, reduces occupational stress. The implications of this work for how organizations can manage emotional labor to the best interests of employees are evident.

Although various studies have investigated the effect of emotional labor on employee well-being, the results of these studies have not been consistent. One shortcoming has been a failure to incorporate the role of affective events present in work settings and the affective environments of those settings. Further, studies generally have not considered contextual factors such as cultural orientation to emotions and emotional workgroup climate. By failing to do so, previous work may underspecify the variables that should be studied and thus conclude that relationships do not exist where, in fact, they do, or find relationships among variables without reference to underlying dynamics. Charmine Härtel, Alice

Hsu, and Maree Boyle address this problem by building a conceptual model of the relationships among emotion labor, emotional dissonance, and emotional exhaustion that incorporates contextual and provider characteristics. They use this model to consider how service provider jobs should be designed; how the work-group climate might be improved; and how selection, training, and counseling might be targeted.

Two chapters conclude the volume, both by the editors. Chapter 16 integrates and extends the chapters in Part IV on Emotional Labor, developing an agenda for future research and collating implications for practice. In Chapter 17, the editors identify twenty-one "tools" for managing emotions in the workplace that arise from the contributed chapters in the volume.

I

CHANGE

2 AN INTEGRATED AFFECTIVE AND COGNITIVE MODEL TO EXPLAIN EMPLOYEES' RESPONSES TO DOWNSIZING

Jan M. Paterson and Charmine E.J. Härtel

Abstract

The organizational change literature offers recommendations about how to manage change to reduce employee resistance and avoid the potentially negative effects of downsizing. This literature suggests that change program characteristics that feature effective communication and change management procedures can increase acceptance of change and have other beneficial outcomes, but there is little agreement on the mechanisms that explain these effects. One popular explanation draws on the stress and coping literature and focuses on the role of emotions by proposing that communication about the change and procedures used to implement it reduce resistance by reducing anxiety. In contrast, the justice-based approach emphasizes the role of cognitions by suggesting that the communication and procedural aspects of change programs reduce resistance by increasing the perceived fairness of the change. This chapter incorporates these two explanations into a single theoretical model. Specifically, the chapter develops a cognitive-affective model that integrates anxiety emotions and justice cognitions to explain the effects of change program characteristics on employees' responses to downsizing, and proposes that the strategies employees use to cope with downsizing represent acceptance and resistance to change.

Although organizations must change and adapt in order to survive (Lawler 1995), employee resistance to change can jeopardize the success of change programs (Hay and Härtel 2000; Iverson 1996). Employee resistance is particularly likely to occur when job security is threatened (Jordan, Ashkanasy, and Härtel 2000), as in downsizing interventions in which the workforce is reduced to try to improve organizational performance (Kozlowski et al. 1993). The resulting job insecurity can have negative psychological consequences for individuals (Dekker and Schaufeli 1995; Zeitlin 1995) and lead to resistance (Jordan, Ashkanasy, and Härtel 2000), which has negative outcomes for the organization (Cascio 1993; Cascio, Young, and Morris 1997; Konovsky and Brockner 1993; Kozlowski et al. 1993).

Current Explanatory Approaches

The organizational change literature offers recommendations about how to manage change to reduce employee resistance and avoid the potentially negative effects of downsizing. This literature suggests that change program characteristics that feature effective communication and change management procedures can increase acceptance of change and have other beneficial outcomes. There is, however, little agreement on the mechanisms that explain these effects. One popular explanation focuses on the role of emotions by proposing that communication about the change and procedures used to implement it reduce resistance by reducing anxiety (e.g., Cummings and Worley 1993; Hay and Härtel 2000). In contrast, the justice framework proposed by Cobb, Wooten, and Folger (1995) emphasizes the role of cognitions by suggesting that the communication and procedural aspects of change programs reduce resistance by increasing the perceived fairness of the change (Cobb, Wooten, and Folger 1995). The purpose of this chapter is to bring these two explanations together into a single theoretical framework. Specifically, the chapter develops a model that integrates emotional and cognitive factors to explain the effects of change program characteristics on employees' responses to downsizing.

Change Program Characteristics

The change management literature suggests that acceptance of change is enhanced by change program characteristics that emphasize the quality and content of communication from change managers, establish procedures that permit participation, and provide support to help employees adapt to the change. High-quality change communications are characterized by their helpfulness (Miller and Monge 1985), openness (Miller, Johnson, and Grau 1994); and accuracy, timing, and completeness (Richardson and Denton 1996; Smeltzer 1991; Smeltzer and Zenner 1992). Content for change communications is advocated to focus on four types of "social accounts." Social accounts are proposed to motivate employees to accept change by explaining the reasons for, and justifying the change (causal accounts), and conveying a vision for the new organization (ideological accounts). Referential accounts establish new frames of reference that help keep the change program moving by setting standards to measure progress and evaluate success. Penitential accounts, on the other hand, are aimed at ameliorating negative consequences by expressing regret for any adversity employees may incur due to the change (Cobb, Wooten, and Folger 1995).

The change management literature also recommends that the procedures used to manage a change allow employees the opportunity for "voice," by soliciting employees' input into the design of changes and by providing opportunities for employees to express views and to appeal decisions. Such opportunities for participation can increase acceptance and commitment to the change by helping employees maintain a sense of control (Cummings and Worley 1993; Kanter 1985). Support mechanisms such as financial compensation, counseling, outplacement services, and training for new jobs within or beyond the downsizing organization can also enhance acceptance of change by helping employees who are to be laid off to find reemployment, and reassuring those who are to be retained that the organization is a caring employer (Kozlowski et al. 1993; Reddy 1994).

Previous research indicates that communication quality (Cameron 1998; Colvin 1993; Smeltzer 1991), communication content (Cameron 1998; Porras and Hoffer 1986), participation (Colvin 1993; Porras and Hoffer 1986; Sagie and Koslowsky 1996), and support mechanisms (Cameron 1998; Colvin 1993; Porras and Hoffer 1986) can increase employee acceptance and the success of an organizational change intervention. These studies, however, did not address the mechanisms that explain the effects of the characteristics of the intervention on employees' responses to change. The present chapter addresses this gap by integrating notions from the emotions and justice literatures.

Change Anxiety

A popular explanation for the effects of change program characteristics on employee responses to downsizing proposes that the major cause of resistance to change is employees' emotional reaction to change, specifically, the anxiety arising from uncertainty over the future and the actual or perceived threat of loss (e.g., Kanter 1985; Robbins, Waters-Marsh, Cacioppo, and Millett 1994). This approach focuses on employees' emotional responses and suggests that high-quality information about the change and the opportunity to participate in planning reduce uncertainty, thereby reducing anxiety and increasing acceptance of the change. Effective support systems that help employees cope with the changes serve similar functions (Kozlowski et al. 1993).

Cognitive appraisal theory offers a theoretical rationale for the change anxiety explanation. Cognitive appraisal theory proposes that an event such as organizational change results in a primary cognitive appraisal in which individuals assess the implications of the change for their well-being. An event that is appraised as having negative outcomes contributes to emotions such as anxiety. Primary appraisals also lead to secondary appraisals, which are more specific assessments that try to make sense of the situation by looking at the consequences of the change, making attributions about the cause, and considering coping potential. Secondary appraisals have the greatest impact on emotions and also influence the strategies individuals use to cope with the situation (Weiss and Cropanzano 1996). Problem-focused strategies attempt to address the actual problem (e.g., by finding out about severance pay or new skills required) whereas emotion-focused coping strategies attempt to alleviate the source of the stress, for example, by seeking social support or using counseling services (Shaw and Barrett-Power 1997; cf. Jordan, Ashkanasy, and Härtel 2000). Thus, effective communication about the change, the opportunity for input into planning, and appropriate support systems can help clarify the nature of the threat. This results in a more accurate appraisal of the event (cf. Hay and Härtel 2000), which gives individuals the chance to use effective coping strategies. This process facilitates anxiety reduction and acceptance of the change.

The literature offers some support for the effects of anxiety on employees' responses to a range of organizational change interventions. Ashford's (1988) longitudinal field study found that uncertainty was linked with higher levels of stress before, and six months after, a restructuring and relocation, and that feelings of personal control and tolerance of ambiguity helped reduce stress. Two field experiments support the effects of change communication by showing that the perceived helpfulness of communication reduced anxiety about the change to an open-plan office (Miller and Monge 1985), and up-to-date relevant information reduced uncertainty and increased trust and job satisfaction during an organizational merger (Schweiger and Denisi 1991). Terry, Callan, and Sartori's (1996) study extended these findings by showing that a composite of supportive leadership, consultation, and communication during an organizational merger was linked with lower levels of appraised stress and higher levels of self-efficacy which, in turn, were linked with the use of problem-focused coping strategies and psychological well-being. In contrast, Miller, Johnson, and Grau's (1994) field study provided little support for the change anxiety explanation. Their results showed that employee ratings of the amount of information they had received about an organizational restructuring were linked with lower anxiety about the introduction of work teams, but the perceived quality of the information was not. Instead, information quality was linked directly with acceptance of change, and anxiety about the change made no additional contribution to acceptance. However, the outcomes of the work team intervention used in this study may have provoked little anxiety and been too innocuous to allow a proper test of the role of change anxiety in explaining employee responses to change.

Individual Differences in Emotional Characteristics

A major weakness of the anxiety explanation of employees' responses to downsizing arises from its failure to recognize the role of individual differences in emotional characteristics. Individual difference variables that appear to be particularly relevant to a model of resistance to change include emotional propensities and emotional intelligence. Considerable research shows that people differ in their propensity to experience positive and negative emotions (Watson and Clark 1984; Weiss and Cropanzano 1996), and that trait anxiety, negative affectivity, and neuroticism are associated with individuals' propensity to experience negative emotions (Spielberger and Sarason 1975–1986; Watson and Clark 1984; Weiss and Cropanzano 1996). Such research suggests that people who have high levels of trait anxiety, negative affectivity, or neuroticism will be predisposed to experience any change as more threatening than those who have lower levels of these characteristics.

People also differ in their emotional intelligence—their individual capacity for emotional self-awareness and expression, use of emotions to facilitate decision making, understanding of emotions, and regulation of one's own and others' emotions (Jordan et al. in press; Mayer and Salovey 1997). Although there is limited research into this relatively recent concept, it is likely that individual differences in emotional intelligence will influence responses to large-scale change so that employees who have high levels of this ability will suffer fewer negative effects and choose more effective coping strategies than those who have lower levels of emotional intelligence.

The research to date suggests that anxiety and stress may explain the effects of change program characteristics on individual coping and well-being, although further work is needed to demonstrate that such emotional responses also help explain reactions to downsizing. However, research showing relatively stable individual differences in emotional characteristics suggests that including emotional factors as an individual difference variable will strengthen the anxiety explanation of employees' responses to change.

Organizational Justice

Organizational justice theory (Greenberg 1990) focuses on employees' cognitive responses to explain the effect of communication and change program procedures on acceptance of change. The basic tenet of this theory is that people evaluate situations that have important consequences for them and respond positively if they perceive the situation to be fair, and negatively if the situation is perceived as unfair. Early work focused on distributive justice and drew on Adams's equity theory (1965) to propose that people compare the ratio of their inputs and outcomes with those of relevant others to determine the fairness of their outcomes. Other criteria that may be used to assess the fairness of allocation decisions include equality and need (Wagstaff 1994). Later work instigated by Thibaut and Walker (1975) focused on procedural justice to examine people's perceptions of the fairness of the procedures and processes used to make decisions. Thibaut and Walker's (1975) self-interest model proposed that people are concerned about procedures because fair procedures give them some control over the process and outcomes of the decision. In contrast, Lind and Tyler's (1988) group-value model argues that the use of fair procedures is perceived as recognizing individuals' standing in the organization, thereby contributing to their sense of self-worth. Most recently, Bies and Moag (1986) differentiated between the organization's formal procedures and the way that decision makers enact those procedures to introduce the concept of interactional justice. This concept proposes that people consider the fairness of the interpersonal treatment they receive, and make judgments on the basis of the interpersonal sensitivity and personal ethicality displayed by the decision maker (Bies and Moag 1986).

Recently, Cobb, Wooten, and Folger (1995) applied organizational justice theory to develop a model that explains responses to large-scale change by proposing that the three justice dimensions mediate the effect of change program characteristics on resistance. This framework proposes that communications that convey causal, ideological, referential, and penitential accounts contribute to employees' perceptions that they receive fair interpersonal treatment from change managers, while procedures that offer employees the opportunity for participation or representation, recourse, and support to adjust to the change, increase perceptions of the fairness of the procedures used to implement the change. Outcomes are generally perceived as fair if they reflect an individual's inputs (the equity criterion), although Cobb, Wooten, and Folger (1995) noted that distributing resources equally or according to need may be perceived as fairer in times of large-scale change when questions about the value of different inputs may make equity difficult to assess. Together, procedural, interactional, and distributive justice are proposed to influence a variety of employee reactions, including acceptance of change, organizational commitment, trust, job satisfaction, quality of work life, productivity, and turnover (Cobb, Wooten, and Folger 1995).

There is considerable evidence that fairness perceptions increase acceptance of performance appraisals (Dailey and Kirk 1992; Taylor, Tracy, Renard, and Harrison 1995), personnel selection decisions (Ployhart and Ryan 1998; Singer 1993; Steiner and Gilliland 1996), drug-testing programs (Konovsky and Cropanzano 1991), labor unions (Skarlicki and Folger 1997), and self-managing work teams (Kirkman, Shapiro, Novelli, and Brett 1996). There is also evidence that fairness perceptions increase both layoff victims' and layoff survivors' acceptance of downsizing. For example, when outcomes are severe, the perceived fairness of a downsizing influences victims' desire for regulation of layoffs and willingness to recruit for their former employer, and survivors' organizational commitment and job satisfaction (Konovsky and Brockner 1993). However, other research shows that the favorability of the outcomes a person experiences influences his or her perceptions of distributive (Brockner and Weisenfeld 1996; Cropanzano and Greenberg 1997) and procedural justice (Ambrose, Harland, and Kulik 1991; Lind and Tyler 1988).

In addition to demonstrating links between justice and acceptance of decisions, the research supports the effect of positive change program characteristics on fairness perceptions. For example, communication about the change (Bies, Martin, and Brockner 1993; Brockner et al. 1990; Konovsky and Cropanzano 1991; Lind, Kanfer, and Earley 1990; Wanberg, Bunce, and Gavin 1999), the procedures used to implement it (Cobb, Vest, and Hills 1997; Konovsky and Folger 1991; Lind, Kanfer, and Earley 1990; Steiner and Gilliland 1996; Taylor et al. 1995), and the interpersonal treatment by change managers (Bies, Martin, and Brockner 1993; Cobb and Frey 1996; Cobb, Vest, and Hills 1997) have been associated with employees' perceptions of the fairness of procedures or outcomes. Moreover, Daly and Geyer's (1994) results offered some preliminary support for the Cobb model by showing that both procedural and distributive justice mediated the effects of causal accounts on intentions to remain with the organization after relocation. This study, however, did not investigate the role of interactional justice, and the proposed effects of voice were not significant. Although the procedural characteristics may play a more important role in interventions that have more severe outcomes, it is also possible that the effects of voice on acceptance of change may be partially mediated by affective, rather than cognitive, responses. Such possibilities suggest that a more comprehensive framework is needed to explain the effects of change program characteristics on employees' responses to change.

Integrated Cognitive-Affective Model

The preceding review indicates that change program characteristics that feature effective communication, allow the opportunity for participation, and provide support to help employees adjust can increase employee acceptance of organizational change interventions. The research also suggests that emotional responses, such as anxiety about the change, or cognitions, such as fairness perceptions, serve as an intervening process that explains why change program communications and procedures increase acceptance of downsizing. Therefore, a theoretical model that integrates cognitive and emotional responses will help increase understanding and serve as a framework to guide the development of effective organizational change interventions.

The cognitive-affective model depicted in Figure 2.1 integrates existing literature by proposing that justice perceptions, change anxiety, and individual differences in emotional characteristics help explain the effects of change program characteristics on employees' responses to downsizing. At the bottom of the figure are the change program characteristics that represent the primary change levers for organizations that wish to improve their change management procedures. Following Cobb, Wooten, and Folger (1995), these characteristics include the criteria used to make decisions, change implementation procedures that feature participation, recourse and support mechanisms, and change communications that convey social accounts. However, the model differs from earlier work by drawing on the communications literature (e.g., Richardson and Denton 1996; Smeltzer 1991) to include quality as a relevant aspect of change communications, and by differentiating between primary and secondary communications. Primary communications refer to the initial announcement that the downsizing will occur, while the secondary communications include the more detailed information conveyed by social accounts. This distinction recognizes that organizational change is a process that unfolds over time.

Depicted at the top of Figure 2.1 are the emotional characteristics of individual employees, which are proposed to moderate different linkages in the model. To the extent that such characteristics are malleable to training, or can be used as personnel selection criteria, these factors represent secondary change levers. The response process depicted in the middle of the figure follows the format of cognitive appraisal theories by proposing that primary appraisal leads to secondary appraisal and change anxiety, which, in turn, result in the use of coping strategies. This model integrates the stress and justice literatures by proposing that individuals' perceptions of the favorability of their outcomes represent primary cognitive appraisals, while justice perceptions represent secondary cognitive appraisals, in which cues from the environment and the person are interpreted in an attempt to make sense of the situation (Weiss and Cropanzano 1996). The model integrates aspects from the stress and change management literatures further by proposing a reciprocal link between justice perceptions and change

34

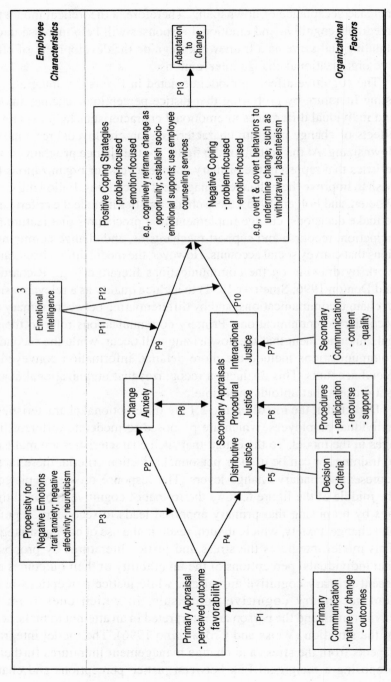

Figure 2.1 A Cognitive-Affective Model of Employee Responses to Downsizing

anxiety, and by proposing that the coping strategies that individuals use to deal with the downsizing represent employee acceptance or resistance to change. Each of the proposed linkages is discussed in more detail below.

Initiation of the response process. As shown in Figure 2.1, the response process is initiated by primary communications relating to the initial announcement that change is impending, the type of change that will be implemented, and information about the outcomes for individuals. These communications are predicted to have a direct effect on individuals' perceptions of the favorability of the change and their own outcomes, which represent the primary cognitive appraisals. This proposed sequence follows Lazarus's (1991a) concept of the cognitive appraisal processes underlying emotional reactions, namely that events appraised as threatening one's well-being produce negative emotional responses. Thus, it is proposed that:

> Proposition 1. Primary communications will initiate primary appraisal processes in employees (P1 in Figure 2.1).

Key intervening cognitive and emotional process variables in the link between change program characteristics and employee acceptance of change. Justice perceptions and change anxiety are proposed as key mediating variables in the relationship between change program characteristics and employees' resistance to downsizing. Specifically, it is expected that unfavorable assessments of the change's outcomes for one's self lead to high change anxiety and low levels of perceived justice. These predictions are consistent with research showing that anxiety emotions are evoked by large-scale change, especially that which involves downsizing (e.g., Dekker and Schaufeli 1995; O'Driscoll and Cooper 1996). Because threats to personal goals are linked with negative emotional responses (Lazarus 1991a; Stein, Trabasso, and Liwag 1993), outcome favorability, or the primary appraisal of the event as threatening, is expected to have a direct impact on anxiety, because unfavorable outcomes constitute a threat to employees' personal goals. Negative affect can be expected even when employees believe the downsizing was handled fairly. This view is consistent with Lazarus (1966; cf. Lazarus and Folkman 1984), who argued that the perception of harm to one's goals can have the same effects as the experience of actual harm. Consequently, it is proposed that:

> Proposition 2. Employees' primary appraisal processes will affect the level of change anxiety they experience (P2 in Figure 2.1).

Emotional characteristics of employees such as trait anxiety, negative affectivity, and neuroticism reflect an individual's propensity to experience negative emotions (Spielberger and Sarason 1975–1986; Watson and Clark 1984; Weiss and Cropanzano 1996). Consequently, it is expected that these characteristics will serve a moderating role by increasing the level of change anxiety that a given individual experiences as a result of hearing about unfavorable outcomes. On this basis it is proposed that:

> Proposition 3. The emotional propensities of employees such as trait anxiety, negative affectivity, and neuroticism will moderate the effect of primary cognitive appraisals on the level of anxiety a given individual experiences (P3 in Figure 2.1).

Factors affecting justice perceptions. Primary appraisal processes affect secondary appraisal processes, as represented by justice perceptions. The link between primary and secondary appraisal processes is consistent with the work of Lazarus (1991a) and Weiss and Cropanzano (1996), and the literature showing that the unfavorable outcomes reduce justice perceptions (Brockner and Wiesenfeld 1996; Cropanzano and Greenberg 1997). Therefore, it is proposed that:

> Proposition 4. Primary appraisal processes will affect secondary appraisal processes, namely justice perceptions (P4 in Figure 2.1).

Change program characteristics and justice perceptions. As previously discussed, the characteristics of change programs have been linked with the three organizational justice dimensions. Distributive justice research draws on equity theory (Adams 1965), which assumes that the criterion used to allocate resources and outcomes is a major determinant of perceived outcome fairness. Because considerable work supports this prediction (e.g., Deutsch, 1987; Giacobbe-Miller, Miller, and Victorov 1998), it is proposed that:

Proposition 5. The criterion that is used to identify people for redundancy will affect perceptions of distributive justice (P5 in Figure 2.1).

Elements of change procedures such as participation, recourse, and support mechanisms have been linked with perceptions of procedural justice (Cobb, Wooten, and Folger 1995). In particular, the extent to which the change program procedures allow employees the opportunity to participate in designing the change program, and to appeal against and have inappropriate decisions overturned, is expected to increase acceptance of change via their direct influence on perceptions of procedural justice and indirect influence on anxiety. The opportunity for participation and recourse are expected to increase perceived procedural fairness by giving employees a sense of control over the process and outcomes of the change (Thibaut and Walker 1975), and by recognizing the value of individuals to the organization (Lind and Tyler 1988). Consequently, it is proposed that:

Proposition 6. Change management procedures will affect perceptions of procedural justice (P6 in Figure 2.1).

The nature of communications about the change has been linked with perceptions of interactional justice (Cobb, Wooten, and Folger 1995). In particular, the care that change managers take to communicate effectively, together with penitential accounts that convey regret for adversity, increases interactional justice by demonstrating the interpersonal sensitivity, personal ethicality, and trustworthiness of the decision makers (Bies and Moag 1986). In line with this research, it is proposed that:

Proposition 7. The content and quality of communication will affect perceptions of interactional justice (P7 in Figure 2.1).

As shown in Figure 2.1, the integrated model predicts that procedural, interactional, and distributive justice impact on change anxiety so that people who rate the procedures, treatment, and outcomes as fair experience less anxiety than those who believe the different aspects are unfair. The justice dimensions are proposed to account for any effects of the communications, procedures, and criteria on change anxiety. Moreover, it is expected that change anxiety and secondary appraisal processes are interacting concurrent mental processes, with the emotional response of anxiety infusing the cognitive process of appraisal and vice versa (cf. Forgas 1995; Izard 1985; Lazarus 1982; LeDoux 1989; Ortony, Clore, and Collins 1988). On this basis it is proposed that:

> Proposition 8. The relationship between change anxiety and fairness perceptions will be reciprocal such that anxiety is inversely related to fairness perceptions and high fairness perceptions help reduce anxiety about the change (P8 in Figure 2.1).

Effect and moderator of fairness perceptions and anxiety on selection of affective and cognitive coping processes. So far, in line with the theoretical perspective that emotion and cognition interact (Izard 1985; Lazarus 1982; LeDoux 1989; Ortony, Clore, and Collins 1988), it is argued that change anxiety affects justice perceptions and vice versa. The dynamic operation of these two factors affects employees' choice of problem-focused and emotion-focused coping strategies. Problem-focused coping strategies link to the cognitive understanding of the anxiety-evoking situation, whereas emotion-focused coping strategies link to the anxiety experience (Folkman and Lazarus 1980). Because each of these types of coping has a positive and a negative pole (Jordan, Ashkanasy, and Härtel 2000), both emotional reactions to and fairness judgments of the change program will influence the extent to which employees select coping strategies that have positive or negative outcomes for themselves and the organization. For example, employees who perceive the change program as fair are more likely to engage in positive problem-focused coping strategies such as cognitively reframing the situation to perceive it as an opportunity rather than a threat (Latack 1986) and establishing socioemotional supports (Vitaliano et al. 1985). Such strategies are positive for the individual employee in that they address the problem and alleviate the source of the stress effectively. They are also positive for the organization because they reflect the behaviors that, from an organizational perspective, are typically considered as representing acceptance of change. Similarly, perceived fairness will facilitate positive emotion-focused coping strategies in employees, such as use of employee counseling services (cf. Kozlowski et al. 1993). In contrast, perceptions of unfairness or high change anxiety are expected to lead to negative problem-focused and emotion-focused coping, including negative talk, covert and overt behaviors to undermine change, withdrawal and absenteeism (Hanisch and Hulin 1990; Lazarus 1991a; Mobley, Griffeth, Hand, and Meglino 1979). Such behaviors typify the organizational construal of resistance to change. Therefore, it is proposed that:

> Proposition 9. Change anxiety will be negatively associated with a range of problem-focused and emotion-focused coping strategies that reflect acceptance and resistance to change (P9 in Figure 2.1).

> Proposition 10. Justice perceptions will be positively associated with a variety of problem-focused and emotion-focused coping strategies that typify acceptance and resistance to change (P10 in Figure 2.1).

Because justice reflects cognitive operations, which are linked to problem-focused coping, justice perceptions may have a stronger effect on the selection of problem-focused coping strategies than on the selection of emotion-focused coping strategies. In contrast, anxiety, as an emotional response, may have a stronger effect on the selection of emotion-focused coping strategies than on the selection of problem-focused coping strategies. Although justice and anxiety are expected to affect both problem-focused and emotion-focused coping, the relative impact of each of these factors should be considered in future investigations.

Following Jordan, Ashkanasy, and Härtel's (2000) argument, the emotional intelligence of employees is expected to moderate the effect of justice and change anxiety on the selection of problem-focused and emotion-focused coping responses (cf. Jordan, Ashkanasy, and Härtel 2000; Mayer and Salovey 1997). Because emotional intelligence refers to the abilities of emotional self-awareness and expression, use of emotions to facilitate decision making, understanding emotions, and regulation of one's own and others' emotions (Jordan et al. in press; Mayer and Salovey 1997), it is expected to enable employees to identify and implement coping strategies that are more productive for themselves and the organization (cf. Cooper 1998). Therefore, emotionally intelligent employees, especially those high on the decision-making and regulation aspects of emotional intelligence, who choose to stay with the organization are more likely to engage in effective problem solving and use available support mechanisms. Individuals low in this ability, on the other hand, are more likely to adopt ineffective coping strategies such as work withdrawal and verbal attacks on management. The selection of positive coping strategies is proposed to typify acceptance of change, whereas the choice of negative coping strategies is proposed to epitomize resistance to change. On this basis, it is proposed that:

> Proposition 11. Employees high in the ability of emotional intelligence will be more likely to engage in effective problem solving, use available support mechanisms, and accept change, even when change anxiety is high. In contrast, employees who are low in emotional intelligence tend to adopt ineffective coping strategies such as work withdrawal and verbal attacks on management, and resist change, particularly when levels of change anxiety are high (P11 in Figure 2.1). It is proposed that the decision-making and regulation dimensions of emotional intelligence will be particularly relevant to problem-solving and enacted coping strategies, since these dimensions of emotional intelligence directly address these response types.

> Proposition 12. Employees high in the ability of emotional intelligence will be more likely to engage in effective problem solving, use available support mechanisms, and accept change, even when justice perceptions are low, whereas employees who are low in emotional intelligence will tend to adopt ineffective coping strategies such as work withdrawal and verbal attacks on management, and resist change, particularly when perceived justice is low (P12 in Figure 2.1). It is proposed that the decision-making and regulation dimensions of emotional intelligence will be particularly relevant to problem-solving and enacted coping strategies, since these dimensions of emotional intelligence directly address these response types.

Because the integrated cognitive-affective model equates the coping strategies used by employees with the attitudes and behaviors that are typically construed as acceptance or resistance to change, the final variable in Figure 2.1 focuses on employees' adaptation to the downsizing intervention. This variable refers to the institutionalization, or long-term persistence, of the change, and reflects the extent to which employees know, perform, and prefer the new behaviors required after the change; agree on the appropriateness of the change; and believe they should support it (Cummings and Worley 1993). Attitudes and behaviors that reflect layoff survivors' adaptation to the downsizing will include affective commitment to the new organization, trust in management, job satisfaction and involvement, and high levels of task performance, innovation, and organizational citizenship behaviors. Responses of lay-off victims that reflect effective adaptation could include undergoing retraining to prepare for new jobs or careers, willingness to recruit for the former employer, and refraining from taking legal action against the organization that made them redundant. Thus, it is proposed that:

> Proposition 13. The use of positive problem-focused and emotion-fo-cused coping strategies that reflect acceptance will have positive effects on employees' adaptation to change within the given organizational set-ting, whereas the use of negative problem-focused and emotion-focused strategies that reflect resistance will have negative effects on adaptation to change (P13 in Figure 2.1).

Conclusion

The propositions put forward in this chapter reflect two distinct theo-retical approaches to explaining employee responses to downsizing, namely, justice-based approaches and emotion-based approaches. This chapter extends theory on the effects of change programs in organiza-tions by integrating these two theoretical approaches into one model, and by including individuals' emotional characteristics and coping strat-egies to help explain the effect of change program characteristics on employees' responses to change. The resulting cognitive-affective model proposes that both emotional responses, such as anxiety about the change, and cognitive justice perceptions that help people make sense of the situation, influence employees' responses to downsizing. However, rela-tively stable individual characteristics of employees, such as emotional propensities and emotional intelligence, will also influence the extent of anxiety people experience as a result of anticipating negative out-comes and the respective coping strategies they choose. Together, these variables are expected to impact on employees' short-term and long-term responses to downsizing. Short-term responses center on problem-focused and emotion-focused coping strategies, with positive strategies that help resolve the problem and alleviate the source of the stress typi-fying acceptance of change, and negative strategies embodying resis-tance to change. Long-term responses to the change reflect the extent to which employees adapt to the downsizing and the change becomes in-stitutionalized in the organizational culture. In this way, change man-agement characteristics can be linked to organizational survival and well-being.

The model proposed here overcomes many of the recent criticisms of current conceptualizations of "resistance to change." For example, Dent and Goldberg (1999) argue that the concept of resistance has moved away from the homeostatic systems notion initially proposed by Lewin's field theory to be viewed as a psychological characteristic of the individual employee. Such a mental model lays the blame for unsuccessful change interventions on employees, and ignores the role of managers who may attempt to implement inappropriate change interventions or use ineffective implementation procedures (Dent and Goldberg 1999; Krantz 1999). The proposed model avoids these pitfalls by drawing on the change management literature to specify the characteristics of effective change programs, and by describing how such procedures impact on employees' emotions and cognitions to influence their choice of coping strategies and long-term adaptation. More importantly, the new model avoids the current "employee-blaming" approach by viewing acceptance and resistance to change as the coping strategies employees use to deal with the losses that result from downsizing. This offers a less judgmental, and more sympathetic and dynamic, view of employee responses than does the traditional approach. This view is also more constructive, in that it encourages managers to identify additional change levers that allow employees to develop appropriate problem-focused and emotion-focused strategies that help them to cope with downsizing and ameliorate the negative psychological and material consequences such interventions can have.

A number of boundary conditions of the model must be noted. In particular, the model does not consider the content of any changes (e.g., restructuring or technological change) that accompany the downsizing, but instead assumes that appropriate changes will be made to ensure that surviving employees will be able to cope with the workload. Failure to address such issues by redesigning jobs and management systems, providing suitable technology and training, or taking other relevant steps to ensure that the accompanying changes are appropriate and feasible will undermine the success of the change effort, even if the process is managed well. In addition, the model does not consider the effect of constant change on employees over the long term. Research shows that the coping process in downsizing situations is dynamic and changes over time (Latack, Kinicui, and Prussia 1995). Future research should consider how the anxiety and justice perceptions of employees undergoing change affect employees' responses on these variables during future change efforts. Changes in perceptions of variables in the model over time should also be explored to identify the relative importance of different factors at different stages in the change process. Moreover, research needs to consider the frequency of large-scale changes in evaluating the ability of an individual's emotional characteristics and change program characteristics to ameliorate negative consequences. Finally, the model does not address the characteristics of the organization directly. Instead, the model assumes that factors such as organizational culture and the nature of employer-employee relations will impact upon justice perceptions via the design of the change communications, procedures, and support mechanisms that represent the characteristics of the organizational change program. This assumption needs to be addressed by further research.

The factors included in the proposed model suggest a number of management activities to consider when organizations undertake downsizing efforts. First, the model highlights the importance of attending to the nature of primary communications and change program characteristics to ensure that they meet employees' informational and procedural needs, and that they encourage effective coping strategies. Second, it suggests that support mechanisms that facilitate employees' emotionally intelligent abilities may promote the use of positive coping strategies and diminish the use of negative coping strategies, thereby improving outcomes for the change effort and for employees. This recommendation is congruent with Goleman's (1998b) suggestion that emotional intelligence training for managers will enable managers to provide supports that help ameliorate subordinates' negative emotions. Third, organizations should consider monitoring employees' level of anxiety and justice perceptions during change initiatives, because this will enable them to improve outcomes and modify elements of change-related activities. Finally, managers should sponsor research that considers the impact of emotional characteristics on responses to large-scale change. Better understanding of the factors affecting individuals' emotional responses to change will enable organizations to develop more effective support and counseling mechanisms. These practices, together with continued research into the management of change, have the potential to improve the outcomes of downsizing efforts for both organizations and employees.

In summary, the cognitive-affective model integrates key elements from the emotions and organizational justice literatures to explain why effective organizational change programs have beneficial effects on employees' responses to downsizing. If further longitudinal research supports the usefulness of the model, it will enhance understanding of the change process and provide an appropriate framework to guide the management of large-scale change. This will help managers design change interventions that avoid the potentially negative outcomes that downsizing can have for layoff victims, layoff survivors, and the organization overall.

3 ANALYZING EMOTIONS FOR A BETTER UNDERSTANDING OF ORGANIZATIONAL CHANGE: FEAR, JOY, AND ANGER DURING A MERGER

Tina Kiefer

In a world of global markets and new technologies, many organizations are going through fundamental change. However, many change projects, especially mergers and acquisitions, do not turn out to be as successful as hoped (Gerpott 1993; ISR 1999; Marks and Mirvis 1992). When trying to explain the low success rates of organizational change, many authors in the merger literature refer to "human factors" or "people problems" as a central cause (e.g., Davey et al. 1988; Müller-Stewens 1991). Some authors see emotional reactions of employees as a major reason for these problems occurring during implementation of change (e.g., Nippa 1996). This may lead in practice to the unfortunate conclusion that emotions need to be "managed away" and "overcome" in order to succeed. Thus, the management of emotions has become a pressing issue for practitioners during change. Unfortunately, there is only little systematic knowledge about how people emotionally experience these change processes and in which context and situations these emotions arise.

This chapter therefore has two aims: First, to start reconceptualizing our understanding of emotions during organizational change in theory and practice. The chapter focuses on specific emotions, their context, and their consequences, drawing on psychological theory and research on emotions. A second aim of this chapter is to illustrate some of the major theoretical notions by recounting stories and explanations behind frequently experienced emotions of a group of people at a specific moment of a merger.

Although the underlying assumption is that there cannot be any recipes for change and emotion management, there is a need to analyze and understand the specific emotions felt in different stakeholder groups in order to understand and manage emotional change (see Figure 3.1). The leading question throughout the chapter is: How can understanding specific emotions help us to better understand organizational change and its management?

Section one briefly summarizes and critically evaluates previous research and theory to better understand emotional reactions and their functions during change. An alternative approach to understanding emotions during change is outlined, drawing on parts of the psychological literature on emotions. Section two presents a qualitative study, which looks at the emotional experience of fundamental changes in a merger of two main competitors within the service sector in Switzerland. Three specific emotions—fear, joy, and anger—are concentrated on as illustrations of the main theoretical issues raised earlier in the chapter. Finally, section three reflects on the implications for understanding and managing emotions during organizational change.

Learning About Emotions from Research and Theory

Lessons from Change Literature

The traditional change literature focuses primarily on negative emotions that play a negative role during change. The main points can be summarized as follows (see Kiefer 2002, for more details):

(a) *Change causes stress and fear.* Many authors suggest that employees find fundamental change in organizations, especially mergers, a stressful, difficult experience and react very emotionally (e.g., Cartwright and Cooper 1992; Hogan and Overmayer-Day 1994; Marks and Mirvis 1992). The emotional reactions in a merger are mainly attributed to the uncertainty as to what the future holds in general, anxiety about loosing one's job, stress (often due to heavy workload), and feelings of loss (e.g., Cartwright and Cooper 1993; Mangham 1973). Survivors of layoffs are reported to feel upset and angry and sometimes even guilty because they are still in a job when former coworkers face unemployment (Brockner and Wiesenfeld 1993; Leana and Feldman 1989).

Figure 3.1   **Steps Necessary to Learn from Emotions for Change Management**

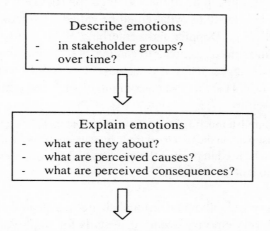

(b) *Negative emotions are an obstruction to change.* Many authors in the change literature believe—implicitly or explicitly—that negative emotions have negative consequences for the individual and the organization (e.g., Zarandona and Camuso 1985). Some authors even view emotions as the reason for withdrawal or destructive behavior (Nippa 1996). Positive emotions during change are rarely discussed.

(c) *Emotions are in need of correction.* Not only in management practice but also in some parts of the change literature, emotional reactions are seen as putting in danger the rationality and thus the effectiveness of people at work (e.g., Piderit 2000). Emotions are often equated with resistance, which needs to be overcome (e.g., see Cox 1997 for similar discussion). A driving assumption is that people fear change in general and therefore oppose it. Resistance is therefore seen as an emotional barrier (Reiss 1995) that prevents people from understanding rational arguments (Trzicky 1998). Fear or anxiety, for example, are usually perceived as a problem of the individual, who is either being irrational or lacking self-confidence. Thus, developmental training, such as stress management (e.g., Cartwright and Cooper 1992: Marks and Mirvis 1992), or better communication of the organizational goals (e.g., Saleker 1995) is seen as necessary managerial action and intervention.

Some of the more practitioner-oriented management literature tries to deal with resistance by what could be called a paradox of "emotion management" (e.g., Doppler and Lauterburg 1994). Although these authors view emotions as a barrier to change, at the same time they realize its power and suggest using it to achieve successful change. Hammer and Stanton (1994) are a typical example of such an approach:

> To accomplish this [to catalyze potential leaders for the change process] you must play on the two most basic human emotions: fear and greed. . . . Fear can be used in many different ways as a catalyst for change. (Hammer and Stanton 1994, 52)

In summary, radical organizational changes, especially mergers, certainly can be very emotive events, especially for employees. *Emotive* in the change literature predominantly means accompanied by *negative* emotions, especially fear and stress. Sometimes negative emotions are viewed as an expression of resistance, leading to negative outcomes for the individual and organization, and thus need to be overcome and managed (sometimes even by management of fear). Thus, this part of the literature has a rather narrow understanding of emotions, as it portrays a simple dichotomy between good and bad. There are, however, different ways of viewing emotions at work and during change (see, e.g., Fineman 2000). One way of starting to broaden our understanding is by drawing on some important approaches from the psychology of emotion.

Lessons from the Psychology of Emotion

Emotional reactions—in others and ourselves—contain a lot of information that we use in our everyday lives and hence help us understand emotions during change. Most of the psychology of emotions suggests that emotions in theory are best viewed as rule based (Lazarus 1991a, 1991b; Parkinson 1995; Scherer 1984) and not chaotic or irrational, as most of the change literature implies. This means that there is a specific logic behind the experience of emotions (which will be described in more detail later on). Therefore the quality and intensity of emotions gives us some insight into the way in which the person interprets the ongoing events in his or her environment (see "core-relational themes" farther down, Lazarus 1991a). Emotions indicate also that there is something of relevance going on and certain events either put goals in danger or support their achievement (e.g., Scherer 1984). The observation of emotions gives us information about what is important for the person. Emotions also reveal values, needs, basic understandings, or beliefs about what is good or bad for us and others. Furthermore—in line with the interpretation of the environment—prototypic emotions also express a specific action tendency (e.g., Frijda 1986).

Most emotion theorists view emotion as a multifaceted concept, which includes a cognitive, a motivational, a communicative, and a physiological component (e.g., Parkinson 1995; Scherer 1984). For the purpose of this chapter, two components are drawn on, namely the cognitive component and its relational aspect and the motivational component, the main pillars of Lazarus's cognitive-motivational-relational theory of emotion.[1]

(a) *Cognitive component.* Theoretically, emotions by many authors are seen as a result of cognitive appraisals following an event relevant for the individual (e.g., see Parkinson 1995 for a summary). The theoretical description of these appraisals helps us understand and differentiate specific emotions, for example fear and anger in a specific culture. According to Ortony, Clore, and Collins (1988), anger in a Western culture indicates disapproval of somebody else's action or the related consequences. Whereas fear or anxiety is a negative reaction to an event that has not happened yet and that is anticipated to happen in the future.

Lazarus (1991a) specifies "core-relational themes" to theoretically map out prototypical emotions. A core-relational theme is "simply the central (hence core) relational harm or benefit in adaptational encounters that underlies each specific kind of emotion" (Lazarus 1991a, 121). The term *relational* points to an important theoretical notion: the relatedness of the individual and its environment. It describes the way in which an emotion is always a result of an individual's appraisal of the environment, based on societal rules. Table 3.1 exemplifies such cognitive appraisal patterns and core-relational themes for a selection of emotions.

(b) *Motivational component.* Interwoven with the theme of an emotion lies its motivational function (see Table 3.1, last column). Different emotions are seen to be linked with different behavioral tendencies or

Table 3.1

Theoretical Dimensions of Selected Emotions

Emotion category	Description after Ortony, Clore, and Collins (1988)	Core-relational theme after Lazarus (1991a)	Reaction tendency after Frijda (1986)
Disappointment/ frustration	Displeased about the disconfirmation of the prospect of a desirable event	—	Submission: tendency to submit control
Anger/rage	Disapproving of someone else's blameworthy action and being displeased about the related undesirable event	Demeaning offence against me and mine	Antagonism: tendency to remove obstacle, hurt, oppose, resist
Fear/anxiety	Displeased about the prospect of an undesirable event	Facing uncertain, existential threat	Avoidance: tendency to avoid, flee, or protect oneself
			Inhibition: action readiness in the absence of action
Hope	Pleased about the prospect of a desirable event	Fearing the worst but yearning for better	—

Pride	Approving of one's own praiseworthy action	Enhancement of one's ego-identity by taking credit for a valued object or achievement, either our own or that of someone of group with whom we identify	—
Joy/happiness	Pleased about a desirable event	Making reasonable progress toward the realization of a goal	Approach: tendency to get closer
			Exuberance: general-ized action readiness
Relief	Pleased about the disconfirmation of the prospect of an undesirable event	Distressing goal-incongruent condition that has changed for the better or gone away	—

action tendencies (Frijda 1986). These behavioral tendencies have a strong adaptive function, helping the individual to adjust to the changing environment. However, the author does not suggest that individuals necessarily act according to the emotion-specific action tendency in an everyday situation, as there are many other factors influencing our situational behaviors. Due to the specific action tendencies, it is not helpful per se to assume that negative emotions have negative consequences for the individual and the environment (or organization), or that positive emotions have positive outcomes as is often implied especially in the managerial change literature.

This section gave brief and selective theoretical input into the possible role of emotions during change from a psychology of emotion perspective. However, in order to manage organizational change, we need to know more specifically what emotions are experienced in an organization, what these emotions are about, and what the consequences of the emotional experience are. This is vital because emotions are likely to vary between different phases, for different groups of the organization as well as in different types of change projects. So basically, before we can start to think about managing emotional change processes, we need to first describe emotions during a specific change, and second explain what these emotions are about (see Figure 3.1). The next section presents some results of a qualitative study aimed at portraying the emotional experience during a merger and illustrates what can be learned from analyzing emotions during change.

Learning About Emotions from Human Resource Managers During a Merger

The Study

The study presented here is part of a larger project that attempted to explore the role of emotions during a merger (Kiefer and Eicken 1999). The research questions relevant for this chapter are: Which emotions are felt during the merger? and What is the context and consequences of the emotions reported?

The study was conducted in a large company in the service sector, resulting from the merger of two of the biggest competitors in Switzerland. Both partner organizations had been undergoing major change processes in the years before the merger was announced. Although stemming from the same sector, they were perceived to have rather different organizational cultures and structures. Previous to the merger, both partner organizations were seen as very secure and reliable employers.

The sample consisted of eight human resource managers working in the same team in one specific area of the country. The interviewees came from both partner organizations. We interviewed four men and five women and their ages ranged from mid-twenties to early sixties. In order to guarantee anonymity, further description of the participants has been omitted.

The data were collected by conducting semistructured interviews, which lasted between sixty and ninety minutes. These interviews were conducted fourteen months after the announcement of the merger and seven months after the integration actually started. Based on our experiences in the pilot study, we chose to structure the interview with the help of an emotion taxonomy (based on Schmidt-Atzert and Ströhm 1983). The taxonomy lists the most common German emotion expressions according to their perceived similarity (see Tables 3.2 and 3.3). The taxonomies with the negative and positive emotions were presented to the participants, and they were asked to indicate the emotions that were most typical for their personal experience during the merger. In a second step, the participants were asked to report an event where they actually experienced one or several of the reported emotions. The procedure was conducted separately for the positive and negative emotions.[2] The interviews were recorded and transcribed. Figure 3.2 shows the process of the data analysis. First, the reported emotions and the description of the circumstances in which they arose were isolated in the text; second, the circumstances of the emotions were further analyzed, by asking: What or who was the trigger of the emotion? In which thematic context did the emotion occur? What is the relational aspect of the interaction between individual and organization? What consequences were reported, if any at all?

For this chapter, quotations were translated from Swiss German to English. In so doing, the quotations lost some of their originality. It is not the intention, however, to use the data to prove a theory but rather to illustrate the emotional experience of this group.

Positive and Negative Emotions Reported

Which emotions were felt during the merger? Tables 3.2 and 3.3 show a wide range of negative and positive emotions reported by the participants as typical for their daily working life during the merger.

Figure 3.2   **Approach to Data Analysis**

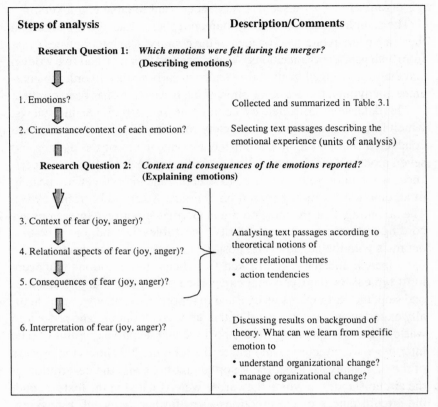

What do these results mean for change management? First of all, they mean that the emotional experience is not limited to stress and fear, but that there are many more negative and also many positive emotions dominating everyday life during change. It is argued in section one that for managing change it is a vital prerequisite to know what kind of emotions are felt in an organization or in a specific team (see Figure 3.1). It is therefore important to keep in mind that these emotions listed in the tables are not representative for the merger in all of the company, but are an illustration of the felt emotions at the time of the interviews for this sample. Obviously different groups would have experienced different events and are thus likely to report different emotional episodes. Change management interventions would therefore have to be designed differently.

Just knowing and being able to describe the emotions felt is yet not sufficient; we need to be able to explain these emotions (see Figure 3.1).

Table 3.2

Negative Emotions Reported

Dislike	Anger	Envy	Frustration	Void	Fear	Resignation	Weariness	Sadness	Shame	Restlessness
Dislike (4)	Anger (29)	Jealousy (2)	Frustration (33)	Boredom (1)	Fear/Anxiety (28)	Hopelessness (—)	Being fed up with (7)	Homesickness (2)	Remorse (1)	Impatience (13)
Contempt (1)	Aggression (7)	Envy (7)	Annoyance (9)	Void (2)	Horror (—)	Resignation (8)	Having enough (11)	Longing (5)	Guilt (1)	Restlessness (12)
Disgust (—)	Resentment (—)	Mistrust (19)	*Dissatisfaction (7)	Listlessness (13)	Panic (1)		Disappointment (12)	Grief (4)	Shame (—)	
Aversion (5)	Rage (14)	Malicious glee (3)			Shock (—)			Sadness (4)	Embarrassment (—)	
*Disapproval (8)	Hatred (—)				Despair (2)			Worry (8)		
	Defiance (3)				*Insecurity (41)					
Total: 18	Total: 53	Total: 31	Total: 49	Total: 16	Total: 72	Total: 8	Total: 30	Total: 23	Total: 2	Total: 25

Note: Taxonomie after Schmidt-Atzert & Ströhm 1983. *Additional emotions reported that were not included in the original.

Table 3.3

Positive Emotions Reported

Joy	Pride	Affection	Surprise	Hope
Enthusiasm (7)	Pride (15)	Thankfulness (15)	Surprise (19)	Hope (28)
Desire (11)	Triumph (1)	Admiration (—)	Astonishment (7)	Anticipation (15)
Joy (38)		Goodwill (1)	Amazement (7)	
Happiness (1)		Affection (3)		
Satisfaction (22)		Confidence (6)		
Relief (12)		Empathy (3)		
Total: 91	Total: 16	Total: 28	Total: 33	Total: 43

Note: Taxonomie after Schmidt-Atzert & Ströhm 1983.

In the next section the emotions fear, joy, and anger are described in more detail and their underlying patterns are analyzed according to Research Question 2.

Fear was chosen because it is a very common emotion reported in the organizational change literature, anger is described because it was often reported in the study but hardly discussed at all in the change literature, and joy was chosen because it was by far the most common reported positive emotion. The emotions differ strongly according to the theoretical core-relational themes and action tendencies. The similarity between the three chosen emotions is that they were frequently mentioned by the interviewed human resource managers.

Regarding these three specific emotions, the contexts in which they arose are described, their relational aspects are worked out, some of their consequences are outlined, and their implications for understanding and managing change are discussed (see Figure 3.2).

Explaining Fear

The category of fear (along with anxiety, despair, panic, and insecurity) has been reported as a typical emotion during the merger. The next subsection describes the context and consequences of fear for this particular sample, following steps 3 to 6 in Figure 3.2.

The Context of Fear

Table 3.1 suggests that fear is about being displeased with the prospect of an undesirable event (Ortony, Clore, and Collins 1988), or is seen as an existential threat (Lazarus 1991a). The merger literature suggests that fear arises due to the uncertain future and especially due to the possibility of job loss (Cartwright and Cooper 1992). The participants in this study did indeed report being anxious with respect to their job:

> P4 (Participant 4): I want to come back to the motive of fear. That is simply unconscious, even if it is not in the foreground right now, but I think somehow it is always with us. Nowadays much more than in the past. . . . Maybe this [fear] would be less strong, if I only had to look after myself.

This person refers to fear unspecifically, not due to a specific event, but makes a very general comment about the changing times (in society in general). His important concern is to feed his family. The next quotations make clear that some reasons for this fear are seen to lie within the company. For example, redundancies have been announced months ago, but no clear figures have been released since:

> P3: Fear really comes to the light, because we still don't have the headcount figures, how many people are we allowed to keep? These figures are discussed on the quiet, but officially they are not known yet . . . and this is of course why this fear emerges—am I still going to be needed then?

Here, the topics connected to the emotion of fear and anxiety go beyond mere job insecurity, reflecting other existential issues and forthcoming changes: Will I still be needed? Am I still good enough to do the job? Have I got the adequate education? Will I still personally be able to have an impact on the place?

> P1: Will I still be needed, and will I stand my ground in this new organization? Look, we have got many problems . . . will I still master my daily routine? Will I be able to meet these new demands? Demands will rise; there is already talk of headcount pressure. You can't say it openly, but it is a topic.

In the last two quotations the organization is seen as a cause for fear. Due to the merger, the insecurity about the future has risen, but in the eyes of P1 and P3, the organization is fueling this fear by not communicating openly about the headcount. There is a noticeable suspicion toward the organization.

Not only unsatisfactory communication is interpreted as a cause for fear, but also decisions by senior management, which are uncontrollable for the participants but impact upon their lives:

> P4: Yes, and especially [fear as a reaction to] certain decisions, made out of the blue, taken by the CEOs and then you wonder permanently, what is going to happen next? Somebody is going to make a decision somewhere, which is of course going to affect my own decisions. Fear is everywhere, where my own existence or that of my family is touched.

P4 refers to "two or three" occasions where management has made unexpected decisions, making the employees feel helpless and vulnerable.

Relational Aspects of Fear and an Excursion on Mistrust

Some of these quotations illustrating context of fear already indicated that fear can be seen as a consequence of interpretations of organizational actions. The participants indicate this by pointing out that fear is based on the fact that the organization has still not released the headcount figures. Fear is theoretically seen as an anticipation of a possible future event. Perceived lack of control over the future event is a typical aspect of fear. Once the organization releases the figures and decides who will be made redundant, the emotion of fear will most likely change into a different emotion (e.g., relief, anger, despair). The quotation of P4 about the "decisions, made out of the blue" also indicates another aspect of this relationship, which can be observed in other participants in connection with fear as well: lack of trust.

Events surrounding the emotion of mistrust are mainly causally attributed to the organization (including policies and strategies, culture, and the way employees are treated):

> P6: The situation we experience now, we experience for the third time. . . . I can't avoid thinking about the past and how things have been sorted in the past, especially how jobs have been assigned, and that a lot did go very differently from what had been announced or promised.
> P5: I try to communicate in every team meeting that there will be something like justice and fairness, but the people simply don't believe it, because it never happened that way in the past before.

These quotations illustrate that the lack of trust is not due to the events happening in the recent merger, but rather they are the consequence of a more-or-less long history of experiences with the organization.

Consequences of Fear

Frijda (1986) describes fear and anxiety as linked either to inhibition (action readiness in the absence of action) or to avoidance (tendency to avoid, flee, and protect oneself) (see Table 3.1). The participants in this study report both. Examples for inhibition are "feeling helpless" or "continuing as before but hoping it will change."

> P2: It looks as if this position [of a coworker] is not going to continue, but you cannot tell just now. And here we are, waiting helplessly.
> P2: Fear is certainly with us. Not knowing what is going to happen, it is hanging somewhere above us. You suppress it—as long as there is work you just continue and you hope that nothing is going to happen, but this fear that something is going to happen is here.

Examples for avoidance are not daring to speak up or criticize, resigning, or taking concrete actions to reduce insecurity:

> P4: If I make a wrong comment in the wrong place, then I am the first to go, when they cut staff.
> P4: Clearly in this phase of insecurity, it is natural that one doesn't criticise openly. . . . It would affect my bonus, wouldn't it!?
> P8: Many were active [as a response to their insecurity], and went talking to the bosses, got active in order to get a position back, as this remained open for a long time.

These quotations illustrate that there are differences between the team members in how they react to the existential threats. On the one hand, participants are constantly aware of the threats, enduring the constant anxiety, trying to continue their work as before. On the other hand, the last quotations make clear that fear can have very concrete and active outcomes, which aim at reducing the insecurity. The quotations suggest that in this group—from the organization's point of view—there are some positive outcomes of fear (e.g., working constructively toward a solution) as well as negative outcomes (e.g., not speaking up) for the organization.

Interpreting Fear for Understanding Change and
Its Management

The analysis of fear in this sample reflects the issues discussed in the change literature, but also broadens the understanding of what fear is about during this merger. Fear is connected to a variety of themes, which can be summarized as potential threats: from job insecurity issues to a much wider range of existential topics such as fear of not being able to contribute to organizational goals any longer. I suggest that these perceived threats are referring to the professional identity of the participants, revealing some basic values and needs, such as to feel needed and to be able to have an impact.

The organization is seen as partly responsible for their fear, which is reinforced by the perceived lack of control, of being at the company's mercy. This suggests that fear is not merely an expression of individual weakness and inadequacy, but is based on a strong interaction with the organization. An important factor here is the previous experience with the organization, which forms the relationship between individual and organization over time. Past events are part of this relationship at present. In order to understand the emotional experience of the merger at this stage, it is on the one hand important to know and acknowledge the history of the organization, and on the other to understand the ongoing formation of the relationship between individual (or teams) and the organization and its representatives. Maintaining a relationship based on trust and esteem once again seems vital for change (Elangovan and Shapiro 1998). For the management of change, these results also suggest that for this group it would not be sufficient to simply send them off to stress management courses, as suggested by much of the practitioner oriented change literature. This could, in turn, make the team feel that the organization denies responsibility for their employees and that the organization is not acknowledging their part of the interaction. This is likely to reinforce their suspicion. Not taking people's anxieties seriously can be interpreted as devaluing the individuals and in this situation is likely to be felt that way by team members.

The interviews indicate that there are several negative consequences of fear to be expected for the organization. Especially the "wait and see" attitude and the "not speaking up" make clear why some authors and managers may find the idea of "management by fear" appealing at first sight. These employees do not dare to speak up and openly "resist."

However, the consequences of such a "wait and see" attitude or "not speaking up" seriously put in question the ability of the team to actively improve the quality of organizational processes (e.g., see Piderit 2000).

Explaining Joy

In this section we are going to look closer at the context and consequences of the emotion "joy" or "happiness," the most frequent positive emotion reported by the participants.[3]

The Context of Joy

What do people feel joyful about during a merger? Table 3.1 suggests that, in general, "joy" means being pleased about a desirable event (Ortony, Clore, and Collins 1988) and about making reasonable progress toward the realization of a goal (Lazarus 1991b). The participants reported a wide range of different events and themes surrounding the emotion joy, which are often mixed with other emotions. First of all the participants reported joy related to the activity itself:

> P2: I felt joy to work on something conceptual as compared to before.

Further examples are "loving a new task" or "feeling enthusiastic about working on the new structure." In other quotations, the theoretical notion of getting closer to a goal is also clearly expressed:

> P7: Joy, because of relief, joy or enthusiasm that we could make the processes work, that we could get rid of old ballast, that something new comes, with more or better structures, or relief, because the whole migration actually turned out to work OK, that despite the heavy workload and the problems with IT that we made it, despite all that.
>
> P3: Joy, because you can bring something about and joy also because it depends a little bit on you, that things work out.

These two quotations illustrate that joy is often combined with other emotions, for example, relief (reaching a goal that was thought impossible) or pride (making things happen due to own abilities). In both quotes the sense of personal achievement is in the foreground. Other examples of joy are theoretically closer to the emotion "surprise," as they express an unexpected turn. Here is a typical example:

P7: Joy when somebody [in the team] tells me, thank you, you have done this really well.

Here the need for social esteem is expressed, despite the heavy workload, where nobody has time for even a little chat. The participant feels acknowledged by either the immediate social surrounding (e.g., team members or line manager) or by the organization itself.

In summary, there are many events causing joy and happiness in the merger. They can be summarized as follows, reflecting streams in the well-being literature: (a) Activity-related joy (e.g., flow; Csikszentmihalyi and Csikszentmihalyi 1988), here often mixed with enthusiasm; (b) Joy through reaching goals (e.g., telic theories; Carver and Scheier 1990), here often mixed with pride or relief; (c) Event-specific joy (e.g., emotion theories; Lazarus 1991b; Scherer 1984), here often mixed with surprise or being thankful.

Relational Aspects of Joy

Because joy is a very broad emotion reflecting a variety of events, the relational aspects differ quite a lot. There are several important relational aspects that clarify the interaction between individual and organization. The organization is often included when the participants talk about joy and happiness. However, there is an obvious distinction. Joy is felt (by getting closer to a goal) on one hand despite the organization (and its merger). This is underlined by participants' reporting to be thrilled by the new possibilities or feeling relief and joy because the team "made it" despite the heavy workload or thankfulness and joy because somebody showed appreciation even though everybody feels stressed. On the other hand, joy is felt due to the organization and because of the organization (and its merger). P8 illustrates this:

P8: I feel happy to be in this organization, we have changed so many things, I have been offered the possibility to learn so much.

In this sample it is interesting to see that the participants refer positive experiences to their own abilities and their will, but also to the organization, despite their strong mistrust expressed elsewhere. In another study conducted in a different industrial sector the positive emotions were never directly attributed to the organization (Kiefer, Müller, and Eicken 2001).

Consequences of Joy

Frijda (1986) suggests that joy and happiness are linked either with exuberance (generalized action readiness), with approach (tendency to get closer), or with being-with (tendency to stay close). This is clearly stated by one of the participants:

> P8: [The feeling to do the job well] triggered off joy and a certain satisfaction, although there was a lot of work, . . . but I didn't mind, that didn't count.

The participant continues to explain that without the feeling of enthusiasm and pride, he wouldn't have been able to cope with all the changes. Another participant refers to the changes that the merger offers:

> P2: Pride, joy, hey, it's you, you can do something new, the catch word they always say, that change and merger aren't only about danger, but also about chances. I have experienced this one to one, and experienced an enormous motivation to start something new. I wanted to do this for a long time, I wanted to get out of the old routine. And now, full of motivation, I am doing something new.

Joy and satisfaction were vital to this group of employees at this stage of the merger, essential for their motivation to go the "extra mile" and not give up.

Interpreting Joy for Understanding Change and Its Management

The participants clearly do not talk only about negative emotions, but also experience positive chances and challenges and also approve of and even enjoy many changes occurring due to the merger. For a more comprehensive understanding of organizational change, it is thus important not only to focus on negative emotions, but also on positive ones. Furthermore, the positive emotions joy, happiness, enthusiasm, thankfulness and pride are vital for the personal performance and motivation and thus for the success of the change process in the change literature. This claim is strongly supported by the literature focusing on the functions of positive (goal congruent) emotions (e.g., Fredrickson 1998). Analyzing joy and happiness, for example, in combination with relief or pride, highlights the importance of feeling a sense of achievement and acknowledgment during change.

For the management of change, this means that it is important not only to try and avoid negative reactions but to more actively create space for personal action and positive experiences and to acknowledge the achievements of the team.

Explaining Anger

This subsection deals with the emotion anger, which has hardly been discussed in the change literature but has been reported frequently by the participants. Also, from my personal experience, managers often interpret anger as an emotional barrier, as resistance to change.

The Context of Anger

What evokes anger during the merger? Demeaning offence against me and mine is the core-relational theme of anger (Table 3.1). Ortony, Clore, and Collins (1988) describe anger more neutrally as disapproving of someone else's blameworthy action and being displeased about the related undesirable events. The events reported in connection with anger are quite broad. Anger is often mentioned in everyday work situations, frequently because of inefficient work processes due to changes created by the merger (running on the spot, doing things twice).

> P1: Many mistakes are made there [in that department] whenever we commission work with them. My colleagues have to make a copy of every single mutation, we have to check and control if it had been done and how it has been done and in over 50% of the cases the work has been done wrongly . . . and that causes anger, and rage, and frustration, as we actually want to do the work ourselves but we are stuck in between.
>
> P5: Anger for me is of a technical nature, that the stuff simply doesn't work and that the structures are not here to support us.

Anger, of course, sometimes arises in social interactions (colleagues who are not doing their work), but in this team is more often reported on a more abstract level in the context of the organization. The following two examples exemplify the latter:

> P8: I think a big part of our annoyance is due to the fact that many mistakes happen, that much of the information doesn't flow properly, that

many corrections need to be made, not between us or because of us, but coming from others, wrongly communicated by the organization, or there were instructions released and then three days later, oh, a mistake has crept in, in some cases very big, bad mistakes, that is a real annoyance and you think why does this need to happen.

P1: [Anger] about the problem as such, about our daily business, which is not working. It is not bound to specific people, then in such companies things are always impersonal, it is somewhere somebody making decisions and it gets communicated in some form, but it is not personal, not Mr. X or Mrs. Y.

Relational Aspects of Anger

What does analyzing the context of anger of this group tell us about their interaction with the organization and how they view the organization? It becomes clear that the participants strongly state their disapproval of certain events and the way in which things are sometimes handled. The organizational actions in their view are in parts badly organized, making their lives more difficult than necessary, and feelings of being "thrown back" start to emerge. Furthermore, the annoyance and anger of the team lay open a very positive and strong work and professional attitude. The participants want to do their job properly but feel hindered by the organization (nonworking processes, etc.). In this sense the organization is—in their eyes—demeaning their position.

Consequences of Anger

Which consequences does the experienced anger have for the participants and the organization? The participants only indirectly mentioned consequences of anger, by talking about the consequences of the events triggering anger (rather than the emotion itself). Frijda (1986) names resistance as an element of the action tendency of anger. Thus, anger triggers the tendency to remove the obstacle or to oppose and resist. Participant 7 expresses this also symbolically, when talking about the daily business where things go wrong:

P7: And that makes my blood raise, also [laughing] it drives me up the wall, and I have the feeling, there is not much I can do to change that, I will always say what I think and I will stand by my opinions, but it takes energy and strength, and my adrenaline keeps exploding, and then in the end again [I feel] frustration and emptiness . . . or simply a listlessness for the whole thing.

Other participants in different contexts express more control and seem to move the obstacle to continue their own way:

> P3: For me this certainly has the consequence that I surely know that the realization of that project, . . . I will do it almost certainly my way. And I won't permanently feel that when they utter a grunt down there in Zurich that I'll jump and run after them, . . . but I will set the dates according to my liking so that I have the feeling I will manage until end of January.

Another person refers to her rising aggression as a consequence of anger and annoyance:

> P5: When it touches my own concerns, I feel that I can react very aggressively, and this against anybody. . . . That is when I realize that with respect to myself and with respect to others I feel that actually me too, I am frustrated.

It becomes clear in most of the quotations that anger and frustration lie very close to each other. Frustration, an emotion that also comprises of helplessness and resignation, is seen here as one consequence of anger.

Interpreting Anger for Understanding Change and Its Management

How can looking at anger help us better understand how organizational change is perceived in this group? Although there is some indication that participants start to go their own way in order to get through their work, anger here does not seem to be an expression of resistance at all, but rather illustrates how the change challenges the team members' sense of efficiency and professionalism. The process of the changes—not the change in itself—is interpreted as hindering them to carry out their job according to their professional standards.

The amount of anger and the reported consequences of anger seem to call for a change management intervention, as dealing with their anger costs them far too much time and energy (to put it in terms of a participant). For change management, the analysis of this emotion made clear that—again—for example, communicating clearly for change in this situation would be inadequate, as none of the participants objected to the aims of the changes (but rather the process of change). In this case it would be important to integrate the experiences of the team to improve the process and the changes.

Summary and Conclusion

The implications of the specific illustrations of fear, joy, and anger for change have already been discussed. Here, the more general implications for change management are summarized. Emotions certainly play a part in management thinking, and previous research has shown how difficult the experience of radical change can be and what some of the crucial issues are that need to be paid attention to when managing organizational change. However, I have argued that there is a downside to some of this literature, as emotions are usually reduced to a simple dichotomy of good and bad with the implications that emotions need to be managed merely by reducing or avoiding negative emotions. This simplification can have a problematic impact on change management, as it may prevent management from taking a close and specific look at different stakeholder perspectives and may lead to stereotypical actions. This is likely to be ineffective or even counterproductive as it does not pay sufficient attention to specific stakeholder perspectives. This chapter aimed to show how a differentiated understanding of emotions can open up possibilities for managing emotions and change. These four general points summarize why emotions should not, and need not, be managed away or reduced, but that they actually give valuable insights into the change process.

First, from a psychological perspective, experiencing emotion also means that the ongoing events are important to our life and our identity. If change does not provoke emotions, it may be either not relevant for the individual or not really noticed. Hence, organizational change is bound to lead to emotional reactions if the changes are radical and fundamental. These emotions are likely to be varied, negative emotions from frustration to envy, and positive emotions from enthusiasm to thankfulness.

Second, emotions during change are not irrational but have their own logic. If we understand this logic, we get valuable insights into specific perceptions of the change process, which are likely to differ between stakeholders (e.g., customers, top-management, or employees). By studying emotions, we learn about goals and needs of people involved as well as about their values concerning the organization (e.g., see Kiefer and Müller 2001). Furthermore, I would argue that an adequate understanding of the mix of emotions is a necessary prerequisite for managing organizational change, as otherwise interventions and management actions are not going to be successful. The case of anger, which may be misunderstood as resistance, is a good example of an emotion that is often misinterpreted. The example also makes clear that labeling others as being resistant is an expression of an inherent (top-down) power position. Understanding emotions in the process of change can overcome this top-down position, specifically as it puts at center stage the ideal that different perspectives on the change process are justified and valid, as it takes into account the different stakeholders in the process of change.

Third, it is important to bear the relational aspects of emotions in mind. Emotions are not merely a product of a specific individual (and his or her personality traits), but are more helpfully viewed as a result of the interactions with the (mainly social) environment. For example, ongoing change events are interpreted on the basis of one's relationship with the organization and its representing actors such as CEO, managers, personal supervisors, and coworkers. This relationship can have a long and varied history. This means that it is important to know the history of emotional episodes in order to lead change adequately. It is also important to be aware of the fact that interpretations of what is happening in an organization at present will impact the future and cannot later be reversed.

Fourth, specific emotions drive action in specific directions. Thus, various emotions are likely to have different impacts on the change process. They can be seen as a personal "engine" and serve an important adaptive function in everyday life. This is a further reason why emotions cannot be "managed away" and are not required to be "overcome" by management interventions. Understanding the adaptive function of emotions prevents us from falling into the trap of dismissing all negative emotions as having negative outcomes. It also helps us keep in mind the vital function of positive emotions such as pride and enthusiasm for successful change.

This chapter suggests that these four basic aspects are a starting point for broadening our understanding of the emotional experience of change. For managing emotions during change, this means that it is vital to first perceive, and then to appreciate, our own and others' specific emotions and acknowledge that there might be a great mix of specific emotions. Managing mistrust in the organization due to an unfair early retirement scheme, for example, calls for different managerial action than a high level of anger due to the feeling of being frustrated in doing a good job by poor organizational procedures. Change management can try to deal with negative emotions either directly, by acknowledging emotions and thus taking human beings and their specific experiences seriously, or indirectly, by dealing with emotions by shaping or managing the underlying events, which again asks for a profound analysis of the situation. However, this chapter also suggests that change management needs to focus more specifically on positive emotions as well, which are a vital part of managing change on an individual as well as on an organizational level.

Acknowledgments

The project was financially supported by the Research Foundation (Grundlagenforschungsfonds) of the University of St. Gallen and the Büchner-Stiftung. I thank colleagues Peter Dachler and Thomas Eberle for their very valuable input on an earlier version of this manuscript.

Notes

1. I consider the communicative function of emotions to be enormously important in the context of work and organizations, especially for the social construction of the change process. However, as this is not the focus of this chapter, I will not discuss it further.

2. With Lazarus (1991a), we define positive emotions as goal-congruent, and negative emotions as goal-incongruent.

3. The translation from Swiss German into English does not always allow to distinguish between the two terms properly, and even Lazarus (1991a) discusses these two emotions together, as they are difficult to separate.

4 MYTHS ABOUT EMOTIONS DURING CHANGE

Charmine E.J. Härtel and Wilfred J. Zerbe

As is often the case with emotions in organizations generally, emotions during change are easily viewed as problematic. From the perspectives of managers pushing change on seemingly reluctant organizational members, felt and expressed emotion is readily seen as representing resistance to be overcome and irrationality to be conquered. Chapters in this section take a different view of employee resistance, arguing that the emotions that accompany change are a natural and useful adjunct to change, and that their likelihood depends upon how the change program is managed. Examined from this perspective, emotions become not the indicators of failing or flawed individuals in the organization, but important indicators of the relevance and effectiveness of change processes. In this section, we explore some of the myths associated with employee emotion and organizational change, concluding with observations on how organizations can exercise emotional intelligence in their management of change.

Myth 1: Employees' Negative Emotional Reactions Reflect Resistance to Organizational Change

Both the Paterson and Härtel and Kiefer chapters point out the dangers of blaming reactions to change on individuals, with labels such as "employee resistance." They argue that employees' emotional responses to change are normal manifestations of coping with the way change is being managed, rather than an irrational response on the part of employees. To remedy this, Paterson and Härtel present a "new model" of change that avoids the "employee-blaming" approach by viewing acceptance and resistance to change as legitimate coping strategies that employees adopt to deal with the real or perceived losses associated with change initiatives. This perspective recognizes that change and the adaptation to it is a dynamic and unfolding process. Consequently, organizations are admonished to provide supports and training that enable employees to develop appropriate problem-focused and emotion-focused strategies for coping with the changing workplace they face in contemporary working life.

Myth 2: Emotions Need to Be Managed Away or Overcome in Order for Change Initiatives to Succeed

In the change literature, emotions are often equated with resistance or the failure of change interventions. This view, Kiefer points out, may lead managers to the unfortunate conclusion that emotions need to be "managed away" and "overcome" in order for a change to materialize. Additionally, Kiefer warns, this view may lead organizations to ignore the possibility that managers may be attempting to implement inappropriate change interventions or to use ineffective implementation procedures.

Myth 3: Emotions Are the Reason for Employee Withdrawal and Destructive Behavior During Organizational Change

The traditional change literature primarily portrays negative emotions such as fear, stress, anxiety, anger, loss, guilt, and uncertainty as having a negative role during change. Some authors, Kiefer notes, even view emotions as the reason for employee withdrawal or destructive behavior. Positive outcomes of negative emotions or positive emotions during change are rarely discussed. Paterson and Härtel and Kiefer explain that it is not the emotions themselves that produce positive or negative outcomes for the individual and the organization but, rather, it is the coping strategies employees engage in as a response to their emotional reactions.

Myth 4: People Fear Change in General and Therefore Oppose It

Kiefer remarks that an implicit and sometimes explicit assumption of the change literature is that people oppose change because they generally fear it. As borne out by Kiefer's research, when sufficient support and coping strategies are available, people facing change can find satisfaction and even joy and enhanced self-esteem.

Myth 5: Emotions Represent Chaotic or Irrational Responses

Authors such as Ashforth and Humphrey (1995) have pointed out that emotions have often been equated in organizational studies with irrationality. Agreeing with this observation, Kiefer asserts that emotions are not chaotic or irrational but, rather, the outcomes of applying societal rules to the appraisal of one's environment.

Myth 6: Negative Emotions Have Negative Consequences for the Individual and the Organization While Positive Emotions Have Positive Consequences

The traditional change literature depicts negative emotions as having negative consequences for the individual and the organization. This view, Kiefer points out, is neither true nor helpful. Her research clearly revealed that a negative emotion, such as fear, could lead to positive actions that have positive outcomes, such as the reduction of insecurity. Just as other scholars have noted (e.g., Jordan, Ashkanasy, and Härtel 2000), negative emotions can lead to positive outcomes for the individual and the organization (e.g., working constructively toward a solution) or negative outcomes for the individual and the organization (e.g., avoidance, not speaking up).

Myth 7: Emotions Are Solely the Product of Individuals

In the change literature, Kiefer notes, emotions such as fear or anxiety, are usually perceived as a problem of the individual, who is either being irrational or lacking self-confidence. Both chapters in this section, however, provide persuasive evidence for defining emotions as the product of individual emotional characteristics interacting with environmental characteristics.

Replacing the Myths of Change with Informed Action

The "Reason" Behind Emotions

Emotions are not without their reason and they are not necessarily unreasonable. What the chapters in these sections have lucidly demonstrated is that emotions are, using Kiefer's words, "always a result of an individual's appraisal of the environment, based on societal rules." Thus, the emotional responses experienced during organizational change are the consequence of interpretations of organizational actions. Indeed, Kiefer notes, emotions are ways humans indicate that there is something of relevance going on and that personal goals are either being supported or threatened. Emotions, therefore, are crucial indicators of what an individual sees as important, valued, needed, understood, and believed as good or bad for themselves and others.

Emotionally Intelligent Change Management

Paterson and Härtel's integrated theoretical model depicts the relationship between change program communications and procedures and acceptance to change as being affected by the emotional responses, such as anxiety about a change, and cognitions, such as fairness perceptions, that it generates. This framework and the findings of Kiefer's research provide extensive advice for those designing organizational change interventions. A few of the implications of their work are depicted in Table 4.1 and elaborated below.

Foster a Culture of Emotional Awareness

One of the implications apparent from the chapters in this section is that organizations need to have the same sort of ongoing awareness of employees' emotional states as they do for the state of employees' skills. It is also apparent that organizations need to develop their members' awareness of emotional processes in the workplace. Individuals need to understand that emotions are the result of assessments of situations. They also need to understand what are beneficial and detrimental problem-focused and emotion-focused coping strategies (cf. Jordan, Askhanasy, and Härtel 2000).

Conclusion

In this chapter we have used the term *myth* in the sense most often used in everyday language—that of a collective belief that is false. However, *myth* also refers to the expression of themes that are understood as universal truths and that offer advice for everyday living (Campbell 1988; Dundes 1984). The truthfulness of myths is irrelevant—their power comes from our unquestioning faith in them (Barthes 1957). The influ-

Table 4.1

Advice for Designing Organizational Change Interventions

DOs	DON'Ts
• Foster a culture of emotional awareness	• Blame resistance on the individual
• Maintain open and quality communication	• Equate negative emotions with negative outcomes
• Provide opportunities for stakeholder input into planning	• Equate positive emotions with positive outcomes
• Provide appropriate support systems	• Overlook the role of the change intervention or implementation in employee response to change
• Safeguard a history of positive change efforts	
	• View emotions as irrational
• Ensure that decision makers display interpersonal sensitivity	• Assume that people fear change
• Monitor emotional reactions in change stakeholder groups	• Leave people to fend with the change themselves
• Identify perceived causes and consequences behind the emotions	• Withhold information about the effect of the change on personal goals
• Match intervention to the results of the emotional reaction analysis	• Ignore the emotional states of stakeholders of change

ence exercised by myth on the structure of society and its institutions is perhaps best recognized by adherents of institutional theory, who repeatedly emphasize its influence on the structure and functioning of different kinds of organizations (Meyer and Rowan 1977; Scott 1994).

Even as the chapters in this section have highlighted the need to broaden our understanding of the emotional experience of change, the challenge facing us is that of overturning accepted truths. We offer two suggestions: First, by studying emotions we are better able to understand the goals and needs of people and the values they hold for their organizations. Understanding the adaptive function of emotions prevents us from falling into the trap of assuming that all negative emotions have negative outcomes and helps us help individuals and organizations come closer to their goals. Second, by promoting constructive alternative conceptions of the role of emotions in change and trumpeting the effectiveness of emotionally intelligent change management practices, we may be able to influence what people understand as myth and reality.

II

CONFLICT/INTERPERSONAL

THE ROLE OF EMOTION AND EMOTION MANAGEMENT IN DESTRUCTIVE AND PRODUCTIVE CONFLICT IN CULTURALLY HETEROGENEOUS WORKGROUPS

5

Oluremi B. Ayoko and Charmine E.J. Härtel

Abstract

One of the major changes facing organizations in the twenty-first century is the prevalence of culturally heterogeneous workgroups (CHWs). Although the diversity literature suggests that diverse workgroups can be more innovative and better problem solvers than homogeneous groups, it also acknowledges that diverse workgroups often fail to achieve this potential because of task and emotional conflict. The kinds of conflict that are generated in CHWs and leader and member responses to them lack thorough documentation in the literature. This chapter examines the emotions experienced with conflict in diverse workgroups and the ways in which group members and leaders respond to conflict-related emotions. We conclude with recommendations to assist organizations in improving the suitability of their management practices for a diverse workplace.

Introduction

One of the major challenges facing organizations in the twenty-first century is the management of increasing heterogeneity, especially cultural heterogeneity at the workplace (Härtel et al. 1999). Managers' attempts to manage heterogeneity and capitalize on the above advantages, however, have met with mixed results (Chatman et al. 1998). For example, in spite of the above advantages, studies have also shown that diverse workgroups compared to homogeneous groups suffer from poor cohesion and social integration (Hambrick 1994), more conflict, higher turnover, less trust, less job satisfaction, more stress, more absenteeism, and more communication difficulties (Alder 1990; O'Reilly, Caldwell, and Barnet 1989; Tsui, Egan, and O'Reilly 1992; Zenger and Lawrence 1989). Also, people different from their coworkers in terms of race, gender, tenure, and other characteristics report feelings of discomfort and less organizational commitment (Tsui, Egan, and O'Reilly 1992). Diverse teams are hampered by more short-term problems, particularly with establishing appropriate processes and relationships with coworkers (Härtel and Fujimoto 2000; Nemeth 1986). These findings show that the affective and behavioral costs often outweigh the cognitive benefits achieved by diverse workgroups (Härtel and Fujimoto 1999). Consequently, organizational leadership still struggles with the management of heterogeneity in the workplace.

Furthermore, the above negative affective and behavioral outcomes suggest that conflict is eminent in heterogeneous workgroups. Triggers of intragroup conflict events may be task- or social-related, the latter being referred to as relationship or emotional conflict (Ayoko and Härtel 2000; Jehn 1997). Emotional conflict, for example, has a propensity to negatively affect general group outcomes (Jehn 1995). Since people tend to dislike others who disagree with them and who do not share similar beliefs and values (Raven and Rubin 1976), and since diversity is related to lower interpersonal attraction (Fujimoto et al. 2000; Hartel and Fujimoto 1999), the potential for relationship or emotional conflict is higher in diverse workgroups.

A primary cause of the problems observed in culturally heterogeneous workgroups (CHWs) is task and interpersonal conflict (cf. Jehn 1997; Tsojvold 1991). Conflict at the individual, group, and, sometimes, organizational levels affects outcomes of diversity positively or negatively (Jehn 1997; Tsojvold 1991). Group member and leader strategies for coping with emerging conflict, we argue, are important predictors of the nature and outcomes of conflict experienced in diverse workgroups. In particular, strategies that enable group members to promote productive conflict while minimizing destructive conflict are expected to facilitate task and social outcomes. This article considers the role of emotion and emotion management in destructive and productive conflict in CHWs.

Even where research has addressed the determinants of group performance in organizations, findings suggest that success often hinges on the ability of the workgroup to embrace experience and manage (rather than avoid) disagreements that arise (Gruenfeld et al. 1996; Tjosvold 1991). Considerable evidence points to the detrimental effects of unmanaged conflict (Jehn 1997; Pruitt and Rubin 1986). Since most conflict produces emotional responses (Gayle and Preiss 1998; Kolb and Putnam 1992), the present research will further the course of successful management of conflict in CHWs by examining the conflict-related emotions and ways that group members and leaders cope with them. Such work is required to harness the potential of CHWs, and to reduce the negative experiences of diverse minority member of the workforce.

Conflict

The above discussion suggests that conflict is eminent in a diverse work team. Yet, the conflict literature reveals that few studies have empirically tested the effects of conflict in organizations (Jehn 1997) and fewer still have looked at conflict and its associated emotions in diverse workgroups or ways in which group members and leaders manage it.

This chapter adopts the social psychology approach to the study of conflict, which focuses on the perceptions of the parties, regardless of any overt displays of hostility (Deutsch and Shichman 1986). In particular, conflict is defined as the perceived incompatibilities by parties of the views, wishes, and desires each holds (Jehn 1992). Although most researchers have conceived conflict as damaging and disadvantageous with adverse effects for individuals, groups, and organizations, research shows that conflict can be beneficial (Jehn 1997). Few of the plentiful studies on conflict, however, have examined the positive effects of conflict (for a notable exception see Jehn 1997). Consequently, we consider the role of emotion in the production of both destructive and productive conflict processes.

Emotion and Conflict

Triggers of intragroup conflict events may be task-related or social-related, the latter sometimes being referred to as relationship or emotional conflict (Jehn 1997). Emotional conflict arises from negative affect and dislike (Berscheid 1983) and, as such, is associated with personal and relationship issues manifested as friction, frustration, and personality clashes within the group (Ross 1989). Since people tend to dislike others who disagree with them or have dissimilar beliefs and values (Raven and Rubin 1976), and since diversity is related to lower interpersonal attraction (Härtel and Fujimoto 1999), the potential for emotional conflict is likely to be higher in diverse groups.

Emotional conflict produces negative reactions that inhibit personal relationships, which limits group cohesion and efficiency. In addition, emotional conflict is increased by dissimilarity in race and tenure attributes because people find it difficult to identify with (and easy to stereotype) those of a different race or tenure. Thus, race and tenure differences tend to encourage heated interactions in workgroups (Pelled, Eisenhardt, and Xin 1999). Pelled, Eisenhardt, and Xin (1999) therefore suggest that managers should pay particular attention to group processes in multirace and mixed-tenure settings.

Task conflict, in contrast to emotional conflict, pertains to the conflict of ideas in the group and disagreement about the content and issues of the task. It is the awareness that there are disagreements about the actual tasks being performed in the group (Jehn 1997), although the ultimate goal of the group may be shared (Brehmer 1976). Group members may therefore experience task-related conflict even when they share the same goal and objective about the task. These conflicts can produce better outcomes for the group, or create emotional angst, occupy the group in disputes over how to accomplish tasks, and fail to inform better decision making. Task conflict is closely linked with value diversity in diverse workgroups (Jehn 1997) and, by extension, CHWs. Task conflict is more likely in CHWs as work orientation and style are features that differentiate cultures.

Heterogeneity and Conflict and Group Consequences

Observable heterogeneity refers to the differences that are visible in people that more often than not arouse responses founded on biases, prejudices, or stereotypes (Milliken and Martins 1996). Biases, prejudices, and stereotypes are themselves founded in social identification and self-categorization . On the one hand, social identity theory postulates that group members establish a positive social identity and confirm affiliation by showing favoritism to members of their own social category (Tajfel and Turner 1986). This discrimination and self-segregation, in turn, disrupts group interaction (Jehn, Northcraft, and Neale 1999).

Social category membership provides naturally occurring lines along which conflicts can be drawn. Categorizing individuals into different groups can provoke hostility or animosity within the workgroup. Categorization effects can surface as emotional conflict over workgroup members' personal preferences or disagreements about interpersonal interactions, typically about nonwork issues such as gossip, social events, or religious preferences (Jehn 1995, 1997).

The self-categorization paradigm refers to the process by which people define their self-concept in terms of their memberships in various social groups. Categorization can be based on the situation, because different aspects of a person's self-concept may become salient in response to the distribution of the characteristics of others that are present in a situation (Markus and Cross 1990). A salient social category is one that functions psychologically to influence a person's perception and behavior and how others treat the focal individual (Turner et al. 1987). To the extent that a particular in-group membership is salient, one's perceived similarity to the others in the in-group is increased (Brewer 1979). Increasing salience of in-group membership, on the other hand, causes a depersonalization of the self, defined as perceiving oneself as an interchangeable exemplar of the social category (Turner 1985). Members of a salient group are more likely to cooperate with in-group members and to compete against out-group members (Wagner, Lampen, and Syllwasschy 1986).

Studies in this area also reveal that people frequently use demographic characteristics (basing salient social categories on demographic attributes) to categorize others and predict their likely behaviors (Allport 1954). This tendency may become more pronounced when the demographic diversity is historical, such that demographically similar people tend to share similar backgrounds and experiences and may therefore expect one another to understand and react to situations similarly (Pfeffer 1983). In addition, perceived dissimilarity based on observable attributes is likely to produce negative short-term effects driven by evoked stereotypes (Härtel and Fujimoto 1999). These evoked stereotypes and prejudices for the dissimilar others in a heterogeneous group, no matter how short-lived (Milliken and Martins 1996), may be a source of negative conflict, which, in turn, inhibits optimal performance.

The negative affective and behavioral effects of diversity can be explained by humans' disposition to be attracted to others perceived to be similar, which has as its consequence the exclusion of dissimilar others (cf. Bryne 1971). Studies reveal that a sharply differentiated in-group is likely to create feelings of resentment and undermine team identification among subordinates who are excluded from the in-group (McClane 1991). Consequently, we propose that emotional conflict will be greater in CHWs where in-group/out-group differentiation is greater.

So far, we have shown that the genesis of conflict is often emotional (emotional conflict), and where it is not (i.e., task conflict), that it produces emotional reactions. We have also shown that diverse groups are more likely to experience conflict than homogeneous groups because of their greater differences in values and norms relating to interaction and work style. Next, we consider some of the ways in which group members and leaders respond to conflict-related emotions.

Responses to Conflict-Related Emotions

It is generally agreed by organization theorists that organizational conflict should be managed rather than resolved to enhance individual-, group-, and system-wide effectiveness (Rahim, Garrett, and Buntzman 1992). The management of organizational conflict involves diagnosis and intervention at the interpersonal, intragroup, and intergroup levels. Diagnosis involves identifying whether there is need for an intervention and the type of intervention needed. Intervention may be designed to attain and maintain a moderate amount of productive conflict and to enable organizational members to learn styles of handling interpersonal conflict so that individual, group, and overall organizational effectiveness are enhanced (Rahim 1986).

Because emotional conflict arises from and perpetuates negative emotions generated by confrontation with values, wishes, and desires dissimilar to one's own, we argue that emotion management skills are crucial in CHWs. Research relevant to the management of emotions includes the literature on interpersonal intelligence (Gardener 1983, 239), social intelligence (e.g., Thorndike 1920), and emotional intelligence (Jordan et al. in press). These areas indicate that effective emotion management involves the ability to identify, monitor, and regulate one's own and other's emotions (Jordan et al. in press). Good emotion management skills enhance information-processing capability in a way that enables greater ability to motivate, plan, and achieve (Salovey and Mayer

1990). The successful regulation of emotion allows individuals to refocus their own and others' attention on more important problems (Salovey and Mayer 1990). On the other hand, if emotional conflict is not minimized and resolved in a positive way, group efficiency and effectiveness suffers (Agyris 1962). Instead, much of the group's effort is turned away from task accomplishment to the resolution of personal conflict or the attempt to ignore conflict.

Emotional conflict is compounded in the heterogeneous workgroup because such groups diverge more in held values and beliefs. Therefore, members and leaders of heterogeneous workgroups need to be able to monitor their own emotions and the emotions of others in order to facilitate effective outcomes in the group. In particular, CHWs need to possess the emotional capability to acknowledge, recognize, monitor, discriminate, and attend to group members' emotions (Huy 1999). The consistent application of this capability will be manifested in the group's norms and routines related to feeling (cf. Schein 1992), which we refer to as emotional climate (cf. Härtel, Gough, and Härtel in press). Thus, it is argued that the level, amount, intensity and frequency of conflicts experienced in CHWs will be related to the extent of the leader's emotional capability.

Summary

To summarize our discussion so far, cultural diversity within a workgroup increases the delineations along social and task lines, which increases the likelihood of emotional and task conflict respectively. In the short-term, group members respond cognitively and affectively to each conflict event. These reactions may initiate a cycle of productive or destructive conflict. Over time, the types of cycles experienced by the group impact upon the group's social (e.g.,, emotional climate) and task characteristics. This conflict sequence, we argue, is affected by the emotion management capability of group members and leaders. In particular, we propose that:

> Proposition 1: CHWs' emotional climate, group norms, and in-group/out-group distinctions will moderate the type, frequency, duration, and emotional outcomes of conflict produced in the group.

> Proposition 2: CHWs will have more instances of productive conflict and fewer instances of destructive conflict when their members and leaders possess good emotion management skills.

Overview of Study

A multimethod qualitative study was undertaken to explore some of the issues raised in the foregoing review. Group meetings with a total of six culturally diverse workgroups from two large Australian organizations were observed and recorded over a period of twelve weeks to gather data about the types, intensity, frequencies, and amount of conflict in these workgroups. Structured follow-up interviews were also conducted and recorded individually with all group leaders and at least 50 percent of the members in each of the participating workgroups in order to clarify and validate informants' prior comments and to enable a check of the accuracy of the researcher's interpretation of transcripts. Transcripts were analyzed using systematic interpretative techniques, namely linguistic text analysis, content ratings, and content analysis, to examine the types, intensity, frequency, and amount of conflict exhibited in these groups (cf. Jehn 1997). Following Jehn's (1997) conflict analysis procedures, the applicability of the types of conflict experienced in workgroups in general to the types of conflict experienced in CHWs was assessed. An independent analysis was also conducted to determine the types, frequencies, and amount of conflict present in the groups. In each unit, a number of members independently identified and reported on the same conflict, which provides a cross-check across informants and increases the reliability of the reports of conflict (Taylor and Bogdan 1984).

Results

The data were analyzed using systematic interpretative techniques (i.e., content coding, content analysis, linguistic text analysis; cf. Jehn 1997). The results of this systematic analysis are presented below.

Triggers of Conflict

Analysis of the data revealed that the triggers of conflict in CHWs are often related to cultural differences such as values and beliefs. An informant from Group 1 summed up comparing the frequencies of conflict in diverse workgroups compared with homogeneous workgroups by saying:

> We have more conflict because we are a really diverse group and actually we talk about it . . . we are diverse and certainly working out how we work together is part of that diversity and that richness and yes, it means

more struggles than other groups. So I think we have more conflict because there are more differences and we are coming from different backgrounds and cultures and we're having to come together and work together for the same thing. So the conflict is there because we have strong people who rightly also are saying, hey I am here and you need to value my diversity. This is good, but if this is not well facilitated, other people may have to leave their diversity outside the door.

The majority of interviewees reported that 50 percent of the conflict in CHWs is triggered by cultural differences. Respondents indicated that cultural differences underpinned member differences in work orientations and views of how individuals should interact with one another. For example, a respondent from Group 4 stated:

There were a lot of differences because of values. ". . . I would probably put differences because of values at 80%, yeah, 80%." Another informant said, "I think the biggest problem was due to values, . . . probably the majority, it would be over 50%. . . . Yeah."

The other conflict triggers identified were poor training, the way people talk, communication styles, and office space. The latter was a strong trigger of conflict and also represents a trigger previously unidentified in the literature. Illustrative excerpts from the transcripts are presented below for each of the identified triggers.

Work Orientation and Styles as a Trigger of Conflict

An interviewee from Group 4 referred to work orientation as a trigger of conflict when she said:

She had difficulty with my work style and . . . yeah, the role that I take as leader in brainstorming sessions . . . and she would often sit back and when I asked [Name] what do you think? And . . . she would not offer anything generally. And she would say that, when I said that to her, I put her under too much pressure. . . . So wanting to pick her brain was like I was putting her under too much pressure. So her work style is quite different.

Another informant from Group 1 spoke about work orientation as a trigger of conflict in this way:

As I said, we come to work and have our tasks and have our things that we need to do, but then we start to interact in a group, the methodology in which we work ends up competing.

Language as a Trigger of Conflict

Most of the informants said that language plays some part in conflict in diverse work teams. The leader from Group 3 put it to the fact that speakers of English as a second language use English differently, which leads to misunderstandings. The group leader from Group 1 identified language as a trigger of conflict when she said:

I suppose behind each word we think a whole lot of different things. Although in our group English is our first language even though we come from different cultural settings, we perceive different things around words, so it is how we understand them that generates some problems . . . the way the language is used generally, should be of concern . . . a culturally appropriate language should be used.

Poor Skills as a Trigger of Conflict

About 70 percent of the informants talked about poor skills as a trigger of conflict. An informant from Group 4 said, "she had had some experience, but she hadn't the broadness of experience in skills that we have had in that area." Another informant from Group 1 said about the team leader:

I did initially feel that she had enough experience to be in that position at that time. But any time we had to work together there were always issues, I felt I was always teaching and I don't like that. When you're working with people I like to be able to be, if I am lower than them, I like to feel that I am grabbing stuff from them. In here I don't. I feel I am teaching [the leader] all the time. I am continuingly giving and [the leader] doesn't give that back. . . . I feel like a bit of a rag . . . and that becomes a problem.

Space as a Trigger of Conflict

When asked to describe her workplace, an informant from Group 1 responded this way:

My work space is what I created. I have a flag [minority ethnicity flag]. I brought in my own furniture with my ethnicity artwork on it . . . my role is counseling employees from my . . . [ethnic group]. . . . My space, because of the things I put in there, was saying welcome to staff of my ethnicity but was saying something opposite to the mainstream staff. The mainstream staff were hesitant to come in here.

On the issue of space, an informant from Group 1 said:

> When we came out here . . . we had our own spaces so we weren't always together. You did not see how people were working at that time. . . . But now, because of the open space, someone saw somebody's paper, read it, and saw that it was written by T and gave it to [the leader] to read to make an issue of it.

The Group 1 leader independently referred to the same conflict, corroborating the informants' comment that space was a great trigger of conflict in culturally diverse workgroups. An informant from Group 3 referring to the effect of space on conflict said "it may have an impact on the disagreements in that I wouldn't have been exposed to M's moods." Even the lack of space to keep resources intact created conflict as reported by an informant from Group 4 who said:

> We had resources and we didn't have any special place for our resources and my colleague used to take resources to the field and when she brought them back there was no place to put these resources, so she put them in her car. Things you know, things get lost. This created problems. . . . We argue, where is this, where is that, oh it's here, I don't know where it is, you know, and sometimes we wouldn't talk . . . and this made for a lot of speculations and problems. . . . If you have an environment where you can access things easily, naturally you would have less frustration and you can function better, you know . . . it became a big issue, yeah it became a heavy duty issue.

This report was confirmed by another informant from the same group independently who said:

> Space is an issue . . . X carries some resources for fieldwork in her car and the other members of the team do not like that idea at all but then there is no place to keep those things.

Conflict Characteristics

The conflict literature indicates that conflict can be classified into two types, task and emotional (also known as relationship conflict). Furthermore, conflict varies along the dimensions of intensity, frequency, and duration. Characteristics of conflict were examined in the present study and are reported next.

Conflict Types

Analysis of the data revealed that the conflict types in CHWs, with the exception of the space-related conflict uncovered in the present research, can be characterized by the task-related and relationship-related problems reported in the general literature on conflict in groups (see Jehn 1995, 1997). For example, an informant from Group 1 in response to the question regarding the kinds of problems encountered daily at work said:

> We have had a steady range of people here that have created a lot of difficulty, but I think there's a lot of difficulty just in cultural diversity. There are things that I experience as a black lady here in the organization that are not always understood. Also, I think at times you react in different ways under different circumstances that people think, gee, that's odd, but had they been in my shoes, would have probably thought, oh gee, I would have been even more curious than that. If I was to categorize the problems, my frustration here would be more personal, the lack of understanding of issues and people, it is really just diverse people skills. Not understanding that people come from different backgrounds and people just talking out of their narrow experiences, they just don't realize that they are insulting you.

The leader of this informant's group independently reported:

> We have had our fair share of interpersonal issues . . . we had people leave because they, you know, there has been too much dominance and they probably thought that I as the team leader have not given enough direction . . . so there have been real, yeah, quite a lot of interpersonal issues going on . . . so there was a reasonable amount of conflict and I certainly felt quite um, what is the word, um, out in the open as being criticized.

In Group 4 an informant said "difficulties here are interpersonal and task, and they do go together."

Interaction Between Task- and Interpersonal- and Space-related Conflict

In addition to identifying space-related conflict, the data revealed an interaction between task-, emotional-, and space-related conflict at work.

An informant from Group 1 reported, "There are some things related to tasks. While they are personal, they do spill over into the task and especially into group dynamics." When further asked whether or not the reverse may happen, she responded in this way:

> It's a good question. I think we all do work with tasks. But there is a cultural perspective. . . . I've worked with indigenous areas and I've then worked in the mainstream areas and my experience has always shown that with indigenous areas, we look after the interpersonal first. We say our hello's. . . . Interpersonal issues are more important. But when I work in the mainstream areas, task-oriented issues are more important.

Referring to the interaction of individual and space, an informant from Group 3 said:

> I guess perhaps I'm the sort of person, who in some way feels responsible for the mood of a place, so that if people are sad or cranky, perhaps I take on some responsibility to lighten that . . . yeah, with my own space I could probably cut myself off and not be bothered by it.

Conflict as an Episode or an Ongoing Event

Informants distinguished between episodic and ongoing conflict. The majority said that conflict in these teams was usually not episodic but rather an ongoing event where, according to an informant from Group 4, "the partial resolution would have lots of little ups and downs and then a big one . . . probably coming again from the little ones."

Conflict Intensity

All of the informants reported that conflict in culturally diverse workgroups could be, as one interviewee from Group 4 put it, "very intense." Another informant from the same group, referring to a conflict, said, "it became extremely intense . . . we were upset and it became extremely intense after that . . . there were just two camps and no one was talking to each other."

Conflict Frequencies

The frequency of conflict in culturally diverse workgroups is high. The informants described the frequency of conflict as an everyday occurrence. For example, an interviewee from Group 4 said, "Quite often, I

would say every day." Another informant from the same group, referring to the same conflict, said, "Initially it would be less common, it
may happen once every couple of weeks. As time went by, it became
very regular, sometimes to the point of almost every day."

Another informant from Group 1 said:

> On a daily basis there would be things that are said that you really have to
> walk away from sometimes or otherwise you'd be making a big deal of it.
> . . . Oh I get three or four things a week at least that really upset me.

Conflict Duration

Conflict in culturally diverse work teams can be prolonged. The majority of informants stated categorically that conflict lasted from four to
nine months. Data revealed that many of the conflicts never resolve.
Resolution for 95 percent of the conflict events referred to by the
interviewees in this study involved the turnover of one of the parties in
the conflict. Responding to the question, "How long did the disagreement or difficulty take to be resolved," an interviewee from Group 4
said, "six months." Also, from Group 1, an informant said, "She had a
distrust for me for a good six to nine months at least and sometimes,
from time to time, things still crop up in that area."

Displays During Conflict

Behavioral Displays During Conflict

When asked to describe what behaviors indicate a conflict, informants
said things like "not talking to each other," "no eye contact between
parties that are involved in the conflict," "not saying hello to each other,"
"a thick air in the room," "an argument," and "gossip." An informant
from Group 4 said:

> She walks in without saying hello to anybody . . . no, you don't say hello
> to each other . . . we argue about who used the resources last.

Conflict, however, rarely resulted in physical aggression. A possible explanation for this was offered by an informant from Group 1
who said:

Some people can become physically aggressive. I think that people understand the legal ramifications of becoming physical and so have become, I think, a little bit wiser in a way.

Emotional Displays During Conflict

A number of emotional displays were reported, most frequently mentioned were verbal aggression and crying. For example, an informant from Group 4, reporting on a disagreement among group members, said, "we could hear their voices," suggesting raised voices. Another informant from the same group, talking about the same conflict, said, "The staff member and her husband came around to my house . . . the husband of the staff tried to tell me how to run the unit and abused me on the phone." Other examples of verbal aggression given by informants were yelling, screaming, and swearing. Although verbal aggression was commonly mentioned by informants, tears were reported as being the most frequently sighted emotion with conflict.

Outcomes of Conflict

Conflict was associated with a number of behavioral, emotional, physical and social outcomes. For example, an informant from Group 1 reported:

> It can be all consuming at times. It can result in stress, but it can also result in absenteeism, being physically sick or not participating. It can result in misunderstanding in work tasks, work competency you know, the whole work. You can be competing in things but your energies and all that are taken up on other issues.

Illustrative excerpts of behavioral, emotional, social, and positive outcomes are provided below.

Emotional Outcomes of Conflict

All the interviewees agreed that there are emotional outcomes for the conflict in culturally diverse workgroups. Informants commonly referred to "resentment," "anger," "bitterness," and "frustration." An informant from Group 1 said, "If this happens on a regular basis, which it does, about two or three times a day, I'm cantankerous by the end of the afternoon, you're just wanting to swear all the time."

Social Outcomes of Conflict

The data revealed that conflict in CHWs also has social outcomes. When asked, "What is the outcome of conflict on your social relationship in the group?" an informant replied:

> We deal with employment of diverse people. Employment basically has effects on death, custody, suicide, all the social drugs and alcohol—all the social things. That is why there is a conflict, because I have a social urgency and you come to an organization like this and you have to go through processes . . . or you work with mainstream people who know nothing about other groups and so they are not personally affected by the social outcomes of what they are doing for a particular group of people. But I am personally affected. I have members who have committed suicide so you know what it's all about. In this work place, that causes disagreement because there is a lack of understanding of why you try to put through things and why so quickly.

Negative Outcomes of Conflict

The majority of informants agreed that other outcomes of conflict in CHWs are poor cohesion, absenteeism, sick leave, and turnover of dissimilar staff or one of the parties in the conflict, which in turn negatively affects the productivity of the group. For example, a minority member from Group 1 said:

> It would have been very difficult to stay if I had not got support, . . . I think I would be resigning and trying to get another career. A lot of [mentions her ethnicity] have different career paths. They go from here to there, they are not always getting to the top cause they are changing sideways, just to get away from certain people or try to find where their niche is.

In all cases where a conflict event was reported, people turned over. For example, a leader from Group 1 indicated that two to three staff members left because of conflict. One left because "swearing offended him so much . . . he never ever got over that and he ended up leaving so he did not finish, he did not complete his training." Another informant corroborated this report, saying, "actually there was absenteeism, the trainee who just resigned had lots of absenteeism . . . he was very stressed." Poor cohesion was also mentioned to be a direct consequence of conflict:

We probably went our different ways and not coming socially together as a group because nobody wanted to come together as a group . . . not cohesive . . . operating quite separately.

Positive Outcomes of Conflict

Analysis of the data also indicated some positive outcomes of conflict. For example, an informant from Group 1 said it has a positive influence on her:

> In that I decided I would not let this overcome me and I had to learn from it. So for me perhaps I'd been a victim too much of my life—I'm not going to be any more. So for me it was moving from personally devastated to how do we make this work.

Another informant from Group 1 said:

> I drew a lot of strength from it. I learned how to communicate . . . my communication repertoire has broadened. It does every time you have something like that and you reflect back on it, you can actually see how you can do things better.

From Group 4, an informant said, "I've learnt to do things differently." Another informant from the same group put the conflict up as "a learning experience."

Conflict Resolution

The analyses revealed that conflict in CHWs never really resolves and that it takes a very long time, five to nine months, for a conflict to settle. When asked if the conflict was completely resolved, an informant from Group 1 said:

> No, no. That's why I probably hesitated when I said nine months. I 'd even say today depending if there are cultural issues that do arise . . . I still think there will be things that come up in the workplace and if I say I am pissy about something, it instantly has this aggressiveness as a reaction. And I think there will be a lot of blockages there, I don't see them coming to an end.

An explanation for this provided by an informant from Group 4 was, "Certainly, you do feel like meat in the sandwich when you are trying to keep peace."

Responses to Conflict and Conflict-related Emotions

In-Group/Out-Group Differentiations

Sometimes cultural differences are perceived by group members as signals of subgroup membership. For example, an informant from Group 1
recounted:

> I brought all these sort of things into my workplace as a way of making
> the workplace identify with me. But I got some objections to it. . . . I
> guess I was making a statement . . . saying this is me and this is how I feel
> comfortable. It was more of a statement to my ethnic [staff] out there,
> come, you are welcome here. It is an indigenous and friendly environ-
> ment. . . . But unknown to me while that was probably my aim, . . . and
> while I personally like seeing that stuff on the walls, I wasn't really aware
> of how much the staff had seen it and then it became a bit of an issue.

In other cases, group members appeared to reject deviation from their
respective cultural norms. For example, an informant from Group 1 said:

> Accepting that there are other languages . . . it becomes a barrier if we
> don't understand or pick it up early that there are language differences.
> And even the way that people analyze things, people often just talk and
> then think people are hearing what they are saying and they are not, they
> are hearing something different. People don't realize the language they
> are using and what they are actually saying . . . they just don't know they
> are insulting you. . . .Their listening skills are turned off, all broad listen-
> ing skills are just turned off.

Manager's Response to Conflict

Avoidance was identified as the most commonly used strategy by leaders to manage conflict. For example, an informant from Group 1 said:

> They [the team leader and branch manager] say I will deal with it. I've
> actually brought up two issues . . . one was the swearing one, and another
> issue with another lady that seemed to be ongoing. So I brought both of
> those to my branch manager and the branch manager said I will deal with
> these and neither was fed back to me. I never heard anything.

In the same group and referring to the same issues, the group leader
said, "I mentioned the problem to [the branch manager] once." When
asked what the branch manager did to manage the conflict, she responded,

"Not a whole lot. I suppose he would counsel me but he would just say, yes, ok."

Managers' Response to Emotions Arising from Conflict

The analysis revealed that leaders do not know how to deal with the emotions that arise from conflict, and that most of the time they use an avoidance strategy to deal with conflict and its resultant emotions. For example, when asked how emotions are dealt with or whether there was anybody who managed emotions produced by the conflict, an informant from Group 1 said:

> No, emotions are the hardest thing that I've found in this team to deal with. I personally come from a background where emotions are very much part and parcel of life, because you know you've got to fight the fight . . . but in an organization like this, I find that as soon as somebody shows emotion, management does not know how to deal with it and it is frowned upon. It is almost like it is not professional and its even sometimes said that "it's a women's thing." Or people have to stereotype things to deal with certain things, but I think we have got to deal with that because sometimes it is highly emotive, especially in cultural diversity . . . we got to deal with people who are upset.

One informant from Group 1 said that rather than deal with the emotion, leaders become patronizing. When asked to elaborate on what patronizing means, the informant said:

> They say, we need to talk, we need to talk now . . . I think patronizing is horrible, it just becomes a blockade and they will stand there and be professional. . . I think if we've got an issue like this we should give people privacy, we take them one-on-one, we don't do group talk. Management wants you to get a group thing happening, then it's a big shame, you know and it's a shame when somebody is really made to communicate with emotion in front of a crowd and that's how they deal with it . . . I think one-on-one would be better.

Other Approaches to Managing Conflict

Other approaches to managing conflict identified were the use of consulting firms, creating rules and guidelines for conflict management, and helping one of the parties involved in a conflict turn over. For example, an informant from Group 4 said:

We set up guidelines, like we actually put them up on the walls, downstairs in our office. . . . We had two, two conflict management workshops from some people outside our organization.

The leader of Group 4 said, "The most positive thing that happened was that she left. I wrote a glowing reference for her to get another job."

Leader Behaviors Perceived as Necessary for Effective Management of Diverse Workgroups

When asked a broad question on what they would see as the role of leaders managing diversity, an informant from Group 1 said:

I think the role of the leader in managing diversity needs to be firstly, recognizing diversity and then knowing that part of a team being able to work together with diversity is understanding that diversity is for individuals. Where we each come from, what makes up that diversity, and how each of us utilizes that diversity in a team way, so it is about recognizing, encouraging and facilitating that diversity to be expressed openly and open up.

An informant from Group 1 said:

Often times managers are chosen because of their expertise rather than their human resource abilities. . . . They should take time to manage people in a respectful way and in a way that makes people feel included in the organization and valued. If they can do that and not be task orientated on everything in order to get the dollar, they will start to realize that their bottom line will increase . . . they will have happy staff, the turnover will be less and it will be just a better place to work . . . they have got to be flexible in their management style and strategies, they need to show that they can demonstrate strategies for wide scenarios that happen in culturally diverse teams . . . they need to be able to have a repertoire of diverse ways they can actually deal with different things and get rid of stereotyping . . . we need managers who just value their staff. . . . They should feel free to be able to go out and seek help.

Another informant from Group 4 said:

The manager should be very understanding and equal to everybody . . . what I am saying is respect, respect personal beliefs, values . . . meet the needs of her employees, have respect of their employees' needs, treat everybody equally for what they are and recognize their experiences, expertise.

Other comments made by informants referred to the need for leaders to be open, to be tolerant, to possess people skills, and to have "a taste of other cultures" by traveling abroad.

Conclusion

In this chapter, we examined the processes and outcomes of emotional conflict and conflict-related emotions in culturally diverse workgroups. We also argued that the course of conflict and the extent to which it is productive or destructive depends upon how group members and leaders react and manage emotional conflict and conflict-related emotions. Finally, we reported the findings of a qualitative study, which provided powerful evidence for the prevalence and intense consequences of conflicts in CHWs.

A MODEL OF EMOTIONAL AND MOTIVATIONAL COMPONENTS OF INTERPERSONAL INTERACTIONS IN ORGANIZATIONS

6

Robert G. Jones and Andrea L. Rittman

Abstract

A perspective derived from basic psychological research and theory on emotion, motivation, and social cognition is developed to describe and explain emotional and motivational aspects of interactions in organizations. The Motivation and the Experience and Display of Emotion (MEDE) model blends taxonomic content categories with process analysis (i.e., description of expected events in encounters). This blending illustrates how stable categories (e.g., attributions) may be used only at critical moments in event processes (e.g., when a problem is identified). Tenets of the theory include (1) emotions serve an external signaling function for motive, (2) motives fall into approach and avoidance categories, (3) motives are constructed by actors and perceivers using a combination of emotional signals and situational characteristics, (4) active and passive emotional signals are a pivotal basis of responses by perceivers, and (5) these responses may profoundly influence the outcomes of encounters. Propositions and implications are derived.

Introduction

Continuing interest in socioemotional organizational behavior (SOB) has bred a group of perspectives aimed at putting these behaviors into a meaningful context (Ashforth and Humphrey 1993; Morris and Feldman

98

1996; Rafaeli and Sutton 1987; Wharton and Erickson 1993). This work has enhanced our understanding of important outcomes and predictors of these encounters, but the procedural dynamics of SOBs are not well informed by existing psychological theory. We suspect that using these theories to explain emotional and motivational dynamics of interactions in organizations holds promise for improving practice.

In this chapter, we will use theoretical frameworks from basic research into emotion, social cognition, and motivation to construct a model for describing and explaining the dynamics of socioemotional encounters in organizations. We derive the motivation and the experience and display of emotion (MEDE) model to provide answers to primary questions associated with the outcomes of these encounters. MEDE is a process-analytic model designed to capture the temporal nature of socioemotional encounters; however, the taxonomic categories and variables of basic research will be used to inform choice points in the analysis of socioemotional processes. Using MEDE, we will derive broad propositions and draw implications to guide future work.

Constructing the MEDE Model

The MEDE model uses Lang's (1995) emotional probe and recent social cognitive taxonomies of emotion (Ekman 1992; Fridja 1986; Higgins, Kuiper, and Olson 1981; Russell 1994) within the context of a process analysis. Lang (1995) has marshaled evidence that emotional responses serve as internal signals for "motive-readiness." Beginning with subcortical arousal systems associated with both "desired" (appetitive arousal) outcomes and outcomes to avoid (aversion arousal), Lang posits that "positive" emotions arise as we *approach* desirable outcomes, and "negative" emotions come about as our efforts to obtain these objects are being thwarted. For example, a smiling offer to mate from an attractive other leads to "positive" emotion, while being told to "shove off" by an attractive other leads to "unhappy" feelings, such as sadness and frustration. Regarding aversive arousal, fear, anger, and disgust arise as we approach undesirable outcomes, while relief results from *avoiding* them. These constructs are summarized in Table 6.1.

Passive Emotions

While these emotional responses provide "motive-readiness" signals that orient us toward action, Lang's theory does not explicitly deal with

Table 6.1

Summary of the Emotion Probe Theoretic

		Type of outcome	
		Desired	Aversive
	Approaching	pleasure, excitement	fear, disgust
Environmental information			
	Avoiding/Missing	frustration, anger	relief

emotional responses that occur after attainment of desirable and undesirable ends. When outcomes actually occur, there are also emotional responses. For example, we may experience joy or gratification when a desirable end is attained or sadness when negative outcomes come to pass. However, because these emotions may signal periods of repose, even they have motive-signaling functions.

It is notable, however, that these outcome-related emotions are more or less passive, while ongoing approach and avoidance quests appear to generate more "active" emotive responses. For example, sadness, relief, and joy, though they all carry with them physiological responses, appear to serve less of an active signaling function than responses associated with fight-flight or sexual arousal systems. Thayer (1996) has shown that there are both active and passive coping responses. Although these have been linked more to moods than to specific experienced or expressed emotions, it certainly makes sense that a more active orientation is adaptive when outcomes are not yet certain. Once a desire has been met or a fear realized, there is no longer a reason to try to exert control to achieve or avoid these outcomes. Active responding is generally reserved for dealing with uncertain situations.

Social Interactions

Apart from exploring this distinction between active and passive responding, considerable research supports the emotion probe theoretic. However, despite the long-standing interest in the role of emotional expression in social interactions, Lang's theory has not been applied to these. In order to accomplish this, the emotion probe theoretic must move beyond *internal* signaling functions to include *external,* social signaling functions of emotion displays (Ekman 1992; Russell 1994). There is some consensus that certain facial displays (smiles, frowns, etc.) are recognizable across cultures as such external indicators of emotive or mood states. Given this nearly universal understanding of emotional displays, it is quite plausible to suggest that humans use others' emotive displays to infer motive readiness. That is, when someone sees you smile, they infer you are anticipating a desirable outcome.

Although it has never been tested, there are both theoretical and empirical reasons for believing that emotional displays serve external motive signaling functions. For starters, there is the evidence for an internal signaling function of emotional experience. Given awareness of the congruence between our own emotional experiences and display inclinations, it is entirely reasonable for us to expect such congruence in others. In fact, wide recognition of certain emotional displays strongly suggests that we understand others' smiles to mean the same thing as our own. Furthermore, recent neurological research shows that the same brain regions associated with our own internal emotional experiences are involved in making sense of others' emotional displays (Adolphs et al. 2000). The use of others' emotive displays to infer motive readiness is therefore quite likely.

Another reason for believing that we infer motive readiness from others' emotive signals also relies on an important argument drawn from the universal recognition position. Specifically, universality is used to argue for an "unlearned" basis of behavior. Why would we be "hardwired" to recognize emotional displays if they did not serve some sort of signaling function? Given the evidence about the internal signaling function of emotions, the external signal function provides a parsimonious explanation for universality.

Both basic and applied research regarding the accuracy of person-perception also provide empirical support for the external signaling function hypothesis. Evidence from management assessment centers suggests that it is socially inferred motive information that makes these personnel selection systems accurate predictors of future behaviors (see Howard and Bray 1989; Jones 1997). Similar support comes from personality research showing self-other congruence regarding motive and emotive characteristics such as extroversion and emotional stability (Kenny et al. 1994; McCrae and Costa 1985).

In summary, there are compelling reasons to believe that emotional displays communicate motive-readiness information in social situations.

However, this basic assumption of the MEDE model—that we use emotional displays to provide and gather information about our motives to others—may be constrained by contextual information. Specifically, our own motive readiness responses (emotions) rely on some processing of situational cues about whether our desires and fears are being met or avoided (Higgins, Kuiper, and Olson 1981; Smith and Kirby 2000). So, how do we use such situational features to make sense of others' emotional signals?

Context

Just observing others' emotional responses does not provide enough information to infer motive. There is, presumably, something about the situation or context that has triggered an emotional response. Correct inferences about motive readiness must also take into account the stimuli that elicited emotional responses. For example, I may see a poker player smile after looking at his or her cards, and infer that the motive of winning the hand has been forwarded by the cards she or he was dealt. Inferences about behavioral (playing poker, smiling) and motivational (winning money) aspects of the situation must be used to arrive at conclusions about the motive. Specifically, I would assume that people who sit down to play poker want to win, as a rule. Their emotive responses are used as a "progress report" about the veracity of these assumptions in a given circumstance (e.g., smiling at a particular hand of cards). Given enough emotional display evidence, I may change my view to see an individual as unconcerned with winning. Thus, the signaling function of emotional responses serves as continuous evidence to test motive hypotheses in a given circumstance. As emotive responses conform to our expectations about motive in a given situation, we learn (and make inferences) about others' motives.

This poker player example also calls attention to problems in this inferential process. Specifically, poker players may deliberately display emotions that are not congruent with actual motive readiness responses. This sort of acting, where it relates to me (i.e., I am also in the poker game), however, still illustrates the importance of the motive signaling function of emotional display, even though the signal may be misleading. That is, people use even incorrect or misleading emotional displays as a basis for signaling and inferring motive. Thus, our first proposition:

Proposition 1: Emotional displays serve as signals of motive readiness with respect to a particular stimulus environment.

Attributes of the Stimulus Environment

So far, we have begged the question of which aspects of the stimulus environment people use to infer motive, based on emotive displays. While the emotion probe theoretic does not provide information about stimulus arrays outside very controlled laboratory situations, applying this theoretic to broader social situations requires some discussion of stimulus environment. One possible explanation for how stimulus environment and emotional display are used to infer motive is based on the distinction between strong and weak situations (Davis-Blake and Pfeffer 1989). In strong situations, outcomes with high valences are quite salient. For example, not conforming to unanimous group pressures or to authority tends to have very clear consequences (social rejection and sanctions, respectively). In these situations, motives are generally fairly clear and can be easily inferred. In "weak" situations, motives may not be as widely shared and understood. Consequently, only observers who are knowledgeable about the stimulus environment should be able to accurately infer motive from emotive responding in weak situations. For example, experienced managers may be better able than inexperienced managers to infer motives from management assessment center participants' emotional responses (see Lorenzo 1984).

Proposition 2: Motive salience and observer expertise interact to influence the accuracy of inferences about motive drawn from emotive displays, such that observer situational expertise plays a significant role in only weak situations.

Meeting of the Motives

So far, we have described the taxonomic categories associated with the person (motive and emotive categories) and the situation (salient, strong, and weak situations). We will now use an exemplar interaction to unfold these categories in a process analysis. Because they are a very common social circumstance in which motive inferences occur, we will use customer service interactions as an exemplar to complete the development of the MEDE model. However, there are many other social situations in organizations to which this model may apply.

Strong Situations

Customer service situations tend to be fairly scripted affairs, with clear expectations on the part of both customer and service provider. For now, therefore, we will assume that customer service personnel need only modest expertise to adequately perceive customers' motives. Where actual events do not conform with customer expectations, service providers can anticipate emotional responses from customers. This may happen when events do not fulfill scripted expectations, or when events surpass scripted expectations. Given propositions one and two, service providers can use knowledge of expectations associated with a situation, plus the emotive responses of customers to infer current motive readiness. To the extent that these inferences are correct, service providers can use their own emotional displays to signal "motive sharing" with recipients.

Appropriateness

Here, the focus of the MEDE model changes to the service provider's management of emotional display in response to inferences about service recipients' motives. The definition of "appropriate" emotional displays (see Ashforth and Humphrey 1993) can be understood in terms of congruence between the service recipient's motives and the service provider's apparent emotional responses. Specifically, following the emotion probe theoretic, if the service recipient is frustrated in obtaining some desired outcome, then the appropriate provider display should reflect the emotions appropriate to frustration of desired outcomes. If the recipient displays discomfort (mild fear) over some threatening outcome, appropriate provider displays should reflect sharing of this concern.

There is virtually no theoretical or empirical guidance about what the content of these "appropriate responses" might be. Consequently, we will return to the phenomenological approach to understanding the process of service interaction used by early theorists (e.g., Hochschild 1979; Rafaeli and Sutton 1987) and, using MEDE, derive further propositions. One possible definition of appropriateness could be that emotive responses of service providers should directly mirror the emotive signals of service recipients. So, if the recipient smiles, it is appropriate for the provider to smile; if the recipient frowns, the provider should frown, and so on. But, this straightforward answer to the appropriateness question may belie the complexity of the process of inferring motive from both emotional display and stimulus environment. For example, a slight smile may mean that the service recipient, while partly satisfied with some aspect of service, is also ambivalent about some other aspect of the stimulus environment. The job of the service provider, then, may be to answer the slight smile with a slight frown, in order to signal that he or she is actively concerned with "what's missing."

This is because service recipients are also busy inferring motive from provider emotive displays. The question being asked implicitly by the recipient is, "Will this person help me to achieve desirable ends and avoid aversive ones?" The answer from the recipient's view should generally be "yes" or the provider becomes a further block or threat in the recipient's stimulus situation. Answering the question with a "yes" in situations where an event has already occurred is straightforward. When a recipient has gotten something desirable or avoided something aversive, mirroring of passive provider emotions may send the appropriate signal. So, when the service recipient has received good service and is smiling, the provider should smile, too. When the recipient is relieved at having avoided a problem, the provider should also express relief.

Proposition 3: After outcomes have occurred, appropriate emotions are those in which service providers signal similar (passive) emotions to recipient expressed emotions (mirroring).

Sending the "yes" signal when the outcome of service is still in doubt may require a different sort of emotional signal. In these conditions, the active/passive dimension of emotion described earlier needs to be invoked. Specifically, when a recipient is expressing an active emotion (approaching something aversive or being blocked from something desirable), it seems most appropriate for the recipient to express an active emotional orientation as well. So, for example, when a resort customer is hoping to get a massage (desirable outcome), the concierge should respond by expressing concern (very mild fear) and assuring the customer that they will "get right on it." Similarly, when a flight attendant encounters a fearful flier, the attendant can express active concern as well, perhaps suggesting means for relaxing (pillows, alcoholic beverages, etc.). Interestingly, a reassuring smile (signaling that all has already turned out well) may serve an important function at some point in this interaction. These relationships are described in Table 6.2.

Table 6.2

Service Recipient Emotions and Appropriate Provider Response Content

	Likely recipient emotion	Service provider response
Post-outcome	Passive	Passive/mirror
Desirable (approach)		
Obtained	*pleasure*	*pleasure*
Blocked	*sadness*	*sadness*
Undesirable (avoid)		
Obtained	*anger/pain*	*anger/pain*
Avoided	*relief*	*relief*
Pre-outcome	Active	Active
Desirable (approach)		
Blocking	*anger/frustration*	*fear/concern*
Undesirable (avoid)		
Obtaining	fear/concern	anger/frustration

There may also be circumstances where gathering information about the recipient's perception of the situation and providing information about the provider's view of the situation may serve important functions prior to expressing any emotion. This would presumably occur in ambiguous situations where motive is not easily inferred, either because emotions are not clearly displayed or because the situation itself is not well scripted. However, the best bet for providers even under these circumstances may be to express concern in order to signal active motive readiness. In more obvious situations, where important outcomes have occurred and are evident in recipient emotional displays, direct mirroring seems more likely to hold.

In summary, following the emotion probe theoretic, before an outcome has occurred, recipient emotions signal *active* dispositions toward outcomes. This means that there may be action that providers can take, and an *active* orientation should be signaled in emotional displays. Once an event has already occurred, there may be much less that a provider can do, hence simply mirroring emotions sends an appropriate signal.

One study has looked at the relationship between provider and recipient emotional displays. Using bank tellers, Pugh (2001) showed that, when providers displayed "pleasant" emotions, recipients were more likely to evaluate service positively. The small effect sizes (rs from .18 to .24) and the mediated relationships found in this research suggest that "positive" emotional displays are only part of the picture. Incorporating this into the process modeled here, it could be that service providers should smile or show positive emotions at the soonest possible time after (1) establishing the situation's meaning to recipients and (2) expressing appropriate active/passive emotions. This leads to a series of propositions.

> Proposition 4: Before outcomes have occurred, effective service providers will display active emotional signals.

> Proposition 5: In ambiguous situations, effective providers will display active emotional signals, will gather more information about service recipient perceptions, and will provide information about the situation to recipients.

> Proposition 6: Expressing positive affect as soon as possible after establishing a situation's motive meaning and displaying mirror or active emotions will positively affect the outcomes of service.

Which active emotional signals are appropriate for which recipient displays? There are several possible answers here. When recipients signal anger or frustration, providers can either express these, too ("missing something desirable" signals), or some degree of fear ("approaching something undesirable" signals). Similarly, when recipients express fear, providers can mirror this or express anger. We suggest that "opposite mirroring" may be appropriate under these circumstances. That is, fear-related emotions should be displayed to angry customers, and anger-related emotions to fearful customers. Of course, verbal communications should signal that these emotions are directed at the barriers or threats customers are encountering, and not at the customers themselves.

> Proposition 7: Prior to outcomes, provider active emotional displays should be the opposite of recipients,' and should be directed at objects that are threatening or frustrating (avoidance) or desirable but not yet attained (approach).

Instrumental Value of Provider Emotional Display

This suggests, of course, that opposite and direct mirroring themselves have instrumental value. The term *appropriate emotion* suggests that more "appropriate" emotional displays will lead to greater service effectiveness, from the organization's viewpoint. From the provider's viewpoint, however, there is still much to know. Which of these interactions, if any, are associated with burnout? Which are likely to enhance or detract from performance in the long run?

Based on a small research literature, there is reason to believe it is the suppression of unpleasant emotions that relates to emotional exhaustion and the expression of negative emotions that is associated with depersonalization (Best, Downey, and Jones 1996; Wright and Cropanzano 1998). Expressing positive emotions is perhaps less likely to have unhealthy consequences, or may even enhance service provider well-being. However, direction of these relationships has not been established, and there may be coping capacities that mediate the more unhealthy relationships (Etzion, Eden, and Lapidot 1998).

Also left in question are the means by which situational and emotional display information are used to infer that an outcome has occurred. For example, extreme emotional displays probably signal an outcome having occurred. How do we decide that an emotion is extreme? At what point do emotional displays become extreme for most observers? Part of the answer to this may be vested in cultural differences among perceivers. For example, recent interactions of one of this chapter's authors with colleagues from Finland brought to light the fact that there are no words in Finnish to describe extreme positive emotions (e.g., "Great!" "Terrific!" "Wonderful!"). Such lack of emotional labels may belie cultural differences in perceptions of the extremity of emotions.

Valence of outcomes may also be signaled through emotional "intensity" (Frijda 1986; Higgins, Kuiper, and Olson 1981). That is, where outcomes are greatly desired (e.g., to win the lottery) there is greater energic arousal associated with emotional responses than when outcomes are less valent (e.g., to win $10 in a prize drawing).

Individual Differences

This suggests a further set of questions related to individual differences in both recipients' and providers' abilities to infer motive accurately. For example, those high in authoritarianism have been shown to be less sensitive to social information than those low in authoritarianism (Gabennesch and Hunt 1971). This example presents particular problems to providers who must try to get across their active motive readiness to recipients high in authoritarianism (i.e., recipients insensitive to the meaning of emotional displays).

Other individual differences may also have effects on the service encounter. For example, emotional expressiveness, the tendency toward demonstrating experienced emotions (Gross and John 1995, 1998), may mediate some of these dynamics. For service recipients who are expressive, inferring motive may be easier for service providers. Less expressive recipients may create ambiguities and lead to greater problems for providers and the organization. The question of which individual differences may influence the service encounter requires further exploration.

Service Provider Outcomes

Assuming for a moment a direct relationship between service provider emotional displays and the troubling outcomes described in early emotional labor research, several questions concerning provider well-being also need to be answered. Specifically, how can providers, who may be required to display "appropriate" emotions, be given means to avoid burnout? Perhaps simply taking a "hypothesis testing" approach to recipient emotions will help providers to establish a sense of control over the service encounter. This sense of control may decrease stress responses, including burnout (see Van Dierendonck, Schaufeli, and Buunk 1998). Similarly, although establishing clear expectations for emotional displays may not always lead to effective responding, knowledge about what actually works will help to make such clear expectations more usable. So, more than just telling service providers to "smile," employers may be able to provide more effective customer service training, based on the MEDE model.

Broader Applications of MEDE

Given some research support, MEDE has broader applications than just customer service. For example, MEDE may explain how certain team interaction processes influence team outcomes. Specifically, it may not be simply the forming of group norms (per several models), but the specific content of these norms with respect to emotional displays, that influences team effectiveness. Presumably, emotional displays that communicate shared core values contribute to the success of effective teams. This may apply to leadership, organizational culture, and to practices such as training, interviews, orientation, and performance appraisal discussions as well. In general, understanding how different emotional displays signal important motive information may enhance the effectiveness of many organizational practices.

Summary

In our view, the use of emotional display information and situational knowledge to infer motive direction and intensity is a central issue for applied research and practice in organizations. The MEDE model provides a starting place for this work that we believe is both broadly applicable and well founded in the basic research literature. As such, the promise of this model is great for improving organizational practices associated with service encounters, conflict and negotiation, team development, performance assessment and management, and other practices involving motive-rich interpersonal interactions.

7 HOW ARE MOODS INSTIGATED AT WORK? THE INFLUENCE OF RELATIONAL STATUS ON MOOD

Stéphane Côté and D.S. Moskowitz

Abstract

The present research examined the proposition from the resource versus demands model (Morris 1999) that events that reflect the adequacy of currently available resources given impinging demands trigger experiences of mood. We hypothesized that high status, which reflects adequate resources, would be associated with positively valenced moods, and low status, which reflects inadequate resources, would be associated with negatively valenced moods. Study 1, a field study, supported the hypothesis that compared to equal and high status, low status in interpersonal interactions is associated with low pleasant mood and high unpleasant mood. Study 2, a laboratory study, supported the hypothesis that individuals experience less pleasant mood and more unpleasant mood after imagining being in a low status situation than after imagining being in an equal or high status situation. Study 3 supported the hypothesis that individuals experience less pleasant mood and more unpleasant mood when they hold low status than when they hold high status in interpersonal interactions in the laboratory. The pattern of findings suggests that relational status influences mood and, more generally, that mood is at least partially triggered by the adequacy of currently available resources given impinging demands.

How Are Moods Instigated at Work? The Influence of Relational Status on Mood

Moods are transient yet pervasive affective phenomena with profound effects on a wide range of cognitions and behaviors (Clark and Isen

1982; Clore, Schwarz and Conway 1994; Frijda 1993; Forgas 1995; George 1996; George and Brief 1992, 1996a; Morris 1989, 1999; Rosenberg 1998; Schwarz and Clore 1996; Watson and Clark 1994; Weiss and Cropanzano 1996). In organizational settings, moods influence several important outcomes (see Arvey, Renz, and Watson 1998; Bagozzi, Gopinath, and Nyer 1999; Baron 1993a; Pekrun and Frese 1992; Weiss and Cropanzano 1996, for reviews) such as task performance (Côté 1999; Estrada, Isen, and Young 1997; George 1991), organizational spontaneity behavior (George and Brief 1992), creativity (Estrada, Isen, and Young 1994; Isen, Daubman, and Nowicki 1987), systematic information processing (Bless et al. 1990; Bless, Mackie, and Schwarz 1992), stereotyping (Bodenhausen, Kramer, and Süsser 1994; Park and Banaji 2000), decision making (Kahn and Isen 1993), leadership effectiveness (George 1995; George and Bettenhausen 1990), absenteeism (George 1989), and job satisfaction (Weiss, Nicholas, and Daus 1999).

The effects of moods on organizational outcomes call for an understanding of the factors that elicit moods and the processes through which moods are elicited at work (George 1991; George and Brief 1992; Weiss and Cropanzano 1996). However, researchers have principally focused on the consequences of mood, and as a result, very little is known about the instigation of moods. The goal of the present research was to test one process through which moods may be instigated in organizational settings. Specifically, the possibility was examined that some events trigger mood because they reflect the adequacy of currently available resources given impinging demands (Morris 1999). Before describing the mood elicitation framework in greater detail, we define mood and its dimensions.

Mood

Moods are transient affective experiences that last for minutes, hours, or days (Clark and Isen 1982; Ekman 1994; Frijda 1993; George 1996; Morris 1989, 1999; Rosenberg 1998; Schwarz and Clore 1996; Totterdell 1999; Watson 2000; Watson and Clark 1994; Weiss and Cropanzano 1996). There is considerable evidence that moods vary within persons over time (Eid and Diener 1999; Larsen 1987; Larsen and Kasimatis 1990; McConville and Cooper 1993, 1997, 1999; Moskowitz, Brown, and Côté 1997; Penner et al. 1994; Stewart and Barling 1996; Teuchmann, Totterdell, and Parker 1999; Totterdell 1999; Vittengl and Holt 1998;

Watson 2000; Weiss, Nicholas, and Daus 1999), and, therefore, a good theoretical model of the instigation of moods should predict their level at any specific point in time. Moods are also pervasive and diffuse and impact a broad range of psychological processes that are not necessarily tied to their causes (Clark and Isen 1982; George 1996; Morris 1989, 1999; Rosenberg 1998; Schwarz and Clore 1996). In laboratory studies, moods induced using affectively laden film clips impact outcomes unrelated to the clips such as information processing, creativity, and task performance (see Clore, Schwartz, and Conway 1994; Isen 1999; Martin 2000; Schwarz and Clore 1996, for reviews). Thus, any mood experienced at work might influence a wide range of organizational outcomes. For example, a worker's bad mood elicited by marital difficulties at home could impact this person's performance and organizational spontaneity behavior at work. This property of mood makes it especially important to understand how moods are instigated in applied settings.

Dimensions of Mood

According to some researchers, pleasant and unpleasant mood have separate antecedents and differential effects on cognition and behavior, because distinct mechanisms underlie their experience (cf. Burke et al. 1989; Cacioppo, Gardner, and Berntson 1999; Davidson 1992; Goldstein and Strube 1994; Watson 2000; Watson and Tellegen 1985; Watson et al. 1999). Further, the literature on mood effects in both social and organizational psychology has traditionally treated pleasant and unpleasant mood as separate dimensions (cf. Clore, Schwarz, and Conway 1994; Côté 1999; George 1991; Isen 1993, 1999; Martin 2000; Schwarz and Clore 1996; Wegener, Petty, and Smith 1995). The present research thus treated pleasant and unpleasant mood as separate dimensions.

Mood Instigation Process

There is considerable evidence that mood fluctuations over time are associated with life events such as social support, social activity, and health concerns (Clark and Watson 1988; Eckenrode 1984; Stone and Neale 1984; Watson et al. 1992; Zautra 1983; Zautra and Simons 1979). However, there is virtually no agreement among theorists about the processes through which moods are instigated. Past research has devoted more attention to the instigation of emotions than moods (see Frijda 1993; Rosenberg 1998; Schwarz and Clore 1996; for detailed discussions of the differences between moods and emotions), and the field currently lacks a broad theoretical framework to predict which events elicit different experiences of mood and why. In the present research, we examined one framework that might allow researchers and practitioners to predict when and under what circumstances different moods are experienced at work.

Resources versus Demands Model

Morris (1999) proposed that moods are influenced by events that reflect the adequacy of one's currently available resources given impinging demands. According to the resource versus demands model, favorable evaluations of one's currently available resources elicit pleasant experiences of mood, and unfavorable evaluations of resources elicit unpleasant experiences of mood. The resources versus demands model explains fluctuations in mood over time. Assessments of the adequacy of one's resources given impinging demands can change over time depending on how many resources are possessed and what the demands are at any specific point in time. According to this model, for example, it is possible for a person to favorably evaluate resources one week and experience pleasant mood that week and to unfavorably evaluate resources the next week and experience unpleasant mood that week.

Support for the resources versus demands model was provided by a study by Diener and Fujita (1995). In this study, several resources of college students rated by informants (friends or family members) were positively associated with pleasant mood and negatively associated with unpleasant mood. These resources included social skills, social support, assertiveness, intelligence, knowledge, and self-control. Resources were even stronger predictors of mood if they matched participants' goals, suggesting that resources that corresponded to demands are especially predictive of mood.

Many events that reflect the adequacy of one's resources given demands might instigate moods at work. In the present research, we examined the possibility that relational status instigates moods at work, because status presumably reflects the adequacy of one's resources in organizational settings.

Relational Status

We define relational status as an individual's standing in the hierarchy of an organization during a particular interpersonal encounter (Lovaglia and Houser 1996). A person's status varies over time; for example, an employee can have low status during an interaction with the boss but high status during the next interaction with a subordinate.

There is theoretical evidence that status is associated with resources in organizational settings. The literature suggests that individuals who hold high status gain control over resources, and that individuals who possess resources gain status. Structural approaches to social exchange posit that status provides the ability to generate rewards and control outcomes (cf. Lawler and Thye 1999). Further, the notion that individuals who possess valued resources in the organization attain and maintain high status in the organization is central to the strategic contingency approach to organizational power (Hickson et al. 1971; Salancik and Pfeiffer 1977). This approach posits that individuals gain status in organizational settings when they are central to information and resources, when they reduce uncertainty for others with information, and when others depend on them to get their jobs done.

There is also considerable empirical evidence supporting the association between status and resources in organizational settings. Social resources as reflected in the size and complexity of one's social network are associated with several indicators of socioeconomic status (education, family income, and occupational prestige; Campbell, Marsden, and Hurlbert 1986). Resources are also associated with the prestige of jobs found by individuals searching for employment (Wegener 1991). Further, perceptions of other persons' status are heavily based on assessment of targets' resources (Ridgeway et al. 1998).

If relational status reflects the adequacy of one's resources, and moods are instigated by events that reflect the adequacy of resources, then relational status might elicit experiences of mood in organizational settings. When an employee has high status (e.g., when giving instructions to a subordinate), that employee may experience positively valenced mood at that moment. However, when the same employee has low status (e.g., when discussing a project with a boss), that employee may experience negatively valenced mood at the moment. In the present research, we tested the possibility that experiences of mood are instigated by one's relational status during interpersonal interactions.

Overview

Three studies are presented that test the theoretical proposition that relational status, an event that reflects the adequacy of one's currently available resources, triggers experiences of mood. The association between relational status and mood was first examined during interpersonal interactions occurring within organizations in Study 1. An event-contingent sampling methodology (Alliger and Williams 1993; Wheeler and Reis 1991) was used in which organizational members reported on their relational status and their mood during several interpersonal interactions over a twenty-day period. This study allowed us to examine associations between relational status and mood in an organizational setting. However, this study did not permit us to make definitive claims that relational status precedes mood during interpersonal encounters. Consequently, Study 2 manipulated imagined relational status with vignettes in the laboratory to test the effects of relational status on mood. Study 3 provided a more realistic setting to test the influence of relational status on mood by manipulating status and examining its effects on mood in real interpersonal interactions in the laboratory.

Study 1: Relational Status and Mood in Organizations

The goal of Study 1 was to explore the possibility that relational status during interpersonal interactions in actual organizational settings is associated with mood.

Relational Status

The focus was on three relational status conditions during interpersonal interactions: low status, equal status, and high status (Kemper 1978; Kemper and Collins 1990). These conditions corresponded to interpersonal interactions with a boss, a coworker, and a subordinate, respectively. These three conditions are (1) conceptually distinct, (2) generalizable across organizational settings, (3) psychologically powerful, and (4) variable over time, and, thus, it seemed reasonable to expect that changes in one's relational status over time could elicit different experiences of mood.

Hypotheses

High, equal, and low status conditions are presumably associated with different evaluations of one's resources at a specific point in time. In low status conditions, individuals presumably rate their resources unfavorably. Thus, low status conditions were expected to be associated with experiences of low pleasant mood and high unpleasant mood.

Hypothesis 1a: Pleasant mood is experienced less intensely in low status situations than in equal status or high status situations.

Hypothesis 1b: Unpleasant mood is experienced more intensely in low status situations than in equal status or high status situations.

In equal status situations, individuals presumably rate their resources as being similar to others'. Thus, equal status conditions were not expected to exhibit an association with mood. However, in high status conditions, individuals presumably rate their resources favorably. Thus, high status conditions were expected to be associated with experiences of high pleasant mood and low unpleasant mood.

Hypothesis 2a: Pleasant mood is experienced more intensely in high status situations than in equal status or low status situations.

Hypothesis 2b: Unpleasant mood is experienced less intensely in high status situations than in equal status or low status situations.

Method

Participants

Participants were recruited from the community through advertisements in newspapers. Two samples of individuals were collected. Sample 1 was recruited by inviting 100 people who held stable paid employment and worked at least thirty hours a week to participate in a study on social interaction. Of these, 89 people completed the study. Sample 1 was composed of 41 men (46%) and 48 women (54%); these individuals ranged in age between 19 and 63 years old ($M = 33.05$, $SD = 9.74$). A second sample was recruited two years after Sample 1. Sample 2 was recruited by inviting 124 people who held stable paid employment and worked at least thirty hours a week to participate in a study on social interaction. Of these 124 individuals, 115 completed the requirements for the study. Sample 2 was composed of 61 women (53%) and 54 men (47%), and the age range was 20 to 69 ($M = 33.83$, $SD = 10.19$). The two samples were combined for data analysis. The combined sample of 204 people included participants ranging in age from 19 to 69 years old. Individuals held a variety of occupations (e.g., engineer, teacher, data analyst, secretary). The heterogeneity of the sample with respect to occupation should increase the generalizability of findings to a variety of "white collar" occupations. Results for this sample concerning the association between behavior and mood have previously been reported (Côté and Moskowitz 1998; Zuroff, Moskowitz, and Côté 1999). However, results concerning the association between relational status and mood have not previously been reported.

For the purposes of this study of the association between relational status and mood, only individuals who were in each status condition (i.e., low, equal, and high status conditions) at least once were kept in the sample. The final sample for the interpersonal situations study was composed of 24 men (41.4%) and 34 women (58.6%); these participants ranged in age between 21 and 57 years old ($M = 36.29$, $SD = 9.87$).

Procedure

Participants first attended a meeting during which the procedures for the study were explained. Participants were informed of their responsibility to complete event-contingent recording forms to monitor their social interactions every day for twenty days. Participants were asked to complete a form for each significant interpersonal interaction as soon as possible after the occurrence of the interaction. An interaction was considered significant if it lasted at least five minutes. Participants were provided with ten forms per day. Participants were asked to distribute the completion of forms evenly throughout the day. Only forms completed at work were used in the present study. Participants completed an average of 55.21 forms at work.

Participants were also given beepers and told that they would be signaled three times a day during the week and twice a day on the weekend. Individuals did not complete forms when they were signaled. Rather, beepers were used to remind individuals of their responsibility to complete forms regularly; it was not expected that the completion of forms would necessarily match the signals. Participants were asked to record the times of the signal on a separate daily form. Records of signal times were kept so we could be assured that participants were keeping records for the study throughout the day. Records of signals were approximately 90 percent accurate in Study 1 and 81 percent accurate in Study 2.

Participants mailed each day's forms on the day following their completion. After instructions for the event-contingent recording part of the study were given, participants completed a battery of questionnaires. After the twenty-day testing period, participants were given $100 compensation for their participation.

Event-Contingent Recording

Event-contingent recording forms requested information about participants' relational status, mood, and interpersonal behavior during the social interaction.

Relational status. On each form, participants were asked to indicate with whom they interacted during that interaction. The options were: supervisor, coworker, support staff, subordinate, casual acquaintance, friend, romantic partner, and other. The focus of the present study was on social interactions with either a supervisor, a coworker, or a subordinate. Interactions with more than one type of partner were excluded from the analyses to clearly distinguish the association between different relational status conditions and mood.

Mood. Nine mood items were listed on every form. These items had been previously used to assess affect valence by Diener and Emmons (1984) and represent each pole of the pleasant/unpleasant valence dimension of some circumplex models of affect (i.e., Larsen and Diener 1992; Russell 1980). The following items indicated pleasant mood: happy, pleased, enjoyment/fun, and joyful. The unpleasant mood items were: worried/anxious, frustrated, angry/hostile, unhappy, and depressed/blue. Participants were asked to rate the extent to which they experienced each mood item using a 0 (*did not occur*) to 6 (*extremely*) scale. Diener and Emmons (1984) provided support for the validity and the reliability of these items.

Interpersonal behavior. Four scales of twelve behavior items for four dimensions of interpersonal behavior (i.e., agreeable, quarrelsome, dominant, and submissive behavior, see Wiggins 1991) were derived from an earlier study (see Moskowitz 1994, for a complete list of items and validity evidence). On each form, participants checked the behavior items they had engaged in during the interaction being recorded. Four different versions of the form were used to avoid response sets. The items representing agreeable, quarrelsome, dominant, and submissive behavior were divided equally among the four versions of the form.

Construction of event-specific mood scores. Pleasant affect and unpleasant mood scores were constructed for each participant for each episode. The intensity ratings of pleasant mood and unpleasant mood items were averaged separately. This procedure yielded two mood scores for each episode: one pleasant mood score and one unpleasant mood score. The internal consistency reliability of items of the pleasant and unpleasant mood scales were .92 and .86, respectively, for this sample.

Construction of event-specific interpersonal behavior scores. Scores for each dimension of interpersonal behavior (i.e., agreeable, quarrelsome, dominant, and submissive) were created by averaging the number of items corresponding to each dimension that were checked. Scores ranged from 0 (*none of the items corresponding to a dimension of behavior were checked*) to 1 (*all of the items corresponding to a dimension of behavior were checked*).

Results

The data analysis procedure consisted of testing a multilevel model for predicting event-level mood (cf. Kreft and De Leeuw 1998; Singer 1998). The model tested examined effects of relational status and interpersonal behavior on mood. The model tested was a multilevel model, because observations corresponding to interpersonal interactions were nested within individuals. The effects of relational status and interpersonal behavior on mood during the ith event by the jth individual ($mood_{ij}$) can be estimated as follows:

$$mood_{ij} = \beta_{0j} + \beta_{1j} BOSS_{ij} + \beta_{2j} COWORKER_{ij} + \beta_{3j} SUBORD_{ij} + \beta_{4j} AGR_{ij} + \beta_{5j} QUR_{ij} + \beta_{6j} DOM_{ij} + \beta_{7j} SUB_{ij} + r_{ij}$$

$$\beta_{0j} = \gamma_{00} + u_{0j}$$
$$\beta_{1j} = \gamma_{10} + u_{1j}$$
$$\beta_{2j} = \gamma_{20} + u_{2j}$$
$$\beta_{3j} = \gamma_{30} + u_{3j}$$
$$\beta_{4j} = \gamma_{40} + u_{4j}$$
$$\beta_{5j} = \gamma_{50} + u_{5j}$$
$$\beta_{6j} = \gamma_{60} + u_{6j}$$
$$\beta_{7j} = \gamma_{70} + u_{7j}$$

In this model, β_{0j} represents the jth person's typical level of mood, and the coefficients β_{1j} to β_{3j} represent the jth person's estimates of the relations between each of the three interpersonal situations and mood. The variables BOSS, COWORKER, SUBORD are dichotomous variables coded +1 if the person interacted with this type of partner during the jth individual's i^{th} observation and 0 if the person did not interact with this type of partner during that same observation. The variables AGR, QUR, DOM, and SUB are continuous variables that represent how much individuals engaged in agreeable, quarrelsome, dominant, and submissive behavior, respectively. The coefficient r_{ij} represents a within-person random effect on aff_{ij}. The coefficient γ_{00} represents the mean of all momentary mood experiences by all participants. The coefficient u_{0j} represents a between-person random effect on γ_{0j}, the jth person's typical level of mood. The coefficients γ_{10} to γ_{30} represent the general association between each of the interaction partners and mood. The coefficients γ_{40} to γ_{70} represent the general association between each of the dimensions of interpersonal behavior and mood. The coefficients u_{1j} to u_{3j} represent between-person random effects on β_{1j} to β_{3j}, the estimates of the relation between interpersonal situations and mood. Finally, the coefficients u_{4j} to u_{7j} represent between-person random effects on b_{4j} to β_{7j}, the estimates of the relation between interpersonal behavior and mood.

The "SAS" procedure "PROC MIXED" was used to simultaneously test the effects of all three interpersonal interaction partners and interpersonal behavior on mood experiences during events (Singer 1998). Interpersonal behavior variables were centered within persons (Hofmann and Gavin 1998; Kreft, De Leeuw, and Aiken 1995).

Inspection of Table 7.1 indicates that individuals interacted with their coworkers more frequently than they interacted with their bosses or their subordinates. Pleasant mood was on average more intense than unpleasant mood.

Inspection of Table 7.2 suggests that Hypotheses 1a and 1b were supported. Interactions with bosses were negatively associated with pleasant mood and positively associated with unpleasant mood. That is, individuals experienced less pleasant mood and more unpleasant mood when they had low status than when they had equal or high status. There were no significant associations between interactions with coworkers and mood. Hypotheses 2a and 2b were not supported. There were no significant associations between interactions with subordinates (high status) and mood.

Table 7.1

Study 1: Descriptive Statistics for Interpersonal Situations and Mood

	N	M	SD
Low status (with boss)	3436	0.12	0.32
Equal status (with coworker)	3436	0.35	0.48
High status (with subordinate)	3436	0.14	0.34
Pleasant mood	3434	2.00	1.43
Unpleasant mood	3434	0.63	0.93

Note: Means for low, equal, and high status represent the percentage of interactions reported in each of these situations.

Table 7.2

Study 1: Prediction of Mood from Relational Status and Interpersonal Behavior

	Pleasant mood			Unpleasant mood		
	Parameter estimate	SE	t ratio	Parameter estimate	SE	t ratio
Intercept	2.11	0.14	15.13***	0.61	0.07	9.15***
Low status (with boss)	−0.39	0.09	−4.53***	0.29	0.07	4.23***
Equal status (with co-worker)	−0.02	0.05	−0.43	−0.01	0.03	−0.45
High status (with subordinate)	−0.10	0.07	−1.46	−0.03	0.04	−0.68
Agreeable behavior	0.79	0.09	9.17***	−0.37	0.06	−5.98***
Quarrelsome behavior	−0.80	0.13	−6.14***	1.05	0.13	8.04***
Dominant behavior	−0.02	0.07	−0.23	0.09	0.06	1.51
Submissive behavior	−0.60	0.09	−6.45***	0.48	0.07	7.00***

Note: $df = 1, 3369$ for all tests except $df = 1, 57$ for tests of intercept. ***$p < 0.001$.

Consistent with past research (Côté and Moskowitz 1998; Moskowitz and Côté 1995), agreeable behavior was positively associated with pleasant mood and negatively associated with unpleasant mood. Further, both quarrelsome and submissive behavior were negatively associated with pleasant mood and positively associated with unpleasant mood.

The findings of Study 1 suggest that when individuals are with their supervisors, they are less likely to experience pleasant mood and more likely to experience unpleasant mood, independent of the behavior they engage in during those interactions. The findings can be interpreted in the framework of the resources versus demands model. High unpleasant mood and low pleasant mood are experienced in low status conditions because assessments of currently available resources are unfavorable. The findings of Study 1 did not provide evidence that individuals are more likely to experience pleasant mood or less likely to experience unpleasant mood when they interact with subordinates. To the extent that being in the supervisor role is associated with resources, these findings do not support the resources versus demands model.

Study 2: Imagined Relational Status and Mood

Study 1 examined associations between relational status and mood in organizational settings. However, the data obtained in Study 1 do not permit us to make definitive claims concerning effects of status on mood as proposed by the resources versus demands model. The goal of Study 2 was to obtain explicit evidence that relational status influences mood. A study was conducted in which imagined relational status (high versus equal versus low) was manipulated and mood was assessed as an outcome.

Hypotheses

The hypotheses of Study 2 mirrored the hypotheses of Study 1.

Hypothesis 1a: Pleasant mood is experienced less intensely in low status situations than in equal status or high status situations.

Hypothesis 1b: Unpleasant mood is experienced more intensely in low status situations than in equal status or high status situations.

Hypothesis 2a: Pleasant mood is experienced more intensely in high status situations than in equal status or low status situations.

Hypothesis 2b: Unpleasant mood is experienced less intensely in high status situations than in equal status or low status situations.

Method

Participants

Participants were thirty female and twelve male undergraduate students who took part in this study as part of a course requirement.

Procedure

The study was a one-factor within-person design with status (high, equal, low) varied within persons. Between one and six participants were welcomed by an experimenter in a large laboratory room that contained several desks and chairs. The experimenter administered a packet that contained a demographics questionnaire and a series of vignettes, each followed by a mood scale. There were a total of six vignettes of approximately equal length depicting two high, two equal, and two low status situations. An example of a high status situation was:

> You are a manager of a large organization. You directly supervise a group of 25 employees. You assign several tasks to your subordinates. These tasks include totaling sales and generating possible new sales strategies. Your subordinates work on these tasks and produce a written report. They turn in their completed work to you.

An example of an equal status situation was:

> You are a member of a five person team working on an advertising campaign. Your decisions are taken seriously by the other team members, but all members can equally influence the final outcome of the meetings. You have to evaluate each member's suggestions, including your own, carefully, and decide whether or not they should be incorporated in the advertising campaign.

An example of a low status situation was:

> You are a sales clerk in a retail store. Your supervisor orders you to greet all customers with a smile and to try to sell as much merchandise as possible. You need to report all of your sales to your supervisor, and your supervisor often gives you feedback concerning your performance and how to increase your sales.

The order in which the vignettes were presented was counterbalanced. Participants were instructed to read each vignette and to rate the extent to which they would experience a list of affect items in the situation depicted in the vignette. Participants were given one hour to complete the packet; all of them finished before the end of the allotted hour. After completing the packet, participants were debriefed and thanked for their participation.

Measures .

Mood. Participants were instructed to rate their mood after reading each of the six (two high, two equal, and two low status) vignettes. The items used to measure pleasant and unpleasant mood were the same as in Study

1, and participants were asked to rate the extent to which they experienced each mood item on a scale of 1 (*not at all*) to 5 (*extremely much*). As in Study 1, pleasant and unpleasant mood scores were calculated by averaging scores on the pleasant and unpleasant mood items, respectively. The scores were also averaged across the two high status vignettes to create pleasant mood and unpleasant mood in high status scores. This procedure was repeated for equal and low status conditions. The internal consistency reliability of items of the pleasant and unpleasant mood scales ranged from .73 to .94 (with an average of .84) depending on the condition.

Results

Effects of Status on Mood

The effects of relational status on mood were tested using repeated measures analyses of variance (ANOVAs) with one within-person factor (status: high vs. equal vs. low). The omnibus test revealed significant differences between the conditions for both pleasant and unpleasant mood. *T* tests provided support for Hypothesis 1 that individuals experience less pleasant mood in the low status condition than in the equal and high status conditions (see Table 7.3). *T* tests also provided support for Hypothesis 1b that individuals experience more unpleasant mood in the low status condition than in the equal and high status conditions. However, Hypotheses 2a and 2b were only partially supported. Pleasant mood was higher in the high status condition than in the low status condition, but there was not a difference in pleasant mood between the high status and equal status conditions. Similarly, unpleasant mood was lower in the high status condition than in the low status condition; there were not a difference in unpleasant mood between the high status and equal status conditions.

Study 3: Relational Status and Mood in the Laboratory

Study 2 examined effects of imagined relational status on mood by assessing the mood of individuals after reading vignettes depicting high, equal, and low status situations and imagining being in these situations. One limitation of Study 2 was that it did not examine mood responses to status in real interpersonal interactions. Thus, we conducted an addi-

Table 7.3

Study 2: Descriptive Statistics and Prediction of Mood from Status

	High status		Equal status		Low status		Com-parison
	M	SD	M	SD	M	SD	F
Pleasant mood	2.92[a]	0.86	2.95[b]	0.63	2.16[ab]	0.70	36.37
Unpleasant mood	1.71[c]	0.54	1.79[d]	0.50	2.33[cd]	0.71	25.40

Note: $N = 42$. $df = 2, 82$, for omnibus tests and $df = 1, 41$ for paired comparisons. Omnibus tests were significant at the $p < 0.001$ level. Paired sample T-tests with the same superscript were also significant at the $p < 0.001$ level. Significant T's ranged between 5.33 and 7.81.

tional study in which status was manipulated in interpersonal interactions in the laboratory, and mood was assessed as an outcome.

Hypotheses

The hypotheses of Study 3 mirrored the hypotheses of Studies 1 and 2.

Hypothesis 1: Pleasant mood is experienced less intensely in low status situations than in high status situations.

Hypothesis 2: Unpleasant mood is experienced more intensely in low status situations than in high status situations.

Method

Participants

Participants were twenty-seven female undergraduate students who took part in the study as part of a course requirement.

Procedure

The study was a one-factor within-person design with status (high versus low) varied within persons. Two participants were scheduled to take part in the study in each session. Participants came to the laboratory twice, where they were assigned once to the high status condition and once to the low status condition. Participants were randomly assigned to the high or low status condition in the first part of the experiment. Individuals who were in the high status condition in the first part of the study were in the low status condition in the second part, and the reverse assignments occurred for the other participants. An odd number of participants completed both the first and second sessions of the study, because three participants missed one of the two sessions.

An experimenter welcomed participants in a room that contained one desk and two chairs. They were asked to complete a resume form on which they described their last three jobs (including their current job if they had one). After both participants completed the resume forms, the experimenter asked them to complete a set of questionnaires and left the room. The experimenter came back to the room and announced that she had picked one of the two participants to be the boss and the second person to be the subordinate in the next part of the study based on their relative work experience. Participants were actually randomly assigned to the boss or subordinate role, but to strengthen the status manipulation they were led to believe that the assignment to roles was based on their resume forms.

Participants were then taken by the experimenter to a second room that included two desks. The boss's desk was large and modern with a comfortable chair. The subordinate's desk was small with a relatively uncomfortable chair. Participants were asked to sit at their respective desks and were given instructions about the task on which they were to work. The subordinate was told that she had to complete a series of ten tasks that would be evaluated by the boss. The subordinate was told that she would have sixty seconds to complete each task and to turn in her work to the boss. Then, the boss would assign a new task, until all ten tasks were completed. The boss was told to evaluate the subordinate's performance on each task using a set of answer keys.

The experimenter then told both participants that the tasks consisted of finding specific numbers within large grids of numbers (see Sandelands, Glynn, and Larson 1989). The subordinate had to inspect each grid of numbers and to circle numbers based on a different rule for each grid. For example, one rule was "circle all the numbers that are larger than 100 or smaller than 50." The boss was told to use a set of answer keys with all correct answers circled to evaluate the subordinate's performance. The boss was also given a clock and instructed to warn the subordinate when time expired (after sixty seconds) by saying "Stop."

The boss was then asked to provide feedback to the subordinate, but only between tasks (i.e., never while a subordinate was working on a task).

Bosses and subordinates were asked to practice the task once, and then participants went though the ten tasks to be completed or evaluated. The experimenter stayed in the room to verify that participants followed the instructions. After the series of tasks was completed, participants were asked to complete an experiment feedback sheet that included manipulation checks for status and mood measures. After the feedback sheets were completed, appointments for the second session were made. Participants were not scheduled with the same partner twice, because the cover story used to assign participants to roles could be used only once with a given dyad.

The procedure for the second session was the same as in the first session. Participants were assigned to the reverse role that they had been assigned during the first session. This was possible because a given participant could report more work experience than her partner the first time but report less work experience than a different partner the second time (participants were never aware of the actual work experience their partners reported on the form).

Measures

Manipulation check for status. The experiment feedback sheet included two manipulation checks for status. Participants were asked to rate on a scale of 1 (*none*) to 5 (*extremely much*) the amount of power or control they had over their partner (power-self) and the amount of power or control their partner had on them (power-other) during the session.

Mood. The items used to measure pleasant and unpleasant mood were the same items as in Studies 1 and 2. The internal reliability of the pleasant mood scale was .81, and the internal reliability of the unpleasant mood scale was .79.

Results

Manipulation Checks

The status manipulation checks (power-self and power-other) were submitted to repeated measures ANOVAs with one within-person factor

Table 7.4

Study 3: Descriptive Statistics and Prediction of Mood and Perceived Power from Status

	High status		Low status		Comparison
	M	SD	M	SD	F
Pleasant mood	2.38	0.78	2.10	0.82	3.02+
Unpleasant mood	1.29	0.41	1.75	0.68	12.21**
Power-self	3.22	1.22	1.48	0.70	43.25***
Power-other	1.48	0.70	3.81	1.18	68.25***

Note: N = 27. *df* = 1, 26, for all comparisons. + $p < 0.10$, ** $p < 0.01$, *** $p < 0.001$.

(status: high versus low). As expected, individuals reported having more power or control over their partner in the high status condition than in the low status condition (see Table 7.4). Further, individuals reported that their partner had more power or control over them in the low status condition than in the high status condition.

Unpleasant Mood

A repeated measures ANOVA with one within-person factor (status: high versus low) was tested to examine the effects of relational status on unpleasant mood. As predicted by Hypothesis 1, individuals experienced more unpleasant mood in the low status condition than in the high status condition (see Table 7.4).

Pleasant Mood

A repeated measures ANOVA with one within-person factor (status: high versus low) was tested to examine the effects of relational status on pleasant mood. There was a marginally significant finding in support of Hypothesis 2 that individuals experienced more pleasant mood in the high status condition than in the low status condition (see Table 7.4).

Discussion

The goal of the present research was to test a theoretical framework that describes one possible process through which moods are instigated in organizational settings. The theoretical framework examined was

Morris's (1999) resources versus demands model, which posits that moods are triggered by events that reflect the adequacy of one's currently available resources given impinging demands. According to this framework, favorable evaluation of the adequacy of resources elicits pleasant moods and unfavorable evaluation elicits unpleasant moods. Previous research had indicated that relational status is associated with the adequacy of currently available resources given impinging demands in organizational settings (cf. Campbell, Marsden, and Hurlbert 1986; Wegener 1991). Consequently it was posited that relational status would be predictive of mood.

Three studies were presented that supported the resources versus demands model by demonstrating that relational status is associated with mood. Study 1, a field study, indicated that having low status (i.e., interacting with a boss) is associated with less pleasant mood and more unpleasant mood than having equal status (i.e., interacting with a coworker) or having high status (i.e., interacting with a subordinate). Low status was presumably associated with negatively valenced mood because low status reflected inadequate resources. This finding occurred despite controlling for interpersonal behavior, such that negatively valenced moods were not simply due to behaving more submissively.

Studies 2 and 3 used experimental designs to test explicitly the influence of status on mood. In Study 2, individuals experienced more unpleasant mood and less pleasant mood when responding to vignettes in which participants imagined having low status positions relative to imagining themselves in equal or high status positions. When status was manipulated in interpersonal interactions in the laboratory in Study 3, individuals experienced more unpleasant mood in the low status than in the high status condition. The pattern of findings from the three studies supports the proposition that events that reflect the adequacy of one's resources given impinging demands elicit experiences of mood (Morris 1999).

Low status was clearly associated with mood in all three studies. Individuals generally felt worse in low status situations than in either equal or high status situations. However, there were no differences in the experience of mood between high status and equal status conditions in Studies 1 and 2, the two studies that included an equal status condition. We had predicted that low status would be related to negatively valenced mood because low status indicates that one's resources are inadequate at a specific moment. We had also predicted that high status would be related to positively valenced mood because high status indicates that one's resources are adequate. However, we found the expected pattern of results for only low status. It is possible that unfavorable assessment of resources has more consequences for mood than favorable assessment of resources does. Conditions in which resources are deemed inadequate have to be rectified quickly, but conditions in which resources are deemed adequate do not necessarily have to be acted upon (see Clore, Schwarz, and Conway, 1994; Schwarz and Clore 1996, for similar arguments). Therefore, unpleasant mood states triggered by unfavorable assessments of resources might be stronger than pleasant mood states triggered by favorable assessments of resources.

Applied Implications

As stated previously, several organizational outcomes are associated with moods (Bagozzi, Gopinath, and Nyer 1999; George and Brief 1996a; Weiss and Cropanzano 1996). To indirectly influence these organizational outcomes through moods, the factors that influence moods need to be identified, because mood might mediate the relation between work events and organizational outcomes (Weiss and Cropanzano 1996). In particular, relational status influences mood, which, in turn, influences important organizational outcomes. The finding that status influences mood has important implications for both supervisors and subordinates.

Implications for Supervisors

It should be expected by managers that subordinates will experience a relatively unpleasant mood when interacting with them. Consideration should be given to what kinds of supervisory behaviors may minimize unpleasant mood states. It is possible that supervisors can reduce these unpleasant responses by reducing visible status differences, by controlling some of their dominating behaviors such as providing criticism and advice, and by increasing supportive behaviors such as providing praise and reassurance. Consideration should also be given to the scheduling of supervisory meetings. While supervision is necessary, frequent supervision may not be necessary. Perhaps the goal should be to schedule sufficient meetings to maintain effective control and management while minimizing meetings to reduce the frequency of events that are typically experienced as unpleasant by subordinates.

If a meeting with a supervisor is a signal for the subordinate to evaluate resources, then supervisors should consistently review with the subordinate whether the resources are perceived to be sufficient for meeting demands. For example, are there sufficient time and personnel for meeting short-term and long-term goals. Moreover, supervisors should view comprehensively the demands on subordinates from all sources within the organization. Work hassles such as equipment malfunction, mechanical difficulties, and incomplete information increase demands on workers, which in turn leads to heightened strain in the form of exertion, fatigue, and cardiovascular reactivity (cf. Evans, Johansson, and Rydstedt 1999; Zohar 1999). Supervisors should provide resources that will reduce the negative effects of work hassles. For example, managers should regularly verify that none of their subordinates' equipment is defective, and should repair any malfunctioning equipment.

Implications for Subordinates

Subordinates should explicitly state their evaluations of demands and resources because the perspectives of supervisors and subordinates may be different. Subordinates should be prepared to request realistic resources for meeting demands when they experience sufficient disparity between resources and demands to impact on mood. Subordinates should also be prepared to negotiate decreased demands when additional resources are not available to address a disparity between demands and resources. For example, when subordinates work with equipment that is defective or outdated, subordinates should request better or more recent equipment. If new equipment is unavailable, subordinates should negotiate reduced demands for output quantity or quality.

Implications for Well-being

We also maintain that increasing pleasant mood and decreasing unpleasant mood represent important goals for managers above and beyond the influence of mood on organizational outcomes such as performance. Pleasant mood is associated with well-being (Diener, Suh, Lucas, and Smith 1999), and increasing subordinates' levels of well-being ought to be an important goal for managers. Increasing the frequency of social interactions that elicit pleasant mood and decreasing the frequency of interactions that elicit unpleasant mood represent one route through which high well-being among subordinates can be obtained.

Limitations and Suggestions for Future Research

The data we presented consist exclusively of self-report measures. Although some of the variables explored in the present research are unlikely to have been biased (e.g., identification of status in the event-contingent sampling study), other variables may be more susceptible to distortion or response bias (e.g., mood). In future research, a wider variety of measures of mood such as observations of facial expressions, could be obtained.

In the past, we have studied how personality traits moderate the relations between interpersonal behavior and affect (Côté and Moskowitz 1998; Moskowitz and Côté 1995). We found that deviations from normative patterns of association between interpersonal behavior and affect (e.g., dominant behavior is associated with positively valenced affect) were predicted by personality traits such as extraversion, neuroticism, and agreeableness. In a similar way, deviations from normative patterns of association between organizational events and mood could be predicted from personality traits. Specifically, the possibility that individuals differ in the extent to which low status is associated with negatively valenced mood depending on some personality characteristics could be explored in future research.

Conclusion

Little is known about the processes though which moods are instigated in organizational settings. The present research tested one theoretical framework through which moods might occur. Specifically, we tested the resources versus demands model, which posits that events that reflect the adequacy of one's resources given impinging demands elicit moods (Morris 1999). We focused on one event that reflects the adequacy of one's resources in organizational settings, relational status. The findings of three studies indicated that, compared to high and equal status, low status is associated with low pleasant mood and high unpleasant mood. These findings provide preliminary evidence that events that reflect the adequacy of organizational members' resources trigger experiences of mood in work settings.

Acknowledgments

Study 1 was supported by grants to D.S. Moskowitz from the Social Sciences and Humanities Research Council of Canada and the Fonds pour la Formation de Chercheurs et l'Aide à la Recherche du Québec. This chapter was written while Stéphane Côté was supported by a fellowship from the Social Sciences and Humanities Research Council of Canada.

We thank Cynthia Fisher, Lance Sandelands, and Wilf Zerbe for their comments on previous versions of this chapter. Thanks are extended to E.J. Suh, Kirk Brown, Ximena Bernardin, and Donna Prahacs for their assistance with data collection for Study 1; Marci Gordon for her assistance with data collection for Study 2; and Steph Scott, Judy Baracz, and Jen Harrison for their assistance with data collection for Study 3.

8 MANAGING EMOTION IN WORKPLACE RELATIONSHIPS

Charmine E.J. Härtel and Neal M. Ashkanasy

The chapters in this section consider some of the emotional displays occurring in the workplace and their function in social communication. The chapters are especially relevant in this book because they deal with the emotion management skills required to respond to the emotional displays employees are likely to encounter in their workplaces.

Emotional Displays in the Workplace

In Chapter 5, Oluremi Ayoko and Charmine Härtel describe research on the emotional displays observed during conflicts in culturally heterogeneous workgroups (CHWs). The emotional displays most frequently reported by the team members were verbal aggression, crying, resentment, anger, bitterness, and frustration. Robert Jones and Andrea Rittman, in Chapter 6, describe some of the positive emotions displayed in the workplace, including pleasure and excitement. Together, these studies vividly illustrate that workplaces are indeed places of emotion. Consequently, it is important as organizational scholars and practitioners to understand the function that emotional displays play in organizational life.

The Social Signaling Role of Emotional Displays

Jones and Rittman point out that much of the attention on emotional displays has focused on their function as internal signals of "motive-readiness." They note, however, that emotional displays also function as external social signals, which assist people in conveying desired messages about themselves to others as well as interpreting the motives and needs of others. These displays may be unregulated or manipulated, and they may aim to correctly inform others of one's motives and needs, or, as in the case of a poker player, to mislead others regarding one's motives and needs.

Drawing on Lang's work, Jones and Rittman describe "positive" emotions such as excitement as indicating that one is *approaching* **desirable outcomes** whereas "negative" emotions such as frustration indicate that **desirable outcomes** are eluding one. Aversive arousal such as fear, anger, or disgust arises, on the other hand, as we approach **undesirable outcomes**, while relief results from *avoiding* them.

Jones and Rittman note that there are also emotional responses when outcomes actually occur. They suggest, nonetheless, that outcome-related emotions are more passive, while ongoing approach and avoidance pursuits are more active. In other words, the level of activation an emotion is likely to generate depends upon whether there is uncertainty and there is a reason to try to exert control to achieve or avoid an outcome. This proposition is congruent with Stéphane Côté and D.S. Moskowitz's proposition in Chapter 7, where they argue that unfavorable assessments of resources may have more consequences for mood than favorable assessment of resources.

Signaling the Anticipation or Occurrence of a Desirable or Undesirable Event

So far, and based on the chapters in this section, we have shown that emotional displays do occur in the workplace and also that they function as external social signals. From the research presented, we are able to develop a list of some of the work-related events that signal the anticipation or occurrence of a desirable or undesirable event, as follows:

Task-Related Conflict

Even when groups share the same goal and objective about a task, they can have conflicts over how to achieve the goal. Task-related conflicts, as Ayoko and Härtel show, can produce better outcomes for the group or lead to emotional angst.

Availability of Resources

Côté and Moskowitz, in Chapter 7, provide evidence that unfavorable assessment of resources negatively affects employees' mood.

Dissimilar Beliefs, Views, Values, and Interaction Styles

Ayoko and Härtel's review of the literature reveals that people tend to dislike others who disagree with them or have dissimilar beliefs, values, and interaction styles. Consequently, dissimilarity in beliefs, views, and values tends to evoke negative emotional responses while similarity tends to evoke positive emotional responses.

Diversity in Culture, Race, and Tenure

Ayoko and Härtel draw on the literature to show that emotional conflict is increased by dissimilarity in race and tenure attributes because people find it difficult to identify with (and easy to stereotype) those of a different race or tenure. Additionally, they note that diverse groups are more likely to experience conflict than homogeneous groups because of their greater differences in values and norms relating to interaction and work style.

Drawing upon social identity theory and social categorization theory, Ayoko and Härtel further highlight that social category membership provides naturally occurring lines along which conflicts can be drawn. Categorizing individuals into different groups can provoke hostility or animosity within the workgroup. Consequently, they propose that emotional conflict will be greater in CHWs where in-group/out-group differentiation is greater.

Interpersonal Attraction

Emotional conflict, as Ayoko and Härtel show, arises from negative affect and dislike. This lower interpersonal attraction is associated with personal and relationship issues manifested as friction, frustration, and personality clashes within the group.

Emotion Management of Others' Emotional Displays

It is clear that emotional displays occur at work, and that these serve important social functions. What is less apparent, however, is how we interpret and manage the emotional displays of others. We conclude this commentary by considering some of the advances made in this area as well as noting some of the important questions that remain.

With respect to interpreting the emotional displays of others, Jones and Rittman suggest that we draw upon the understanding we have of our own emotional responses together with our interpretation of the cues we have about a situation. Jones and Rittman's motivation and the experience and display of emotion (MEDE) model appears to assume a one-to-one correspondence of emotion with the perception of one's goal state. However, as the emotional intelligence literature underscores, some people lack emotional awareness. Consequently, people can fail to express an emotion properly because they lack the ability to differentiate between emotions or to accurately label an emotion. If, indeed, the extent to which one expresses emotions, as predicted by the MEDE model, positively correlates with one's emotional intelligence level, it could well be that emotional intelligence (see Chapter 10, this volume) may be developed by training people in the MEDE approach.

As Jones and Rittman note, recipients of communication will vary in their sensitivity to emotional displays. This means that effective interaction with others is quite likely to require not only emotion management skills, but skills in logical argument and persuasion. Ayoko and Härtel take account of this, in that skills in conflict management as well as emotion management are included in their model.

The Ayoko and Härtel and Côté and Moskowitz chapters both highlight the importance of the emotion management skills of leaders or supervisors. Côté and Moskowitz, for example, suggest that supervisors should view comprehensively the demands on subordinates from all sources within the organization. Additionally, they advise supervisors to increase the frequency of social interactions with subordinates that elicit pleasant mood and decrease the frequency of interactions with subordinates that elicit unpleasant mood.

Ayoko and Härtel's research reveals that many group leaders do not know how to manage emotional displays and consequently avoid them to the detriment of team members and team climate. They argue that leaders need to possess the emotional capability to acknowledge, recognize, monitor, discriminate, and attend to group members' emotions. Indeed, they go even further than this, and suggest that leaders need to develop and maintain a positive workgroup emotional climate, manifested in the group's norms and routines related to feeling.

Questions that Remain

The chapters in this section clearly reveal the need for emotion management skills in the workplace. While offering important new information on what skills employees require to manage the emotional displays they encounter in the workplace, the chapters also raise important questions. For example, Côté and Moskowitz ask, What kinds of supervisory behaviors minimize unpleasant mood states? Jones and Rittman highlight the need for additional research on guidelines for how employees should respond to others' emotional displays. They ask, Would a "hypothesis testing" approach to others' emotional displays be useful? They also ask, as do Ayoko and Härtel, How can team norms with respect to emotional displays improve team effectiveness? This question is, as yet, not answered definitively.

III

DECISION MAKING

DETERMINANTS OF INTUITIVE DECISION MAKING IN MANAGEMENT: THE MODERATING ROLE OF AFFECT

9

Marta Sinclair, Neal M. Ashkanasy,
Prithviraj Chattopadhyay, and Maree V. Boyle

Abstract

In this chapter, we propose a model of managerial intuitive decision making based on problem characteristics, decision characteristics, environmental factors, and individual factors. We propose also that affect moderates the intuitive decision-making process. Based on the affect infusion model (AIM), we suggest three interaction scenarios between the determinants of intuitive decision making and affect: moderate mood, high-intensity emotions, and affective feelings. We theorize that positive mood encourages the use of intuition while negative mood discourages it. We argue further that high-intensity emotions serve as a conduit to intuitive processing, but only if the decision maker focuses on the decision outcome. Conversely, we propose that high-intensity emotions can act as a barrier to intuition if the decision maker focuses on the emotion itself. Lastly, we hypothesize that managers will be more likely to use intuition in subsequent decisions if they receive affective confirmation as a result of their earlier use of intuitive decision making.

Determinants of Intuitive Decision Making in Management: The Moderating Role of Affect

This chapter explores factors conducive to the use of intuition in managerial decision making, and the moderating role of affect. Our model is based on the premise that, if identified, affective states can be used as conscious triggers or modifiers of the intuitive processing. As a result, and depending on the nature of the decision task and situation affect, affect may determine whether managers will use either an analytical or an intuitive decision-making style.

Based on Epstein (1998) and Shapiro and Spence (1997), we define intuition as:

> Non-sequential information processing, comprising both cognitive and affective elements, that results in direct knowing without any use of conscious reasoning.

Within this definition, affect is treated as an umbrella term for all emotional feelings, such as emotions and mood (Forgas 1995; Weiss and Cropanzano 1996). In this chapter, we develop propositions about the determinants and affective moderators of intuitive decision making within three theoretical frameworks: contemporary decision-making approaches (see Eisenhardt and Zbaracki 1992; Langley et al. 1995; Sauter 1999), Epstein's (1990, 1998) cognitive-experiential self-theory (CEST), and Forgas's (1994, 1995) affect infusion model (AIM).

We argue that the need to study intuition in management contexts (e.g., see Mintzberg 1989; Simon 1987) is a direct result of changes in business environment since the 1980s. In particular, this is an environment that has been plagued by high uncertainty (Schon 1983) and rapidly evolving technology (Stepanovich, Uhrig, and Armstrong 1999). Under these conditions, managers are often forced to decide expediently under pressure (Nutt 1999) or without adequate information (Agor 1984; Goodman 1993), often facing multiple alternatives in unprecedented situations (Eisenhardt 1989). These issues have led to a search for new approaches to decision making that hold potential to supplement the traditional analytical processes (Agor 1989; Andersen 2000; Sauter 1999).

Managerial Decision Making and Intuition

Psychologists (e.g., Damasio 1999; LeDoux 1996) have identified the existence of parallel cognitive systems: cognition and affect. In respect to information processing, Epstein (1990, 1998) has argued that this is reflected in rational and experiential cognitions, where cognitions at the nonconscious level are primarily emotionally driven. This view opens new possibilities for the study of intuition and its intentional use in organizational decision making. Denes-Raj and Epstein (1994) stipulate that information is processed in parallel. In their view, moreover, the experiential mode, which encompasses intuition and other nonconscious processes, is the default. This notion concurs with Cappon's (1993) interpretation of intuition as an *evolved instinct.*

Our position is that intuition and instinct are two related yet *separate* constructs. This implies that, even though experiential information processing and intuition appear to overlap, we do not view them as identical. We suggest instead that experiential cognition encompasses other aspects of information processing besides intuition, such as instinct. Conversely, and as we discuss in more detail later in this chapter, we theorize that intuition may also function on other levels of consciousness, where it might utilize different processes. Similarly, it could also be argued that analysis is only one of the tools used by rational processing. In order to mitigate readers' confusion, in this chapter we will refer to the experiential information processing mode as the *intuitive style,* and the rational mode as the *analytical style,* of decision making.

Similar to Boucouvalas (1997) and Shirley and Langan-Fox (1996) in their literature reviews, we have found a number of conflicting definitions of intuition. Petitmengin-Peugeot (1999) explains these inconsistencies by the lack of appropriate language to describe the intuitive process. Her interpretation concurs with Crossan, Lane, and White's (1999) conclusions about the nonverbal nature of intuition, pointing to a frequent use of images and metaphors in the intuitive process (see also Vaughan 1979). Similarly, Petitmengin-Peugeot (1999) and Rowan (1986) describe intuition as subconsciously perceived and synthesized impressions that are difficult to verbalize. Despite the conceptual differences, most definitions acknowledge three commonalities: (1) the intuitive event originates beyond consciousness, (2) the information is processed holistically, and (3) an emotional aspect frequently accompanies intuitive perception (Shapiro and Spence 1997).

The focus of this chapter is on the use of intuition in intentional decision making in business settings (Harbort 1997). This environment-specific definition is based on Isenberg's (1984) and Simon's (1987) research that delineates managerial intuition as a nonconscious, quick pattern recognition and synthesis of past professional experience and expertise. In addition, as suggested by Bastick (1982), Shapiro and Spence (1997), and other researchers, our concept of intuition includes an affective component. Further, we incorporate in our model Burke and Miller's (1999) findings that the use of an intuitive decision-making style is subject to situational contingencies.

Analytical and Intuitive Decision-Making Styles in Management

The pressures of today's dynamic business environment are often addressed by an integrated use of analytical and intuitive decision-making styles. This approach builds on Simon's (1987, 61) notion that analytical and intuitive management styles are "complementary components of effective decision-making systems." These styles, according to Mintzberg (1989), enable "non-sequential processing," critical for fast digestion of dense but ambiguous data. Mintzberg (1989) further argues that analytical (or rational) and intuitive styles counterbalance each other's weaknesses in terms of error introduction, processing ease, problem complexity, and use of creativity. Sauter (1999) describes the interaction of both styles as a symbiosis, where analytical and intuitive styles contribute complementary components to decisions. In this model, analytical processes deal with objective information, while intuition covers those areas not amenable to objective analysis, such as uncertainty and complexity (see also Langley et al. 1995).

Moving to a higher level of consideration, Parikh, Neubauer, and Lank (1994) argue that thought processes may have to reach to the "supra-conscious" level (see also Vaughan 1979). In this instance, explanation of intuitive insights goes beyond the scope of decision makers' experience-based pattern recognition. We speculate that, on this level, intuition might even act as a conduit to direct knowing (Brockman and Simmonds 1997; Parikh et al. 1994) and, as such, could use different processes than the experiential system. In particular, the notion of higher levels of consciousness seems to be supported by controversial developments in physics and biology, such as the theory of morphogenic fields, where Sheldrake (1987) has proposed that knowledge can be communicated across space and time through "morphic resonance." This theory carries the implication that people can tune intuitively into any thoughts accumulated during human evolution. This concept, however, has yet to be tested scientifically and is, therefore, beyond the scope of the present discussion.

Based on our outlined position, we propose that there are two parallel modes of information processing, anchored on different levels of consciousness, and testable by currently available scientific methods. These are the rational (or analytical) mode on the conscious level, and the experiential (or intuitive) mode operating predominantly on the nonconscious level. Both modes are assumed to function in an integrated manner, interacting mostly beyond an individual's awareness (Denes-Raj and Epstein 1994). The dominance of either mode seems to be determined by contextual factors, such as degree of novelty, and other parameters, including cognitive style preference, level of experience and expertise, and degree of emotional involvement (Epstein et al. 1996), and their cumulative effects seem to be moderated by different affective states, as discussed later in this chapter.

In summary, we argue that each information-processing mode supports a different decision-making style, suitable for a different type of problem solving. The analytical style of the rational mode is intentional, predominantly verbal, and comparatively affect-free (Epstein et al. 1996). It follows abstract, general rules of analysis and logic and is suitable, for example, for solving complex mathematical problems (Denes-Raj and Epstein 1994). In contrast, and again according to Epstein et al. (1996), the intuitive style of the experiential mode is intrinsically automatic, preconscious, holistic, associationistic, primarily nonverbal, and strongly linked to affect. It adheres to context-specific, heuristic rules. This style therefore deals with complex situations by means of prototypes and metaphors (Epstein 1998).

Figure 9.1 depicts the three decision-making styles we have discussed, incorporating the various influences on intuitive decision making. In particular, we argue that intuitive decision making is affected by characteristics of the problem, the decision, the environment, and the decision maker. Affect is also shown in our model as a moderator of individual and environmental factors. A corollary of this argument is that decision makers are likely to benefit from consciously matching their decision-making style with the decision task and situation. In the following sections of this chapter, we develop the model shown in Figure 9.1 in more detail. We begin with a discussion of the principal underpinnings of analytical and intuitive decision-making styles, and go on to consider the specific determinants of intuitive decision making identified in the

Figure 9.1 **Decision-Making Model**

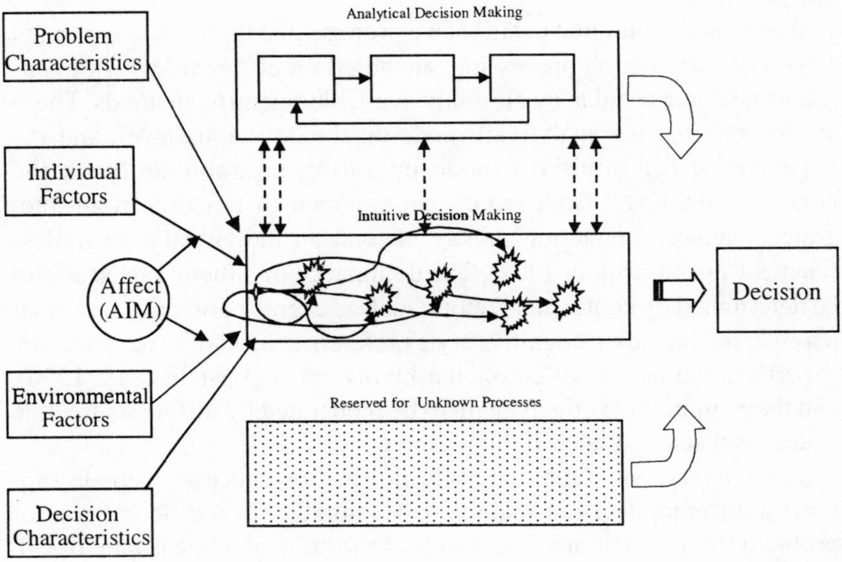

figure. In the final part of this chapter, we deal with the effect of mood, high-intensity emotions, and affective confirmation based on previous history of success in making intuitive decisions.

Rational Decision Making

Classical decision-making models are based on a cognitive process that usually occurs in a linear temporal sequence and leads to a logical and objective outcome (see Langley et al. 1995; Nutt 1999). These models assume the existence of perfect rationality, which requires an unambiguous problem definition, well-defined goals, known alternatives and their outcome, clear and stable preferences, no time or cost constraints, and a decision choice aimed at maximizing the economic payoff (Plous 1993). Since many of these conditions are not met in organizational life, decision makers usually operate within "bounded rationality" (Simon 1997). This implies that the chosen decision does not have to be ideal or even optimal, so long as it satisfies the individual's most important needs (Plous 1993). Despite various attempts to elaborate on Simon's (1960) original model by adding dynamic factors (e.g., Mintzberg, Raisinghani, and Theoret 1976), rearranging the sequence (e.g., Nutt 1984), or focusing on particular stages of the process (e.g., Pounds 1969), recent findings indicate that the success rate of rational decision-making tends to be only around 50 percent (Nutt 1999). Indeed, Mumby and Putnam (1992) have gone so far as to suggest that decisions in organizations are more appropriately characterized as "bounded emotionality." Clearly, as Carroll, Pandian, and Thomas (1993) have concluded, analytical models still fall short of providing all of the answers.

Intuitive Decision Making

Intuitive decision making addresses the need to process information and to arrive at a decision at a speed that precludes an orderly sequential analysis (Simon 1987). Aided by intuition, Eisenhardt (1989) suggests, decision makers can not only act quickly, but can also adjust their response to changing stimuli. Most literature on intuitive decision making in business context has been linked to experience and expertise (e.g., Isenberg 1984; Klein 1998; Simon 1987). According to this interpretation, experienced decision makers are inclined to forsake the analytical model in favor of a holistic scanning of memory for similar events or situations. Upon retrieving this information, they creatively reorganize these information chunks into a new interrelated pattern. This intuitive processing depends on years of experience and the level of expertise (Behling and Eckel 1991; Härtel and Härtel 1996; Isenberg 1984; Simon 1987), and therefore does not seem to be applicable to novice managers or unprecedented situations.

Hammond et al. (1987) contradict this position by pointing out that such a narrow definition might degrade intuition to a form of nonconscious analysis. Similarly, Mintzberg (1989) and Langley et al. (1995) argue that less experienced decision makers may also arrive at creative solutions to complex problems in unprecedented situations. As a consequence, they suggest that managers in general can draw on their subconscious to grasp instantaneously a whole new structure. The discrepancy regarding the role of experience has been partially addressed by Crossan, Lane, and White (1999), who distinguish between "expert intuition," which relies on past pattern recognition, and "entrepreneurial intuition," which enables decision makers to connect patterns in a new way. This typology seems to provide a common ground for the expert-based (Simon 1987) and the inventor-based (Mintzberg 1989) interpretation of how intuition works. We argue that both types of intuition can coexist. In this respect, they represent narrow aspects of the same more broadly defined construct, and therefore relate to the same group of factors and affective states.

Factors Determining Decision-Making Styles

We have organized the identified factors that influence managerial decision-making style into four groups (see Figure 9.1): (1) problem characteristics, (2) decision characteristics, (3) environmental factors, and (4) individual factors. These factors are similar to Kelley's (1967) three-dimensional cube of attribution theory, dealing with person, task, and environment. Since our research focuses on determinants of intuitive decision making, we will limit our discussion to key factors conducive to the use of intuition, listed in Table 9.1.

Problem Characteristics

We argue that decision makers tend to use intuition when they face problems characterized by ambiguity, information complexity or inadequacy, and lack of precedence. This position concurs with Behling and Eckel (1991), who suggest that intuition is useful in situations where problems are poorly structured. The results of Parikh, Neubauer, and Lank's (1994) survey also indicate that managers are more likely to use intuition when solving ill-defined problems where there are no precedents available. Mintzberg (1989) has hypothesized that important management activities rely to a large extent on holistic and intuitive processing because of problem ambiguity and complexity. Agor (1984) arrived at a similar conclusion: that intuitive decision making is employed when managers face conflicting facts or inadequate information. In addition, Burke and Miller (1999) have reported the use of intuition in unprecedented or novel situations. Thus:

> Proposition 1: The more ambiguous a problem is, the more likely it is that managers will use intuition in decision making.
>
> Proposition 2: The more complex or inadequate the available information is, the more likely it is that managers will use intuition in decision making.
>
> Proposition 3: The less precedence there is for a problem, the more likely it is that managers will use intuition in decision making.

Table 9.1

Determinants of Intuitive Decision Making

Problem Characteristics
    Ambiguity
    Information complexity or inadequacy
    Lack of precedence
Decision Characteristics
    Nonprogrammed
    High importance
    Significant impact
Environmental Factors
    Organizational Characteristics
        Configuration
        Encouragement of tacit knowledge
        Industry category
    Situational Variables
        Time pressure
Individual Factors
    Personal Characteristics
        Cognitive style
        Attitude to intuition
        Affective orientation
        Creativity
        Risk tolerance
    Personal Variables
        Experience
        Expertise

Decision Characteristics

We identify three decision characteristics conducive to intuitive processing: (1) nonprogrammed, (2) high importance, and (3) significant impact decisions. Nonprogrammed decisions are defined as nonrecurring or nonroutine decisions that require a unique approach (see Simon 1960). This description implies that such decisions are prone to ambiguity and lack precedents. Wally and Baum (1994) have supported this assumption by identifying the use of intuition as a key personal determinant of speedy strategic decision making, which tends to require unique solutions because of the ambiguity and unprecedented nature of most strategic issues. In addition, Goodman (1993) has listed the perceived importance of the decision as one of the contextual factors leading to nonsequential processing of information because of time pressure. Again, this is a scenario that might be conducive to intuition. Based on Kriger and Barnes's (1992) findings that decision events have different organizational and individual significance, however, we will treat this characteristic from two separate perspectives: the importance of the decision for the organization on the one hand, and the perceived impact of the decision for the manager on the other. Therefore:

Proposition 4: The less routine the nature of a decision is, the more likely it is that managers will use intuition in decision making.

Proposition 5: The greater the importance of a decision is for an organization, the more likely it is that managers will use intuition in decision making.

Proposition 6: The more significant the perceived impact of a decision is for the manager, the more likely it is that he or she will use intuition in decision making.

Environmental Factors

We have divided environmental factors into two groups: (1) organizational characteristics, which are fairly stable, and (2) situational variables. We deal with each of these groups in turn.

Organizational Characteristics

In our model, we consider three broad organizational characteristics that seem to influence the use of intuition: configuration, encouragement of tacit knowledge, and industry category. We deal with each of these in turn in the following.

Configuration. It describes the way in which an organization functions in terms of its structure and formalization of procedures (Mintzberg, Ahlstrand, and Lampel 1998). Mintzberg and his associates have identified seven configuration types: entrepreneurial, machine, professional, diversified, adhocracy, missionary, and political. Mintzberg argues that each configuration influences the degree to which analytical or intuitive decision making is encouraged and used. Specifically, entrepreneurial, innovative organizations with a flat informal structure tend to be more intuitive in terms of decision-making style. Mintzberg's position is supported by the findings of Crossan, Lane, and White (1999) concerning the use of the entrepreneurial type of intuition in situations prone to innovation and change. It seems reasonable to conclude, therefore, as Maidique and Hayes (1984) suggest, that a lack of formal procedures, common in entrepreneurial organizations, leads to ambiguity, and therefore is conducive to the use of intuition. Hence we posit:

> Proposition 7: The more entrepreneurial is the configuration of an organization, the more likely it is that managers will use intuition in decision making.

Encouragement of tacit knowledge. Leonard and Sensiper (1998) have defined tacit knowledge as knowledge that a decision maker has acquired through nonconscious learning and is either unaware of or cannot explain it fully. Reber (1989) has shown further that nonconscious learning and knowledge development can be more effective in decision making than rational methods. He concluded that this is because tacit knowledge increases with a more developed knowledge base and higher levels of expertise. On the other hand, research findings by Brockmann and Simmonds (1997) indicate that the use of tacit knowledge is influenced by a combination of a decision maker's experience and his or her use of intuition, which serves as a conduit. Studies in group tacit knowledge (Leonard and Sensiper 1998) and collective intuition (Eisenhardt 1999) have shown that successful organizations utilize tacit knowledge in decision making by encouraging their managers to use intuition. Therefore we propose:

> Proposition 8: The more an organization encourages the use of tacit knowledge, the more likely it is that managers will use intuition in decision making.

Industry category. Based on Parikh, Neubauer, and Lank (1994) and Agor (1984), we propose that intuition is used more in industries characterized by ambiguous problems and lack of adequate information. We propose further that intuition is associated with unprecedented situations (Burke and Miller 1999). Consistent with Wally and Baum (1994), we therefore argue that the use of intuition is likely to be more prevalent in fast-paced industries where time plays a major role in decision making:

> Proposition 9: In more fast-paced industries, it is more likely that managers will use intuition in decision making.

Situational Variables

The most important situational variable we have identified, and there-fore included in our model, is time pressure. Schoemaker and Russo (1993) state that, when time is short, intuition might be the only option for the decision maker. Similarly, Thompson (1967) has determined that nonrational methods are best used when the time is limited. In addition, Wally and Baum (1994) have identified time pressure in terms of deci-sion speed as a factor encouraging the use of intuition. We argue that, under time constraints, decision makers might have to resort to rapid nonsequential processing, as described by Simon (1987), and therefore will be more inclined to use intuition. Hence:

> Proposition 10: The more time pressure is exerted on managers, the more likely it is that they will use intuition in decision making.

Individual Factors

We have grouped the individual factors emerging from literature into two categories: (1) personal characteristics based on personality traits and attitudes and (2) personal variables of contextual nature. Out of each category, we have selected factors that have the strongest theoreti-cal support and are viable for measurement.

Personal Characteristics

The personal characteristics considered in our model include (1) cogni-tive style, (2) attitude to intuition, (3) affective orientation, (4) creativ-ity, and (5) risk tolerance.

Cognitive style. Messick (1976, 5) has defined cognitive style as "con-sistent preference in preferred ways of organizing and processing infor-mation and experience." Based on this definition, other researchers (e.g., Allinson and Hayes 1996) have argued that cognitive style influences managers' preferences for analytical or intuitive decision making and other managerial activities. Similarly, Taggart et al. (1997) have stressed the role of personal style in determining a manager's preferences for a rational or an intuitive approach to work situations. These findings are supported by earlier research (e.g., Agor 1984; Herrmann 1982;

Mintzberg 1989) which established that managers have a distinct mental preference for analytical or intuitive information processing, where the latter is more holistic, creative, and emotional. As Mintzberg, Ahlstrand, and Lampel (1998) pointed out, this mental preference has an impact on managers' leadership styles. Pitcher (1997) has identified three leader types, with "the artist" as the most intuitive manager, characterized by an entrepreneurial, imaginative, and emotional nature, similar to Mintzberg's concept of a holistic "thinking style," or approach to strategic thinking. Hence, we argue:

> Proposition 11: Managers who have a more holistic thinking style are more likely than managers with less holistic styles to use intuition in decision making.

Attitude to intuition. Regardless of cognitive style, the use of intuition seems to be influenced by an individual's attitudes. Burneko (1997) has hypothesized that denial or trivialization of intuition might inhibit its use. Similarly, Epstein et al. (1996, 394) have concluded that the use of intuition depends on "confidence in one's feelings and immediate impressions as a basis for decisions and actions." Therefore, we propose:

> Proposition 12: Managers with a more positive attitude toward intuition are, compared to managers who are less positively inclined, more likely to use intuition in decision making.

Affective orientation. It is defined as the degree to which managers are aware of affective cues, and subsequently use them as guidance in their decision making (Booth-Butterfield and Booth-Butterfield 1990). As mentioned earlier, the use of intuition seems to depend on whether the decision maker is in touch with his or her feelings (Epstein et al. 1996). Booth-Butterfield and Booth-Butterfield have argued that some individuals make decisions based on their feelings because they use affect as information consciously. Conversely, we theorize that non–affectively oriented managers may be more inclined to ignore the influence of their feelings and will attempt to base their decisions on a logical analysis (Epstein 2001). We therefore argue that:

> Proposition 13: Compared to less affectively oriented managers, managers who are more affectively oriented are more likely to use intuition in decision making.

Creativity. According to Bowers, Farvolden, and Mermigis (1995), creativity implies a mental process that generates a novel form or product through an unprecedented insight. Creativity seems to mediate especially the inventor-based or "entrepreneurial intuition" where creative decision makers "discern possibilities that have not been identified previously" (Crossan, Lane, and White 1999, 526; Mintzberg, Ahlstrand, and Lampel 1998). Creativity is closely related to intuition through imagination (Cappon 1994; Crossan, Lane, and White 1999) and associative thinking (Epstein, 2001) and, according to Pitcher (1997) and Westley and Mintzberg (1989), leads to innovation and visionary leadership. Creative problem solving thus seems to assist decision makers especially in unfamiliar, complex, or ambiguous situations (Bowers, Farvolden, and Mergigis 1995; Simonton 1975). Hence:

> Proposition 14: Compared to less creative managers, more creative managers are more likely to use intuition in decision making.

Risk tolerance. Wally and Baum (1994) define risk tolerance as the ability to tolerate ambiguity and a willingness to decide under such conditions. This characteristic describes a decision-maker's ease in dealing with ill-structured situations and vaguely defined problems, prevalent in intuition-conductive scenarios. By the same token, this definition implies a lower level of active involvement than "risk propensity" (Sitkin and Weingart 1995) or an individual's tendency to take risk per se. As Wally and Baum point out, risk tolerance is associated with psychological flexibility, another feature linking it to intuition. Therefore, we posit:

> Proposition 15: Compared to less risk-tolerant managers, more risk-tolerant managers are more likely to use intuition in decision making.

Personal Variables

As the final group of factors in our model, we examine two personal variables: (1) experience and (2) expertise. We view them as two distinct factors, even though they tend to be treated jointly in the literature (see, e.g., Crossan, Lane, and White 1999; Simon 1997).

Experience. According to Isenberg (1984), managers develop their intuitive decision making through trial-and-error experiences in similar situations. In other words, as Klein (1998, 34) puts it, "some aspects of intuition come from our experience to recognize the situations and know how to handle them," especially how to respond to the nonconsciously registered missing or unusual elements of the scenario. This position is congruent with the results of Burke and Miller's (1999) study, where 56 percent of interviewed managers acknowledged that they based intuitive decisions on their work and personal experience. The importance of knowledge beyond one's domain of expertise is echoed by Monsay (1997), who argues that the creative aspect of intuition is enhanced by experience in a broad range of areas. Our model focuses on intentional decision making in management context, so we limit our scope to experience gathered through management-related activities, and:

> Proposition 16: Compared to less experienced managers, more experienced managers are more likely to use intuition in decision making.

Expertise. Even though closely related to experience, expertise is limited in our model to occupational domain (Härtel and Härtel 1996). In this view, the level of job-related education and years of professional experience in the specific field determine expertise. Our position is based on Härtel and Härtel's (1996) conclusion that an expert's judgment is superior to a novice's only within his or her domain of expertise. For example, an accountant may decide intuitively about a tax issue but analyze carefully all options when learning how to play chess. On the other hand, some researchers suggest that expertise is nothing but rapid pattern recollection, frozen into habit (Simon 1987). Epstein (2001) and Hammond et al. (1987) argue in particular that expertise is more closely linked to nonconscious analysis than intuition. Our definition, however, encompasses also the inventor-based aspects of intuition (Crossan, Lane, and White 1999; Mintzberg 1989). Consequently, it seems reasonable to conclude that experts differ from skilled managers in their ability to combine existing patterns in a novel and creative manner. Once more, this is related to intuitive processing, leading to:

> Proposition 17: The higher the level of the professional expertise, the more likely it is that a manager will use intuition in decision making.

In summary of this section of our chapter, we have identified the four groups of factors, shown in Figure 9.1, that are conducive to the use of

intuition in managerial decision making: problem characteristics, decision characteristics, environmental factors, and individual factors. We
have also formulated specific propositions, based on the extant literature, suggesting how each is related to intuitive decision making. In the
following section, we argue that their compounded effects are moderated by the affective state of the decision maker.

The Role of Affect

A central tenet of our argument in this chapter is that affect plays a role
in decision making. This view is based in part on recent empirical studies (e.g., Elsbach and Barr 1999; Petitmengin-Peugeot 1999) indicating
that decision makers are inclined to use or eschew intuition depending
on their affective states. In this context, Simon (1987) argues that "emo-
tion-driven intuition," which represents response without careful analysis or calculation, leads to "irrational" decisions. Other researchers have
adopted a more neutral stance. For example, Shapiro and Spence (1997)
concluded that an affective aspect generally accompanies intuitive events.
Their position is consistent with Epstein's (1998) findings that the experiential processing uses affect as a cue for action. As we noted earlier,
affect is defined as an umbrella term for emotions and mood (Forgas
1994), where emotions are directed at a specific object or person, while
mood lacks object-specificity (Frijda 1993). Moreover, moods tend to
be less intense and of longer duration (Frijda 1993). Another distinction, important for our proposition development, is that affective states
have two components. The first of these is intensity, measuring the
strength of the affect. The second is direction; whether the affect is negative or positive (Petty, Gleicher, and Baker 1991, 183–184). In the following section, we develop specific hypothesized relationships between
intuition and affect, based on the affect infusion model (AIM; Forgas
1994, 1995) and findings about the confirmatory role of affect (Bastick
1982; Cappon 1994; Petitmengin-Peugeot 1999).

The Affect Infusion Model

The AIM (Forgas 1995) stipulates that there are four information-processing strategies: direct access, motivated, heuristic, and substantive.
The selection of a strategy is determined by a cumulative effect of problem, decision, and individual characteristics. Each strategy has a differ-

ent potential for affect *infusion*, which indicates how much the processing and its outcome are influenced by affectively loaded information. In the instance of our model, the direct-access mode is not relevant because it is not focused on affective elements. Therefore, we will discuss the motivated, heuristic, and substantive modes, and interpret them in the light of our arguments concerning proclivity to use intuitive versus analytical decision-making styles.

The Role of Affect in Heuristic Versus Substantive Strategies

The heuristic and substantive decision-making strategies of the AIM (Forgas 1995) correspond respectively to Epstein et al.'s (1996) rational and experiential information processing modes. Forgas (1995) argues that decision makers tend to use heuristic processing when in a positive mood, which indicates favorable conditions to proceed. Negative mood, on the other hand, evokes a sense of danger and, therefore, prompts substantive processing. This implies that the selection of intuitive versus analytical decision making might be influenced by the current mood of the decision maker. Elsbach and Barr (1999) have identified a similar trend in their study of complex decision making. Their findings indicate that positive mood is likely to encourage simplified, heuristic processing while negative mood leads to a reliance on rational decision-making protocols.

Furthermore, recent research by Ashby, Isen, and Turken (1999) indicates that positive and negative affective states are mediated by independent neural pathways and, as such, are not necessarily opposites. Based on results of their studies, Ashby, Isen, and Turken (1999) concluded that different affective states appear to have different effects on memory, judgment, processing strategies, and social behaviors. Isen's earlier work also indicates that moderate positive affect has an important role to play in decision-making outcome (see Nygren et al. 1996; Estrada, Isen, and Young 1997). Isen and her colleagues (e.g., Ashby, Isen, and Turken 1999) stress that this holds true for only moderate levels of emotion. Based on these findings about the asymmetrical nature of negative and positive affect, we treat the impact of each separately:

> Proposition 18a: Managers in moderately positive affective states are more likely to use intuitive decision making than managers in moderately negative affective states.

Proposition 18b: Managers in moderately negative affective states are more likely to use analytical decision making than managers in moderately positive affective states.

Motivational Strategy

In contrast to the heuristic and substantive strategies, the motivational strategy in the AIM is relatively affect-free during actual information processing (Forgas 1995). This strategy is guided by the decision maker's strong motivation to arrive at a desired outcome; nevertheless, the processing is likely to be *triggered* by a high-intensity affect. Forgas (1995) notes that the impact is independent of the negative or positive direction of the affect. For example, anger is just as likely as elation to trigger a motivational strategy.

The affect, however, appears to have a different effect on the use of intuition depending on the focus of the decision maker. Expanding on the AIM, and consistent with Palmer (1998), we argue that *high-intensity* affect is likely to trigger intuitive processing so long as the decision maker focuses on desired outcomes and goals. In other words, emotion can be used to reinforce an individual's intent to find a solution, therefore activating intuition. This notion is supported by Monsay's (1997) depiction of intuitive process as inevitably accompanied by a strong desire to solve a particular problem.

On the other hand, it appears that high levels of affect are likely to *preclude* access to intuition when the decision maker focuses on the affect itself, rather than finding a solution to the problem at hand. This position is consistent with Elsbach and Barr's (1999) findings that stress can impede intuition. Further, Petitmengin-Peugeot (1999), in a study of highly intuitive people, found that strong emotion disturbs intuitive listening. Similarly, Vaughan (1979) found that emotions such as fear and anxiety tend to interfere with intuitive perception by blocking subtle incoming signals.

In summary, our arguments suggest that the impact of high-intensity emotions on the use of intuition depends on whether the decision maker focuses on the problem or the affect. Hence, we propose:

Proposition 19a: For managers in high-intensity affective states, affect is likely to facilitate the use of intuition in decision making, but only if the manager's focus is on the decision outcome.

Proposition 19b: On the other hand, if the manager's focus is on the affect, then affect is likely to block the use of intuition in decision making.

Affective Elements of the Confirmatory Process

The final topic we discuss is the effect of a manager's confirmation that intuitive decision making is useful and successful. This process is in addition to the interactions we have outlined already. In this respect, the function served by affect depends on whether it is perceived in the first place and, if so, how it is perceived. Many researchers (e.g., Agor 1986; Bastick 1982; Cappon 1994; Petitmengin-Peugeot 1999; Vaughan 1979) point out that some decision makers tend to use feelings as their preferred mode of perception. For example, Petitmengin-Peugeot identified that an intuitive insight might be transmitted by means of a kinesthetic, sensational, or affective feeling. Research findings indicate that these feelings take on a specific quality, which serves as confirmation of "true" intuition. Cappon (1994) and Petitmengin-Peugeot (1999) have independently concluded that the genuine nature of the intuitive outcome tends to be confirmed by an emotional signal such as suddenly feeling calm, certain, or relieved. Cappon (1993, 45) describes "a feeling of certitude through the stomach," while Petitmengin-Peugeot (1999) refers to a feeling of certitude and coherence. Similarly, Bastick (1982, 85) talks about the "warm feeling of being right."

In line with our earlier arguments that positive affect leads to more use of intuition in decision making, we argue that the positive affect generated by intuitive decision making would likely be self-reinforcing, and would therefore encourage further use of intuition. Thus, our final proposition is:

Proposition 20: Managers who receive affective confirmation of the successful and useful nature of their intuitive experience are more likely to use intuition in future decision making than managers who do not receive this confirmation.

Discussion

In this chapter, we have described a model of the determinants and affective moderators of intuitive decision making in management context. This model is especially timely because the pace and complexity of modern business life has led to a greater interest in managerial intuition. Consequently, there is an imperative for management scholars to understand these processes. Our theoretical framework is based on contemporary decision-making approaches (Eisenhardt and Zbaracki 1992; Langley et al. 1995; Sauter 1999), CEST (Epstein 1990, 1998), and AIM (Forgas 1994, 1995). We addressed four groups of factors conducive to the use of intuition: problem characteristics, decision characteristics, environmental factors, and individual factors. We also discussed the nature of intuition and affect, and explored the role of affect in the intuitive decision-making process. The model we propose incorporates the moderating effect of positive and negative mood, high-intensity emotions, and the confirmatory affective feelings on the use of intuition.

As a final note, we acknowledge four limitations in our model. First, there may obviously be additional factors that affect decision-making styles that we have not considered. Second, the testing of our model is likely to be limited by the reliability and validity of the available scales used to measure the identified factors. In particular, most measures (e.g., the Positive and Negative Affect Scale (PANAS), Watson, Clark, and Tellegen 1988) are based on self-reports. Third, it is to be noted that our framework is limited to intentional decision making in business context. Finally, it might be necessary to identify more specifically the effect of industry type on decision-making styles, and to determine whether there are any significant differences across cultures or gender. Irrespective of these limitations, however, we believe that our model constitutes another step toward facilitating systematic and rigorous research of intuitive decision making and will further our understanding of the role of affect in this process.

In conclusion, identification of the determinants and affective moderators of intuitive managerial decision making has important implications for management practice. In particular, if empirical testing bears out our propositions, the knowledge can be used to train managers to become more aware of their affective states and the important factors involved in the decision-making process. Managers can subsequently use this newly acquired skill to shift from one decision-making style to another, and thus access intuition consciously whenever appropriate. For example, if a manager does not have adequate information, or is under pressure to make a decision too fast to apply analytical decision making, he or she could consciously trigger intuitive processing. Conversely, if a manager arrives at an intuitive decision, he or she could consciously switch to the analytical process to scrutinize the outcome.

This way, the use of managerial intuition could complement analytical decision making and thus possibly contribute to an improved speed, accuracy, and quality of decisions.

Acknowledgments

This research was funded in part by a grant from the Australian Research Council. The authors would like to thank Seymour Epstein and three anonymous reviewers at the Emotions At Workplace Conference for their valuable comments to the previous version of this chapter.

10 EMOTIONAL INTELLIGENCE: THE CONCEPTUAL ISSUE

Aaron Ben-Ze'ev

The concept of "emotional intelligence," although quite recent in psychology, has gained tremendous popularity. It almost seems as if everything in our lives today somehow has to do with emotional intelligence: We have problems at work, no doubt this is because of our poor emotional intelligence; if we have problems with our kids, it is probably our poor emotional intelligence that is at fault; if there are problems in our sex life, of course this is because of poor emotional intelligence. When a concept is as broad as this, it soon becomes meaningless. Nevertheless, it is possible to be more specific on the concept of "emotional intelligence," thereby making it more meaningful and fruitful. The concept is not entirely new.

Intelligence is our ability to function in an optimal manner in complex situations. Emotional intelligence is an intelligence in which the emotional system plays a major role. This chapter will first clarify the notions of "rationality" and "intelligence" and suggest that these notions be used in a normative sense only, when referring to optimal functioning; the question of which type of system can function in this way is a separate, descriptive issue. The different psychological mechanisms and logic underlying the emotional and intellectual systems will be described, and it will be demonstrated that emotional, and not merely intellectual reasoning, is an integral part of human intelligence. This chapter will then examine whether the two systems can be integrated. Also, the psychological notion of "emotional intelligence" will be described. Finally, some implications of the suggested conceptualization of emotional intelligence for the study of emotions at work will be discussed.[1]

Two Senses of Rationality and Intelligence

There are two senses according to which something has usually been considered rational: (a) a descriptive sense, in that the generation of X involves intellectual calculations, and (b) a normative sense, in that X may express an appropriate response in the given circumstances.

The two senses are not interdependent—something can be rational in one sense or both. Emotions are essentially nonrational in the descriptive sense, since they are typically not the result of deliberative, intellectual calculations. Emotions are often rational in the normative sense: frequently, they are the most appropriate response. In many cases, emotions, rather than deliberative, intellectual calculations, offer the best means to achieve our optimal response. This may be true from a cognitive point of view—emotions may supply the most reliable information in the given circumstances; from a moral point of view—the emotional response is the best moral response in the given circumstances; or from a functional point of view—emotions constitute the most efficient response in the given circumstances. In such cases, it is rational (in the normative sense) to behave nonrationally (in the descriptive sense). The failure to distinguish between these two senses of rationality underlies much of the heated dispute about the rationality of emotions.

There is a long tradition criticizing the rationality and functionality of emotions. In this tradition, which pervades much of current culture, emotions are regarded as nonrational in the descriptive sense—they are not the product of intellectual thinking—and hence as irrational in the normative sense—they are an impediment to rational reasoning and an obstacle to normal functioning and moral behavior. While I accept that emotions are nonrational in the descriptive sense, I reject the assumption that they are irrational in the normative sense. Typical emotions are not the product of intellectual thinking, but this does not imply that they are not the optimal response in many circumstances.

A similar analysis can apply to the notion of "intelligence." Intelligence may be characterized as our ability to function in an appropriate (or even optimal) manner in complex situations. It has often been assumed that such ability is basically an intellectual ability. I reject this assumption as well and argue that this ability usually consists of both emotional and intellectual capacities. Hence, we may speak about emotional intelligence; that is, intelligence in which the emotional system plays a major role.

In order to avoid confusion between the normative and descriptive senses of "rational" and "intelligent," these terms should be used in only the normative sense; that is, referring to an appropriate or optimal response to the given circumstances.

The Rationality (or Intelligence) of Emotions

Although emotions are nonrational or nonintelligent in the descriptive sense, namely, they are not products of intellectual thinking, emotions may be rational or intelligent in the normative sense; that is, they are often the appropriate, or even the optimal, response.

Emotions are the optimal response in many circumstances associated with their generation; namely, when we face a sudden significant change in our situation but have limited and imperfect resources to cope with it. In these circumstances the emotional response is often optimal, because optimal conditions for the normal functioning of the intellectual system are absent. For example, in circumstances when much of the relevant data are missing but speed may be more important than accuracy, our decision making must be done in a more or less predetermined form without having to think about what to do exactly. Deliberative calculations are not required for the emotional system to behave rationally in the normative sense: reason in emotions is not simply a matter of calculation but first of all a matter of sensibility. Moreover, in many situations the calculated pursuit of self-interest is incompatible with its attainment. In light of its evolutionary origin, behaving emotionally may in many cases promote our own interest (see also De Sousa 1987; Elster 1999; Frank 1988; Oatley 1992; Solomon 1990).

Emotions constitute an adaptive mechanism in the sense that they are flexible, immediate responses to changing stimuli. They are useful urgent responses to emergencies. Indeed, emotions are often the most practical and useful states that we can assume. Grief over the death of a person is of value; it is a natural evaluative response conveying our appreciation of the worth of a fellow human being and is important for the development of moral behavior. Likewise, love is of value in helping us to establish a more intimate and stronger bond with other people, and fear is an alerting mechanism, important in ensuring self-preservation. Strong emotions also rouse us to perform in ways that might otherwise be beyond our capability. Thus, fear spurs humans and animals to run faster and longer than they ordinarily can. Emotions discontinue normal functioning either by disrupting it or by significantly strengthening it. Both cases have an adaptive function.

The functional value of emotions does not imply that emotions are beneficial in all circumstances. Although emotions are often rational in the functional sense of being an appropriate response, this kind of rationality may be characterized as local, since it does not take into account global implications, but only those limited to the local present situation (Frank 1988).

Emotions are rational in the normative sense also in the moral domain: they are morally valuable. Emotions are especially important in our relationships with those near and dear to us. In such circumstances, which constitute the bulk of our everyday behavior, partial emotional attitudes are not only possible but also morally commendable. Sincerity and particular attention to specific needs, both typical of emotional attitudes, are of crucial importance. Emotional attitudes are also a moral barrier against many crimes. Emotional evaluations have emerged through a long process of evolutionary and personal moral development. Accordingly, they are significant in expressing some of our deepest values and commitments and in providing basic guidelines for moral behavior. However, the crucial role of emotions in moral life does not imply their exclusivity; the intellectual capacity is important as well (Ben-Ze'ev 2000).

The adaptive value of emotions is to be found in the way emotional patterns have evolved. The burden of explaining emotions should shift from reasoning to developmental processes. Evaluative emotional patterns have emerged and have been modified throughout the evolution of the species and personal development of the individual agent. Explaining emotional phenomena cannot be limited to the fractions of seconds in which we are supposed to make the various intellectual calculations, but has to account for many evolutionary and personal factors. The process of evolutionary and personal development has modified, or tuned, our emotional system in such a way that our surroundings immediately become emotionally significant.

The Psychological Mechanism Underlying Emotions

So far, it has been shown that the emotional system, and not merely the intellectual one, can be regarded as rational or intelligent in the normative sense of providing the most optimal response in the given circumstances. Now, two major aspects in which the emotional system differs from the intellectual one—(a) the psychological mechanism underlying emotions and (b) the logic of emotions—will be described.

A word of warning is in order. When speaking about intellectual and emotional systems, we do not assume the existence in our mind (or brain) of a little person driving a car termed *intellect* and another person driving a tram named *desire*. Rather, we refer to two modes of the mental system: one is typical of our being calm and cool, and the other is typical of intense emotions. Another mental mode is the perceptual mode. The borderlines between these modes are not clear.

A distinction can be made between two major types of psychological mechanisms: schematic and deliberative. Whereas the schematic mechanism is more typical of the emotional mode, the deliberative mechanism is more typical of the intellectual mode.

A deliberative mechanism typically involves slow and conscious processes, which are largely under voluntary control. Such processes usually function on verbally accessible, semantic information, and they operate in a largely linear, serial mode. A schematic mechanism typically involves spontaneous responses depending on a more tacit and elementary evaluative system. Schematic activity is typically fast, automatic, and with little awareness. It is based upon ready-made structures or schemes of appraisal, which have already been set during evolution and personal development; in this sense, history is embodied in these structures. Since these schemes are part of our psychological constitution, we do not need time to create them; we just need the right circumstances to activate them. Schematic activity largely occurs outside of focal awareness, can occur using minimal attentional resources, and is not wholly dependent on verbal information. This distinction has been suggested in various forms concerning different phenomena (e.g., Ben-Ze'ev 1993; Clore and Ortony 1999; Ekman 1992; Lazarus 1991a; Lyons 1980; Sloman 1996; Smith et al. 1993; Van Reekum and Scherer 1997. Physiological evidence for the presence of such a schematic emotional system is presented in LeDoux 1996).

The two types of mechanism may clash. Thus, we may persist in being afraid even when our conscious and deliberative judgment reveals that we are no longer in any peril. We can explain such cases by assuming that certain schematic evaluations become constitutive to a degree where no intellectual deliberation can change them. This corresponds to situations in which intellectual knowledge fails to influence illusory perceptual content. Spontaneous evaluations are similar to perceptual discriminations in being immediate, meaningful responses. They entail no deliberative mediating processes, merely appearing as if they are products of such processes.

The schematic nature typical of the emotional evaluations enables us to consider emotions not as an isolated result of a cognitive inference, but as part of ongoing interaction. Deliberative evaluation is a preparatory process that precedes and is separate from its product. A schema is an active principle of organization, which is constitutive in nature; it is not separate from the organized state, but part of it.

The spontaneous and schematic nature of emotions does not imply that deliberative thinking has no role in generating emotions: we may think about death and become frightened, or think about our mates and become jealous. Deliberative thinking, however, has a preparatory, rather than constitutive role in emotions. Thinking may prepare the system for the activation of schematic evaluations: it brings us closer to the conditions under which evaluative patterns are spontaneously activated. Deliberative thinking may be the immediate stimulus for the activation of an evaluative pattern, but the emotional evaluation itself is nondeliberative. This gives the mental system, while being in the emotional mode, the ability to react almost instantaneously to significant events and yet to draw fully upon the power and flexibility of complex cognitive and evaluative capacities such as abstract thinking (Smith and Lazarus 1990).

The biological function of emotions provides a clear explanation for the development of an automatic appraisal mechanism: to provide a quick response to urgent situations. The great role of personal and social circumstances in generating emotions does not change the spontaneous and unreflective nature of emotions. Such circumstances mold our character so that some of our spontaneous and natural emotional responses assume a certain form. Here we may speak of "learned spontaneity"; this spontaneity is an immediate response but has been shaped by our personal and social history (Oakley 1991).

Although the above description of the psychological mechanism underlying emotions is, generally speaking, correct, it is up to empirical research to determine the exact nature of such a mechanism. It may be the case that the distinction between deliberative and schematic processing does not exhaust all the types of processing underlying emotional and intellectual responses.

The Logic of Emotions

There might be some synthetic principles underlying emotional reasoning that are different from those associated with intellectual reasoning. The principles of both emotional and intellectual reasoning do not violate the analytic rules of formal logic, but they follow different principles from the point of view of their content.

The logical principles underlying the emotional and intellectual modes can be divided into three groups, each concerned with a different type of information. Those types refer to (a) the nature of reality, (b) the impact of the given event upon the agent, and (c) the background circumstances of the agent.

a. The Nature of Reality

The Emotional Mode

1. The emotional world consists of the environment I actually perceive or in which I imagine myself to be;
2. Changes are more significant than stability;
3. A personal event is more significant than a nonpersonal event.

The Intellectual Mode

1. The environment that I actually perceive or in which I imagine myself to be constitutes a small portion of the intellectual world;
2. Changes are not more significant than stability; on the contrary, we should assume that there are stable regularities in the world;
3. A personal event is not necessarily more meaningful than a nonpersonal event.

b. The Impact of the Given Event

The Emotional Mode

1. The perceived strength of an event is most significant in determining its impact;
2. The more real an event is perceived to be, the more significant it is;

3. Those who are relevant and close are more significant than those who are irrelevant and remote.

The Intellectual Mode

1. The objective strength of an event is what is most significant;
2. The significance of an event is not always connected to its perceived reality;
3. My psychological distance from a certain person is of no relevance in evaluating this person.

c. Background Circumstances of the Agent

The Emotional Mode

1. The more responsible I am for a certain event, the more significant the event is;
2. The less prepared I am for a certain event, the more significant the event is;
3. The issue of whether the agent deserves a certain event is greatly significant in evaluating this event.

The Intellectual Mode

1. My responsibility for a certain event is in many cases not relevant to its present significance;
2. My preparedness for a certain event is in many cases not relevant to its present significance;
3. The issue of whether the agent deserves a certain event is not always significant for evaluating this event.

It is beyond the scope of this chapter to discuss these different logical principles (for detailed discussions, see Ben-Ze'ev 2000, 2002), but even the above headlines describing these principles can illustrate the different types of logic associated with each mental mode.

Is It Possible to Integrate the Emotional and Intellectual Systems?

The differences between the emotional and intellectual modes cast doubt on whether they can ever be integrated into one system. Hence, they are usually described as contradictory, and the dispute focuses on which of the two should be preferred.

A prevailing tradition has seen these differences as an indication of the shortcomings of the emotional system and hence drawn the conclusion that the intellectual system is the true essence of the mental realm. Plato, Descartes, and Kant are prominent representatives of this tradition that considers intellectual thinking to be the essence of the mental realm. In Plato's metaphor, intellectual reason is the shepherd and emotions are the dogs (Plato 1963). In a modern formulation of this view, the mind is an intellectual processor of knowledge that sorts out information in a relatively unbiased manner and emerges with carefully drawn conclusions and well-considered decisions. From this perspective, the mind is envisaged as a sober little creature seeking the most intellectual answers. This attitude is still common in philosophy and psychology. It is clearly expressed in the computational approach to the mind that constitutes the prevailing view in the fields of the philosophy of mind and cognitive psychology.

The opposite view, represented by Hume and Bergson, considers the emotional system to be of greater cognitive value. Hume (1978, 415) argued that "reason is, and ought only to be the slave of the passions." Bergson's (1907, 155) view is in clear opposition to the tradition that assumes that intellectual thinking is the best and in many cases the only means to know reality. He considers the ultimate cognitive tool to be the instinct, which in many respects is similar to emotions.

The differences between the emotional and intellectual systems are genuine; nevertheless, integrating the two is still possible. The starting point for describing this possibility may seem surprising: Spinoza's (1985) view of the different levels of cognition.

Most people consider Spinoza as belonging to the intellectualist tradition; a contention that is inaccurate. Spinoza believes that the ultimate cognitive tool combines both the emotions and the intellect. Spinoza distinguishes between three different levels of cognition (or knowledge): perceptual (and emotional), intellectual, and intuitive. Cognition stemming from singular (or unique) things, and that is based on the senses and imagination, is considered to be confused and false. Emotional cognition usually belongs to this type. Intellectual cognition that is based upon common and universal notions is considered as necessarily true. However, according to Spinoza, the highest form of cognition is not intellectual knowledge, but rather an intuitive knowledge that combines elements from the other two types: it proceeds from singular things but expresses universal knowledge concerning the essence of things. For Spinoza this kind of cognition is related to an emotional attitude: the intellectual love of God (Spinoza 1985 II, 40s1,2; II, 47; V5, 33).

We may say that Spinoza's first level of cognition, perceptual and emotional cognition, uses the spontaneous mechanism, whereas the second level, intellectual cognition, uses the deliberative mechanism. The content of the first level is partial and that of the second level general. The third level of cognition is similar to emotional knowledge concerning its mechanism—it is a type of schematic mechanism; it is similar to intellectual cognition in the sense that its content has a broad validity as it refers to many circumstances.

We may identify the third level of knowledge as a kind of intuition. Intuition may be characterized as expressing a claim whose content is correct but seems to be unfounded. The spontaneous mechanism underlying the intuitive claims seems to be insufficient for substantiating these claims; this mechanism refers to limited data that have no necessary connections to the broader content implied in intuitive claims. Such lack of foundation can lead to many errors and distortions—and indeed this is a common situation concerning emotional claims. How can we explain that a type of cognition, which is basically unfounded, is considered to be the highest type of cognition? How can we distinguish between the lowest and highest type of cognition?

The psychological model that may explain intuitive knowledge is that which refers to expert knowledge. Like emotional knowledge, expert knowledge is intuitive in the sense that it is not based on a careful intellectual analysis of the given data, but rather on activating cognitive structures such as schemata. Acquiring cognitive schemata is like acquiring skills. Before acquiring the cognitive schema associated with riding a bicycle, riding is a controlled thoughtful activity done in stages; the transition from one stage to another is usually accompanied by conscious deliberations. Once the schema is acquired, the mediating stages disappear along with the reasoning processes. These learned activities can then be performed automatically since the intellectual rules have become part of the agent's cognitive structure. In these circumstances, the cognitive effort is mostly restricted to a trigger function. Take, for example, wine experts. These people have developed perceptual sensitivity that enables them to discern perceptually different types of wine without using mediating intellectual deliberations. Other evidence suggests that people can sense intuitively in the first thirty seconds of an encounter what basic impression they will have of the other person after fifteen minutes—or even after six months (Ambady and Rosenthal 1992; Goleman 1998b).

Expert knowledge, which is a type of intuitive knowledge, expresses the highest form of knowledge. Emotions also typically involve such type of intuitive or immediate knowledge, but this is so because of the urgency of the situation and not necessarily because we are experts in the matter of emotions. This may lead to many distortions that indeed are associated with partial emotional attitudes. It is interesting to note that the cognitive mechanism of the highest form of knowledge, expert knowledge, is similar to that of knowledge that is frequently distorted, namely, emotional knowledge (see also Ben-Ze'ev 1993).

The intuitive mechanism is not a mysterious entity that necessarily contradicts the results of intellectual deliberations. A person using the intuitive mechanism does not use the deliberative one because the latter necessarily leads to false claims, but because in these particular circumstances this person does need it.

The regularities typical of emotions should be described as assumptions structured into our personality, not as intellectual calculations carried out inside our heads. The emotional agent is not necessarily aware of premises and does not therefore necessarily infer conclusions from them. Instead of assuming an intelligent agent who makes explicit intellectual calculations, we should assume a well-designed and somewhat inflexible system, thus providing a more economical explanatory mechanism. Indeed, simple mechanisms often underlie what seems overwhelmingly complicated when described by formal idioms.

Our emotional behavior is clearly not rule-following behavior. When we fall in love or become angry, we do not calculate our emotional response; in most cases the relevant data and the general principles of calculation are simply unknown to us. Although we do not actually make intellectual calculations, the emotional response, being in accordance with such calculations, may be perceived *as if* it were the result of such calculations. When one is angry with the right person to the proper extent at the right time, one acts in accordance with what reason dictates, but not because of it. Here anger speaks with the same voice as reason, but this does not mean that we employ reason through deliberative, intellectual processes. We do not need such processes here; we simply act in accordance with our character (see also Aristotle 1984, *Nicomachean Ethics*, 1102b28).

Generating emotions consists mainly of activating basic evaluative patterns rather than a process of intellectual persuasion. This explains why, from an emotional point of view, it is true that "one picture speaks louder than a thousand words." The emotional system is more easily activated by visual than by verbal stimuli, whereas the intellect is more susceptible to verbal stimuli. Poetry, so successful in inducing emotions, is, of course, verbal, but it affects us in the way that pictures do: it does not present long intellectual arguments, but rather excites points of sensitivity that activate the emotional system. This process is also one of the ways in which music induces emotions.

Having shown that the integration between the emotional and intellectual systems is conceptually possible, the notion of "emotional intelligence" that presupposes such integration is discussed.

Emotional Intelligence

The presence of two systems of reasoning has been indicated, each with its own set of basic principles. Accordingly, something that may be regarded as reasonable in one system may not be regarded so in the other system. Hence, we can understand expressions such as, "Emotionally, you're an idiot." The different principles of the two systems stem from their different focus of concern: whereas the emotional system is concerned with the personal and volatile, the intellectual system is concerned with the general and stable. Both concerns are of great importance in our lives; hence, our ability to combine them is of great value for us. We may say, therefore, that intelligence in its broad sense, which includes both intellectual and emotional intelligence, is the ability to use in an optimal manner both types of intelligence.

Strictly speaking, emotional intelligence is an emotional ability to function in an optimal manner in complex situations; similarly, intellectual intelligence is an intellectual ability to function in an optimal manner in complex situations. In themselves, both types of intelligence are not sufficient for optimal behavior in most everyday circumstances. Circumstances in which only intellectual capacities are required for arriving at the optimal solution include, for example, abstract problems and taking account of remote consequences. Circumstances in which only emotional capacities are required for arriving at the optimal solution may exist in very close and intense relationships. But is seems that the integration of intellectual capacities may benefit us in these circumstances as well. Accordingly, it makes more sense to speak about intellectual intelligence as consisting merely of intellectual capacities than to speak about emotional intelligence as consisting merely of emotional capacities. When speaking about emotionally intelligent behavior, we therefore mean behavior in which emotions play a major, but typically not an exclusive, role. Hence, emotional intelligence typically combines, in an optimal manner, emotional and intellectual capacities.

The concept of "emotional intelligence" is of quite recent stock in psychology. The first paper about emotional intelligence was published in 1990 (Salovey and Mayer 1990). This may well be because researchers were slow to realize the role of emotions in intelligent behavior and because combining intelligence and emotions was previously considered a contradiction in terms, something like "dry rain" or "a sexually experienced virgin." However, once we have recognized the value of emotions in optimal behavior and the existence of the two types of reasoning, the idea that emotions play a major role in intelligent behavior becomes important to our understanding of human intelligence.

From a psychological point of view, emotional intelligence can be characterized as the capacity to process emotional information accurately and efficiently, and accordingly to regulate the emotions in an optimal manner. We may speak about two domains of emotional intelligence: (a) recognizing emotions, in us and others, and (b) regulating emotions, in us and others.

Emotional intelligence consists of recognizing and regulating emotions in an optimal manner. A person who can easily recognize and regulate her emotions, or those of others, is emotionally intelligent. Someone who knows that anger is destructive or useless in a particular situation and who repeatedly behaves angrily in spite of such knowledge, may be considered emotionally unintelligent. This person may either misidentify her anger or may identify it correctly but, while angry, evaluate it positively. Emotional intelligence expresses the skills, rather than knowledge per se, that an individual can attain in order to function adequately from an emotional point of view. Unlike intellectual intelligence, emotional intelligence involves a unique type of sensitivity rather than deliberations (e.g., Goleman 1995, 1998b; Mayer and Salovey 1995, 1997). In light of the integral role of emotional sensitivity in intelligence, it has been claimed that if we want computers to be genuinely intelligent, then they will need to have emotional intelligence (Evans 2001; Picard 1997).

Our ability to be accurate in identifying our emotions and those of other people is not merely a cognitive ability, but also an evaluative ability that largely depends upon our emotional sensitivity. Identifying emotions in other people requires emotional closeness to them, just as the ability to perceive a certain value, like the normative belief in the goodness of God, requires the adoption of certain values. Proper emotional attitudes are sometimes necessary for proper cognition. Emotional intelligence is not merely intelligence; it is emotional as well.

It is not obvious whether it is easier to recognize and regulate our own emotions or those of others. Thus, recognizing our own emotions seems to be easier than recognizing the emotions of others; however, this may be true concerning only positive emotions since in negative emotions the mechanisms of denial and repression are common and hinder our ability to recognize our own emotions. Similarly, the capacity to regulate the emotions of others seems to be more indicative of emotional intelligence since such regulation requires a more complex understanding of circumstances; however, in some cases, it is easier for us to give advice to others rather than to ourselves.

Recognizing and regulating the emotions requires both emotional self-awareness and empathy; but it also requires an intellectual ability that can calculate the various implications of different alternatives. For example, to know how and why I, or other people, feel, requires not merely emotional acquaintance, but intellectual thinking as well. We cannot adequately recognize and regulate emotions without some intellectual ability.

Some aspects of emotional intelligence may be innate, while others are acquired through engaging in various activities—usually both emotional and intellectual—until general rules and past experience are embodied in our mental system, thus sensitizing this system to more complex and general circumstances and regularities. To a certain extent, emotional intelligence, which is a kind of expert knowledge, can be learned. It can be learned to a greater degree than intellectual intelligence. Unlike intellectual intelligence, which hardly changes after teenage years, emotional intelligence continues to develop. In fact, it appears that as we mature, we acquire a greater degree of emotional intelligence (Goleman 1998b).

How is emotional intelligence related to emotional intensity? Is there a correlation between the two in the sense that a person with high emotional intelligence is also a highly emotional person? The connection between the two is complex. Emotional intelligence may influence emotional intensity in various manners. On the one hand, emotional intelligence includes the capacity to identify emotions easily—our own and other people's emotions—and this capacity is usually related to high emotional sensitivity. On the other hand, emotional intelligence includes the capacity to regulate and utilize emotions and this capacity involves a certain type of indifference and detachment that is not typical of emotional people. Emotional intelligence involves flexibility and comfortable relationships—these are not typical of very intense emotions. Also the ability to stop something that we have started and found to be harmful, which is typical of emotional intelligence, is not typical of highly emotional people. Accordingly, we may assume that emotional intelligence will not be very high both among indifferent people, whose distance from the emotional circumstances will make it hard for them to identify such circumstances, and very sensitive people, whose tremendous emotional involvement will make it hard for them to keep the distance that is required for emotional regulation. I would speculate, therefore, that people with high emotional intelligence will have moderate emotional intensity; people at the extremes will have low emotional intelligence.

Emotional responses are often expressed in extreme behavior, and it is this type of behavior whose moral consequences are most harmful. In these circumstances emotional intelligence is of utmost importance. Intellectual reasoning should allow emotional responses to direct our moral conduct as long as these are, for example, moderate; when the responses tend to become extreme, we should in most cases consult intellectual reason before behaving in light of these responses. Intellectual reason allows certain degrees of freedom to the emotional system, but this is not a complete freedom. The ability to manage our emotions plays a key role in improving our well-being. However, we must remember that such an ability should not be understood as implying that we should disregard our emotional tendencies; this may prevent us from enjoying the many advantages of the emotional system. The popular advice to count to ten before expressing our anger reflects an awareness of the risks of an immediate emotional response. Such advice, however, does not completely dismiss the functional value of emotional responses: it does not go so far as to count to a thousand.

Another way in which emotional intelligence deals with the shortcomings of emotional partiality is to be acquainted with many partial emotional perspectives. Learning to appreciate the diversity of partial human perspectives is crucial for giving our own perspective its proportionate weight.

Emotional intelligence provides guiding principles—such as "drive safely"—rather than specific rules—like "don't exceed 100 kilometers per hour." What constitutes safe driving may vary considerably, depending on several factors such as the competence of the driver, the conditions of the road, and the driving of other people (Averill, Catlin, and Chon 1990, 34). Optimal, rational behavior, which combines both emotional sensitivity and general intellectual rules, may vary considerably, depending on several personal and contextual features. We may provide some specific rules that may help us achieve optimal, rational behavior, but at the end of the day, personal and contextual features will have a crucial role in determining our rational behavior.

A spontaneous, emotional system and a deliberative, intellectual system are both important for conducting a valuable life. The different systems often express opposing tendencies and competing interests; yet each system retains a somewhat independent voice and influence. It is as important for an individual as it is for a state to have potential sources of dissent from within. The possibility of internal conflict is sometimes a wellspring of vitality and sensitivity, and a check against one-sidedness and fanaticism (Adams 1985).

Some Implications for Emotions at Work

The above characterization of emotional intelligence is clearly relevant to the study of emotions at work. Many types of work, such as those performed by lawyers, doctors, nurses, therapists, teachers, hairdressers, police, waiters, and prostitutes, require some kind of regulation of the emotions. Regulating the emotions is an important aspect of emotional intelligence.

There is no doubt that we often regulate our emotions at work. Regulating the emotions does not mean being nonemotional; rather, it means changing our emotional attitudes. Being professional is not synonymous with being emotionless; of course, professionalism should exclude excessive emotional intensity, which prevents normal functioning. Often, it is necessary for professional work to involve the emotions. Accordingly, Betty Bender is correct in arguing: "When people go to work, they shouldn't have to leave their hearts at home."

An important division of the means of regulating emotions is related to the three intentional aspects of emotions: motivation, cognition, and evaluation. Thus, emotions can be regulated by using *behavioral, cognitive,* and *evaluative* means. Behavioral means facilitate or prevent certain types of changes, thereby regulating emotional intensity. Cognitive interpretations can focus not merely on the presence or absence of the changes themselves, but on the manipulation of their significance. The evaluative method of regulating emotions focuses on changing our evaluative structure rather than on the interpretation of particular circumstances.

Behavioral means of regulating emotions are common and involve popular activities such as exercise, reading, working, listening to music, watching TV, going for a walk, being with people, eating, and shopping. Some of these means, such as exercise, listening to music, going for a walk, being with people, and eating, can be used at work.

Behavioral means are limited in their usefulness, since they usually modify our encounter with reality, but change neither our personality nor reality. There is always the possibility that we will have to face the reality at some future time, and the accompanying emotional intensity may then be increased. Many behavioral means are types of escape devices that can be compared to taking aspirin: they fail to cure the illness, but they help us to cope better with its symptoms. Nevertheless, behavioral means are generally adaptive because they are readily available and have immediate results (Eisenberg and Fabes 1992).

Cognitive means of regulating emotions are very popular and emerge quite early in our development. Examples of such means include diverting our attention, thinking positively, giving ourselves a "pep talk," and interpreting the situation in a way that avoids unpleasant implications.

Cognitive means can take the form of attention deployment or manipulating the emotional content. When we use the means of attention deployment, we divert our attention from the emotional concern to something else. Thus, it is often better to ignore an insult than to respond to it. An example of manipulating the emotional content can be found in the story of a husband who, when asked whether he cared that his wife was having an affair, answered: "I'd rather have 50 percent of the shares of a good business, than 100 percent of a poor one."

In using behavioral means, we approach or avoid certain people, places, or objects in order to regulate our emotions; in using cognitive means, we distract our attention from or concentrate on certain aspects of people, places, or objects. Cognitive means reduce emotional intensity by avoiding thinking about certain emotional circumstances, while escapist behavior actually removes us from these circumstances. Cognitive means are valuable in that they require less investment of resources than does escapist behavior. However, in cases where physical proximity to the emotional event may prevent us from ignoring it, the usefulness of cognitive means is limited, and they may need to be supplemented by behavioral means.

A most useful and common cognitive means is changing, and in particular broadening, our perspective. Many people involved in service work use this method. Flight attendants, for example, use a broad array of techniques to avert their anger toward obnoxious passengers. A common tactic is to conceive of such a passenger as suffering, and thus deserving of pity rather than anger. They focus on what the other person might be thinking and feeling—that is, they imagine a reason that excuses his behavior, such as fear of flying. Similarly, nurses often interpret the situation in a way that facilitates compassion toward their patients. The choice of a different emotional perspective makes all the difference.

There are many circumstances in which behavioral escape devices are not available and evaluative means are hard to achieve—thus leaving cognitive means as the most feasible option. In modern service work, one cannot use behavioral escape devices such as avoiding clients, and it is unlikely that workers could change their evaluative patterns in a short period of time. When flight attendants are required not only to appear happy but also to be happy, and bill collectors are expected to be angry, the most efficient way to fulfill their work requirements is to use cognitive means. Accordingly, they might reinterpret the situation by adopting another perspective—usually that of the client or employer. This practice may, in the end, facilitate an evaluative change.

Evaluating means are the most profound and difficult means of regulating emotions, as they often involve modification of specific norms and personal architecture. Whereas cognitive means are mainly concerned with changing our interpretation of the emotional object, evaluative means are concerned with changing our attitude toward the emotional object. The cognitive interpretation may turn out to be inadequate to our surroundings; for an evaluative change, the requirement for some correspondence with reality is less relevant.

Profound evaluative means do not merely involve surface behavior, where we try to change our outward appearance, but a deep change in which we alter ourselves and spontaneously express a real emotion that has been self-induced. In surface behavior, we may deceive others about our real emotions, but we do not deceive ourselves. Such a separation of display and emotion is hard to sustain. With a profound change, however, our behavior is a natural consequence of that change, and feigning is unnecessary (Hochschild 1983).

Since it is hard to maintain a separation between an emotion and its display for a long time, one needs to reduce the strain by altering either the display or the emotion. If, for professional reasons, the display is important, then the best way to reduce the strain is to assume the required emotion. Take, for example, social workers who need to exhibit positive emotional attitudes toward their clients. If someone tends to find needy people irritating, then this person is not suitable for social work, as the role will demand a continuous discrepancy between emotional experience and emotional display. Adopting a basically favorable tendency toward the needy may avoid the discrepancy, but since this would involve a change in attitude, it would be difficult to achieve. On the other hand, it may be the case that a certain social worker possesses a basic positive tendency, but because of temporary circumstances, such as a bad mood, finds it difficult to exhibit the necessary positive attitude. In this situation, behavior and cognitive means of regulating emotions are the most appropriate.

Regulating emotions is a quite common practice in our everyday life. Nevertheless, reaching an optimal level of regulation requires emotional intelligence. Given that there are many means of regulating emotions, the best way of succeeding in such regulation is to combine several means at the same time. Hence, it is useful to be aware of these means in order to utilize them in our daily life.

Bearing in mind the proliferation of new types of work and the rapid changes in the structure of organizations, emotional intelligence is of great importance in all types of work.

Conclusion

Contrary to the long tradition that considers emotions to be irrational and harmful, in many circumstances the emotional response is the optimal one, and, hence, emotions can be regarded as rational in this normative sense. Our conduct is more valuable when it is determined by both the emotional and intellectual systems. The optimal integration of the two systems expresses emotional intelligence. Such integration is possible and desirable. Increasing emotional intelligence is a feasible task that requires deeper understanding of the ways the emotional and intellectual systems operate. This is particularly true of the emotional system, whose nature has been far less the object of academic research.

Ernest Hemingway said: "Happiness in intelligent people is the rarest thing I know." He might be right if by intelligence he meant merely intellectual intelligence. Such intelligence in itself may reduce or even eliminate many types of emotion, in particular happiness, a state in which our perspective is sometimes illusory. However, emotionally intelligent people are precisely those who are from time to time able to be happy despite everyday hardship. In emotionally intelligent people happiness is not rare.

Note

1. The discussions in this chapter are based on the book, *The Subtlety of Emotions* (Ben-Ze'ev 2000).

11

GRINNING, FROWNING, AND EMOTIONLESS: AGENT PERCEPTIONS OF POWER AND THEIR EFFECT ON FELT AND DISPLAYED EMOTIONS IN INFLUENCE ATTEMPTS

Donald E. Gibson and Scott J. Schroeder

Power often defines how people think and feel in organizational settings. Social psychologists have long argued that power relationships are inherent to social interaction (French and Raven 1959) and organizational theorists stress the ubiquity of power and influence acts in organizations (Kanter 1977; Kipnis 1984; Kipnis, Schmidt, and Wilkinson 1980; Kotter 1985; Pfeffer 1981, 1992; Yukl and Falbe 1990). The "thinking" side of dyadic power is well developed in cognitively oriented models of social influence (see Barry 2001; Kipnis 1976; Raven 1993, 2001; Kelman and Hamilton 1989). A common theme in all these models is the assumption that the influence agent is a rational decision maker who engages in a primarily cognitive process of determining effective influence strategies based on a cost/benefit analysis (Bruins 1999). An element missing in the extant models, however, is the "feeling" side of power: the effect of agent *emotions* on the influence process. In the influence tactic literature, for example, emotions are considered primarily in terms of a marginal cost for the agent: in their rational decision-making process, agents are encouraged to consider the possible negative emotions of their targets as a potential cost exacted on the relationship. They are not, however, urged to consider their own emotions about having and using power in the workplace.

At the same time, theorists of emotion in organizations are increasingly emphasizing that a person's control over his or her emotional feeling and display can be a potent form of influence. Criminal interrogators use a combination of positive and negative emotional displays to influence their targets to confess to crimes (Rafaeli and Sutton 1991); lawyers use anger displays as "rambo litigators" to intimidate witnesses and "strategic friendliness" to soften them up (Pierce 1995); flight attendants induce positive feelings in themselves in order to manage the anxiety of airline passengers (Hochschild 1983); organizational leaders express passion about mission and goals to engender positive emotions in employees (Goleman 1998b). Given the importance of emotion in influence processes and the importance of influence in emotion processes, we propose that the time is ripe for an integration of these two theoretical approaches.

The purpose of this chapter is to advance the study of dyadic workplace influence through a review and analysis guided by the social psychology of influence agents' emotional feeling and display. We ask three interrelated research questions: In organizational settings, how does the agent's perceiving that he or she has greater power than an influence target in a dyadic situation shape the agent's felt emotions? How do agents' strategic displays of emotions potentially enhance the effectiveness of influence attempts? And, How do agents' perceptions of power affect whether they express authentic or strategic emotions in their influence attempts? Understanding how agents feel and display both authentic and strategic emotions has important implications for understanding the use and abuse of power in organizations.

The chapter is organized as follows. First, a brief literature review summarizes research in the fields of interpersonal influence and emotion management, providing current definitions, clarifying the need for theory, and providing a rationale for including emotions in the influence process. We then propose a dyad-level model of emotions in interpersonal influence, from the agent's point of view. We outline research literature supporting links in the model, depicting an influence episode as driven by agents' perceived level of power, which then affects both the feelings they have about using that power and the displayed emotions they use in the actual influence attempt. The chapter concludes with a discussion of the model's implications for researchers in both influence and emotion management processes and managers using influence in organizations.

The Interpersonal Power and Influence Tactics Literature

The following is a brief conceptual synopsis of the extant interpersonal influence literature. It is not considered comprehensive, but rather is aimed at providing a rationale for including emotions in the influence process (for a more complete summary of this literature, see Kipnis 1976; Barry and Watson 1996).

Power and Influence Defined

We draw on French and Raven (1959) in defining power as the potential influence that one person, the agent, has over another person, the target. We define perceived power as the extent to which the agent believes he or she is instrumental to the achievement of a target's goals, such as the agent's felt capacity to apply sanctions, or his or her possession of expert knowledge that would hinder or help the target achieve a desired outcome. The agent must also feel that he or she could or would in fact use the capacities (see Kelman and Hamilton 1989, 84). Influence is the process by which agents exercise their perceived power to successfully persuade others to follow their advice, suggestions, or orders (Kolb, Osland, and Rubin 1995). The social influence process, overall, can be defined as the use of both verbal and nonverbal actions by a person (the influence agent) directed at another person (the target) with the expectation that those actions will bring about a desired change in the attitudes, feelings, or behaviors of the target that would not have otherwise occurred (adapted from Barry 2001, 20).

Research in Power and Influence

Conceptual models of social influence commonly identify the sources of power, stages and events, particular influence tactics, and contextual elements that comprise an influence attempt. Models differ in the degree to which they focus on the agent (or powerholder), the target, or the interaction between agent and target. Kipnis (1976) presents the stages of the influence process from the perspective of the agent, or as he terms it, the powerholder. The agent's motivation to influence another's behavior initiates a decision-making and action sequence in which the agent (1) chooses to make an influence attempt based on an assessment of costs and benefits, and (2) determines the appropriate influence tactic depending on the sources of power available and those most likely to overcome target resistance. The agent then engages in the influence attempt, the success or failure of which can impact the agent's need to influence, values, and perceptions of him- or herself and the target. Pfeffer (1992) outlines a similar approach in managerial settings. Other models are target-centered, identifying the conditions that facilitate target acceptance of influence; Kelman (1974; Kelman and Hamilton 1989) specifies that targets comply when they perceive that accepting an influence attempt will assist in goal attainment. Cialdini (1988) identifies conventions in social interactions that engage targets' inclinations toward automatic compliance. Social rules predispose targets to accept an influence attempt when they are called upon to reciprocate, to behave in a manner consistent with their commitments, and to heed authorities, for example. Still other models elaborate agent/target relations in interpersonal influence. Indicative of this perspective is Raven's (1993, 2001) power/interaction model, which includes consideration of agent and target characteristics such as age and gender, motivations, and cost/benefit assessments as central to understanding the process of interpersonal influence. Barry's (2001) expectancy approach to interpersonal influence suggests that agent and target behaviors and responses are dependent on their expectancies and social perceptions concerning each other, their relationship, and the situation. Kotter (1985) offers that constructing effective influence relationships in organizations requires that agents and targets understand and seek compatibility in their respective personal styles, goals, and expectations.

Empirical research in interpersonal influence in organizations has focused primarily on attempting to classify the tactics used by managers in upward, downward, and lateral influence attempts (Kipnis, Schmidt, and Wilkinson 1980; Yukl and Falbe 1990; Yukl and Falbe 1991; Schriesheim and Hinkin 1990). This literature has generated several overlapping sets of influence tactics (though consistency in their identity has eluded researchers [Yukl and Falbe 1990]) ranging from "harder" tactics of pressure, threat, and intimidation to "rational" tactics of providing information and logical persuasion to "softer" tactics of ingratiation and inspiration (Kipnis and Schmidt 1985). Emotions are clearly implied in the way agents might use these tactics—for example, negative emotional displays to accompany pressure; positive emotional displays to accompany ingratiation—and emotions are also implied in the reaction of targets to hard or soft tactics. In general, however, this research focuses on the empirical tendency of managers to use particular tactics and their potential consequences rather than the importance of emotions per se.

Theory and research in social influence, then, suggest a process in which agents assess their goals, their sources of power, and potential target resistance, and then strategically determine the available tactics that will most likely induce compliance and overcome that resistance. The approaches are universally cognitively and rationally based. A description of Raven's (2001) model is illustrative: "In essence, the model describes the agent as a rational decision maker who weighs various costs and benefits of the power bases available to him before invoking one of them to influence the target" (Bruins 1999, 9). Likewise, targets decide to comply with or resist an influence attempt based on their cognitive appraisal of the episode and the likely outcomes of their actions (Barry 2001). Consequently, both the agent and target are viewed as rational participants in influence events (Koslowsky and Schwarzwald 2001). Consideration of the role of emotions in interpersonal influence is largely absent; at most, emotions are viewed as marginal contributors to the power process.

The Management of Emotions Literature

Emotions, long considered as physiological and subjective feeling states largely out of the control of the people feeling them, are increasingly being conceptualized as manageable and potentially strategically used (see Parkinson 1997; Frijda 1986). This change in conception has increased recognition by theorists and researchers that emotional feeling and display are potentially important as contributors to social influence. This section summarizes this emerging theory and research.

Emotions Defined

Defining affective phenomena remains controversial and elusive, with terms such as *moods*, *feelings*, and *emotions* often used differently by different researchers (Forgas 1992). As used here, we define *emotions* as states of action readiness elicited by events appraised as meaningful (Frijda 1986)—they are relatively intense, short-lived states focused on a particular target or cause (Arvey, Renz, and Watson 1998; Weiss and Cropanzano 1996). *Moods* take the form of a general positive (pleasant) or negative (unpleasant) appraisal, and differ from emotions in that they tend not to be focused on a specific cause, but may be evoked by several relatively insignificant events (Frijda 1986; Tellegen 1985). Following Frijda (1986, 251), we define *feelings* as an awareness of a situation having meaning for the agent, plus anticipation that actions could be taken (the feeling could turn into an emotion) if the situation becomes urgent.

We further distinguish these emotional *states* from dispositional affect, which is a personality *trait* referring to a person's relatively stable, underlying tendency to experience positive and negative moods and emotions (Staw, Bell, and Clausen 1986; Watson and Clark 1984). Individuals characterized by dispositional negative affectivity tend to be distressed, upset, and have a negative view of self over time and across situations; positive affectivity is the tendency to experience positive moods, such as pleasure or well-being, across situations (Larsen and Ketelaar 1991). By focusing on interpersonal interaction, we wish to highlight a further characteristic of emotion: that a person's felt emotion may be more or less congruent with his or her *displayed emotion* in an encounter. The latter will be defined as "facial expressions, bodily gestures, tone of voice, and language" conveying—or attempting to convey—emotional meaning (Rafaeli and Sutton 1989, 4).

Managing Emotions As a Form of Social Influence

Recent studies of emotion in organizations have emphasized the degree to which individuals control or manage their outward emotional display (Hochschild 1983). Two interrelated forces motivate people to control their emotions: first, to respond to organizational "display rules" that are in place to enhance the presentation of the organization to external audiences, such as customers (e.g., that airline flight attendants should be upbeat and smiling), and second, to induce appropriate emotions in others (e.g., to make airline passengers happy). Hochschild's elucidation of emotional labor neatly captures both aspects of emotion management. She defines emotional labor as "the management of feeling to create a publicly observable facial and bodily display," and notes that this labor requires individuals to suppress certain feelings "in order to sustain the outward countenance that produces the proper state of mind in others" (Hochschild 1983, 7). Most emotion labor research has focused on the first aspect, the dynamics of controlling one's feelings, and the theorized cost this control might entail for people, in the form of stress (Adelmann 1995), feelings of alienation (Erickson and Wharton 1997), and loss of a sense of identity (Hochschild 1983). Much less examined is the notion that the purpose of emotion labor is to manage the emotions of others, and thus emotion labor is an influence process (see Thoits 1996). From our viewpoint, in the influence process, agents engage in varying degrees of emotion management to display emotions in order to influence the attitudes, behaviors, and emotions of targets.

The primary focus of influence in emotion labor studies has been the service provider–customer interaction, in which the service provider primarily tries to induce positive emotions in customers to enhance their attitudes about the organization (Hochschild 1983; Wharton 1993; Parkinson 1997; Van Maanen and Kunda 1989; Lively 2000). The primary thrust of Hochschild's initial work was that lower-power service workers would be called on to manage their own emotions in the quest to make higher-powered clients feel good. Much less examined is the notion that more powerful agents might manage their own emotions to influence less powerful targets, though there is suggestive research. Sutton (1991), in his study of bill collectors, argues that collectors use particular emotion strategies to induce debtors to pay on time. Collectors were instructed to display warm emotions to extremely anxious debtors; irritation, even anger, to friendly, sad, or indifferent debtors; and calmness to angry debtors. These specific emotional displays were encouraged by the organization because it was thought that by expressing particular emotions—in response to, and in anticipation of, particular target emotions—collectors could bolster their primarily coercive power base. Rafaeli and Sutton (1991) further argue that contrasting positive and negative emotional displays used by criminal interrogators are a strong means of social influence to bring about compliance by criminals in confessing crimes.

Thoits (1996) investigated encounter group sessions and observed emotional displays explicitly used to manipulate the feelings of others. Specifically, the group used a combination of acting personal events out, provoking strong negative emotions as a way of "purging" or catharsis, then providing support and warm emotions to draw the group closer together. Thoits (1996, 86) argued that "evoking not only positive but negative emotional states in others can be a useful social tool in attaining solidarity, behavioral compliance, social change, and/or identity change," but she notes that with a few exceptions, these aspects have not been the focus of serious study.

These studies suggest that agents in influence interactions use emotional displays as important means of influence over targets. Missing from them, however, is a guiding theoretical framework that attempts to link the level of perceived power, agent felt emotions, and the emotions they display in the influence attempt, yet these linkages are critical to understanding the influence process. These studies tend to treat the agents' displayed emotions as separable from emotions they feel, yet few studies have examined how the two might relate. Moreover, existing studies do not draw on the substantial social influence literature to bolster the case for emotion as an influence tool; in few of the studies is reference to social influence research made at all. What is needed in this field is a framework for theory that integrates social influence theory with theories of emotion management and display.

An Integrated Approach to Perceptions of Power and Emotions in Influence Attempts

The model presented in Figure 11.1 depicts the relationships between an influence agent's perceived power and his or her felt and displayed emotions in an influence episode. The model focuses on the process of cognitions, emotions, and behaviors an agent undertakes in devising and implementing an influence attempt, analogous to the approach used by Kipnis (1976). We assume, as did Kipnis, that the motivation to influence another person arises in the agent when he or she "experiences an aroused need state that can only be satisfied by inducing appropriate behaviors in others" (1976, 16), and might include a need to satisfy organizational role requirements, a need to enhance his or her self-esteem and self-efficacy, a desire to harm or benefit the target, or other motivations (Raven 2001). We first outline the role of the agent in this theoretical model, then examine the links between the agent's perceived power and felt emotion, his or her perceived power and displayed emotion, and then the potential reciprocal effect of felt emotion on displayed emotion.

The Agent's Role

The model suggests two broad categories of variables that influence the agent's level of perceived power (and indirectly affects felt and displayed emotions): agent attributes and agent perceptions of the influence situation.

Figure 11.1   **A Model of Agent Perceived Power and Felt and Displayed Emotions in a Dyadic Influence Attempt**

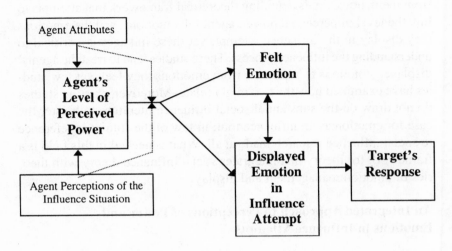

In terms of agent attributes, research suggests several personality traits that would affect an agent's perceived level of power, his or her felt emotions, and his or her tendency to use particular kinds of emotion in influence attempts. Barry (2001) cites Machiavellianism, dogmatism, and locus of control as personality variables that have been associated with influence strategy choice. Our focus on emotion suggests that this list be expanded to include emotional individual difference variables, specifically, an agent's dispositional affectivity—that is, his or her tendency to experience positive or negative moods and emotions. It is likely—though as yet largely untested—that these would also affect agent feelings about and use of power (Barsade et al. 2000). A suggestive study by Iverson, Olekalns, and Erwin (1998) found that high PA is associated with a preference for actively controlling the environment and autonomy, both of which should enhance feelings of power, even if, in fact, the sense of control is an illusion (Alloy, Abramson, and Viscusi 1981). Empirical work by Caldwell and Burger (1997) is also suggestive on this point: they show that individual measures on the Big Five personality dimensions were correlated with reported use of influence strategies. They found, for instance, that high levels of agreeableness and conscientiousness are associated with relatively low self-reported use of assertiveness and exchange tactics and relatively high self-reported use of rational persuasion and involvement.

Individual differences are also likely to attend the agent's tendencies in terms of emotional display. Recent research has suggested that individuals differ in the extent to which they outwardly display their emotions (Kring, Smith, and Neale 1994), and also differ in their ability to monitor and control their own verbal and nonverbal behavior with respect to social cues—that is, they differ in expressive self-control (Snyder 1974). Other potentially important agent traits include demographic variables, particularly agent sex. In terms of emotion, research indicates that women are more emotionally expressive than men are (see summary in Hatfield, Cacioppo, and Rapson 1994), and are particularly more likely to express warmth and liking during interactions with others (Bem 1974; Rafaeli 1989a). However, research that has considered potential differences in the way men and women may feel about and use influence tactics is contradictory and inconsistent (see Dreher, Dougherty, and Whitely 1989; DuBrin 1991; Offerman and Schrier 1985; Thacker and Wayne 1995).

In terms of the agent's perception of the influence situation, at least five assessments by the agent impinge on his or her level of perceived power, and indirectly, his or her feelings about the influence attempt. First, following Kipnis (1976), the cognitive attributions agents make for why a target might resist are an important determinant of the agent's decisions about means of influence as well as the emotions he or she is likely to feel in the attempt (see Weiner 1986; Graham, Hudley, and Williams 1992). Second, the agent must assess the *likelihood* of resistance by the target. There is substantial evidence that individuals feel negative affect such as irritation and annoyance when their efforts to exercise power are blocked or frustrated (Dollard et al. 1939; Berkowitz 1978, 1982). The third potential aspect is the agent's prior experience with the target in influence attempts, and the resulting level of liking for the target. Negotiation research, for example, suggests that the existing and past interpersonal relationships between negotiators will shape perceptions of current negotiation interchanges (Polzer, Neale, and Glenn 1993; Sondak and Moore 1993; Barry and Oliver 1996). These past experiences affect the level of liking, affection, or attraction of the agent toward the target, which shapes both the agent's emotions and his or her inclination to use particular power bases (Michener and Schwertfeger 1972). Fourth, organizational contextual variables will also be important, particularly cultural norms surrounding power and authority (Hofstede 1984), and norms for emotional feeling and display (Rafaeli and Sutton 1989; Van Maanen and Kunda 1989).

Finally, the agent's current mood is likely to affect perceived power. On the positive side, studies have shown that inducing positive moods enhances feelings of control, cognitive creativity, task activity, and persistence (Isen and Baron 1991; Seligman and Schulman 1986; Staw and Barsade 1993), which may enhance an agent's ability to discern appropriate power bases and effectively influence others. On the negative side, laboratory studies suggest that moderate negative affect increases aggressive tendencies (Bell and Baron 1990), and subjects experiencing negative moods tend to interpret ambiguous stimuli in a negative or threatening manner (Watson 1988; Watson and Clark 1984). Thus, being in a negative mood may lead an influence agent to interpret targets as likely to resist their influence, when, in fact, they do not intend to resist at all.

The model shows agent attributes and perceptions of the situation as having a direct effect on the agent's level of perceived power, as well as a mediating role in the agent's felt and displayed emotions. For example, an agent's dispositional affect (e.g., tendency to feel positive emotions like optimism) is likely to shape both the agent's level of perceived power as well as his or her tendency to feel and display particular emotions in the influence attempt. Likewise, the agent's attribution of why the target might resist (e.g., because he's lazy) will affect the agent's emotions in the attempt (e.g., feeling and displaying anger to motivate the lazy target to succumb to the agent's influence).

The Effect of Agent Perceived Power on Felt Emotions

Research is generally supportive of the notion that perceiving that one has more power than another person, and increasing that power (e.g., being promoted and increasing one's legitimate power, acquiring additional expertise, finding out critical information), are associated with positive emotions (Kemper 1978; Lovaglia and Houser 1996; Mulder 1977; Ridgeway and Johnson 1990). This connection is consistent with long-held views that individuals are strongly motivated to gain ability, mastery, competence, and power, and that securing them brings satisfaction (Sullivan 1940). These motive theories are consistent with more recent sociological theory linking perceptions of power directly to emotion. Kemper (1990, 222) argues that an elevation of an agent's power in a dyadic interpersonal relationship leads to a greater sense of ease and security; elevation of the target's power leads to fear or anxiety for the agent. Kemper (1991) explored this contention through an empirical study of emotion episodes, confirming that by reading respondents' descriptions of power relationships, coders could correctly identify their likely felt emotions better than chance, and found that "power gained by self" in these episodes was associated with increased happiness/security (Kemper 1991). Mulder (1977) argues that individuals have a basic need to gain power and to be independent of more powerful others by increasing their own power. In a series of experimental simulations, he showed that those who were assigned more powerful roles were more satisfied than those who were in less-powerful roles. Lovaglia and Houser (1996) found that participants assigned to leadership positions in groups reported more positive emotions during task interactions than did other group members.

These studies emphasize that increasing one's power in general leads to positive emotions. Positive emotions might also be indirectly generated by the fact that an agent increasing his or her power in an interaction reduces the possibility of target resistance. Since target resistance and the prospect of conflict over the influence attempt is likely to increase negative emotions or at least reduce positive ones on the part of the agent, reducing this possibility is likely to increase positive feelings. In general, our proposition is that increasing one's power in a situation gives one an enhanced sense of freedom of choice—increasing power gives an agent more options in the influence attempt. Increasing freedom and choice, we propose, leads to increased positive emotions about the prospects of successful influence.

The Possession/Use Paradox

Though perceiving that one has power in relation to another has generally been associated with positive emotion, anticipating *using* that power, at least in the form of dominating behaviors, has been associated with more ambivalent, or even negative, emotion. Some theorists have argued that the exercise of power in general is satisfying (see Mulder 1977), and clearly there are individuals for whom dominating behavior results in increased positive emotion. In organizational settings, however, the use of dominating behavior may not bring satisfaction. Milgram (1963) argues that agents who must influence others because their authoritative role dictates that they should may not experience any personal satisfaction from influencing others and indeed may find the act of influencing distasteful. Moskowitz and Côté (1999), in a recent field study, found that while being in subordinate roles and engaging in submissive behaviors is related to unpleasant affective states, possessing supervisory roles or using dominant behavior is not necessarily associated with positive ones. In a variety of work settings, dominant behavior was positively associated with unpleasant affect but not associated with pleasant affect.

Cognitive appraisal theorists emphasize the degree to which an actor experiences agency or responsibility for events determines emotional response. To the degree that agents feel powerful, they will be more likely to take responsibility for positive outcomes, producing emotions of pride (Weiner 1986); and conversely, for negative outcomes, the more likely they will attribute responsibility to less powerful others and feel anger. Tiedens, Ellsworth, and Moskowitz (1998) have attempted to directly study this association between power, agency, and emotion. By inducing status differences in participants by assigning them roles of "boss" and "subordinate," they found, in line with their hypotheses, that given a negative outcome, the low status subordinate was more likely to be blamed, and in a positive outcome, the high status boss was more likely to receive credit. More importantly, though, these attributions of agency were related to differences in feeling specific emotions: subjects assigned to low status roles felt more sadness, guilt, appreciation, and gratitude, depending on whether they were held responsible for an outcome; subjects in high status roles felt more anger, frustration, pride, and self-satisfaction. These investigations suggest that there are predictable differences in the emotions agents tend to feel depending directly on their level of perceived power.

We argue that there is a *possession* versus *use* paradox in emotional responses to having and using power: the perception of increasing power by an agent vis-à-vis a target in itself will be satisfying, but using that power—since it inevitably raises the potential for target resistance—will arouse more ambivalent emotions. As long as resistance is minimal, influence agents should regard increases in their power as positive and contribute to good feelings. To the degree that agents think that the target will resist their use of power, agents will tend to feel negative emotions, even if they know they possess sufficient power to carry out their intended actions.

The Effect of Perceived Power on Displayed Emotions

The preceding research suggests that an agent's perceived level of power vis-à-vis a target will affect his or her felt emotions about influencing that target. In this section we argue that an agent's perceived level of power will also be an important determining factor in the *displayed* emotion that accompanies the influence attempt. In this section we temporarily analyze displayed emotion in isolation from felt emotion to assess the possible direct effects of perceived power. We do this because the agent's display of emotion itself is meaningful in communicating power (e.g., displays of pride or anger regardless of actual feelings may communicate perceived power levels), and knowing that particular emotions illustrate power, agents may be motivated to display emotion strategically; that is, they may manage their emotional display to enhance their appearance of power. We will discuss the relative congruence and discrepancy between the agent's felt and displayed emotions in the next section; in this section we essentially hold felt emotions constant.

Strategic Emotional Display

In social influence interactions, knowing that emotional displays signal levels of power, agents will be motivated to align their displays of emotion with their perceived level of power. This relatively conscious management of emotion suggests that emotions are not only inherent, natural responses to events, but they are also expressed *intentionally* to produce the desired appraisal by others. This means that there are two kinds of emotion: "A reactive variety that is fundamental, authentic, and natural, and a strategic variety that is secondary, simulated, and manufactured" (Parkinson 1997, 74). Salter (1995, 137) echoes these two types: "Emotional signals can be genuine expressions of how the sender feels. They can also be false, posed expressions chosen for their impact on receivers." Thus, an agent's use of influence is characterized by interpersonal emotional signals that can express genuine emotion or be used instrumentally to have a desired effect (see also Buck 1988; Bailey 1983). Because agents know that their emotions will be appraised in certain ways by others (e.g., anger will be taken as a signal that someone is to be blamed), they may use this knowledge to strategically display particular emotions to enhance their influence.

By arguing that agents will be motivated to use their emotions strategically, we do not mean to imply that we can predict what specific emotional display will emerge. For a given level of perceived power, the range of possible displayed emotions in influence attempts is wide, both in terms of valence (negative, neutral, or positive emotions) and intensity (little to no emotion to strongly intense passions). Rather, what we are arguing here is that the relative discrepancy of power will be critical in determining the options that an agent has in terms of emotional display. Increasing the power of the agent vis-à-vis the target will increase the flexibility of the agent to choose different valences and levels of intensity; decreasing the power of an agent or making it more ambiguous vis-à-vis a target will tend to constrain both the valence range and intensity of emotional displays available to the agent.

Depending on their perceived level of power and an assessment of their relationship with the target, research suggests that agents may draw on three general emotional display strategies: positive, negative, and cloaked, or concealed. Morris and Feldman (1996, 991), for example, capture the potential for these different emotion valences to be used in the employee-customer setting: "Positive emotional displays are aimed at increasing bonds of liking between employees and customers; display rules emphasizing emotional neutrality are used to convey dispassionate authority and status; negative display rules emphasizing anger and hostility often are employed to intimidate or subdue clients (e.g., bouncers)" (see also Thompson, Nadler, and Kim 1999 for similar distinctions in the negotiation literature). We are interested in displayed emotions used as influence in a variety of organizational settings, not limited to the customer service interaction (see Ashforth and Humphrey 1995), since we regard this phenomenon as generalizable to a range of dyadic influence attempts. In this section we outline studies supporting the idea that agents use displayed emotions for social influence purposes, and the proposed reasons why these emotion-as-influence strategies contribute to the effectiveness of influence attempts.

The Grinning Agent: Strategic Displays of Positive Emotions

There are three mechanisms that contribute to the effectiveness of positive emotions as enhancements to an agent's influence tactics: inspiration through contagion, softening, and increasing likability. First, agents may display positive emotions—such as happiness or optimism—in the belief that these emotions may be contagious—that is, agents may seek to "infect" the target with their positive emotions (Hatfield, Cacioppo, and Rapson 1994). If targets catch the positive emotion, they will be less likely to resist, since resistance implies conflict and potential negative emotions, and targets will be motivated to maintain a positive state

(Staw, Sutton, and Pelled 1994). Locke (1996) found in an ethnographic study of pediatric physicians that effective use of humor by doctors and nurses in "comedic performances" could successfully turn negative emotions felt by patients and their families—such as anxiety and despondence—into liking, reassurance, and resilience. The contagious effect of this humor made it more likely that patients would follow the doctors' medical recommendations for treatment, an important influence outcome. Second, the persuasion literature suggests that if agents can induce a positive mood in targets, they are more likely to be effective because targets may not pay as close attention to the quality of the arguments made by an agent (Bailey 1983; Petty and Cacioppo 1986). Schwarz, Bless, and Bohner (1991) show that weak arguments made by a persuader can be just as persuasive as strong arguments for those in positive rather than negative emotional states. Thus, an agent expressing positive emotions may "soften up" the target for an influence attempt.

Third, positive emotions increase the potential for interpersonal attraction and likability on the part of the agent. There is evidence that expressions of positive emotions (specifically, happiness), increase likability. Clark, Pataki, and Carver (1996) found that subjects increased their level of liking for a stimulus person who expressed happiness versus a stimulus person who expressed no particular emotion at all. In turn, likability has been shown to be a potent form of social influence. Cialdini (1988) cites the use of techniques by professional salespeople as evidence that generating a "liking bond" between agent and target dramatically increases the tendency for the target to assent to social influence. Citing the techniques of highly successful car salespeople, Cialdini notes that the "world's greatest car salesman" attributes his success to two things: a fair price and someone they *like* to buy from. In the tradition of Dale Carnegie's *How to Win Friends and Influence People* (1936), the strategy is to initially generate liking by the target for the agent through expressing positive emotions, and this liking, in turn, decreases the target's potential resistance to agent influence attempts.

Empirical studies have demonstrated that agents frequently use strategically displayed positive emotions in influence attempts. Pierce (1995, 72) argues that trial lawyers use positive emotional displays to influence their witnesses, and simultaneously, their impression on the jury: "Being nice, polite, welcoming, playing dumb, or behaving courteously are all ways that a trial lawyer can manipulate the witness in order to create a particular impression for the jury. I term this form of gamesmanship strategic friendliness." Rather than attempting to bully a witness or scare them through the use of negative emotions, lawyers may influence a witness—particularly a sympathetic one—by displaying positive, friendly emotions. Given the effectiveness of the mechanisms cited above, it is not surprising that organization norms are developed and enforced specifying the use of positive emotions, particularly in customer service interactions. Rafaeli and Sutton (1991, 749) argue that in these settings, service providers-as-agents use "expressed positive emotions as tools of social influence," a contention explored in roles as diverse as flight attendants (Hochschild 1983), hairdressers (Parkinson 1991), amusement ride wranglers (Van Maanen and Kunda 1989), secretaries (Wichroski 1994), supermarket clerks (Tolich 1993), and cruise ship entertainers (Tracy 2000). Organizations socialize agents and enforce particular positive emotion display rules because these have been shown to be effective in garnering increased client satisfaction, compliance, and, ultimately, profit (Rafaeli and Sutton 1989).

The Frowning Agent: Strategic Displays of Negative Emotions

From the agent's perspective, strategically displaying positive emotions can enhance influence attempts by generating similar positive emotions in the target; the contagion of the emotion itself and the desire by targets to maintain that positive emotion may make resistance less likely. Agents strategically displaying negative emotions enhance their influence through a different process: they generally do not desire to generate similar emotions in the target, but rather complementary ones. The archetypal emotion indicating power is agent-expressed anger, which is intended to generate the complementary feeling of fear. There is substantial evidence that people express anger when they wish to intimidate others, that is, to show that they are more powerful than a target (thus demonstrating outwardly their perceived level of power). Impression management theory suggests that control over one's emotional expression is a way of securing power in social situations (Jones and Pittman 1982). Specifically, expressions of anger can enhance an agent's power through intimidation, that is, convincing the target that the agent is dangerous, by advertising his or her available power to "create pain, discomfort, or all kinds of psychic costs" (1982, 238). Empirical research supports the notion that anger expressions are used strategically to intimidate targets. In one experiment (Clark, Pataki, and Carver 1996), subjects were told that their job would be to get another person to agree to work on a set of math problems—a task the experimenters expected would be unpopular with the student targets. The study found that subjects increased the amount of anger they expressed—and reduced the amount of happiness—when given the task of persuading another to complete an unpopular task. "Expressing anger increases others' perceptions that we are dominant and intimidating and, as a consequence, people often will choose to strategically present anger . . . when motivated to get another to go along with their preferences," assert Clark, Pataki, and Carver (1996).

Why are agents motivated to use anger displays as an intimidation strategy? First, agents believe that targets will attribute greater power to those who express anger. Recent work by Tiedens (2001) confirms this belief. She argues that not only are people expressing anger seen by others as dominant, strong, competent, and smart, they also believe that "individuals with angry facial expressions tend to occupy more powerful social positions than do individuals with different emotional expressions, such as sad facial expressions" (2001, 87). In a series of studies, Tiedens found that political figures and business leaders were seen as more powerful if they expressed anger than if they expressed disappointment or sadness. For example, students who viewed President Clinton in grand jury testimony defending himself through the use of anger expressions viewed him as more deserving of status and power than when he expressed sad emotions. Participants in a job interview experiment thought that an applicant expressing anger about a past event should get a higher status position—and higher pay—than an applicant expressing sadness about a past event. Agents are correct to believe, then, that "emotional expressions are diagnostic of the social position of the expresser" (2001, 87), because "People used anger expression as a signal of competence and the ability to wield power" (2001, 93).

The second reason that agents express anger to enhance their influence attempts is their belief that negative emotional displays are themselves a direct form of punishment. Targets will wish to avoid agent expressions of negative emotion, because it arouses undesirable negative feelings in themselves. For example, bill collectors "believe that expressed emotions such as anger, irritation, and mild disapproval serve as tools of social influence when such conveyed feelings induce anxiety in debtors," because debtors believe that as a result of complying they will reduce or escape that unpleasant anxiety (cited in Rafaeli and Sutton

1991, 750). Lawyers are trained to intimidate uncooperative witnesses, for example, by expressing anger, or "acting mean." Pierce (1995, 61) argues that "the most common form of emotional labor associated with lawyers is intimidation. . . . Cross examination [for example] involves not only acting mean but creating a specific impression on the witness . . . one author describes a case in which cross-examination was so aggressive that the witness had a heart attack on the witness stand."

Third, displays of anger, particularly extreme anger, may enhance the perception by targets that the agent will use extreme influence tactics such as direct force or coercion. The extremity of the emotional display is a signal of how far the agent might go to influence change on the target's part. Raven (1990) argues that expressions of out-of-control emotions may be important as stage-setting devices for use of a coercive power base. He cites the example of Hitler's attempting to influence the Austrian prime minister to join the Nazi cause in World War II by "ranting like a maniac," suggesting that Hitler's very expression of passion made it more likely that Hitler would deliver on his bizarre threats. "By behaving like an uncontrolled madman, Hitler may then have made his most extreme coercive threats seem credible" (Raven 1990, 515). Thompson, Nadler, and Kim (1999) summarize this approach as the "rant 'n rave" tactic in negotiation, arguing that the appearance of "irrationality" is quite rational: the "out of control" emotions help to convince targets that the agent is willing to take great risks that could hurt both parties if the agent does not get what he or she wants (see also Schelling 1960; Frank 1988).

The Emotionless Agent: Strategic Cloaking of Emotions

A final emotion display strategy for agents is to display no emotion. We regard this as an emotion strategy because first, as we argue above, it is unlikely that the agent actually has no authentic feelings about an influence episode, and thus it is likely that the agent has to exert some effort to present a nonemotional demeanor; and second, the no-emotion expression is intentionally used to control the emotions of the target. The strategy is to appear emotionally neutral, but the underlying feelings and the intended effect are anything but emotionally neutral. The reasons that cloaking emotions is an effective influence strategy are that (1) emotional displays by managers and employees are seen as a weakness in organizational settings, and, by contrast (2) lack of emotion is considered a strength. In a similar polarity, emotions are considered irrational and threatening to the logic of bureaucratic authority; lack of emotion is associated with rationality in decision making that is essential to maintaining bureaucratic authority.

Displays of strong emotion—positive or negative—have generally been considered anathema to the workplace. From a scientific management perspective, emotions distract from the efficient operation of work; they are unpredictable, disruptive, and promote feelings of instability (Taylor 1911; see also Stearns and Stearns 1986). From a power perspective, expressions of emotion signal weakness—they indicate a person who is "out of control" and attending more to personal needs and feelings than to the rational qualities of an organizational role. From a negotiating perspective, expression of emotion is a signal that an agent has departed from rational analysis and is vulnerable to losing his or her share of the bargaining zone. Negotiators are advised to keep a "poker face" that does not reveal their true preferences, since these preferences are potentially vital information for their opponent (Thompson, Nadler, and Kim 1999). The notion of emotion-expression-as-weakness is also implicit in the treatment of women at work: feminist studies have emphasized that the understood stereotype that women are more emotionally expressive than men is also associated with less power in organizational settings (Hochschild 1983). Women are expected to take on more roles requiring emotional nurturance and support, roles that are also consistently less well remunerated and less status-rewarded than those accorded to men (see Lively 2000).

The idea that emotional displays—particularly of "vulnerable" emotions such as sadness, fear, guilt, and joy (see Gibson 1997)—are associated with weakness makes its opposite appear inherently true: lack of emotion implies power. This notion is bolstered by a long history of bureaucratic authority being associated with affective neutrality. Though we have emphasized the degree to which emotions are linked—both behaviorally and experientially—to perceived power, the tendency to express emotion in organizations is muted by an ideology depicting rationality as the basis of legitimate authority and power, and simultaneously, rationality as the opposite of emotionality (see Ashforth and Humphrey 1995; Fineman 1993; Gibson 1997; Mumby and Putnam 1992). From this vantage point, power is equated with the control of emotions. One source of this ideology derives from Weber's conception of bureaucracy, which depicts rationality as the absence of emotion:

ideal-type bureaucracy was to be "'*Sine ira et studio*,' without hatred or passion, and hence without affection or enthusiasm," and organizations were successful only to the extent that they eliminated "all purely personal, irrational and emotional elements which escape calculation" (1946, 216). Jackall (1983, 128) consequently argues that managers who wish to succeed in authority hierarchies need to "mask all emotion and intention behind bland, smiling, and agreeable public faces."

This association of lack of emotion with influence is bolstered through norms associated with what it means to be professional. Professionalism has long been associated with "affective neutrality" (Parsons 1951); that is, the ability to remain impassive and unemotional in interactions with potentially volatile clients is itself a source of power. Studies of medical doctors (Smith and Kleinman 1989) and police detectives (Steinross and Kleinman 1989) show that norms for controlling emotion displays are an explicit aspect of socialization, primarily because a lack of emotional display provides power through distancing:

> Because we associate authority in this society with an unemotional persona, affective neutrality reinforces professionals' power and keeps clients from challenging them. One element of professional socialization, then, is the development of appropriately controlled affect. (Smith and Kleinman 1989, 56)

Expressing no emotion is an essential part of agents' attaining and maintaining power as part of the professional role. Lively (2000, 38) finds that professionalism comprises not only behavioral rules, but also feeling rules; she argues that "Professionalism refers to the blend of expressed and suppressed emotional expressions that are required for a person to claim the status associated with a professional role." Thus, the professional norms stipulating neutral or no-emotion expressions are in themselves feeling and display rules for agents intending to preserve and extend their power.

Combinatory and Sequence Effects

The preceding analysis should not be construed as suggesting that consistency in expressed emotions—only positive or negative—is most effective. Rather, combining different valenced emotions, and using them in particular sequences, may also contribute to the effectiveness of an influence attempt. This strategy is explicit in criminal interrogators' use of "good cop, bad cop" strategies, which exhibit both positive and negative emotion expressions, strengthening the overall effect by explicitly contrasting the intimidation of negative emotions with the relief of positive ones (Rafaeli and Sutton 1991). A second potential pattern is an escalation strategy, which may begin with low-level positive emotions to denote likability and friendliness, then shift to cloaked, neutral emotions to denote seriousness and legitimacy, then build up to negative emotions to denote coercion; this strategy has the advantage of the agent's being able to stop the process when resistance is overcome, without resorting to potentially relationship-damaging strategies needlessly.

Perceived Power and Degrees of Congruence Between Felt and Displayed Emotions

Summarizing the previous two sections suggests (1) that perceptions of power directly produce patterns of agent felt emotions, and (2) perceptions of power affect agents' emotional display. The latter finding is not complete, however, in the sense that though we posit that perceived power has an effect on display, we do not predict what the valence of the display will be, whether positive, negative, neutral, or a combination. Rather, we argue that increasing levels of perceived power by the agent vis-à-vis the target will increase the agent's *freedom of choice* of emotional display, particularly its level of intensity and its degree of authenticity. This relationship is critical to understanding the dynamics of power and emotion, yet has not been explored in extant literature.

This line of reasoning, however, first begs the question of how the felt emotions aroused in an influence attempt affect the emotions actually displayed. Though the literature on strategic emotions implies a substantial degree of control by agents over their displayed emotions, it is unlikely that their felt emotions are not also an important factor. Thus, while we recognize that felt and expressed emotions are conceptually distinct—in the spirit of emotional labor research (Hochschild 1983)—we also recognize the reciprocal effects likely to occur between felt and expressed emotions (see Staw, Sutton, and Pelled 1994 and our Figure 11.1). We argue that even strategic emotional expressions tend to be the result of a management process in which "real" felt emotions are exaggerated or suppressed for presentation purposes rather than a process in which a strong felt emotion (such as hate) is covered by a completely different emotion (such as smiling admiration—see Clark, Pataki, and Carver et al. 1996).

The degree of discrepancy we are likely to find between felt and displayed emotions will depend on many factors, including the strength and identity of the emotion felt (see DePaulo 1992), the motivation of the agent to control his or her emotions, the strength of organization rules for appropriate display (Hochschild 1983), and the ability of the agent to monitor and control emotional displays (Snyder 1974), among other factors. It is our contention that agents will vary to the degree that they express their authentically felt emotions, depending on their level of perceived power. Specifically, the greater the perceived discrepancy in power between an agent and target, the more likely the agent will express his or her authentic emotions (thus greater congruence between felt and displayed affect), and similarly, the greater the intensity and range of emotion the agent will perceive he or she has the freedom to display to a target.

There is some evidence that agents' power level leads to a potentially wider variety and higher intensity of emotional expression. Salter (1995) in an ethnographic study of organizations ranging from theatrical groups to the military to a corporate bureaucracy, found asymmetrical emotional behavior between individuals of different status rank. Superiors were more likely to display anger-threat and happiness-reassurance emotions; subordinates were more likely to display fear-evasion and sadness-appeasement. Power provided superiors more latitude to express happiness and joking behaviors as well as more negative affect, particularly anger, illustrating allowance of a greater emotional range. Differential emotional behaviors have also been demonstrated in powerful and less powerful group members. Ridgeway and Johnson (1990, 1207) suggest that depending on a group member's status, felt emotions are either suppressed or expressed, and thus, "The expression of socioemotional behavior in task groups is deeply intertwined with the status hierarchy of the group." They propose that high status members are more likely to feel mastery of situations, take responsibility for successful outcomes, and feel pride and express positive emotions. If they encounter disagreement from lower-status group members, they are free to express anger or other negative emotions toward them. Lower status members, however, are not free to express negative emotions upward, and thus power produces an asymmetry in the kinds of emotional behavior allowed. Similarly, at the organizational level, Van Maanen and

Kunda (1989, 55) speculate that attention to emotional labor (in the sense of suppressing felt emotions) is strongest in the middle of organizational hierarchies: those with either very low power or very high power have fewer normative constraints in emotional feeling and display:

> Perhaps only the dominant and the doormat in organizational life have a relative freedom from emotional constraint. Those proverbial tycoons or founders of organizations can more or less feel and express what they want, as can the (equally proverbial) day laborers or temps who have little or nothing to risk in the workplace.

The Law of Power and Authenticity

This line of reasoning suggests that in the case of strategic emotions, influence agents have more latitude to devise emotional displays that support their influence tactics. It also suggests that with increasing perceived power, agents are less likely to have to engage in strategic behaviors; that is, they are more likely to express their authentically felt emotions. We more formally state this as the Law of Power and Authenticity in organizations:

> The greater the perceived discrepancy in power between an influence agent and target, the greater the tendency for congruence between an agent's felt and displayed affect.
> *and*
> The greater the perceived discrepancy in power between an influence agent and target, the greater the intensity and range of affect the agent will perceive he or she can display to a target.

Two normative processes keep this Law of Power and Authenticity in place. First, emotions expressed by the powerful are regarded as more important. An authentically expressed emotion is likely to have a larger effect for more powerful agents, because their power implies that their feelings should be attended to, deferred to, and resolved by others, if possible. Hochschild (1983) argues that emotion norms typically allow the powerful to vent their negative feelings and ignore the emotional consequences for inferiors. In situations where there is a wide discrepancy in power between organizational roles, agents are allowed freedom of emotional expression while targets are expected to show deference to these emotional displays, that is, to show ritual appreciation and support (Goffman 1956). In observing attorneys and paralegals, Lively (2000) notes that attorneys are able to vent their frustrations without fear of retaliation, interrupt the activities of paralegals, and ignore them; paralegals, on the other hand, are expected to absorb attorneys' anger, not fight back, and not demand attention. As Clark (1990, 319) puts it, "superiors have a right to have their feelings 'count'; inferiors' emotions are discounted or invisible." Authentic emotions, for the higher power agent, are more likely to be recognized and *work* in the influence attempt than are authentic emotions from less powerful agents.

Second, increasing power for the agent typically implies less sensitivity of the agent to target reactions, that is, a possible check on authentic emotions. Two important reasons for agents to strategically control emotions are to decrease target resistance and to protect themselves from the target's feeling negative emotions, since these might harm longer-term relationships. As the agent's power increases, both of these reasons become less salient: there is less possibility of resistance, and less sensitivity on the part of the agent to a target's emotional reaction.

Support for this idea can be found in recent research suggesting that increases in an agent's level of power generally result in less sensitivity to what less powerful people are thinking and feeling. Fiske (1993) argues that powerful people have stereotypical notions of less powerful people because they pay less attention to them. The lack of attention produces simplified thinking that then supports status quo power structures. Moreover, there is evidence that increasing power shapes the capacity of agents to sense the emotions of their targets. Snodgrass (1985), in a lab study of participants in either teacher or learner roles, found that those in the learner (structurally subordinate) role were more sensitive to the feelings and thoughts of the teachers than teachers were of learners. In a replication study using organizational roles, Snodgrass (1992) confirmed her earlier findings, showing that subordinates were more sensitive to how their leaders felt about them than the other way around. Thus, we argue that the greater the perceived discrepancy in power between an influence agent and target, the less attention the agent will pay to the target's feelings and attitudes, leading to less constraint on the agent's displayed affect.

Discussion and Conclusion

This review suggests that perceptions of power change the emotional landscape for agents. Perceiving that one has power in a relationship produces distinctive patterns in the kinds of emotions felt by agents and simultaneously releases the agent from some constraints on what emotions can be expressed. By producing a model that recognizes the effect of power on emotional feeling and expression and the effect of emotional feeling and expression on power, we contribute to research in both arenas.

Existing models of social influence portray an agent logically assessing reasons for and levels of target resistance, selecting from an array of possible influence tactics, and implementing the influence attempt. Our approach is not inconsistent with these models in the sense that felt and displayed emotions can be considered as inputs to the logical process. By introducing emotions into the process, however, we increase both the model's validity and its complexity.

Research Implications

Our model suggests that we cannot fully describe agents' psychological decision process without including how they feel about having and using power, their current mood, and their dispositional tendencies in terms of feeling and expressing emotion. The model secondly suggests that increasing perceptions of power are associated with typical patterns of feeling—increasing one's sense of power increases the likelihood that agents will feel the specific positive emotions of pride and happiness, as well as the specific feelings of anger and intimidation, depending on how they perceive the likely event outcomes (positive or negative) and whether they feel responsible (see Weiner 1986). These strong emotional patterns suggest implications for how influence tactics will be selected and the consequences of those tactics. Though selection of tactics and their consequences have been explored (see Falbe and Yukl 1992), the emotions that might affect both of these variables have not. Third, this model explores the critical place of strategic emotions in the influence process, tying together disparate strands of research suggesting that emotional displays are a critical communicative signal of agents' perceived power and are essential to the tone and consequences of an influence attempt. Researchers have effectively catalogued a variety of influence tactics in organizations (see Kipnis, Schmidt, and Wilkinson 1980; Yukl and Falbe 1990). What remains to be accomplished is also cataloguing a range of emotional tones that may accompany these tactics and their implications for the agent's perception of self (see Rind and Kipnis 1999); the relationship between agent and target; and, at a larger level, the effect on an organization's communication climate.

Finally, the model accentuates that increasing the agent's level of perceived power not only increases the range of influence tactics available, as previous models have emphasized (e.g., Kipnis, Schmidt, and Wilkinson 1980), but it also increases the range of emotional valence and intensity available to the agent to support and illustrate these tactics. Increasing levels of power mean that the agent can become increasingly authentic in his or her expression of felt emotions, and at the same time, increasing levels of power imply that targets will increasingly be called upon to absorb and defer to the emotions of the agent.

The model suggests possible research inquiries at three levels of analysis. At the individual level, our framework suggests that agent disposition affects his or her perceived level of power. But dispositional affect has not been connected with influence behavior. What are the effects of positive and negative affectivity on the choice and use of particular influence tactics and displayed emotions? A second individual level variable is gender. Findings suggest that women are generally more emotionally expressive than men (e.g., Hatfield, Cacioppo, and Rapson 1994). Are women more likely to be strategic in their emotional expression in the sense that we propose here, or more likely to be authentic? And how do these tendencies interact with perceived power?

At the dyadic level, more research is needed to discover the emotional exchange between agent and target. For example, how do relationship variables such as duration, depth or intensity, and degree of interdependence affect an agent's felt and displayed emotions? Work by Gutek suggests that parties in one-time encounters are less constrained in their behavior and emotional displays than those in ongoing relationships, due to their lack of anticipated future interaction and mutual investment (Gutek 1995). How might relationship duration affect an agent's ability to assess perceived power relative to a target? For example, a relationship with short history potentially limits an agent's knowledge of a target's position or resources.

At the contextual level, research is needed to identify different kinds of emotional cultures that are enacted in different organizations and their effect on influence behaviors. Cross-cultural research has identified substantial intercountry differences in norms for emotional feeling and expression (e.g., Scherer, Wallbott, and Summerfield 1986), but little research has examined the contrasting emotional norms of organizational cultures. Display norms present in the cultures of some organizations may constrain the strategic use of emotions, invoking preferences for the "grinning agent," the "frowning agent," and the "emotionless agent."

Implications for Managers

The proposed model offers important implications for managers in their use of power at work. The possession/use paradox suggests that while management consultants and others have emphasized an "empowerment" approach calling for managers to distribute power to people throughout the organization, managers and employees are less well instructed in how to effectively *use* power. The paradox uncovered here suggests that increasing perceived power will generate a combination of positive and negative emotions; training should focus on how to recognize these emotional tendencies and help managers assess when these tendencies are appropriate and inappropriate in influence attempts. The law of power and authenticity indicates that increasing power often comes with less attentiveness to the target's feelings and reactions to an influence attempt. In organizations, increased power may also be associated with increased visibility—making one's simple presence as influential as the use of an influence tactic. Consequently, increasing power may require increased sensitivity to the impact of one's presence on others in the organization, counter, perhaps, to the natural inclinations as identified in this model. Further, the law indicates that increasing power is associated with greater congruence between an agent's felt and displayed emotions. This suggests that the strategic use of emotions by managers might be greatest for those with some but not a lot of power. As a consequence, we would expect that increased burdens of attentiveness to targets and required emotional labor may subject managers in the middle to heightened levels of emotional exhaustion and resultant burnout (e.g., Maslach 1982a; Van Maanen and Kunda 1989).

Researchers have successfully mapped a cognitive model of social influence that may explain parts of individual behavior part of the time. But to gain a richer understanding of the influence agent in action, we must take into account not only the logic of overcoming measured resistance, but also the passion behind the power.

12 MANAGING EMOTIONS IN DECISION MAKING

Neal M. Ashkanasy and Charmine E.J. Härtel

Traditionally, models of decision making have included an implicit assumption that decision-making processes are inherently rational. Simon (1987), for example, while noting that human rationality is bounded, essentially associates emotion with irrational processes and, consequently, to poor decision making. The chapters in this section refute this view, however. Consistent with Ashforth and Humphrey (1995) and Härtel and Härtel (1997), the authors of these chapters argue that emotions and intuition, far from being antithetical to rational decisions, are an inherent part of decision making.

The view that emotions can assist decision making is supported by recent evidence from neuropsychology (see Damasio 1994, 1998, 1999). Damasio (1994), in particular, posits that the different components of the limbic brain play a hitherto unknown central role in rational decision making. He argues that decisions are strongly conditioned by somatic states—bodily sensations—that enable people to make value judgments. He goes on to describe a particularly poignant instance of inept decision making caused by a brain lesion, which blocked access to emotions. In this instance, the patient was able to describe with unemotional precision how he maintained full control of his vehicle while driving on icy roads to his appointment, remaining unruffled by the occurrence of potentially tragic accidents all around him. Although the patient's brain lesions, which had deprived him of emotional feelings, assisted him in driving on icy roads, they also deprived him of the ability to evaluate alternatives in decisions with future implications. The

latter was demonstrated when the same patient, at the end of an appointment, could not make a simple decision about the date of his next appointment. While Damasio and his assistants looked on, the patient
dithered back and forth, weighing up the consequences of each date,
without any decision. In the end, Damasio's assistants had to make the
decision for him.

Conventional wisdom still holds that emotions have no place in organizational decision making (see Ashforth and Humphrey 1995), even
hinting that emotions are beyond management's reach. Damasio's (1994)
conclusions imply that the true situation may be just the reverse; that
emotions and emotional management may be critical to effective management. More recently, scholars and management consultants alike have
begun to question the assumption that emotions are unmanageable, and
that they have no place in rational decision making. Parkinson (1997)
and Frijda (1986) argue that emotions, far from being unmanageable,
are important components of management and can be used strategically.
Hay and Härtel (2000), for example, argue that emotions are an integral
part of leaders' decisions to support or resist change initiatives undertaken by other leaders within an organization. Goleman (1998a, 1998b)
positions the management of emotions at the core of leadership in organizational settings. Similarly, Druskat and Wolff (2001) portray emotions and emotional intelligence as essential to effective group and team
effectiveness in organizations. The chapters in this section advance these
views, explaining how emotions and emotion management can affect
decision making.

In the first chapter in this section, Marta Sinclair and her colleagues
propose that emotion is the crucial determinant of the decision-making
mode adopted by a person. In their model, decision making can be either analytical or intuitive. In this respect, an intuitive mode of decision
making will be adopted when the decision maker is aware of his or her
feelings or is experiencing a moderate level of positive affect. Intuitive
decision making is also indicated when the decision maker receives affective confirmation for this mode of decision making. Further, the use
of intuition in decision making when accompanied by high levels of
positive or negative affect is determined by the decision maker's locus
of attention. When the decision maker focuses on the outcome, then an
intuitive style is anticipated. When the decision maker focuses on his/
her affective state, on the other hand, the "affect is likely to block the
use of intuition."

Although yet to be tested empirically, Sinclair and her colleagues propose a model that clearly has direct impact on the way that decision making can be managed. Thompson (1967) argued that the person-situation match determines what decision-making styles will lead to optimal outcomes. Thompson's arguments, however, were predicated upon a rational model of decision making. If the model proposed in Chapter 9 proves to be correct, then the implication for management is that maintenance of positive affect—not too much and not too little—will be conducive to more effective and efficient decision making by organizational members. This proposition is consistent with Nygren et al. (1996), who reported that positive affect leaders are more optimistic in decision making. Of course, this proposition presupposes that such decision making is necessarily always beneficial. Indeed, this is not the case. As Thompson (1967) noted, there are many occasions when the optimum decision-making mode is analytical. In this respect, there are clearly also situations when positive affect will be suboptimal for decision making. Indeed, it could well be the case that application of Thompson's model is itself contingent upon appropriate management of emotions.

The issue of exactly how to manage emotions to achieve the optimum style of decision making, however, remains unresolved in Chapter 9. This issue is addressed more directly in Chapters 10 and 11. In Chapter 10, Aaron Ben-Ze'ev addresses the issue of emotional intelligence. Ben-Ze'ev, a philosopher, takes an approach that is different from the one that readers of this book are likely to be most familiar with. His focus is on the essence of emotional intelligence—how emotions contribute to the overall effectiveness of human functioning. Thus, emotion and intellect are both viewed as integral components of human intelligence. Here, use of cognitive intellect and emotions in decision making must be optimized for the most effective decision approach and choice. Emotional intelligence was canvassed from a more traditional perspective in Chapter 1, but still in a manner that is entirely consistent with Ben-Ze'ev's perspective. In particular, emotional intelligence implies ability to perceive, to regulate, to understand, and, ultimately, to manage emotions. From this perspective, emotional intelligence could be argued to be the key to emotion regulation in terms of the Sinclair et al. model described in Chapter 9. Such a proposition would be consistent with analyses forwarded by other authors such as Ashkanasy and Tse (2000) and George (2000) that emotional regulation lies at the heart of effective leadership.

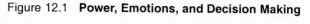
Figure 12.1 **Power, Emotions, and Decision Making**

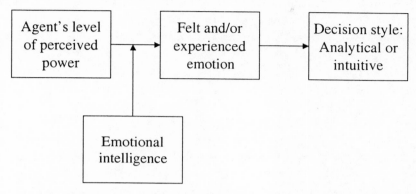

This point is taken a step further in Chapter 11. Here, Donald Gibson and Scott Schroeder present a model where power, manifested in the hierarchical structure of organizations, determines the display and experience of emotions in work settings. In this sense, power is intimately tied to decision making (see Kipnis 1976) and, as Gibson and Schroeder argue, to the management of emotions. These authors also identify a paradox whereby possession and use of power can have opposite effects. Thus, while possession of power is associated with positive affect, use of the same power can often be linked with negative affect. The implication of this is that the use of power requires a special sensitivity to the consequences of power, both for the power holder and for the target of the power. Indeed, they conclude that "the strategic use of emotions by managers will be greatest for those with some but not a lot of power."

The overall picture presented by the chapters in this section is illustrated in Figure 12.1. In this figure, the agent's level of real or perceived power determines the nature of his or her affect (positive or negative), which, in turn, is linked to his or her decision-making style (analytical or intuitive). Emotional intelligence, a dispositional variable, moderates the power-emotion link, such that high emotional intelligence is associated with better perception, regulation, and management of emotion (see Chapter 1). While this representation is stylized, it does present the centrality of both experienced and displayed emotions in the decision-making process. The model also provides some insight into the process of managing emotions to maximize decision effectiveness and efficiency.

IV

EMOTIONAL LABOR

OBSCURED VARIABILITY: THE DISTINCTION BETWEEN EMOTION WORK AND EMOTIONAL LABOR

13

Jamie L. Callahan and Eric E. McCollum

"I'm sorry you've had a bad experience with us," Janet says politely to the disgruntled customer who has just told her he will never again do business with her company. Inside, she thinks to herself, "Good riddance." In a courtroom across town, opposing lawyers Ellen and Sam argue bitterly that the other is misrepresenting the truth as they each try to convince the judge to rule in their favor. After the hearing, they meet for lunch and share stories about their kids, who go to the same daycare center. And in the parking lot at a huge discount store, Toni sits in her car before her shift begins and recites a litany of affirmations to help keep her calm as she anticipates the crowds coming to the month-end sale. As each case illustrates, dealing with emotion in the workplace is a major component of day-to-day life.

Hochschild first drew attention to emotion management in organizations in her book *The Managed Heart,* and "emotion systems" theory, as Hochschild (1983, ix) has labeled her work, is becoming increasingly popular as a framework for scholarship and practice in the organizational literature. Hochschild (1979) originally proposed the terms *emotion work* or *emotion management* to capture the essence of the management of emotions—the control and thoughtful presentation of emotions to others in a variety of interpersonal contexts. Emotion management may take many forms, including suppressing emotional reactions, exaggerating them, or modulating their expression. Hochschild added the term *emotional labor* to capture a very specific meaning associated with the management of emotions, namely being paid to manifest a specific emotional state as part of one's job (Hochschild 1983). A review of the organizational literature addressing the sociology of emotions reveals the use of all three terms. However, there has been a distinct shift in how these terms are used in the organizational literature that "obscures the variability in work role emotional demands" (Wharton and Erickson 1993, 457–458). In other words, we manage our emotions in the workplace both to benefit ourselves and to benefit the organization. Furthermore, we are sometimes expressly required to manage our emotions as part of our job, and other times do so because it benefits us directly, making work more enjoyable, meaningful, or less stressful. While both actions occur in the workplace, they spring from different sets of demands and thus are important to differentiate in studies of emotion in organizations (Callahan 2000a; Lively 2000). In much of the recent literature, however, "emotional labor" has been used to describe both functions, thus obscuring the distinctions between them. This chapter explores the theoretical underpinnings of the two terms, presents a framework for clarifying the distinctions found in emotion management actions, and describes several typical organizational interventions that have implications for emotion management.

Theoretical Underpinnings

Hochschild (1979, 1983) used the general term *emotion work* to refer to any attempt to modify the experience or expression of a consciously felt emotion. However, when specifically addressing emotion work that is conducted as a required part of actual job performance, Hochschild used the term *emotional labor.* Hochschild grounded this distinction in Marx's definitions of the "use-value" and "exchange-value" of commodities (Hochschild 1983).

Marx argued that something has use-value if it has what John Locke called a "natural worth" to "supply the necessities, or serve the conveniences of human life" (1867/1990, 126n). In other words, something has use-value if you can use or gain pleasure from it but not necessarily get something in exchange for it. For example, the air that we breathe or a baby's laugh might be considered to have use-value—neither of these things is generally bought, sold, or traded.

On the other hand, something has exchange-value if it can be "exchanged" for something else of value. Marx argued that "exchange-value appears first of all as the quantitative relation, the proportion, in which use-values of one kind exchange for use-values of another kind" (1867/1990, 126). In other words, something has exchange-value if it can be traded for something else of value. Specialized skill as a computer programmer has exchange-value and so does an ice cream cone on a hot summer day—people pay money to get these things. Sometimes, things that have use-value can be transformed into having exchange-value. For example, we can enjoy a scenic meadow in the middle of an isolated forest for its use-value; however, when a developer builds access roads to the area and makes a bid to buy the property, that use-value is transformed to exchange-value.

Given these definitions of exchange-value and use-value, we argue that the term *emotion work* is appropriate for situations in which individuals are personally choosing to manage their emotions for their own noncompensated benefit. The term *emotional labor,* on the other hand, is appropriate only when emotion work is *exchanged* for something such as a wage or some other type of valued compensation. It is very possible that Hochschild's own words in describing the distinction between her terms may be at the root of the present confusion:

> I use the term *emotional labor* to mean the management of feeling to create a publicly observable facial and bodily display; emotional labor is sold for a wage and therefore has *exchange value.* I use the synonymous terms *emotion work* or *emotion management* to refer to these same acts done in a private context where they have *use value.* (Hochschild 1983, 7n)

Many people have interpreted Hochschild's statement based on the words "public" and "private" and have, therefore, used emotional labor as the management of emotions that is conducted in organizations and emotion work as the management of emotions that is conducted in personal or family settings. However, such an interpretation is somewhat simplistic and misses the essence of the Marxist underpinnings of Hochschild's work. The distinction that is most meaningful for organizational researchers is the distinction between *use-value* and *exchange-value.* Emotion work has use-value, while emotional labor has exchange-value.

For the purpose of this chapter, we make a third distinction between the terms Hochschild (1983) uses. She used *emotion management* and *emotion work* as synonymous terms distinguished from *emotional labor.*

We use *emotion management* to describe the general control of emotions in either form of use-value or exchange-value. This extension of Hochschild's original definitions is important. By having an overarching term for the construct, we can frame a discussion of the general actions within organizations that include elements of both use- and exchange-value.

A Framework for Distinguishing Emotion Management Actions

Wharton and Erickson (1993) argue that the types of occupations or organizations typically studied in this area of research may be a contributing factor to the blurred distinction between the terms. By focusing on the people in the service sector, such as airline flight attendants and store clerks, the fine distinctions between emotional labor and emotion work are more easily lost. For example, the "customer friendly" attitude of a skilled salesperson may both be rewarded on the job through bonus pay, *and* be a source of personal pride for the employee who values providing good service to his or her customers. The same actions, in other words, might contain elements of both emotional labor and emotion work simultaneously. Lumping them together under one or the other label obscures the different determinants of each. In hopes of bringing clarity to this muddle, we suggest that a framework for visualizing the various shades of emotion management would be a useful tool regardless of the type of organization or occupation to which it is applied. While the dichotomy of exchange-value and use-value should be one approach to understanding emotion management in social settings, we also believe that adding a second distinction can be useful.

In her definition of emotional labor, Wharton (1993) says that not only are such actions performed for a wage, they are also under the control of others. The implication is that emotion work is controlled by the individual, while emotional labor is controlled by the organization. The grocery store clerk whose manager instructs her to smile when dealing with customers is being paid not only to manage her emotions as part of her job, but she is also told exactly what emotional state she must manifest. In contrast, the middle manager who works out at the gym over his lunch hour because it helps him feel calmer and more in control is not explicitly paid for feeling relaxed, but he is also free to choose the emotional state he prefers to cultivate. We have

Figure 13.1   **Forms of Emotion Management**

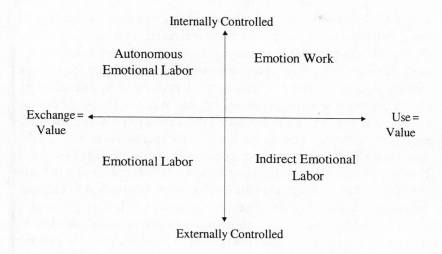

combined the ideas of internal versus external control and use- versus exchange-value to create a framework that we feel brings important distinctions into focus. The intersection of these two dichotomies creates a matrix (see Figure 13.1) that has four variations of emotion management—emotion work, emotional labor, autonomous emotional labor, and indirect emotional labor.

Emotion Work and Emotional Labor

Emotion work and emotional labor served as the starting point for our attempt to understand the variability in emotion management actions, so they will not be defined again. Instead, we present some examples of what emotion work and emotional labor would look like in an organization. We are performing emotion work when we smile and say hello to a coworker in the hallway, even though we are having a bad day. When we stifle a bored expression as we listen to someone explain the latest story making the rounds, we are performing emotion work. These actions serve as the social lubricant of our everyday lives. Emotional labor takes the classic form of the airline attendant smiling at the rude passenger. We also see emotional labor when otherwise cheerful bill collectors growl angrily at debtors to pay their bills. These are actions that are specifically part of the job description.

Autonomous Emotional Labor

Tolich (1993) made a critical distinction in extending the concept of emotional labor based on his qualitative research in a service context. He agreed with others that emotional labor has exchange value, but argued that the concept was more complex than that. He contended that emotional labor, or emotion management performed as part of a specific job task, is not always alienating, and it is not always under the control of the organization. He called this category of emotional management "autonomous emotional labor"—the spontaneous, individually controlled management of emotions during the performance of job tasks. This is an extension of Rafaeli and Sutton's (1989) conception of "faking in good faith," when an employee manages an emotion to conform with organizational standards because she believes it is the right thing to do. In autonomous emotional labor, the employee manages emotions to conform to her own standards not only because she feels it is right, but also because she chooses to.

What does autonomous emotional labor look like in the context of organizations? Tolich (1993) told the stories of supermarket clerks who truly loved their jobs and molded their emotions to create even greater enjoyment on the job. They allowed positive emotion to cascade into even more positive emotion as they performed tasks that were specifically part of their jobs. Autonomous emotional labor "occurs when the conception and management of emotions is regulated by the individual" (Tolich 1993, 378).

Indirect Emotional Labor

Just as autonomous emotional labor can be under the control of the individual but also has value to the organization, other actions in the workplace can have a perceived use-value to the individual but are directed by external requirements. We term such actions "indirect emotional labor." A classic example of this would be the type of organization-sponsored festivities recounted by Van Maanen and Kunda (1989) in their description of a high-technology firm's culture building retreat. These types of organizational events typically require cheer and friendliness, yet they are not a specific part of an individual's job performance. Employees are not paid to go to the festivities as part of their actual position in the organization, but the organization expects them to attend and to be cheerful about it. The emotion management performed at these events may certainly be useful to the individual because it might indirectly influence, for example, future promotions and pay raises. As Van Maanen and Kunda (1989, 45) point out, emotion management in these situations may be "to strike a pose, cut a deal, or further their own careers" or it may be done in "a bemused, if bewildered way, to simply go along with the crowd." On the other hand, some employees may genuinely enjoy the chance to socialize with their colleagues outside the bounds of the formal workday even though the occasion still falls under the broad umbrella of work.

Organizational Interventions

We feel that the distinctions inherent in our matrix can be useful to practitioners as they plan organizational interventions. Given that "emotion is the leading element that organizes responses to significant others" (Johnson 1998, ii), practitioners must be aware that they are intervening in emotional systems when they lead change efforts in organizations. Not all interventions that influence emotion management actions are specifically targeted at emotion management as a presenting issue. However, we contend that any organizational intervention has implications for different types of emotion management and practitioners should be mindful of those implications, and the distinctions between emotion management actions have important implications for selecting the most effective interventions for a wide variety of presenting issues.

Emotion management along the exchange-value continuum is associated with job tasks and the actions associated with autonomous emotional labor and emotional labor are embedded in the structure of the position. Thus, interventions would be oriented toward support structures and explicit management of the task; conversely, interventions that affect those support structures or job tasks may influence emotional labor actions. On the other hand, emotion management connected to use-value is associated with the social life in the organization and more likely reflects the culture of the organization. As a result, emotion management interventions targeted at interpersonal relationships and culture issues would be more effective. Again, those interventions that influence interpersonal dynamics and organizational culture independently of emotion management are likely to have an impact on the emotion work that is conducted in the organization.

The organization has much greater control over instituting interventions associated with emotional labor and indirect emotional labor because they are "externally controlled" actions. Autonomous emotional labor and emotion work emerge from the individual and are "internally controlled" actions. Nevertheless, the organization can take steps to either encourage or discourage these individually determined emotion management actions.

Because of the systemic nature of emotion management, we explore the influence that several different types of organizational interventions have on the different types of emotion management actions. Indeed, any intervention that affects one type of emotion management is very likely to influence other types of emotion management as well.

Leadership Development Programs

The goal of recognizing and engaging in emotion management is a component of many leadership theories, although usually not framed with the same language. The limitations in scope of early approaches to leadership led to a growing interest in the concept of "transforming leadership," a term first proposed by James MacGregor Burns in 1978 (Bryman 1992). Transformational leadership called for a more complex and higher level relationship between the leader and follower that relied on satisfying higher needs and engaging the full person to meet mutual expectations that could convert followers to leaders and leaders to moral agents. This was contrasted with more traditional, supervisory, management approaches of exchange for services/duties, rewards, pay, security, and other compensations that were now referred to as "transactional leadership" (Sashkin and Rosenbach 1993).

Words throughout the literature that have been used to describe transformational leaders and leadership include passion, care, intensity, confidence, self-confidence, respect, values, and trust—each of which is considered an "emotion" or "emotion-laden" word (Clore, Ortony, and Foss 1987; Etzioni 1988; Shaver et al. 1987; Ward and Throop 1989). Bass claims that the emotional arousal initiated by the charismatic (or transformational) leader generates a sense of excitement in the followers (Bryman 1992). Axelrod and Sashkin (2000) found compelling evidence that leadership development programs that focus on increasing these transformational capabilities can make individuals more self-aware and, thus, better able to manage the interpersonal relationships within the organization. So, we contend that leadership development programs can be considered an intervention that indirectly influences emotion work.

On the other hand, the ability to manage the emotions of self and others is a fundamental component of the job task for transformational leaders. In this light, leadership development programs would contribute to helping individuals perform emotional labor.

Stress Management and Wellness Programs

There are a wide variety of stress management and wellness programs that have implications for both emotional labor (e.g., how my actions may influence the customer) and emotion work (e.g., how I can better interact with my coworkers). For example, T-groups enable individuals to see how their behavior affects other individuals, and they also facilitate smoother team operations (Bion 1961, 1994).

Popp (2000) reports on a project designed to train the home-loan loss mitigation specialists of a large mortgage company to understand the patterns of stress that families undergoing mortgage default experience. Loss mitigation specialists contact families whose mortgages are in the process of foreclosure in an effort to work out an agreeable solution that keeps the family in their home and the company from the financial loss of foreclosure. Clearly, knowledge of the dynamics of family stress would be helpful knowledge for workers in such a job.

In the process of delivering his intervention, however, Popp found that the loss mitigation workers were anxious to discuss their own stress reactions that came from working daily with families in crisis. One of the recommendations that came from his project was that the loss mitigation department create a formal arena for the emotion work of managing job stress by holding regular meetings to discuss job stress and the strategies workers use for dealing with it. Thus, an intervention that aimed to improve job performance by providing information also changed the emotion management norms for the organization by legitimizing the public discussion of job stress.

Employee wellness plans might be considered classic workplace therapy. They are primarily formal counseling programs that help employees identify and work through a wide variety of problems, especially those associated with stress management and personal issues stemming from stress (Ramsey 1985). These programs help employees relieve the pressure associated with emotional labor. Establishing formal wellness plans that offer employees a sounding board and the opportunity to actually use that sounding board without penalty may help alleviate emotional labor dysfunctions.

Structural Interventions

Work design is a classic organizational development and change intervention that has particular implications for alleviating emotional labor dysfunctions. Essentially, the goal of work design interventions is to create jobs that foster employee fulfillment in order to increase productivity (Cummings and Worley 1993). Several interventions under the rubric of work design offer relief from emotional labor. For example, vertical loading (Hackman and Oldham 1980) embeds decision making and problem solving in lower level positions. This enables workers to have more control over the job and to create processes that minimize those encounters that are more likely to result in dysfunctional emotional labor. Another example of work design is the sociotechnical systems approach in which individuals should have multiple skills in order to be flexible within the organization. Such flexibility offers employees the opportunity to periodically rotate jobs from those that require intensive emotional labor, "front stage," to those that offer respite from emotional labor, "back stage."

A "back stage" area (Goffman 1959) may be considered any space where the rigors of emotional labor are relaxed. Beyond rotating jobs, the organization may take a more active role in creating a back stage location by providing a physical space in which employees can "let off steam" from emotional labor interactions. This may operationalize organizational attempts to buffer emotions (Ashforth and Humphrey 1995) while maintaining a preferred organizational image. For example, this could very simply involve creating a break room for customer service employees to enact the coping mechanism of physically escaping from the situation (Young 1999).

Organizational Culture and Team Building

Kurstedt et al. (1999) report on an academic program designed to teach engineering students interpersonal skills. The curriculum included such things as communication skills, group development experiences, negotiation strategies, conflict resolution, and the like. Since most of the students were already employed full time in professional positions, they were asked to apply their newly learned skills to difficult situations they encountered at work and then engage in a structured reflective evaluation of the outcome. The reflection asked the students not only to develop alternative actions they might have taken, but also to articulate the emotional process that was part of the situation they were attempting to change. Thus, one goal of the class was to enhance the students' ability to recognize and engage in emotion management in their organizations. Some of the actions identified by students were clearly associated with emotional labor, while other actions were not driven by the job or organization and, therefore, could be considered emotion work.

Large-scale culture change initiatives also can influence emotion work practices in an organization. Callahan (2000b) found that cultural issues around gender and age were the primary source of emotion management in a nonprofit organization loosely affiliated with the U.S. Air Force; this emotion work acted as an inhibitor of much needed cultural change (Callahan, in press). In some cases, culture change may indeed be an appropriate therapeutic step for an organization to maintain a healthy existence. Culture change efforts are designed to create cultures based on those values, beliefs, and norms (Schein 1992) that are most likely to keep organizational members dedicated to achieving organizational goals (Cummings and Worley 1993). Culture change initiatives focus on the basic assumptions that guide interpersonal relationships within an organization and, thus, are presented here as an intervention for emotion work. An outcome of such an initiative may certainly result in changes to emotional labor practices, however.

Friedman (1985) used the revision of a religious community's strategic plan to consciously alter the emotional dynamics of the congregation. While serving as the rabbi of a large, suburban synagogue, Friedman found that a small number of long-standing members of the congregation held a great deal of power and were able to monopolize decision making. Younger members of the congregation were rebelling, suffering in silence, or leaving. Friedman, as rabbi, was being pulled to endorse the views of each side. To break up the stalemate, Friedman proposed a radical shift in the mission and goals of the organization, a change that would not be agreeable to either faction. He then arranged a number of small group conversations to discuss his plan and strategically mingled members of each camp in the groups. Using Bowen's (1978) family systems theory as a guide, Friedman attempted to listen as calmly as possible to both factions in his congregation while siding with neither—a process Bowen calls "detriangling." The result was that a few long-term members of the congregation left the church while the remaining members were able to reconcile their differences and infuse the community with a new sense of vitality and common purpose. Friedman shifted the emotional dynamics of the organization through an intervention that did not overtly target emotion management.

If this example were placed in a for-profit setting, the connection to emotional labor would be even clearer. A radical shift in organizational mission and goals would necessarily require a change in compensated behavior in a for-profit organization. In this case, not only was Friedman applying emotional labor as part of his role as rabbi, but also he was also implicitly incorporating emotional labor in the tasks of the congregation members. Although emotion management has been addressed in the context of nonprofit organizations (e.g., Callahan 2000a), there has not been an explicit comparison of the differences in emotion management between nonprofit and for-profit organizations.

Conclusion

Whenever interest in an area explodes on the forefront of organizational studies, it is not unreasonable for the field to explore different definitions, to search for the right fit of terms. Hochschild's very definition of the distinction between emotion work and emotional labor may have led the field to explore the private/public distinction between the two terms. However, the core of her definition held the most promise for anchoring the study of the management of emotions in organizational life—the distinction between use-value and exchange-value.

One may certainly argue that all emotions in organizations are emotional labor because they represent transactions between individuals (e.g., I hold back my anger because I want you to be my friend). If this is the case, then all instances of emotion management have become commodified and, therefore, the construct is meaningless. However, emotion work can be explicitly distinguished from emotional labor in organizational contexts (Callahan 2000a; Lively 2000), especially when using the economic distinction of exchange-value/use-value.

We argue that the distinction between different types of emotion management is important not only to advance theory development but also to advance practical interventions in organizations. These emotion management phenomena occur in organizations and are necessary elements to successful interactions in social settings. Emotion work, when functional, helps smooth interpersonal relationships in organizational life and has an indirect (and likely positive) influence on organizational outcomes. Emotional labor, when functional, facilitates better job performance and has a more direct influence on associated outcomes.

Weick (1999, 134) noted that some theories "seem to matter more than others" in influencing the practice in and study of organizations. After an overview of some of the most powerful or "moving" theories in organization studies, he and Peter Frost concluded that one of the common factors in all of these was that they centered on emotional concepts. By clarifying our language associated with emotion management, we increase the opportunity to create more moving theories of organization.

14 EMOTIONAL WORK AND EMOTIONAL CONTAGION

Lyndall Strazdins

Abstract

Emotional work is unique and skilled work—it involves handling emotions and social relationships and its product is the change of feeling in others. Data was provided by employees of a health care organization ($n = 261$). Findings indicate that when people do emotional work they can "catch" emotions from others. Handling positive emotions in others improves well-being. Handling negative emotions in others relates to a wide range of psychological health problems. Emotional work may not be sustainable unless the contagion process is recognized.

Introduction

When people do emotional work they are trying to help others' feelings and well-being, but how does emotional work affect those who perform it? Is emotional work hard work and does its performance affect health? Emotional work is defined as the behaviors enacted to meet emotional role demands and improve the well-being of others at work and in the family[1] (England and Farkas 1986; England 1992; England and Folbre 1999). In contrast to physical role demands, such as assembling a product or vacuuming a house, emotional role demands are concerned with relationships and other people's emotions (James 1989). A manager handling staff conflict, workmates organizing a social get-together, and a nurse asking a patient how he or she is feeling are examples of emotional work.

232

Emotional work is distinguished from the related constructs of emotional labor and emotion management (Hochschild 1983; Wharton 1999). First, although emotional work is often part of service work, it is not considered exclusive to the service role. Emotional work is viewed as an important integrative behavior that occurs in other work roles, including the workmate role and manager role, and in family roles (see, e.g., England and Farkas 1986; Strazdins, Galligan, and Scannell 1997). Thus, the term *emotional work* is used to denote its incomplete commodification; it is not always, and not only, performed because it is paid for (Himmelweit 1999). Second, the focus of emotional work, as it is defined here, is on the behaviors performed to affect other people's feelings. Hochschild's definitions of emotional labor and emotion management refer to the management of emotion in the self in order to display a particular feeling, whereas emotional work refers to behaviors used by individuals to alter other people's feelings. The two constructs overlap and may be thought of as describing different aspects of a similar process. When service workers display niceness, warmth, or friendliness, for example, they intend to affect customers' feelings (make them feel welcomed, cared for, attended to, happy). To do this, they manage their own emotions, monitor the other person's feelings, *and* behave (speak warmly, self disclose, listen, soothe, and so on).

Emotional work has also been distinguished in terms of three dimensions. These dimensions—companionship, help, and regulation—are based upon the main integrative functions of social relationships (Rook 1985, 1987, 1990). Each dimension involves different behaviors, and targets different feelings in other people. Companionship primarily involves handling positive emotions in others and includes behaviors such as showing warmth, giving recognition and praise, including others by asking about their thoughts and feelings, playing, joking, and organizing social occasions. In contrast, help and regulation involve dealing with negative emotions encountered in the work role. For example, a manager might help distress and conflict among staff by listening attentively, soothing or calming, acting protectively, talking about the relationship issues proactively, and mediating conflict. Examples of regulating behaviors include giving suggestions and guidance, setting limits, and providing feedback. The distinctions between these dimensions are important because, as will be discussed later, if emotions are contagious, then the impact of emotional work depends upon the sort of feelings handled.

Emotional work benefits organizations. Not only is it widely performed in service work, human services, and health care professions (Strazdins 2000), but it is part of workmate contextual performance and managerial job duties. When people do emotional work, they endeavor to create positive emotions in others, build cooperative and cohesive relationships, and mitigate negative emotions and disharmonious work relationships. These facilitative behaviors are an important part of the social fabric at work, are likely to build organizational social capital, and, to paraphrase Karasek (1999), build capacity.

Health Impact of Emotional Labor and Emotional Work

Since Hochschild (1983) there has been a fundamental concern about the health impact of this type of work. Few studies have examined emotional work per se, nevertheless findings on the related construct of emotional labor are germane. The evidence so far is mixed: emotional labor may exact a health cost, be health neutral, or can even improve employee outcomes (Wharton 1999). For example, feelings of inauthenticity were predicted by low job control, and the perception that job performance required handling people well (Erickson and Wharton 1997), and emotional exhaustion was predicted by emotional dissonance (Morris and Feldman 1996). However, Wharton (1993) found no difference in levels of emotional exhaustion between employees whose job involved contact with the public and employees whose job did not. In fact, employees in public contact jobs were more satisfied with their jobs than those in non-public contact jobs (Wharton 1993). Similarly, Erickson and Wharton (1997) did not find a relationship between amount of emotional labor and depression.

Emotional labor might even improve well-being in those who perform it. As well as creating emotional dissonance and alienation, emotional labor may offer opportunities for self-expression, enjoyment, and social integration (Ashforth and Humphrey 1993). Thus Tolich's supermarket clerks (1993), although they disliked handling the "complainers," also enjoyed interacting with customers. There was a clerk who told jokes, a clerk who gave her customers smiley faces if they looked sad, and a clerk who "show scanned" by tossing groceries in the air and catching them with his other hand, scanning code facedown (Tolich 1993).

In this chapter, it is proposed that emotional contagion helps explain why this type of work can improve *or* impair the health of those who do it. Emotional work targets different emotions in other people, and the health effects will depend upon what these emotions are and how often they must be managed. When emotional work involves handling positive emotions in others, it will not be health damaging. But when it involves handling negative emotions in others, such as anger, anxiety, sadness, and despair, then a health cost can occur. The theory of emotional contagion (Hatfield, Cacioppo, and Rapson 1994) explains this unique occupational risk. If emotional work, as argued earlier, benefits organizations, then understanding and managing contagion is essential to sustaining its performance.

Emotional Contagion and Emotional Work

Emotional work may *invoke* particular feelings in the self; in effect, emotions may be "caught" from others (Hatfield, Cacioppo, and Rapson 1994). To be performed effectively, emotional work involves awareness, judgment, timing, understanding, and engagement with other people's feelings (Steinberg 1999). It is this unique requirement to *engage* with other people's emotions that may help explain how emotional work affects health.

First, emotions can be caught from others via empathy (Hatfield, Cacioppo, and Rapson 1994). Alongside love and attachment, empathy, sympathy, pity, and gratitude are emotions that foster cooperative and integrative social relationships and contain the other person as their referent object (Oatley and Jenkins 1996). Empathy involves the active appreciation of another person's emotions, and usually involves feeling that emotion in the self. Empathy is likely to be integral to emotional work. For example, empathy is a strong predictor of provision of support to others (Trobst, Collins, and Embree 1994). Over time, empathic engagement with others may lead to persisting changes in emotional well-being, and it is the emotional component of empathy (the feelings of distress when engaging with others' negative emotions) rather than the cognitive component of empathy (perspective taking) that appears to be the potent mechanism (Gross 1994). At the extreme, listening to others talk about their traumatic experiences has been linked to a process of "vicarious traumatization" whereby psychological well-being becomes impaired and beliefs about the benign nature of the world are altered (Pearlman and Mac Ian 1995).

Second, emotions can be caught from others via changes to cognitive priming and recall (Hatfield, Cacioppo, and Rapson 1994). Other people's emotions may serve to prime recall of emotionally similar information and recall of similar emotional experiences (Oatley and Jenkins 1996). People who feel happy recall more happy memories than sad memories, and process happy or pleasant words more quickly compared to sad or neutral words (Oatley and Jenkins, 1996). Similarly, people who are sad recall more sad or negative memories and selectively process more sad or negative information (Cacioppo and Gardner 1999). This negative bias of cognitive processing may be one of the factors that contribute to depression and anxiety, suggesting a link between repeated experiences of negative emotions and the development and the maintenance of psychological disorder (Oatley and Jenkins 1996).

Third, handling others' emotions may create an emotional reaction in the self (Hatfield, Cacioppo, and Rapson 1994). Emotions serve a signal function, giving relational meaning about the personal significance of events or stimuli (Lazarus 1991a, 1993). The relational meaning results from a perception of the harms or benefits of a particular event, in this case, an interaction involving emotional work. For example, positive emotions may result when the emotional work interaction conforms to the individual's goals (happiness), enhances his or her identity (pride), and expresses or involves affection (Lazarus 1991a, 1993). These sorts of interactions are more likely to occur when handling positive emotions in other people. Negative emotions are more likely to occur when emotional work involves handling distressed, hostile, or conflictual relationships, primarily the focus of help and regulation. When the emotional work interaction is perceived as threatening, such as handling angry customers, fear and anxiety may result. When the emotional work interaction is perceived as demeaning, such as handling critical or contemptuous others, anger is likely to result.

Emotions can also be caught from others via synchrony and physiological convergence (Hatfield, Cacioppo, and Rapson 1994). During interactions, individuals tend to "synchronise facial expressions, vocalizations, postures and movement with those of another person, and consequently to converge emotionally" (Hatfield, Cacioppo, and Rapson 1994, 5). This involves facial synchrony and mimicry, vocal synchrony and mimicry, and central nervous system activity coordination. For example, when trying to read their spouse's feelings, husbands and wives show physiological changes that mimic their spouse's physiological changes (Levenson and Ruef 1992). The central nervous system directs this mimicry, and this, in turn, feeds back into the central nervous system, resulting in feeling the emotion that was originally mimicked (Hatfield, Cacioppo, and Rapson 1994). Furthermore, those individuals who pay close attention to other people's feelings or are responsible for others, are much more likely to be affected (Hsee et al. 1990).

Emotional work thus alters the "emotional balance sheet" of individuals via empathy, changes in cognitive processes, when the interaction is enhancing or threatening, and via mimicry. All or some of these may occur during emotional work. If emotions can be "caught," the more individuals engage with and handle positive emotions in others (companionship), the more likely they are to experience positive emotions, and this will improve their emotional well-being. However, the more individuals engage with and handle negative emotions in others (involved in help and regulatory dimensions of emotional work), the more likely they are to experience negative emotions, and this will be where the health costs occur. Evidence for an emotional contagion pathway linking emotional work to health would be a negative correlation between amount of companionship and psychological distress (Hypothesis 1), and a positive correlation between amount of help and regulation and psychological distress (Hypothesis 2).

If there is no emotional contagion effect of emotional work, then it would be expected that the correlations between psychological distress and different types of emotional work would be similar. Presumably the effects of non-emotion specific processes such as lack of control, emotional dissonance, or amount of emotional work performed would be similar for each dimension of emotional work. Furthermore, it is *engagement* with other people's emotions that is the key pathway affecting health, not simply awareness of distress in the workplace. Employees may occupy work roles with extensive role demands, and they may be aware of these demands, but those who make the *effort* to engage with others and perform emotional work will be most at risk. A third hypothesis, then, is that emotional work will predict health outcomes over and above the knowledge that other people are emotionally distressed.

Summary

The more people experience positive, as compared to negative, emotions, the more they experience well-being (Diener and Larsen 1993). Conversely, the more people experience negative emotions, compared to positive, the more they suffer psychological distress (Fredrickson and Levenson 1998). Emotional work poses a health risk by "exposing" employees to other people's negative feelings.

This exposure does not occur only in the service role, but in the manager and workmate roles as well. Provision of support to staff, regulating conflict in the work group, and building cooperative relationships with suppliers or other organizations are important parts of the manager role (Muchinsky 1993). Within teams and work groups, workmates provide support and help their peers as part of job contextual performance (Gabbaro 1990; Motowidlo and Van Scotter 1994; Van Scotter and Motowidlo 1996). Although emotional work is likely to be found in nearly all service jobs, when interactions are sustained or repeated and the focus is upon other people's welfare (be they student, client, patient, or customer), emotional work will be much more frequent (England and Folbre 1999; Gutek 1995; Himmelweit 1999). Thus, not just service workers, but managers and workmates, are vulnerable to contagion. This impact may be quite pervasive with both general and work-related psychological health affected. Specific hypotheses are as follows:

> H.1 Psychological distress, goal loss, occupational stress, and intention to leave the job are lower the more employees handle positive emotions and interactions in their work roles (companionship emotional work).

> H.2 Psychological distress, goal loss, occupational stress, and intention to leave the job are higher the more people handle negative emotions and interactions in their work roles (help and regulation emotional work).

> H.3 Emotional work will predict psychological health outcomes over and above knowledge that other people are distressed.

Method

Participants

The sample comprised 261 employees from a health care organization providing a variety of inpatient and outpatient services to the public. The health care workers, mainly nurses, had repeated and sustained interactions with patients and their families, giving opportunity for service relationships to develop and extensive emotional work to be performed (Gutek 1995). The emotional work of employees was an important focus of management and a salient role prescription. For example, giving care and showing respect to clients and patients were part of the organization's core values, which all employees were expected to reflect.

The description of the sample in terms of age, gender composition, country of origin, education, employment status, and occupation is summarized in Table 14.1. The large proportion of women reflects the gender composition of Australian health care occupations. In the Australian labor force 93 percent of qualified nurses are women, 7 percent are men (ABS cat. 6101.0, 1997). The ethnic and indigenous composition of the sample was comparable to the Australian workforce (ABS cat. 6101.0, 1997). Participants were more highly educated and literate than the Australian labor force (ABS cat. 6101.0, 1997). Because the sample overrepresented part-time employees, the average number of hours worked per week (31.5) was lower than the Australian average (ABS cat. 6101.0, 1997).

The study sampled three work roles (manager, workmate, and service) where emotional work was performed. Forty-eight percent supervised, managed, or led staff. Half of the managers supervised between two and five staff, 19 percent supervised one other person, 13 percent supervised between six and ten staff, and 19 percent supervised more than ten staff. Ninety-five percent of participants worked in teams or workgroups of over two people, with most (38%) working in teams or workgroups of more than ten people. Ninety-three percent of those sampled provided a direct service to patients or clients as part of their work role, and of these, 91 percent served at least ten patients or clients per week.

Procedure

Anonymous questionnaires were distributed with paychecks to all employees of the organization and a follow-up letter was sent the following fortnight. Response rate was 34 percent. Informed consent was obtained from all participants prior to questionnaire administration.

Measures

Independent Variables

Emotional role demands. Three items, one for each work role context (manager, workmate, and service role), assessed how distressed participants' staff, workmates, or customers and patients had been over the last year. Scores were summed to assess total emotional role demands

Table 14.1

Demographic Characteristics

Demographic characteristic	Mean (*SD*) or Percent
Age	40.60 years (9.54)
Sex	86% women
Region of origin	75% Australia, 10.5% Britain, 4.3% Asia
Indigenous	1.6% Aboriginal or Torres Strait Islander
Non–English speaking background	11.7% Non–English speaking background
Education attainment	12% Year 10 or less, 10% Year 12, 29% trade qualification, 26% Bachelor, 11% postgraduate
Employment status	45% full time, 45% part time, 10% casual
Occupation group	4% unskilled, plant operator, 11% clerical or customer service, 2% trades, 76% professional or paraprofessional, 6% manager or executive

encountered at work. Participants who did not have a score for the service or manager role (all participants had scores for workmate role) were scored 0. Response categories ranged from 0 (*don't know*) to 4 (*extremely distressed*) (see Table 14.2).

Integrative emotional work (IEW) inventory. The IEW inventory (Strazdins 2000) assesses frequency of participant behaviors for three emotional work dimensions: companionship, help, and regulation. These dimensions are empirically distinguishable across both work and family roles, and, because they are positively correlated, can also be summed to form an estimate of the total emotional workload of individuals within and across roles (Strazdins 2000).

Items were completed for each work role that participants occupied (manager, workmate, and service). Scores were then summed across role contexts to give a total work score. Participants who did not have a score for a role were given a score of 1 for each item (this is the equivalent to responding not at all to the emotional work items for that role). Response categories ranged from 1 (*not at all or not applicable*) to 5 (*frequently or most of the time* [*more than once a day*]).

Table 14.2

Descriptive Statistics for Independent and Dependent Variables

Measure	M	SD	Skew.	α
Emotional role demands	6.95	2.84	0.48	0.70
IEW work companionship	56.571	14.27	0.36	0.88
IEW work help and regulation	91.18	24.58	0.93	0.94
Psychological distress[a]	12.06	9.93	1.23	0.92
Goal loss	2.86	1.01	0.21	0.84
Occupational stress	37.20	13.24	0.74	0.95
Turnover intention	1.78	0.81	1.90	0.73

Note: [a] Psychological distress measured with the CES-D (Radloff, 1977). Scores for this scale range from 0 to 60, with scores above 16 reflecting clinically significant psychological distress.

Work companionship. Companionship behaviors improve positive emotions in others and keep social networks close (e.g., "How often have you expressed appreciation and praise to . . . ," "How often have you organized social occasions and get-togethers for . . ."). Twenty-one items assessing amount of companionship performed in manager, workmate, and service roles were summed to form an aggregated work role measure (see Table 14.2).

Work help and regulation. Help behaviors repair negative emotions and relationship disharmony (e.g., "How often have you listened attentively to another's problems or worries . . . ," "How often have you acted as a third party to resolve problems between . . ."). Regulation behaviors guide or influence another person's negative emotions and social behavior (e.g., "How often have you tried to persuade another to stop doing something that was harmful . . . ," "How often have you discussed social rules or guidelines with . . ."). Scores on help and regulation items for manager, workmate, and service roles were summed to form an aggregated forty-two-item work role measure (see Table 14.2).

Dependent Variables

Scale statistics for all dependent variables are presented in Table 14.2.

General psychological health: Psychological distress. The Center for Epidemiologic Studies Depression Scale (CES-D) measured levels of depressive symptomatology (psychological distress with negative affect) experienced over the previous week (Radloff 1977). The twenty-item scale assessed levels of general psychological distress,[2] with recent studies indicating correlations between CES-D scores and a wide range of psychological problems, including anxiety, mild depression, major depression, nonspecific psychiatric diagnoses, and risk for developing depression (Fechner-Bates, Coyne, and Schwenk 1994; Zonderman et al. 1993). Items assessed depressed mood, feelings of guilt and worthlessness, loss of appetite, sleep disturbance, and other symptoms associated with depression. Participants indicated how often they experienced symptoms using response categories of 0 (*rarely or none of the time [less than one day]*) to 3 (*most or all of the time [5–7 days]*). Scores were summed to form the scale. Radloff (1977) proposed a cutoff point of 16 to indicate clinically significant levels of distress. Twenty-seven percent of participants had CES-D scores above 16.

General psychological health: Goal loss. Based upon Braithwaite's measure (1990), four items assessed the degree to which participants were unable to pursue important life goals or interests. For example, "How often have you felt unable to try new things or pursue new goals?" Response categories ranged from 1 (*not at all*) to 5 (*very often*). Summing and averaging scores formed the scale.

Work-related well-being: Occupational stress. The Stress Arousal Checklist (SACL) (Gotts and Cox 1988; Mackay, Cox, Burrows, and Lazzerini 1978) assessed self-reported negative mood and stress. The measure consists of a series of eighteen adjectives and participants were instructed to show how much they felt, for example, "worried" or "distressed" over the past week about their job. Response categories ranged from 1 (*definitely do not feel*) to 4 (*definitely feel*). Items were summed and averaged to form the scale.

Work-related well-being: Intention to leave. Six items measured intention to leave the current job in the next twelve months (by taking a redundancy offer, by leaving the organization, by a promotion, and so on). Response categories ranged from 1 (*not at all likely*) to 5 (*extremely likely*). Scores for the items were summed and averaged.

Results

Analytic Strategy Overview

Hierarchical multiple regression was used to assess the health impact of emotional work. Work companionship and work help and regulation were entered as a second set after all other variables to assess changes to R^2. Possible interactive effects of emotional work dimensions on health were also tested, but no interactions reached significance. Bivariate correlations for independent variables are appended.

Emotional Contagion Effects of Emotional Work

Tables 14.3 to 14.6 present regression analyses of the effects of emotional work on psychological distress, goal loss, occupational stress, and turnover intentions. Emotional contagion effects of emotional work were found for nearly all outcomes. Supporting Hypothesis 1, companionship at work improved work-related well-being, reducing levels of occupational stress (Table 14.5). Supporting Hypothesis 2, the more employees performed help and regulation, the more psychological distress (Table 14.3) and goal loss they reported (Table 14.4). Furthermore, high levels of help and regulation increased employees' intention to leave their current job (Table 14.6). Supporting Hypothesis 3, emotional work contributed a health effect over and above emotional role demands at work. A significant R^2 change was observed for all outcomes when emotional work variables were entered. However, knowledge of other people's emotional distress also affected health, significantly predicting psychological distress and occupational stress (Table 14.3 and Table 14.5). Table 14.7 summarizes the emotionally contagious effects of emotional work.

Discussion

Emotional work can be hard work. Helping and regulating other peoples' emotions at work increase psychological distress, goal loss, and intention to leave the job. Yet, companionship at work reduces occupational stress. Emotional work is thus both good and bad for health, and the difference lies in the types of emotions handled in others and the types of emotions invoked in those performing it.

People's feelings are *part* of the work and *part* of its costs (Hochschild 1983). Because emotional work requires responsiveness, engagement, and empathy, other people's emotions can get "caught" and affect the self. The effects of emotional work add up, and as the service economy expands, more and more people will work in jobs that require emotional work. But it is not only in the service role where emotional work takes a toll. The emotional wear and tear can occur in any work role where

Table 14.3

Summary of Multiple Regression Analyses Predicting Psychological Distress ($n = 233$)

Predictor	B	SE B	β
Gender	−0.10	0.10	−0.07
Age	−0.01*	0.00	−0.17*
Non–English speaking background	0.05	0.11	0.03
Education	−0.05**	0.02	−0.23*
Occupation	−0.00	0.03	−0.01
Work hours	−0.00	0.00	−0.03
Work emotional role demands	0.04*	0.02	0.22**
Work companionship	−0.00	0.00	−0.14
Work help and regulation	0.01**	0.00	0.26**

Note: Summary statistics not shown for role occupancy dummy variables (manager role and service role) which were entered first. Gender coded 0 = male, 1 = female. Adjusted $R^2 = .08$ ($p < .01$). R^2 change for emotional work variables .03, $p < .05$. Missing data deleted listwise.

*$p < .05$; **$p < .01$.

Table 14.4

Summary of Multiple Regression Analyses Predicting Goal Loss ($n = 230$)

Predictor	B	SE B	β
Gender	0.33	0.19	0.11
Age	−0.02**	0.01	−0.20**
Non–English speaking background	0.08	0.22	0.02
Education	−0.05	0.04	−0.11
Occupation	0.02	0.05	0.03
Work hours	0.01	0.01	0.09
Work emotional role demands	0.07	0.03	0.16
Work companionship	−0.01	0.01	−0.16
Work help and regulation	0.01	0.00	0.29**

Note: Summary statistics not shown for role occupancy dummy variables (manager role and service role) which were entered first. Gender coded 0 = male, 1 = female. Adjusted $R^2 = 0.07$ ($p < 0.01$). R^2 change for emotional work variables 0.04, $p < 0.01$. Missing data deleted listwise.

*$p < 0.05$; **$p < 0.01$.

Table 14.5

Summary of Multiple Regression Analyses Predicting Occupational Stress (n = 230)

Predictor	B	SE B	β
Gender	−0.37**	0.14	−0.18**
Age	−0.01	0.00	−0.12
Non–English speaking background	0.12	0.15	0.08
Education	−0.04	0.03	−0.11
Occupation	0.01	0.04	0.01
Work hours	0.00	0.01	0.06
Work emotional role demands	0.08**	0.02	0.28**
Work companionship	−0.01*	0.00	−0.23*
Work help and regulation	0.00	0.00	0.14

Note: Summary statistics not shown for role occupancy dummy variables (manager role and service role) which were entered first. Gender coded 0 = male, 1 = female. Adjusted R^2 = 0.09 ($p < 0.01$). R^2 change for emotional work variables 0.03, $p < 0.05$. Missing data deleted listwise.

*$p < 0.05$; **$p < 0.01$.

Table 14.6

Summary of Multiple Regression Analyses Predicting Intention to Leave (n = 233)

Predictor	B	SE B	β
Gender	−0.46**	0.15	−0.20**
Age	−0.01	0.01	−0.07
Non–English speaking background	−0.01	0.17	−0.01
Education	−0.01	0.03	−0.01
Occupation	−0.09*	0.04	−0.16*
Work hours	0.01	0.01	0.11
Work emotional role demands	0.02	0.03	0.08
Work companionship	0.00	0.00	0.05
Work help and regulation	0.01**	0.02	0.24**

Note: Summary statistics not shown for role occupancy dummy variables (manager role and service role) which were entered first. Gender coded 0 = male, 1 = female. Adjusted R^2 = 0.10 ($p < 0.01$). R^2 change for emotional work variables 0.04, $p < 0.010$. Missing data deleted listwise.

*$p < 0.05$; **$p < 0.01$.

Table 14.7

Summary of Emotional Contagion Effects of Emotional Work

| | Outcomes | | | |
Emotional work	Distress	Goal loss	Occ. stress	Turnover
Companionship			+	
Help and regulation	–	–		–

Note: – Indicates significantly impaired health. + Indicates significantly improved health.

emotional work is done, and those who do it in many roles at work will be the ones most at risk.

Several assumptions and limitations of the research must be kept in mind. First, emotional work, as it is defined here, is limited to the cultural context in which it was developed and tested, namely English-speaking Western cultures. There are likely to be cultural variations in (a) what defines a positive or negative emotion and what defines a harmonious or adversarial social relationship, (b) the behaviors that are used to help others with their emotions and build positive relationships, and (c) role prescriptions for emotional work. Second, the response rate for the study was relatively low. It may be that those who responded were more likely to be helpful and altruistic. This may have affected the amount of emotional work that they performed at work. The possible effect of self-selection on the associations found between different types of emotional work and health is unclear. Confidence in the findings will be improved if they are replicated in other studies sampling different organizations and types of service work. Third, direct measurement of emotional contagion was not undertaken. Results are consistent with an emotional contagion process, but they do not directly demonstrate the presence of emotional contagion. Experience sampling and the monitoring of physiological responses are required to directly assess whether, and when, emotional contagion occurs.

Previous research on the health effects of emotional work has not distinguished between the types of emotions involved, resulting in mixed and contradictory findings (Erickson and Wharton 1997; Morris and Feldman 1996; Wharton 1999). If emotions can be caught, then these sorts of distinctions are critical, challenging assumptions that any, or all sorts of, emotional work is/are health damaging. Handling positive emotions in others could invoke positive emotions in the self, and so increase well-being (Diener and Larsen 1993). Handling negative emotions in others could lead to negative moods, psychological distress, and, eventually, poor health (Cohen and Rodriguez 1995; Elstad 1998; Leventhal and Patrick-Miller 1993). Knowledge of others' emotional distress does not explain the health impact, because emotional work involves something extra—*engagement* with the other persons' emotion.

Emotional work is a unique form of work because it requires handling feelings rather than producing tangible objects. This "emotionality" has been one reason why it has not been recognized as a form of work, despite its extensive performance in service jobs, by managers, and as part of workplace contextual performance. Companionship aims to enhance other people's emotional well-being and to build positive social relationships. Its focus is on producing positive emotions in others by speaking warmly, giving praise and affection, spending time with others, and organizing social get-togethers. These sorts of behaviors form a cooperative social "glue" (Oatley and Jenkins 1996) and benefit those who perform them, those who receive them, *and* the organization, because it creates and maintains positive and cooperative working relationships.

In contrast, helping and regulating others at work exacts a health cost. Both help and regulation are performed with the intention to repair negative emotions or social relationships and restore emotional equilibrium in others. Help involves the provision of coping assistance to others who are distressed. Regulation involves exerting constraint or giving guidance to others who are upset or angry. Although both of these types of emotional work may repair or restore well-being in others (Rook 1985, 1987, 1990), and be important ways that stress is managed in organizations, they involve handling negative emotions such as sadness, despair, anger, and fear.

At work those who perform help and regulation may find that their own mood becomes altered, and they themselves begin to feel sad, angry, or anxious. They may feel empathy for the plight of others, or their own mood could mimic the other person's mood (Hatfield, Cacioppo, and Rapson 1994). They may find that their cognitive processing has become negatively primed, so that they remember distressing events of their own, or they selectively process negative information and their own decision making becomes affected (Cacioppo and Gardner 1999; Oatley and Jenkins 1996). Helping or regulating others, such as handling "complainers" (Tolich 1993) or abusive airline passengers (Hochschild 1983), can also result in feelings of anger or threat about the interaction itself. Negative emotion can then carry over, "contaminating" subsequent interactions with clients, workmates, or staff. Furthermore, those employees performing extensive help and regulation are more likely to intend to leave their job. This sort of emotional work not only affects employees' well-being, but it may increase labor wastage and impair the health of organizations.

Suggestions for Practitioners

Handling negative emotions in others is hard work. It is both "stressful" (Lazarus 1991a) and effortful, and it means that those who do this type of emotional work at work will need to expend time and energy calming their own negative emotions (Thayer, Newman, and McClain 1994). Just as employees doing repetitive physical movements as part of their job take rest breaks to relax and stretch, those who do emotional work need time to restore their own emotions, calm down, soothe or return their emotions to equilibrium. This is unlikely to occur, particularly in the manager and workmate role, unless emotional work is valued by organizations as an important and desirable organizational behavior, performed as part of, not in spite of, other work duties.

Some emotional contagion may be inevitable, and "emotional workers" will need to be skilled in managing their own emotions in order to deal with it. The skills described in the emotional intelligence literature (e.g., Goleman 1996) seem especially relevant. Training in these skills (self-awareness, emotion regulation, and self-soothing) should be viewed as important and necessary for all employees who do emotional work, not just managers. The notion that emotions can be caught is relevant to research and theory on emotional intelligence in organizations. Generally, being able to manage the emotions of others at work is viewed as desirable and adaptive, and an important part of the people skills involved in successful job performance. This study indicates that sometimes there can be a cost to the self and this also needs to be monitored and regulated.

It is important for organizations to minimize the risks and maximize the benefits of emotional work. As the literature on social support attests, *receiving* emotional work is important for the well-being of employees, and a positive and integrated workplace climate improves their capacity to perform. But delivering emotional work to the public, and creating and maintaining an integrative work climate, takes time and effort. It is hard work and can impair the health of those who do it. Emotional work is not confined to one work role: in the workplace, managers, workmates, and service workers all perform emotional work. Any employee who performs emotional work risks emotional contagion, and those employees who occupy multiple work roles with high emotional demands are the most at risk. It is in organizations' interests to sustain the emotional work of their managers and employees *and* to find ways to mitigate the health costs to those who do it.

Acknowledgments

Thank you to the Psychology Department at the Australian National University for its support of the project, to the men and women who volunteered to participate in the research, to the National Centre for Epidemiology and Population Health for support in preparing this paper, and especially to Dr. Valerie Braithwaite for her help and editorial comments.

Notes

1. This definition of emotional work follows from a definition by England and Farkas (1986) and England and Folbre's (1999) "caring work."

2. The CES-D does not measure major depression, which requires at least two weeks of symptom presence, and in most cases is far more long standing in symptom course. However, participants with major depression would most likely obtain high CES-D scores (Coyne 1994).

Appendix A

Table 14.A

Bivariate Intercorrelation Matrix of Independent Variables Predicting Health and Turnover Intentions: Intercorrelations Among Independent Variables (n = 230)

Predictors	1	2	3	4	5	6	7	8	9
1. Gender	—	0.04	-0.04	0.01	0.06	**-0.23**	0.08	0.14	0.07
2. Age		—	0.12	-0.17	0.04	0.05	0.10	-0.10	-0.04
3. NESB			—	0.19	0.01	-0.04	0.02	0.06	0.13
4. Education				—	**0.49**	0.15	0.16	**0.26**	**0.32**
5. Occupation					—	0.07	**0.23**	**0.24**	**0.22**
6. Work hours						—	0.14	0.13	0.08
7. Work distress							—	**0.41**	**0.42**
8. Work companionship								—	**0.62**
9. Work help/regulation									—

Note: Gender coded 0 = male, 1 = female. "Work distress" denotes work role emotional demands. "Work comp." denotes summed companionship scores for manager, workmate and service roles. "Work help/regulation" denotes summed help and regulation scores for manager, workmate and service roles (nonmanagers). Missing data deleted listwise. Bolded correlation coefficients are significant at the .01 level.

A CONCEPTUAL EXAMINATION OF THE CAUSAL SEQUENCES OF EMOTIONAL LABOR, EMOTIONAL DISSONANCE, AND EMOTIONAL EXHAUSTION: THE ARGUMENT FOR THE ROLE OF CONTEXTUAL AND PROVIDER CHARACTERISTICS

15

*Charmine E.J. Härtel, Alice C.F. Hsu,
and Maree V. Boyle*

Abstract

In response to the increasing interest regarding the emotional consequences facing service providers who perform emotional labor as part of their service roles, this chapter provides a conceptual examination of the causal sequences of emotional labor, emotional dissonance, and emotional exhaustion (the EEE sequence). Specifically, we propose a theoretical model that examines the emotional experience, performance outcomes, and turnover intentions of service providers in a holistic fashion by incorporating affective events theory to integrate the concept of daily hassles and uplifts with the EEE sequence. In addition, the organizational factors of cultural orientation to emotions and workgroup emotional climate, and the individual factors of provider dissonance tolerance, hassle tolerance, and uplift reactivity are introduced and depicted as influencing the EEE sequence. Implications for theory, practice, and future research are discussed.

Introduction

Two key concerns regarding the management of service workers are service performance and turnover (Ashkanasy, Härtel, and Zerbe 2000b). Over the past decade, practitioners and researchers have drawn attention to the emotional labor (EL) requirements of service work and the important role of emotions in retention and performance (e.g., Härtel, Barker, and Baker 1999). In this chapter, we develop a theoretical model of the role of EL, emotional dissonance (ED), perceived affective work events, and provider and environmental emotional characteristics on provider emotional exhaustion (EE), turnover intention, and service performance (see Figure 15.1). Although it is acknowledged that customer factors influence provider emotional experiences, consideration of these is beyond the scope of this chapter.

Recently, academics have theorized that EL can produce ED and that this conflict between what one feels and what one is required to display by the organization produces, in turn, EE (Ashforth and Humphrey 1993; Hochschild 1983; Morris and Feldman 1996). EE, as the core dimension of work burnout (Maslach 1982b), is proposed to be an important determinant of turnover intention in service providers.

In the literatures examining the effects of emotions on workers, work events are theorized to give rise to affective reactions, which have consequences for workplace behaviors such as performance (Weiss and Cropanzano 1996). Research based on this affective events theory shows that hassles and uplifts at work produce negative and positive emotional reactions respectively (Härtel, McColl-Kennedy, and McDonald 1998; McDonald and Härtel 1999). This chapter integrates the concept of hassles and uplifts with the EL-ED-EE sequence. Specifically, the model developed proposes that perceived hassles partially mediate the relationship between ED and EE and that perceived uplifts directly affect service performance.

In addition to examining the relationship of EL and perceived affective work events with providers' reported service performance, turnover intention, and EE, this chapter aims to identify characteristics of the provider and of the environment that enhance positive aspects of service work and buffer against the negative aspects of service work. The two contextual factors identified are emotional workgroup climate (Härtel, Gough, and Härtel in press) and organizational cultural orientation to emotions. The proposed provider characteristics

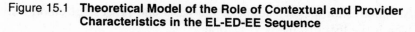

Figure 15.1 **Theoretical Model of the Role of Contextual and Provider Characteristics in the EL-ED-EE Sequence**

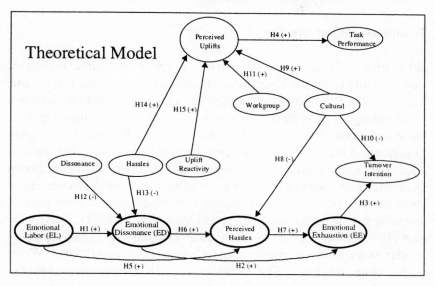

are dissonance tolerance, hassle tolerance, and uplift reactivity. The proposed model depicts workgroup emotional climate and cultural orientation to emotions as enhancing the perception of uplifts, and cultural orientation as also being inversely related to turnover intentions and perceived hassles. The provider characteristic, uplift reactivity, is proposed to enhance the experience of positive work events, namely the perception of uplifts. The provider characteristics of dissonance tolerance and hassle tolerance are both proposed to buffer providers against the negative emotional effects of service work, reducing providers' experience of ED.

The chapter aims to enhance the understanding of the emotional processes and consequences associated with service work. In particular, it identifies that studies of emotional job requirements and EL have overlooked the role of affective events in service work and the affective characteristics peculiar to the work environment within which a provider executes his or her service role. The chapter addresses this research gap by identifying the organizational, workgroup, and individual orientations to emotions and emotional events that shape the emotional experience of service providers on the job. Identifying and understanding the contextual and individual characteristics relevant to the study of EL first requires an understanding of the basis and process of emotions, which is the focus of the next section.

Emotions—What Are They?

It has been said that most of the variance in service encounter outcomes can be explained by consideration of emotional variables (Mano and Oliver 1993). But what are emotions? The concept of emotion, despite a long history of prominence in academic study, has no single agreed-upon definition (see Fineman 1996 for a review). Because this chapter is concerned with the consequences of affective events within the service context, the definition of emotions used in affective events theory is adopted here. Namely, emotions are "affective responses to what happens in the environment and cognitive representations of the event's meaning for the individual" (Frijda and Mesquita 1994, 51). Thus, emotions have a clear cognitive content and, since they are linked with particular events, have a specific cause (Forgas 1995; Frijda 1993; Weiss and Cropanzano 1996). Our interpretation of emotions also considers them to be socially constructed (Oatley 1993), with their situational antecedents and interpretation shaped by cultural, social, and organizational norms (Ekman 1993; Fineman 1996; Frijda and Mesquita 1994; Rafaeli and Sutton 1989).

Within an organizational setting, the displays of emotions expected are typically restricted with the emphasis being on "rational" behavior (Fineman 1996). In contrast, emotionality within organizational life is often viewed as undesirable or dysfunctional for organizational processes, effectiveness, and for achieving its objectives (Mumby and Putnam 1992). Given this view, organizations or management often deem it necessary to impose job requirements through policies or rules through norms and cultures, aimed at controlling or regulating the emotional activities of its members (see Ashforth and Humphrey 1995; Fineman 1993). EL is one salient form of the organizational prescription of emotions.

The Emotional Labor–Emotional Dissonance–Emotional Exhaustion (EL-ED-EE) Causal Sequence

Increasingly, it is recognized that one critical aspect of service work concerns the explicit or implicit requirements for service employees to express appropriate emotions on the job (Ashforth and Humphrey 1993;

Hochschild 1979, 1983; Leidner 1999; Rafaeli and Sutton 1987, 1989; Steinberg and Figart 1999a, 1999b). At the same time, job outcomes for service workers such as service performance and turnover intentions have been theorized to be affected by affective work events (Weiss and Cropanzano 1996). This chapter focuses on EL and its psychological consequences, ED and EE, as the potentially negative aspects of the service job, and proposes a model that depicts the ED induced by EL as contributing to the increased likelihood that a provider will perceive work events as hassles, which in turn increases the chance of EE (the precursor to burnout). Before turning to a consideration of the provider and environmental emotional characteristics that can increase or decrease the negative and positive consequences of EL, the causal sequence among EL, ED, and EE that is established in the literature is described. In particular, the literature reviewed next highlights three findings. First, the literature portrays EL as directly influencing ED, which in turn is expected to directly effect EE. The sequence gives rise to the second point, that ED is expected to mediate the relationship between EL and EE. Third, the literature links EE to turnover intentions.

Emotional Labor

EL is defined in this chapter as the efforts to display or to feel organizationally desired emotions in jobs where face-to-face or voice-to-voice interactions with the public are an important component of the job (Ashforth and Humphrey 1993; Hochschild 1983; Wharton 1999). The concept of EL was first conceptualized by Hochschild (1983, 7) in her seminal work, *The Managed Heart*, as "the management of feeling to create a publicly observable facial and bodily display." Later scholars broadened this concept to include the spoken word and tone of voice (Rafaeli and Sutton 1987, 1989).

Hochschild argued that displaying organizationally sanctioned emotions to customers is a form of "labor" since it requires effort, planning, anticipation, and adjustment on the providers' part in order to publicly display emotions that they may not necessarily feel privately (James 1989). Such displays are hard work, intensive, and have value for the organization (Steinberg and Figart 1999a). In her study of flight attendants, Hochschild raised concern that the requirement of EL to display organizationally prescribed emotions may have pernicious effects upon the well-being of service providers. Understanding the genesis of this concern requires an examination of the nature and forms of EL; this point is taken up next.

Service Encounters

Service encounters are the interpersonal interactions between customers and service providers (Czepiel, Solomon, and Surprenant 1985). Service encounters may be regarded as emotional events that elicit emotional reactions in the interactants (Härtel, Gough, and Härtel in press). For example, emotions influence the outcomes of service encounters by affecting customer satisfaction, attribution, and response to organizational crises (Härtel, Gough, and Härtel in press; Härtel, McColl-Kennedy, and McDonald 1998). Similarly, service encounters, which make up a large part of service providers' work life, have emotional consequences (Härtel, Gough, and Härtel in press).

Features of the service context have implications for service providers and the practice of EL. Service encounters are often high in uncertainty, as they are emergent and dynamic; and the services rendered are intangible, instantaneous, and inseparable from the interactions of the participants, so that service quality is often difficult for customers to evaluate (Ashforth and Humphrey 1993). These combined factors place a premium upon the behaviors and service performance of the providers who are situated in the organization-customer interface (Ashforth and Humphrey 1993; Bitran and Lojo 1993). To ensure task accomplishment and the success of service encounters, providers need to manage the emotions of the customers, for example, try to induce or suppress a particular emotional state in them, while at the same time cope with their own emotions. EL thus involves managing the emotions of the self and managing the emotions of others (Ashforth and Humphrey 1993; Hochschild 1983; Steinberg and Figart 1999a).

Service Jobs Requiring Emotional Labor

According to Hochschild (1983, 147), jobs involving EL entail (1) voice or facial contact with the public; (2) requirement for the worker to produce an emotional state or reaction in the customer; and (3) opportunity for the employer to control the emotional activities of the employee. The burgeoning research in this area has uncovered a whole range of emotional expressions required and regulated in diverse service jobs.

The forms of EL may vary widely in valence, frequency, duration, intensity, and involvement depending on the nature of the service roles (Morris and Feldman 1996, 1997). For example, flight attendants must maintain gracious smiles while bill collectors train themselves to show contempt and anger (Hochschild 1983; Sutton 1991); nurses are expected to be caring, sympathetic, loving, and involved with their patients while the EL of supermarket clerks or fast-food clerks (Leidner 1991, 1993; Rafaeli 1989a, 1989b; Sutton and Rafaeli 1988) is of a shorter duration, more frequent, repetitive, and often entails highly scripted emotional displays such as "smile and say thank you" (Sutton and Rafaeli 1988). Among other service roles examined for their EL requirements are waiters and waitresses (Hall 1993; Paules 1991), amusement park employees (Van Maanen 1991; Van Maanen and Kunda 1989), and also those often regarded as service "professionals" such as paralegals (Pierce 1995), medical staff and nurses (O'Brien 1994), banking employees (Wharton 1993), police or criminal investigators (Steinross and Kleinman 1989), and insurance agents (Leidner 1991).

During service interactions, judgments about the appropriateness of emotional displays are largely influenced by display rules or feeling rules. Display rules are learned norms regarding when and how emotion should be expressed in public (Ekman 1973; Rafaeli and Sutton 1989), while feeling rules refer to the norms and expectations that govern what feelings one should have in a certain situation (Hochschild 1983).

EL is influenced by the social, organizational, occupational, and other localized factors that shape display rules and convey to people what emotional displays are appropriate, acceptable, or expected in a particular context. However, particular attention has been given to organizational norms and rules that entail deliberate attempts to control, regulate, or require emotional expressions. Forms of organizational attempts to control the emotional activities of service providers include scripts (Ashforth and Fried 1988), monitoring and supervision, training, socialization, selection, and recruitment (Mumby and Putnam 1992; Rafaeli and Sutton 1987).

EL may involve more than the displaying of emotions to customers. It is recognized that it is also performed with respect to internal customers of an organization, such as coworkers, supervisors, and management. External customers, however, exert the most influence upon the provider due to the physical proximity and immediacy of the encounter, followed by coworker influence, supervisor influence, and, most remotely, the influence of management (Rafaeli and Sutton 1987). For this reason, the scope of this chapter is limited to the customer-provider aspect of EL.

Influence of Emotional Labor on Provider Well-being

Integrating Thoits's (1985) and Hochschild's (1983) work, Rafaeli and Sutton (1987) described three possible outcomes for providers who perform EL: emotional harmony, emotional deviance, and emotional dissonance. A provider experiences emotional harmony when there is total congruence between inner feelings and the expressed emotions as required by display or feeling rules. For example, when a provider required to express enthusiasm actually feels enthusiasm and expects to feel enthusiasm, that provider is experiencing emotional harmony. When, on the other hand, there are conflicts between the required expressions of emotions and felt emotions, emotional deviance may occur where a provider expresses inner feelings and disregards display rules, such as expressing anger or rudeness toward customers. Emotional deviancies, however, are subject to organizational control or punishments, such as the risk of being fired for displays of rudeness. Thus, rather than the performance of EL resulting in ED, in most cases it results in ED, where a provider expresses the appropriate emotions to satisfy display rules and copes with the clashes of these requirements with inner feelings. Therefore, the first hypothesized link depicted in the proposed model is that EL exerts a direct and positive influence on ED (see Figure 15.1).

Emotional Dissonance and Emotional Exhaustion

ED is defined as the emotional state experienced by a provider who expresses organizationally desired emotions that do not represent his or her true feelings (Hochschild 1983; Middleton 1989). For example, providers displaying positive emotions to rude customers are experiencing ED when their inner feeling is one of anger (Morris and Feldman 1997). Akin to the notion of cognitive dissonance, it denotes a state of incongruence (Hochschild 1983) and gives rise to feelings of conflict and tension.

ED is argued to be an inevitable outcome of EL (Hochschild 1983; Mumby and Putnam 1992) as it is not possible for service providers to sustain a particular emotional state all the time, as required by the nature of service jobs (Ashforth and Humphrey 1993; Hochschild 1983).

Given the discrepancy between felt and expressed feelings, a service provider may perform EL through surface acting and deep acting (Hochschild 1983). Surface acting involves the provider merely feigning emotions and focusing on the outward behavior, such as a supermarket clerk smiling at customers without feeling the warmth. Deep acting, on the other hand, involves the provider forcing himself or herself to actually experience the desired feelings in order to display them. For example, flight attendants are taught to evoke feelings of friendliness by imagining the passengers as guests in their living room (Hochschild 1983, 105). In addition, spontaneous or genuinely felt feelings, such as a nurse feeling sympathy toward patients without prompting, may also be a form of EL (Ashforth and Humphrey 1993).

Hochschild (1983) contends that the performance of EL necessitates an alienation of "true feelings" from "displayed feelings" and thus estranges the "self" from the work role. The resulting "fragmentation of the self" has aversive consequences. Role theory, which identifies such dissonance as a form of person-role conflict (Kahn et al. 1964; Rafaeli and Sutton 1987), also suggests that when a person complies with the role expectations and expresses the desired level of emotions, there are feelings of duplicity and resistance that, over time, may give rise to negative consequences such as job stress.

Empirical Evidence of the ED-EE Link

While Hochschild's stark portrayal of the dichotomy of the "real self" and the "false self" are deemed to be simplistic and problematic by some (e.g., Wouters 1989, 1992), emerging empirical evidence supports the proposition that ED is commonly found among service providers, and that the persistent conflict and tension of ED arising from the performance of EL is strongly and directly linked to EE (Abraham 1998, 1999; Morris and Feldman 1997). Consequently, the second hypothesized link depicted in the proposed model is that ED has a direct effect on emotional exhaustion, with high levels of ED predicting high levels of EE (see Figure 15.1). EE refers to a state of depleted energy caused by excessive emotional demands made on people interacting with customers or clients (Jackson, Turner, and Brief 1987; Maslach 1982a; Saxton, Phillips, and Blakeney 1991). It is a specific stress-related psychological state in which a person may experience feelings of fatigue, irritability, frustration, and being used up and worn out (Maslach and Jackson 1981), which, in turn, give rise to the feeling that "one can not give anymore" (Maslach 1982a).

People who occupy service roles requiring frequent face-to-face interactions that are intense, emotionally charged, and longer in duration are more likely to experience higher levels of EE (Maslach 1982a). EE is an important issue as it denotes the core dimension and the first stage of work burnout (Maslach 1982b), and thus a point where possible and effective managerial intervention in the burnout process may occur (Boles, Johnston, and Hair 1997). In addition, research has suggested that EE may induce or predict the intention to leave one's job. Specifically, EE has been empirically linked to heightened turnover intentions in contact service workers (Saxton, Phillips, and Blakeney 1991). A recent study by Babakus et al. (1999) also indicated that EE is linked to intentions to leave through lowered job satisfaction and organizational commitment. Thus, the third hypothesized link depicted in the proposed model is that EE exerts a direct and positive influence on turnover intention (see Figure 15.1).

Emotional Dissonance as a Mediator of EL-EE

Research findings suggest that EL is not uniformly harmful to all service providers. It is not the mere performance of EL that leads to EE. Wharton (1993), for example, found that providers employed in jobs involving EL were no more likely to experience burnout than nonperformers of EL; and that EL was related to increased job satisfaction for some providers (Adelmann 1995; Wharton 1993; Wharton and Erickson 1995). Instead, it has been found in separate studies that it is the tension and conflict arising from ED that is significantly associated with higher EE and lower job satisfaction (Abraham 1998, 1999; Morris and Feldman 1997; Saxton, Phillips, and Blakeney 1991).

While research on ED remains scarce, the results of the few existing studies suggest that ED is the critical variable in predicting the influence of EL on provider well-being and, thus, job outcomes such as turnover and performance. It is exactly when a provider begins to experience such mismatch and tension that EL becomes problematic (Morris and Feldman 1997). The act of expressing sanctioned emotions as part of the work role appears to be dysfunctional for the individual only to the extent that expressed sanctioned emotions conflict with felt emotions.

Figure 15.2 **The EL-ED-EE Causal Sequence as Established by Contemporary Studies**

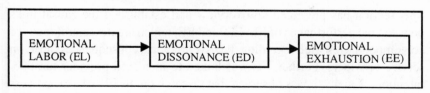

Hence, ED is expected to mediate the relationship between EL and EE. Figure 15.2 illustrates the EL-ED-EE causal sequence presented so far.

Theoretical and empirical attempts to investigate the important ED-EE link have only just begun. Scholars thus far have sought to explain the link between ED and EE by investigating personal dispositions and certain job characteristics. Empirically, Abraham (1999) found negative affectivity to be a moderator of the ED-job satisfaction relationship and a mediator of ED-EE, while Morris and Feldman (1997) showed the same finding for job autonomy. Theoretically, Ashforth and Humphrey (1993) considered examining the ED-EE link from the perspective of social identity theory, while Rafaeli and Sutton (1987, 15) argued that the effect of dissonance depends on the extent to which a provider has internalized feeling rules. For example, providers who display "fake" emotions while believing such acting should not be part of the job (faking in bad faith), have not internalized feeling rules and are more likely to experience ED than those who have internalized the need for presenting false emotions (faking in good faith).

In examining these issues, however, current studies seem to fall short of considering the wider experiences of employees' emotional life at work, and identifying the mechanisms and conditions through which the EL-ED-EE causal sequence operates. Moreover, the inconsistent findings outlined earlier suggest that this sequence is more complex than currently portrayed. It is argued next that research examining the EL-ED-EE process needs to recognize that EL and its consequences do not occur in a vacuum, rather that it is important to take into account the role of contextual factors. The service encounter context comprises emotional events that have the potential to elicit positive or negative emotions in the provider. Furthermore, the emotional experiences of the provider during service work occur alongside and within the organizational and workgroup environment, which offer their own emotional characteristics and potential emotional stimuli.

Summary

This section has presented an overview and established the causal links between the performance of EL, ED, and EE, which are the central focus of contemporary research regarding the psychological consequences of EL on service providers. Further, EE was linked to increased provider turnover intentions. Finally, it was observed that research on the EL-ED-EE process has overlooked the role of the context. In the next section, affective events theory and the concept of daily hassles and uplifts are evoked to link daily affective work events with the EL-ED-EE process.

Integrating Hassles and Uplifts with the EL-ED-EE Sequence

Affective Events Theory

Affective events theory (Weiss and Cropanzano 1996) recognizes that work events give rise to affective reactions, which have consequences for workplace behaviors and attitudes such as performance and job satisfaction (Weiss and Cropanzano 1996). It focuses on the events that happen to people in work settings in contrast to the traditional emphasis on personal dispositions or features of the environment taken in the study of antecedents to organizational job attitudes and behaviors.

Affective events theory incorporates the cognitive appraisal process to explain how events elicit emotions. According to cognitive appraisal theorists, emotional reactions begin with a two-stage appraisal of an event (Frijda 1986, 1988; Lazarus 1982, 1991a; Plutchik 1994; Smith and Ellsworth 1985). In primary appraisal, the first stage, an individual evaluates the event for its relevance to well-being in terms of positive or negative events. Lazarus (1991a, 92) terms this as assessing "harms or benefits." This stage then initiates a secondary appraisal where the individual appraises the more specific context, focusing on consequences, attributions, or coping potential. It is in the secondary appraisal that the experiences of discrete emotions such as anger, sadness, or joy are generated.

Affective events theory and its incorporation of the cognitive appraisal theory of emotions may offer the best way forward in understanding emotions in the workplace. Using these perspectives, this chapter aims to integrate the concept of daily hassles and uplifts, as negative and positive affective work events respectively, with the EL-ED-EE sequence.

Hassles and Uplifts As Negative and Positive Work Events

One promising avenue for the study of psychological well-being in the workplace is provided by the concept of daily hassles and uplifts. Hassles are "the irritating, frustrating, distressing demands or annoying minor events that more or less characterize everyday transactions with the environment" (Kanner, et al. 1981, 3). In contrast, uplifts are the "positive experiences such as the joy derived from manifestations of love, relief at hearing good news, the pleasure of a good night's rest, and so on" (Kanner et al. 1981, 6). Hassles and uplifts can elicit negative and positive affect respectively. Uplifts or positive experiences at work have been empirically linked with favorable outcomes such as performance and supervisory evaluations (Staw, Sutton, and Pelled 1994). Consequently the fourth hypothesized link in the proposed model depicts perceived uplifts as exerting a direct and positive influence on service performance.

The effects of hassles on well-being have long been of interest in the medical and stress literature. Kanner et al. (1981) found hassles to be a better predictor of psychological stress than the traditional major life event approach (Holmes and Rahe 1967), which focuses on major and rare events such as death and marriage. They argued that this is because hassles are almost unavoidable and have powerful cumulated effects on emotions, an influence often overlooked in the stress literature.

Hassles and uplifts are important contextual factors for two reasons. First, over time, these events may be cumulative and produce major effects on health and psychological functioning. Second, hassles and uplifts may symbolize larger ongoing issues and concerns. That is, they may be the daily manifestations of such stable features of life as social roles, personality traits, and psychodynamic conflicts (Kanner et al. 1987).

Emotional Labor and Perceived Hassles

Hassles happen in particular life contexts. Kanner et al. (1981) identified hassles in the social sphere, such as work overload and underload, as well as in the physical environment, such as noise and traffic jams. Hassles on the job represent a type of repeated hassle that often presents consistent and predictable demands to employees; for example, hassles from one's boss or supervisor, misplacing and losing things, or not having enough time to complete tasks. Hassles may vary in meaning, intensity, and importance (Ruffin 1993). They can relate to relational processes (e.g., threat) or more stable characteristics associated with the individual (e.g., the occupation). Because the EL associated with service work largely pertains to relational processes, which also have the potential to be problematic, it is proposed that providers' perceived level of hassles are positively related to the level of EL required by the role. This is the fifth hypothesized link in the proposed model; namely, that EL exerts a direct and positive influence on provider perceived hassles (see Figure 15.1).

Perceived Hassles As a Mediator of the Dissonance-Exhaustion Relationship

A potential hassle becomes a hassle only if the individual appraises it as being a hassle; that is, it is not a hassle by virtue of its occurrence. How a person endorses a particular hassle as having occurred, and its respective aversiveness, is individually conceived (Kanner et al. 1981). The variation in the significance and effect of hassles is a function of how they are appraised relative to the available coping resources of the individual. It is argued here, therefore, that hassle interpretation and intensity will vary between individuals, situations, and over time.

Constant or extra customer demands or complaints are among the major factors found to worry and stress service providers at work (Czepiel, Solomon, and Surprenant 1985). The EL associated with these service work events increases the probability of ED as previously shown. The tension and conflict of ED adds to the challenges providers must face in executing their service and work roles, increasing the chance of perceiving a given work event as frustrating or negative. In other words, ED may heighten providers' tendency to negatively appraise events in the course of executing their work, which results in their perceiving higher levels of hassles than providers experiencing low levels of ED. Moreover, in keeping with the affective events theory framework, hassles represent negative work events that serve as negative emotional stimuli with the potential to exacerbate or magnify an existing negative emotional state (Kanner et al. 1981). Consequently, the perception of the presence of hassles may further exacerbate the negative feelings providers in a state of ED have, increasing the chance of ED developing into EE. Consequently, the sixth hypothesis in the model developed in this chapter is that providers experiencing stronger ED are more likely

to perceive more hassles at work than those experiencing lower dissonance (see Figure 15.1). High perceived hassles is expected to increase,
in turn, the likelihood and intensity of EE subsequently experienced by
the provider. Thus, hypothesis seven is that perceived hassles will partially mediate the relationship between ED and EE (see Figure 15.1).

Summary

To summarize, frequent ED, or person-emotion—role-emotion conflicts,
makes the execution of a provider's role more challenging. It was argued that providers experiencing high levels of ED are more likely to
regard interactions with customers during service encounters as events
that are frustrating or taxing on their emotions. The heightened perception of hassles produced by ED was proposed to lead, in turn, to a higher
likelihood of EE.

Contextual and Provider Characteristics Influencing Emotional Experiences in Service Work

The next section proposes that contextual characteristics of the organization and the individual characteristics of provider influence providers' emotional reactions and perception of work events. Organizational
cultural orientation to emotion (COE), positive workgroup emotional
climate (WEC), and provider reactivity to uplifts are argued to enhance
the positive aspects of work events, while provider dissonance tolerance and hassle tolerance are introduced as emotional buffers against
the negative aspects of service work.

Contextual Factors

Various authors have indicated that EL and its related issues are better
studied in the context or culture within which they are localized (Boyle
1997; Mumby and Putnam 1992; Van Maanen and Kunda 1989). EL as
a work practice does not occur in a vacuum but is, as discussed, one
form of the wide range of emotional expressions and displays occurring
in the workplace. Moreover, as EL represents a more direct and extreme
form of organizational prescription and control over the emotions of
organizational members (Ashforth and Humphrey 1995; Leidner 1999),
there is therefore need to consider the relatively enduring organizational

contextual factors contributing to the emotional experiences of providers. This is especially so since researchers have recently highlighted the lack of attention to the emotional characteristics of organizations in organizational studies (Mumby and Putnam 1992) and the need to recognize the inescapable intertwining of rationality and emotionality (cf. Ashforth and Humphrey 1995; Martin, Knopoff, and Beckman 1998).

Organizational Cultural Orientation to Emotion

Culture represents one approach to assessing organizational context (Denison 1996). It is concerned with identifying the features of the organization's context, which are enduring over time and stably held in the values, beliefs, and behaviors of employees. Thus, organizational culture measures are aimed at describing those dimensions of an organization's context that capture the deep structure of the internal environment. Organization culture is comprised of many dimensions such as structure, support, risk, cohesiveness, and outcome orientation (Denison 1996; Schneider 1990).

Organizational culture, in particular, is argued to exert an overarching influence on how emotions are expressed and experienced by organizational members (Van Maanen 1991). For example, Mumby and Putnam (1992) argued that culture shapes the ways employees perform EL and that EL reciprocally contributes to the development of organizational culture.

In this chapter, a new dimension of culture is proposed, namely organizational orientation to emotion. Cultures high in concern for employee emotional well-being should be characterized by a high level of organizational recognition for EL, defined as the degree to which an organization acknowledges, addresses, legitimizes, rewards, or compensates the existence and demands of EL (Boyle 1999).

Organizational contexts that create and maintain expectations about emotional expressions may include recruitment and selection, socialization, and rewards and punishments (Rafaeli and Sutton 1987). Thus, an organization's COE may be indicated by the organization's level of formal and informal recognition of the emotional job requirements associated with individual jobs (Boyle 1999). Examples are, the extent to which job descriptions contain emotional characteristics of the role, forms of job socialization and training, selection criteria, and level of provision of formal supports to assist in coping with emotional job requirements such as employee assistance programs, time-out breaks, stress leave, leave entitlements for critical emotional job incidents, emotion management skill training, supervisor training that includes how to help subordinates manage emotional job requirements, the level of proceduralization and prescription of emotional responses (e.g., rigidity of organizationally approved emotional responses, number of emotional display rules), and whether mechanisms to monitor employees' emotional well-being are in place (Newton 1995).

Cultures that marginalize emotionality tend to overlook employees' emotional needs in the course of performing their work (Fineman 1993). For example, in a study of emotionality in social work agencies, Meyerson (1998) found that in a highly medicalized culture, feelings of burnout and stress were treated as individual failure or as diseases and were talked about in ways that reflected values and beliefs of traditional medicine where the individual is viewed as the locus of disease and cure. Conversely, in a psychosocially oriented culture, feelings of burnout and stress were treated as normal and inevitable parts of the work, negative emotional experiences were regarded as occupational hazards that a professional is expected to experience on occasion, and emotional control was seen as impossible and sometimes undesirable as social workers are supposed to use emotions as a source of connection and insight.

Organizations that demonstrate a commitment to recognize and legitimize emotion-related issues at work are more likely to implement policies that will reduce perceived on-the-job hassles for providers. For example, in an experimental study of on-the-job hassles for bus drivers, a job environment intervention designed partly to reduce passenger demands on drivers significantly reduced reported hassles by the drivers, which also led to a reduction in occupational stress (Evans, Johansson, and Rydstedt 1999). Therefore, it is proposed that providers' perception of their organization's COE will influence their emotional experience in the workplace. In particular, the eighth and ninth hypothesized links in the proposed model are, respectively, that provider perceptions of COE exert a direct and negative influence on provider perceptions of daily hassles and that COE exerts a direct and positive influence on provider perceptions of daily uplifts (see Figure 15.1). Furthermore, it is expected that a worker's perception of the degree to which an organization is concerned with his or her emotional well-being may influence turnover intentions. This argument is consistent with the framework presented in this chapter, namely, that poor organizational attention to the emotional well-being of workers may be antecedental to the level of negative and positive work events experienced (i.e., daily hassles and uplifts) and thus induce intentions to leave the job. Consequently, the tenth link hypothesized in the proposed model is that provider perceptions of COE exert a direct and negative influence on provider turnover intentions (see Figure 15.1). At this point, it is important to point out that hassles are not linked to task performance in the model as individuals are expected to leave rather than jeopardize their career possibilities because of poor performance. It is acknowledged that contextual performance or organizational citizenship behavior would likely suffer when a high level of perceived hassles is present.

Workgroup Emotional Climate

One contextual factor that may influence providers' emotional experience of work events is the emotional climate of their workgroup. Climate is the "shared perceptions of the events, practices and procedures or behaviors that get rewarded, supported and expected in a setting" (Schneider 1990, 384). Climate is also an assessment of the quality of a given organizational context, but differs from culture in that it is concerned with the more transient and less enduring temporal surface structures of the context (Denison 1996; Schneider 1990). Climate aims to describe the qualitative dimensions of an organization's internal environment that influence behavior (Tagiuri and Litwin 1968).

Emotion can be a group-level phenomenon (Ashforth and Humphrey 1995; Heise and O'Brien 1993) and may be viewed as one dimension of psychological climate (Koys and DeCotiis 1991). The concept of emotional climate is described by De Rivera (1992, 197) as "an objective phenomenon that can be palpably sensed," and that can be observed objectively, such as an emotional climate of fear during wartime. Within organizations, individuals form work-climate perceptions (Burke, Boruski, and Hurley 1992) that are relatively stable over time and that help determine the appropriate behavior in a given situation (Koys and DeCotiis 1991). The emotional climate of a workgroup may influence group members' emotional experiences at work because the social and physical environment influences people's emotions (cf. Rafaeli and Sutton 1987). Härtel, Gough, and Härtel (in press) proposed the construct of WEC, and their research showed a strong and direct link between individual providers' perception of emotional climate and individual providers' reported job satisfaction.

One way by which the emotions of one person can be transmitted to another is through emotional contagion (Hatfield, Cacioppo, and Rapson 1994). Emotional contagion is "the tendency to mimic the verbal, physiological, and/or behavioral aspects of another person's emotional experience or expression, and thus to experience or express the same emotions oneself" (Hsee et al. 1990, 328). That is, people may "catch" another's emotions in a variety of ways through conscious or nonconscious processes (Hsee et al. 1990). This suggests that the emotional expressions a person observes in others more or less impacts one's own emotional expressions. Moreover, facial feedback theorists (e.g., McIntosh et al. 1997; Zajonc 1985) contend that the emotional expressions of an individual can alter the emotions experienced by that individual. For example, the act of smiling can induce one to feel happiness or cheerfulness.

Social support from peers or coworkers is also identified as one dimension of climate affecting the emotional experiences of workers (Kopelman, Brief, and Guzzo 1990). In the service work environment in particular, where providers are required to engage in constant emotional interactions with external customers, coworkers provide each other the emotional climate both "on-stage" and "back-stage" from the service scene (Boyle 1997). When the WEC within which service providers carry out their daily work is perceived as positive, it may foster positive emotional experiences at work for the providers. Consequently, the eleventh link hypothesized in the proposed model is that provider perceived WEC exerts a direct and positive influence on provider perceived uplifts (see Figure 15.1).

Provider Emotional Buffers

Characteristics of the individual influence emotional reactions and the consequences of those reactions (Jordan et al. in press). People differ in their emotional predispositions, reactivity, and the range and level of emotional coping or defense mechanisms (Fridja 1986; Pervin 1993). These relatively enduring individual traits will influence how people respond to a given emotional stimuli and how they experience emotions (Smith and Pope 1992).

Three individual difference variables identified as relevant to provider emotions in the workplace are introduced in this chapter: provider dissonance tolerance, hassle tolerance, and uplift reactivity. These variables all share the underlying theme that individuals differ in their perception, interpretation, and reaction to emotional stimuli (Smith and Pope 1992). Therefore, individuals possessing high emotional buffering abilities are expected to be more protected from the negative aspects of events when they are perceived to occur, whereas the perception of positive experiences at work is expected to be enhanced for these individuals.

Provider Dissonance Tolerance

ED lies at the heart of the proposed model as EL has been shown in previous research to only adversely impact psychological well-being when ED is experienced. However, there is some evidence to suggest that individual providers differ in their degree of tolerance to the constant tension or conflicts arising from the discrepancy of displayed and felt emotions.

First, as mentioned in previous sections, several studies of the EL-ED-EE process produced inconsistent results suggesting that EL is not uniformly harmful to everyone (e.g., Adelmann 1995; Wharton 1993). Further, some scholars contend that gender may be one factor that influences ED. For example, female providers, by virtue of their generally perceived lower social status (Hochschild 1983) or mindfulness of the socially conceived qualities of being a woman (Bellas 1999; O'Brien 1994; Wharton 1993), may tend to be more accepting or resilient to ED. Similarly, both person-environment fit theory (Caplan 1983) and the dispositional approach to attitudes (Staw, Bell, and Clausen 1986) raise the possibility that some employees may not find the expression of organizationally sanctioned emotions as particularly unpleasant. In some cases, employees are able to go on "automatic pilot," experiencing only "emotional numbness" during EL (Hochschild 1983). Together, these studies can be used to argue for the existence of a new individual difference construct, namely differences in tolerating ED, coined herein as dissonance tolerance (DT). Thus, the twelfth link hypothesized in the proposed model is that provider DT exerts a direct and negative influence on provider ED (see Figure 15.1). In other words, DT is predicted to buffer providers against the negative events experienced during the course of performing EL.

The determinants of a provider's tolerance level are likely to be broad and complex. For example, since ED may be partially explained using social identity theory (Ashforth and Humphrey 1993), providers' social identification may contribute to their DT. Keaveney and Nelson (1993) identified two psychological coping variables, individual providers' motivation orientation and perceived role benefits, which were found to reduce perceived role conflicts of marketing personnel. Other possible contributing factors include the provider's education, people orientation, interpersonal skills, extroversion/introversion, emotion-related beliefs, level of internalization of feeling rules (Rafaeli and Sutton 1987), locus of control, age, gender, and self-monitoring ability (Snyder 1974). While self-monitoring ability is the ability to control expressive behavior to match the expression and self-presentation of others in social situations (Abraham 1998, 235), DT refers to the ability to withstand the discrepancy or discomfort of expressing desired emotions when they differ from the emotions actually experienced. In other words, DT is the degree to which a provider does not feel troubled or bothered by the need to "pretend" emotions that are not genuinely felt.

Provider Tolerance to Hassles

Earlier it was established that the perception of a hassle results from a subjective judgment arising from an individual's available resources. In other words, individual predispositions will affect whether a given event is regarded as a hassle or as an uplift. As hassles create negative affect and providers are expected or required to display positive affect even when experiencing hassles during EL, providers having high levels of tolerance for hassles associated with service work are proposed to respond with less negative affect to hassles and consequently will report lower levels of ED. Adapting the definition for hassles, the new individual difference construct of hassle tolerance (HT) may be defined as the relative tendency or predisposition of a person to withstand negative, frustrating, or annoying minor events associated with the everyday interactions in one's environment. Like DT, provider HT may act as an emotional buffer to the negative aspects of EL, thereby reducing providers' experience of ED. This hypothesized link is depicted as Hypothesis 13 in the proposed model, namely that HT exerts a direct and negative influence on ED (see Figure 15.1). Providers with high HT may also perceive more uplifts at work as they are less receptive to the negative aspects of EL. Consequently, the fourteenth hypothesized link in the proposed model is that HT exerts a direct and positive influence on perceived uplifts (see Figure 15.1).

Provider Reactivity to Uplifts

Uplift reactivity is another individual difference variable introduced in this chapter. Similar to HT, uplift reactivity (UR) may be defined by adapting the definition for an uplift. Thus, UR is the relative tendency of a person to react strongly to a given positive event associated with the everyday interactions in one's environment. Similar to HT, different individuals may react to a given uplift with varying degrees of intensity, and therefore the experience of pleasure also varies. For example, a compliment from a superior may elicit in different subordinates emotions ranging from slight pleasure to utter joy. It is argued that people with high reactivity to uplifts will also be more likely to perceive a given event as positive, as they are more receptive to the positive aspects of EL. Thus, it is proposed that provider uplift reactivity is one individual difference variable that enhances the level of uplifts perceived by providers at work. The fifteenth hypothesized link in the proposed model is, therefore, that UR exerts a positive and direct influence on perceived uplifts.

To summarize, the experience of EL, ED, and EE is shaped and influenced by how a provider perceives and experiences daily work events as hassles or uplifts, as well as organizational and individual factors that contribute to these perceptions. A provider's service performance is positively influenced by the level of his or her perceptions of uplifts on the job. A provider's perception of uplifts, in turn, is influenced by contextual factors including organizational orientation to emotions, and the emotional climate of the providers' workgroup. Individual provider's tolerance to hassles and reactivity to uplifts are also expected to predict the level of perceived uplifts. Finally, provider DT and HT both act as buffers, directly reducing providers' experience of ED. The specific hypothesized links are shown in Figure 15.1.

Discussion

In this chapter, we developed a theoretical model of the EL-ED-EE process from an affective events theory perspective. In particular, the negative and positive aspects of EL were linked to the concept of daily hassles and uplifts. Service providers' perceptions of the level of hassles was predicted to be directly influenced by the level of ED they experienced, thereby exerting a mediating effect on the ED-EE relationship. Perceived uplifts, on the other hand, were predicted to directly influence service performance.

In addition, contextual and individual factors were incorporated into the expanded model of the EL-ED-EE process. For the contextual factors, WEC was predicted to enhance service workers' perceptions of uplifts at work, and COE, which was introduced and developed in this chapter, was predicted to positively influence perceived uplifts, and negatively affect perceived hassles and turnover intentions. The individual difference variables, DT and HT, both introduced and developed in this chapter, were predicted to buffer service workers against the negative effects of EL, namely the experience of ED. Finally, provider UR, an individual difference variable also developed in this chapter, was predicted to enhance service perceptions of uplifts at work.

Implications for Theory

Theoretical relationships were proposed between negative work events and the emotional experiences of providers who perform EL as part of their job roles, and between positive work events and service performance. Particular to service jobs, the theoretical model presented here integrated the framework of daily hassles and uplifts into a model of EL and its consequences. Additionally, the proposed model shows that individual difference and contextual factors affect EE, turnover intentions, and performance outcomes, and therefore need to be taken into account in future studies of EL.

Implications for Practice

In view of the rapid growth in the service industry and service jobs, the issues of EL and its consequences at work are increasingly relevant. Numerous scholars from management and sociology contend that management today can ill afford to overlook the need to create and design a psychologically healthy (though not completely stress-free) environment for workers (cf. Abraham 1998; Greenhalgh 1982). For service organizations especially, the key to better service, and thus better organizational outcomes, ultimately rests upon the quality of the service performance of its employees. Service quality, in turn, depends upon providers' emotional experiences on the job. Furthermore, turnover, which is a major issue for many types of service work, is argued to be a direct consequence of providers' on-the-job well-being as represented by ED and EE.

There are three obvious implications for managers that flow from the proposed model. The first pertains to job design for service providers. The mediating role of perceived hassles on the ED-EE relationship suggests that one point of managerial intervention for stress or burnout could be aimed at reducing on-the-job hassles for providers. How service encounters are designed by organizations can make a difference. Management should design the procedures for service interactions to minimize the possibility of unnecessary hassles or job overload for providers; for example, by designing service scripts or procedures that are parsimonious, allowing for reasonable time and resources, and providing avenues for providers to divert customer requests or complaints when necessary. The appropriate designs will be contingent upon the nature of the required service interactions.

The second implication is in regard to the desirability of organizational efforts to foster a positive work environment for service employees. Since perceived uplifts are proposed to affect providers' customer service performance, management may consider enhancing positive events at work. While this may be achieved in various ways, we argue in our model that a high COE and a positive WEC are two contextual factors able to enhance perceived uplifts at work. Thus, management may, for example, look to reduce rigidity of emotional regulation or rules, impose less standardized scripts for emotional transactions, provide opportunities for informal socialization activities among employees, and appraise managers on their ability to foster a positive WEC.

Finally, the findings on provider individual differences in DT, HT, and UR have practical implications for recruitment criteria, training, and employee counseling. In addition to basing selection decisions upon the criteria of outward emotional "expressive behaviors" such as emotional stamina (Hochschild 1983), individual tolerance levels for dealing with situational hassles and conflicting emotions may also prove to be useful indicators for assessing the suitability and compatibility of potential applicants for the service role. In addition, provider training and counseling should include programs to assist existing employees to develop their coping mechanisms and tolerance levels.

Future Research

This chapter introduced and highlighted the importance of various new variables: for example, cultural orientation to emotion (COE) and provider dissonance tolerance (DT), hassles tolerance (HT), and uplift reactivity (UR). Further research on construct and measure development for these new constructs is needed. More efforts are needed to define or refine these new constructs and identify possible dimensions and develop indicators for testing.

Investigations of the links proposed in the model require validation in both positive EL and negative EL settings. Since it has been theorized that positive and negative EL have different consequences for providers, the role of tolerance-related variables in service jobs requiring negative EL may yield very different insights. In addition, since the EL-ED-EE sequence has a time element, future study would benefit from a longitudinal investigation of the issues we identified in our review.

Conclusion

Research efforts toward a holistic understanding of the emotional processes of service providers are relatively new but burgeoning. The central theme of this chapter has been to propose, develop, highlight, and investigate in a holistic fashion the important and intricate relationship between emotional environments and personal factors and the emotional consequences arising from EL performed in the service encounter context. This chapter has sought to contribute to knowledge in this field in three key ways. First, by clarifying the constructs of EL and ED. Second, by identifying, proposing, and operationalizing relevant organizational and individual differences variables. Third, and most importantly, is to present a new angle for understanding and considering emotions in work life by integrating affective events theory in the way of daily hassles and uplifts into the study of EL. The proposed model opens new areas for future research endeavors that have the potential of enriching understanding of the emotional life of people who perform service work.

16 EMOTIONAL LABOR AND THE DESIGN OF WORK

Wilfred J. Zerbe, Charmine E.J. Härtel, and Neal M. Ashkanasy

> *The beginning of wisdom is to call things by their right names.*
>
> —Chinese proverb

What Is Emotional Labor?

Jamie Callahan and Eric McCollum pay heed to the call of this proverb in the first contribution to this section. They begin by pointing out the confusion that exists in our use of the terms *emotion management, emotion labor,* and *emotion work.* Taking us back to Hochschild's (1983) intention, they argue that the distinction between emotion work and emotional labor rests on the distinction between use-value and exchange-value. "Emotional labor takes the classic form of the airline attendant smiling at the rude passenger. We also see emotional labor when the otherwise cheerful bill collector growls angrily at debtors to pay their bills." Emotional labor is performed in exchange for something of value—at work typically pay. In contrast, emotion work is not done as part of an exchange: "We are performing emotion work when we smile and say hello to a coworker in the hallway, even though we are having a bad day."

The "obscured variability" that Callahan and McCollum illuminate is a second dimension that distinguishes emotion work from emotional labor. Besides the use- versus exchange-value distinction, they point out that emotion labor is performed to conform to external expectations whereas emotion work is internally controlled. Thus the two terms differ in not one, but two respects. Further, two other forms of emotion management are possible. *Autonomous emotional labor* is of exchange-value but internally controlled, such as when an employee willingly chooses to manage an emotion in line with organizational expectations, what Rafaeli and Sutton (1989) called "faking in good faith." *Indirect emotional labor* has only use-value but is externally controlled. Callahan and McCollum cite the example of an employee who is cheerful and friendly at an organizational social event in order to meet organizational expectations but has no expectation of reward.

Callahan and McCollum identify the implications of the use-exchange distinction for managerial interventions, pointing out that different kinds of interventions are likely to have differential effects on each of their four kinds of emotion management. For example, they point out that when the kind of emotional management that is the target of the intervention is higher in exchange-value, then interventions that focus on structural factors, such as work design, will be more effective. In contrast, when emotional management that emphasizes use-value is the target, interventions aimed at relationships and culture will have greater impact.

The Effects of Emotional Labor

In the following chapter Lyndall Strazdins also uses the terms *emotional work*, *emotional labor*, and *emotion management*. For Strazdins, emotional labor is about managing one's feelings in order to achieve a particular emotional display. Emotional work, on the other hand, constitutes the behaviors used to alter the feelings of others. Clearly, they are strongly related. Indeed, the focus of Strazdins' chapter is the health effects of emotion work and labor and, more specifically, the dynamic by which these health effects occur. She points out that research results on the relationship between emotional labor and employee well-being are mixed—sometimes the dissonance between true feelings and those that workers display is shown to be related to emotional exhaustion. Yet sometimes emotional labor may "offer opportunities for self-expression, enjoyment and social integration." Strazdins argues that when emotional work involves handling positive emotions, it will not have harmful effects, but that when it involves handling negative emotions, health costs are more likely. The dynamic for this effect—emotional contagion—is the focus of her chapter.

Emotional contagion is the tendency of individuals to "catch" emotions from others, to experience in themselves the emotions they observe in others. Emotions can be caught through a number of mechanisms—empathy with another's experience, the prompting of one's own emotional memories by observing emotionally similar information, by arousing perceptions of the possibility of personal harm or benefit, and by the physiological effects of the tendency of individuals to synchronize facial expressions and other indicators of feelings. Thus, when the emotional labor that employees perform brings them into contact with positive emotions in others, they are more likely to experience positive emotions. When the emotional labor they perform requires engagement with negative emotions, they are more likely to experience negative emotions and attendant health effects.

Strazdins showed support for this framework in a study of health care workers. Employees were asked about how emotionally demanding their work contexts were, how frequently they themselves engaged in two aspects of emotional labor—improving positive emotions through work companionship, and repairing negative emotions through help and regulation. They were also asked about how much psychological distress they felt, their sense of the degree to which their ability to pursue valued goals was diminished, how much occupational stress they felt, and their intentions to leave their jobs. As predicted, the results showed that negative outcomes were associated with greater emotional demands and with greater engagement with negative emotions. Engagement with positive emotions decreased negative outcomes. The implications for managers that wish to maximize employee well-being are clear—foster opportunities for contact with emotionally positive experiences and provide support that reduces the effect of contact with negative experiences, such as opportunities to rest and recover and to receive emotional support, as well as training in emotion management skills such as those associated with emotional intelligence. Strazdins points out that the implementation of such measures is most likely in organizations that recognize and value emotional work and that provide a positive and integrative workplace climate.

When Is Emotional Labor a Problem?

Callahan and McCollum sought to help us understand clearly what emotional labor is, and Strazdins what its effects are. In the final chapter in this section, Charmine Härtel, Alice Hsu, and Maree Boyle combine these objectives with an explication of the characteristics of the workplace context and of employees to build a comprehensive, integrated model of emotional labor and its effects. Like the other chapters in this section, this one starts with emotional labor, which is defined as simply "the efforts to display or to feel organizational desired emotions." The core of the authors' model is the emotional labor—emotional dissonance—emotional exhaustion sequence. Emotional dissonance is the emotional state that employees experience when the emotions they express to fulfill organizational expectations do not match their true feelings. Härtel et al. argue that emotional labor results in emotional dissonance "in most cases" because organizational sanctions mitigate against employees disregarding display rules and expressing their true feelings. This second state is one of emotional deviance. The third possible state is emotional harmony, where felt, expressed, and expected emotions agree. The consequence of emotional dissonance is emotional exhaustion, the stressed state that results from conflict between true and displayed feelings.

Härtel, Hsu, and Boyle integrate everyday hassles and uplifts into their model as instances of affective events (Weiss and Cropanzano 1996). Hassles are irritating minor events, whereas uplifts are positive minor events. In the authors' model, the more emotional labor employees perform, the more hassles they perceive. Further, hassles are likely to exacerbate the effects of emotional dissonance, thus hassles are best represented as a mediator of the dissonance–exhaustion relationship. Härtel and her colleagues go on to consider the role of characteristics of the work context and of the provider. Two context variables are noted: the organization's cultural orientation to emotion and the emotional climate of the workgroup. The former refers to the degree to which an organization's culture reflects a concern for employee emotional well-being that "acknowledges, addresses, legitimizes, rewards, or compensates the existence and demands of organizational labor." Cultural orientation to emotion is posited to be positively associated with perceived uplifts and negatively with perceived hassles and turnover intentions. Workgroup emotional climate is the extent to which employees experience their workgroups as positive and as supportive and is posited to be positively associated with perceived uplifts. Finally, three individual characteristics are captured in the model: provider dissonance tolerance, which decreases the experience of emotional dissonance;

tolerance to hassles, which is positively associated with perceived uplifts and negatively associated with emotional dissonance; and reactivity to uplifts, which is positively associated with perceived uplifts. Finally,
two other constructs are included in the model: task performance, which
is related to perceived uplifts, and turnover intentions, which are said to
result from emotional exhaustion.

The implications of this model are numerous and cluster into three
categories. The first concerns the design of jobs. Härtel et al. say that
service provider jobs should be designed to reduce on-the-job hassles.
This can be accomplished through the use of parsimonious service scripts
and procedures, providing reasonable time and resources for employees
to do their work, and providing avenues for diversion of customer requests or complaints when such diversion is appropriate. Second, organizations should foster positive work environments for service employees
at both the workgroup level and at the level of organizational culture.
They point out the difference between organizational cultures in which
feelings of burnout and stress are viewed as indications of low employee
performance or of illness as opposed to those that see such effects as
inevitable consequences of doing emotion work, and the expression of
emotional reactions as healthy. Third, organizations can consider the
mechanisms of recruitment, training, and employee counseling to enhance the likelihood that service providers will be able to tolerate emotional dissonance and situational hassles and appreciate uplifts.

Making Sense of Terms and Conditions

What the three contributions in this section demonstrate is the complexity of the nature of emotional labor, the involved path from emotional
labor to its effects, and the intricate conditions under which it does or
does not have costs for employees and organizations. The value of each
chapter is its illumination of a part of this chain. Yet each, even the most
comprehensive, does not capture all of what the other chapters pose or
what might also be relevant to an understanding of emotional labor. For
example, in the Callahan and McCollum discussion of the difference
between the use and exchange value of emotional labor (defined broadly),
the distinction is made between internally and externally controlled
emotional labor. Härtel, Hsu, and Boyle acknowledge the argument that
employees who "fake in bad faith," who display fake emotions in response to external rather than internal rules, may be more likely to ex-

perience emotional dissonance. This suggests that the first element of the Härtel et al. model, "emotional labor," could be made more complicated by adding the distinction between the display of emotion to meet internal as opposed to external feeling rules. A second example is the argument that Strazdins makes that it is the valence of the emotion that employees catch through emotional contagion that determines the valence of its effects. Although not acknowledged by Strazdins, a strict reading of this claim is that emotional dissonance does not matter, that it is not the conflict between having to display positive (or negative) emotions even as one experiences negative (or positive) emotions that reduces well-being, but having to deal with negative emotions. The results of Strazdins's study show that contact with positive emotions is a good thing and that contact with negative emotions is a bad thing. Again, although Härtel et al. list three possible states that capture (some of) the combinations of emotional display and feeling, namely, dissonance (feelings ≠ displayed emotions), deviance (display ≠ organizational display rules), and harmony (feelings = displayed emotions = organizational display rules), they incorporate only emotional dissonance into their model and posit that it is dissonance that results in ill health, rather than being in a job that creates negative emotions. To a large extent, the entire literature on emotional labor is biased by an emphasis on research in situations where employees are asked to display positive emotions in situations they experience as negative. When such studies find a relationship between dissonance and health effects, the conclusion is that dissonance is the culprit because the way dissonance is typically measured confounds display and experience. The use of separate measures that allow the assessment of separate effects is one solution. Another would be to look for the effects of dissonance in situations where employees derive a great deal of pleasure from their jobs, but to do them well must display negative emotions.

While the addition of definitional complexity will not make the work of those who investigate emotional labor easier, it may be a route to reliable demonstration of the elusive link between emotional labor and well-being.

Designing Emotion Work

What each of these chapters shares is an implicit or explicit acknowledgment of the role of work design. Emotional labor is not often thought about as a product of work design (see Humphrey 2000, for an exception), but it is clearly about what employees are expected to do, how much control they have over what they do, the process by which they achieve the results they are expected to achieve, and the organizational supports that may or may not be provided. Emotional labor can be approached from a technical point of view, which is the one adopted when these and other authors talk about the use of mechanisms such as training, which all three chapters do, or of selection, rewards, and punishments to motivate emotional display, or job rotation or vertical loading to manage its effects, as the chapters by Callahan and McCollum and by Strazdins do. A the same time, it is clearly a socially mediated phenomenon, embedded in the interaction between the "service provider" and the person who receives the service, whether the latter is a customer or another employee, as each chapter recognizes. Again, all three chapters point out the role of the organizational context in either supporting or ignoring emotion work.

We began this commentary with a call for definitional clarity. The focus of this call was on our "dependent variable," namely, emotional labor. However, we can also critique our conception of what we mean by our "independent variable": work design. Consider, for example, the argument that work design is not something that exists outside of employees, something that is done for them, but rather something that they participate in. Wrzesniewski and Dutton (2001) have recently proposed the notion of "job crafting," in which employees are active shapers of their jobs, rather than passive recipients of jobs created by others. "Job crafters are individuals who actively compose both what their job is physically, by changing a job's task boundaries, what their job is cognitively, by changing the way they think about the relationships among job tasks, and what their job is relationally, by changing the interactions and relationships they have with others at work" (2001, 180). Whereas job design (Hackman and Oldham 1980) treats jobs as composed of static task elements, job crafting views jobs as having malleable task and relational boundaries.

Although the kinds of jobs that they use as prototypical examples are not limited to those commonly found in the emotional labor literature, they do include many. Nurses that expand the relational boundaries of their work to include family members are job crafting, as are hairdressers that solicit personal disclosures from clients despite sometimes being formally prohibited from doing so. Engineers that choose to manage connections among project team members are job crafting. Wrzesniewski and Dutton cite Rafaeli's (1989b) study of how cashiers changed features of their jobs by defining how they interacted with customers as job crafting.

Job Crafting and Emotional Labor

The elements of Wrzesniewski and Dutton's conceptual framework underscore the relevance of their job crafting model to emotional labor. First, the likelihood of job crafting depends in part on the perceived opportunity to do so, which stems from the degree to which job tasks are interdependent with those of others and how much discretion or freedom to job craft is permitted by monitoring systems in the job. Emotional labor, while often organizationally proscribed, is difficult to monitor and ultimately stems from individual decisions about what emotions to display and at what intensity. Second, the motivation for job crafting arises from employee desires to assert control over their work, create and sustain a positive self-image, and build human connections with others. Assertion of control may be the motive behind employee crafting to diminish organizational demands for emotion work, such as "when an overworked employee reduces the scope and scale of work activities to prevent exhaustion" (Wrzesniewski and Dutton 2000, 181). Employees may increase or decrease emotional labor as a way of maintaining their self-image. Ashforth and Humphrey (1993) and Pratt and Dutton (2000) have similarly argued that emotional labor may provide opportunities for self-expression tied to their sense of identity. Finally, the motive to build human connections is common to Wrzesniewski and Dutton's conception of job crafting and emotional labor.

Wrzesniewski and Dutton see job crafting as positive for employees, as resulting in added meaning of work and of desirable identities. They see job crafting as neither positive nor negative for organizations. If the results of actions taken to forge new meanings and identities align with organizational objectives, then job crafting can be a good thing for organizations. Again, the parallels with emotional labor are evident: when employees display emotions that agree with organizational expectations, the result is "harmony"; when they do not, it is "deviance."

The implications that Wrzesniewski and Dutton draw for research and practice are also instructive for the study of emotional labor. They point out, for example, the methodological challenges evident in tracking a dynamic construct and suggest that qualitative, narrative approaches are thus most appropriate. A similar lesson case can be made for emotional labor, given the complexity of constructs and terms discussed earlier. Wrzesniewski and Dutton also say that job crafting is "a process that can be affected only indirectly by managerial action" (2001, 195), through such mechanisms as rewards and incentives that encourage employees to revise relational and task boundaries. Further, organizations that wish employees to shape their own work as a means of employee development should provide active acknowledgment and encouragement.

We began this chapter with a description of Callahan and McCollum's work distinguishing use-value from exchange-value, where use-value was the pleasure that individuals gained from the work itself, as opposed to what it could be exchanged for. We ended with an examination of how employees can increase the personal value of their jobs, independent of what is rewarded by their organizations, by modifying the parts of the job that they control.

17 WHAT ARE THE MANAGEMENT TOOLS THAT COME OUT OF THIS?

Neal M. Ashkanasy, Charmine E.J. Härtel, and Wilfred J. Zerbe

So we come to the last chapter of our book. The question that we ask at this juncture is, What are the management tools that come out of all this? Indeed, one of our key objectives in compiling this collection of papers is that the focus should be on "managing" emotions, rather than on "research, theory, and practice," as in our first book (Ashkanasy, Härtel, and Zerbe 2000a). Papers from the *Second Conference on Emotions and Organizational Life* were selected for this book on the basis of quality *and* on the basis that they had something to say specifically about the management of emotions in workplace settings. Have we succeeded in producing a *practical* guide for managers? After all, the study of emotions in workplace settings is a relatively recent phenomenon and has only really been going at full steam since Ashforth and Humphrey (1995), the establishment of the Emonet discussion list in 1997, and the first *Conference on Emotions and Organizational Life* in 1998. Nonetheless, research to date is beginning to provide some important information that practicing managers ought to be considering in their day-to-day management practices. In this respect, the chapters in this book, including our own linking chapters (4, 8, 12, and 16), can be seen to provide a substantial list of "emotion management tools" that astute managers may wish to apply in their organizations.

The organization of this chapter mirrors that of the book as a whole. Basically, we aimed here to extract, from each of the four summary chapters in this book, a compendium of management tools that can be applied in a straightforward fashion on the shop floor by practicing managers. The topics are managing emotion in a changing workplace, managing emotion in workplace relationships, managing emotions in decision making, and managing emotional labor. In the end, we identified twenty-one such tools that managers can use to manage emotions in the workplace, as follows in Table 17.1.

In the following, we discuss each of these tools in more detail, within the context of each of the four sections of this volume.

Managing Emotion in a Changing Workplace

As Härtel and Zerbe point out in Chapter 4, the management of emotions has developed a mystique of its own. For too long, management orthodoxy has dictated that management is an impassionate, rational process (see Ashforth and Humphrey 1993). As a result, seven myths about change and emotions have developed, as follows:

- Employees' negative emotional reactions reflect resistance to organizational change.
- Emotions need to be managed away or overcome in order for change initiatives to succeed.
- Emotions are the reason for employee withdrawal and destructive behavior during organizational change.
- People fear change in general and therefore oppose it.
- Emotions represent chaotic or irrational responses.
- Negative emotions have negative consequences for the individual and the organization while positive emotions have positive consequences.
- Emotions are solely the product of individuals.

Based on the chapters in Section 1, Härtel and Zerbe systematically debunk these myths. Instead, they advocate a proactive approach to emotion management, where managers work with emotion, rather than regarding emotion as something that has to be controlled or dismissed. This leads to our first six "management tools."

Tool 1: Maintain Open and Quality Communication

Our first tool is based on Chapter 2 (Paterson and Härtel), which argues that communications have a direct effect on individuals' perceptions of the favorability of the change and their own outcomes. Therefore, the open and

Table 17.1

Management Tools

1. Maintain open and quality communication.
2. Provide opportunity for stakeholder input into planning.
3. Provide appropriate support systems.
4. Safeguard organizational history.
5. Display interpersonal sensitivity by conveying regret for adversity and social esteem.
6. Manage "affective events."
7. Provide training and development to foster emotional display recognition and management skills in managers and employees.
8. Teach leaders how to set norms that create positive emotional climates in teams and cultures.
9. Teach employees how to diagnose emotional displays
10. Teach employees and managers what events are likely to evoke emotional displays.
11. Develop emotional intelligence in employees and leaders.
12. Recognize the role of both intuitive and analytical decision making in management.
13. Engender a positive outlook conducive to intuitive decision making.
14. Teach managers and employees that effective decisions require an optimum mix of cognitive intellect and emotional regulation.
15. Teach managers that the strategic use of emotions by managers requires judicious use of power.
16. Align rules for engaging in emotional labor with organizational goals.
17. Use indirect methods (e.g., interpersonal dynamics, culture) to influence indirect emotional labor.
18. Develop specific interventions to improve emotional management: (1) leadership development programs; (2) stress management and wellness programs; (3) work redesign to alleviate "emotional labor dysfunction"; and (4) a formal back stage to permit employees to deal with emotions.
19. Provide employees with the opportunity to "restore their own emotions."
20. Design service provider jobs so that they reduce on-the-job hassles.
21. Create an organizational culture that recognizes the legitimacy of emotion.

regular provision of high-quality information that helps people understand the change's outcomes for them as individuals will help reduce uncertainty and, in turn, anxiety. As much as possible, communications should assist individuals to see how the change can benefit their personal goals. Open, quality information, as well, helps demonstrate the interpersonal sensitivity, personal ethicality, and trustworthiness of the decision makers.

Tool 2: Provide Opportunity for Stakeholder Input Into Planning

Another key way that change leaders can reduce uncertainty and anxiety, and therefore increase adaptation to change, is to provide the stakeholders of the change initiative with the opportunity to participate in planning. As does open and quality communication, the opportunity for input helps employees understand change's outcomes for them as individuals.

Tool 3: Provide Appropriate Support Systems

The provision of appropriate support systems can help clarify the nature of the threat posed by the change as well as help employees to choose beneficial problem-focused and emotion-focused coping strategies that have positive outcomes for themselves and the organization (see Grzywacz and Marks 2000).

Tool 4: Safeguard Organizational History

As Paterson and Härtel note in Chapter 2, organizational change is a process that unfolds over time. And time itself, as Kiefer (Chapter 3) observes, marks in people's minds what change in a given organization means. Consequently, organizations need to safeguard their change history so that future change endeavors are not impeded by past wrongs (cf. Fisher 2000). Additionally, as Kiefer notes, it is important to know the history of emotional episodes in order to lead change adequately.

Tool 5: Display Interpersonal Sensitivity by Conveying Regret for Adversity and Social Esteem

Paterson and Härtel argue in Chapter 2 that perceptions about the interpersonal sensitivity, personal ethicality, and trustworthiness of the change decision makers play an important role in employee adaptation to change (cf. George 2000). One of the ways this is demonstrated is by the expression of regret for adversity brought on by the change. Kiefer points out that the potential threats employees perceive range from loss of one's job to fear of not being able to contribute to organizational goals to loss of one's professional identity. Since these fears, she argues, are grounded in basic values and needs such as the need to have an impact and feel needed, organizations need to pay particular attention to social esteem during periods of change.

Tool 6: Manage "Affective Events"

Similar to Cynthia Fisher's suggestion that emotional events such as hassles and uplifts need to be managed in the workplace (Fisher 1998,

2000; Fisher and Noble 2000), Kiefer alludes in Chapter 3 to the possibility of management indirectly dealing with emotions by shaping or managing the underlying events. In order to effectively do this, she suggests, "a profound analysis of the situation" must be undertaken following each emotion-eliciting event.

Managing Emotion in Workplace Relationships

In Chapter 8, Härtel and Ashkanasy discuss the three chapters in the book that deal with the role of emotional displays in social communication. Given the practical focus of the present volume, the chapters in this section are of special interest. This is because they instruct as to the emotion management skills specifically required to respond to workplace emotional displays. Five tools emerge from these chapters, as follows.

Tool 7: Provide Training and Development to Foster Emotional Display Recognition and Management Skills in Managers and Employees

In Chapter 5, Ayoko and Härtel's research revealed that many group leaders do not know how to manage emotional displays. They consequently try to avoid them. Ultimately, this is to the detriment of team members, team climate, and team effectiveness. They, along with Jones and Rittman, argue that employees' capacity to acknowledge, to recognize, to monitor, to discriminate, and to attend to group members' emotions need to be developed for individual, group, and organizational effectiveness and well-being.

Tool 8: Teach Leaders How to Set Norms That Create Positive Emotional Climates in Teams and Cultures

In Chapters 5 and 6, Ayoko and Härtel and Jones and Rittman argue that leaders need to develop and to maintain a positive workgroup emotional climate, manifested in the group's norms and routines related to feeling. This also implies the need for monitoring and development activities.

Tool 9: Teach Employees How to Diagnose Emotional Displays

In Chapter 6, Jones and Rittman suggest that Lang's work on emotional displays may provide a useful basis for diagnosing the motives and needs signalled by such displays. In particular, employees should be taught that "positive" emotions generally indicate that a person is approaching realization of a desirable outcome whereas "negative" emotions generally indicate that a desirable outcome is eluding one. Aversive arousal, on the other hand, generally signals that a person is approaching an undesirable outcome whereas relief generally signals that an undesirable outcome has been averted. Additionally, employees should be taught that the likelihood of an emotional display driving action will depend upon the level of uncertainty present and whether the person has reason to try to exert control over the outcome.

Tool 10: Teach Employees and Managers What Events Are Likely to Evoke Emotional Displays

Emotional displays are generated by events or the anticipation of events. If employees are taught the types of events that tend to generate, in particular, negative emotions, this will help them manage situations in ways to minimize negative emotion-evoking events as well as to enhance positive emotion-evoking events. Some such events are task-related conflict or conflicts over how to achieve a goal (Ayoko and Härtel), unavailability of resources (Côté and Moskowitz), dissimilarity in beliefs, views, values, and interaction styles (Ayoko and Härtel), diversity in culture, race, and tenure (Ayoko and Härtel), in-group/out-group differentiation (Ayoko and Härtel), and low interpersonal attraction (Ayoko and Härtel).

Tool 11: Develop Emotional Intelligence in Employees and Leaders

Once individuals have diagnosed an emotional display, they also need to know how to respond to it. Consequently, developing emotional intelligence in employees will increase the effectiveness of interventions in emotional displays and minimize the likelihood of taking actions that create harm (see also Chapter 10 and Tool 14). Additionally, as Côté and Moskowitz suggest, leaders can use knowledge of emotion-evoking events to improve their relationships with subordinates. In particular, they admonish supervisors to increase the frequency of social interactions with subordinates that elicit pleasant mood and decrease the frequency of interactions with subordinates that elicit unpleasant mood.

Managing Emotions in Decision Making

Just as traditional management literature has dismissed emotions in the management of change, so, too, have emotions been traditionally viewed as outside the domain of "rational" decision making (e.g., see Simon 1976). In Chapter 12, Ashkanasy and Härtel argue, based on Damasio (1994), that this view is profoundly flawed. Indeed, Damasio makes is clear that emotions lie at the very heart of decision making. The three chapters in Section 3 take up this theme, but do so from different angles, resulting in six more tools.

Tool 12: Recognize the Role of Both Intuitive and Analytical Decision Making in Management

Sinclair and her colleagues point out in Chapter 9 that the use of intuition in decision making depends on the nature of the situation and of the problem being addressed, as well as the personality and style of the manager concerned. Intuitive decision making can therefore be expected when problems are ill defined and/or unusual. Interestingly, Sinclair and her associates also suggest that intuition is more likely to be used when a decision is important or has consequences for the decision maker. Intuitive decision making is also expected in fast-paced and entrepreneurial industries. Finally, intuitive decision making is likely to be the preferred style for experienced managers who are more emotional in outlook, more risk tolerant, and more creative.

Tool 13: Engender a Positive Outlook Conducive to Intuitive Decision Making

According to Sinclair and her associates, effective intuitive decision making is associated with moderate positive affect. If the affect is more than moderate, that is satisfactory, too, so long as the manager's focus is on the outcome and not on the affect itself. It seems, therefore, that a creative intuitive style to management is associated with positive affect where the manager keeps his or her focus on the task ahead. Further, feeling good about the success of intuitive decision making is conducive to continuing to use this approach.

Tool 14: Teach Managers and Employees That Effective Decisions Require an Optimum Mix of Cognitive Intellect and Emotional Regulation

The idea of emotional intelligence has been widely promulgated in the professional literature (e.g., see Cooper and Sawaf 1997; Goleman 1998b)—perhaps even overdone (see Chapter 1). In Chapter 10, Aaron Ben-Ze'ev takes a more considered look at the conceptual issues in emotional intelligence. In this view, emotional intelligence, rather than being a broad social intelligence as suggested by Goleman, is an approach to emotional regulation. From this perspective, rather than emotional intelligence being an end in itself, it may be more appropriately regarded as a means to augment cognitive intelligence. Taken in conjunction with Tools 12 and 13, the picture that emerges is that the most effective approach to decision making does not rule out the value of emotions. Instead, emotions must be managed in such a fashion that the manager's cognitive abilities can be utilized to their maximum effectiveness.

Tool 15: Teach Managers That the Strategic Use of Emotions by Managers Requires Judicious Use of Power

Gibson and Schroeder in Chapter 11 take up the issue of power and its relation to emotion. They argue that managers know little of how to use power effectively in their day-to-day roles. In particular, managers need training in order to understand power and its effects. Managers with too much power become arrogant and oblivious to the effects of their power on their subordinates. On the other hand, by understanding power and its effects, and becoming sensitive to the effects of power on subordinates, managers can learn to regulate the way that they present emotional cues to their subordinates. More tools for managing emotional labor are presented in the following section.

Managing Emotional Labor

In Chapter 16, Zerbe, Härtel, and Ashkanasy summarize the fourth and final section of this volume: managing emotional labor. Indeed, it is here that six of the most useful of the tools for management that we have identified lie. Emotional labor is more directly associated with behavior at the workface than other aspects of emotion discussed in this volume, so this is not surprising. The tools arising from this section are many and varied.

Tool 16: Align Rules for Engaging in Emotional Labor with Organizational Goals

Callahan and McCollum in Chapter 13 make a distinction between emotion management that has "use-value" and emotion management that has "exchange-value." Further, emotional management can be either internally controlled to meet personal expectations and goals or externally controlled to meet organizational expectations. Thus, managers seeking to influence emotional labor (which is externally controlled and which has exchange-value) should use structural mechanisms aligned with organizational goals. The kinds of mechanisms commonly talked about in the literature on emotional labor fit in this category, such as organizationally mediated rewards and inducements, and structures such as job descriptions and direct supervision.

Tool 17: Use Indirect Methods (e.g., Interpersonal Dynamics, Culture) to Influence Indirect Emotional Labor

Organizations seeking to influence indirect emotional labor (which is externally controlled and which has use-value) should use more indirect mechanisms, such as those that influence interpersonal dynamics and the culture of the organization. Similarly, influence over emotion work (which is internally controlled and which has use-value) is best managed through indirect mechanisms. Although not suggested by Callahan and McCollum, organizations might be wise to ensure that indirect emotional labor or emotion work that conforms with organizational goals not be discouraged through the overuse of externally mediated exchanges. Extending hypotheses from the work on intrinsic motivation, the argument could be made that individuals' motivation to engage in emotion work that they enjoy for its own sake (the definition of use-value) might decrease with the addition of external rewards. Indeed, autonomous emotional labor is at risk from such overjustification. Emotion management that employees perform because they want to, but that has exchange-value, is desirable in that it meets organizational goals without the possible costs of emotional labor. Although Callahan and McCollum propose the use of structural mechanisms to encourage it, softer, more culturally based support might be wiser.

Tool 18: Four Specific Areas of Intervention Through Which Organizations Can Improve Emotional Management

18.1. Leadership Development Programs should develop the connection between transformational theories of leadership and emotional expression and control (see also Ashkanasy and Tse 2000). As such, these programs can be used to increase the interpersonal capability of an organization's members.

18.2. Stress Management and Wellness Programs have the potential to increase self-awareness and thus interpersonal relationships, as well as provide avenues for the release of stress that can accompany emotional labor.

18.3. Work Redesign to alleviate "emotional labor dysfunction," which can be inferred to be the negative effects of the emotional dissonance that can be part of emotional labor. Callahan and McCollum point out that vertical loading can provide individuals with more control over work and thus alleviate the feeling of loss of control that can come with emotional labor. Increasing employee flexibility through job rotation can facilitate movement from the emotional labor intensive "front stage" to the "back stage," where respite is possible.

18.4. A Formal Back Stage area may also contribute to the creation of an organizational culture that acknowledges the importance of emotion management and legitimizes its existence.

Tool 19: Provide Employees with the Opportunity to "Restore Their Own Emotions"

Like Callahan and McCollum, Strazdins in Chapter 14 identifies the importance of providing employees with the opportunity to "restore their own emotions." The presence of an organizational culture that recognizes and values emotional work is key to supporting such opportunities. Based on the conclusion that handling positive emotions has benefits to employees and that handling negative emotions does harm, Strazdins identifies ways that organizations can seek to minimize the risks and maximize the benefits of emotion work. In particular, employee skill at managing emotions that arise as a result of emotional contagion suggests that training in skills such as those that are part of emotional intelligence would be beneficial.

Tool 20: Design Service Provider Jobs So That They Reduce on-the-Job Hassles

In the final contributed chapter in this volume (Chapter 15), Härtel, Hsu, and Boyle point out that service provider jobs should be designed to reduce on-the-job hassles, such as by designing parsimonious service scripts and procedures, allowing reasonable time and resources, and providing avenues for diversion of customer requests or complaints.

Tool 21: Create an Organizational Culture That Recognizes the Legitimacy of Emotion

Our final tool is also from Chapter 15. By creating an organizational culture that is oriented to emotion, management can foster a positive work environment for service employees. Such a culture "acknowledges, addresses, legitimizes, rewards, or compensates the existence and demands of organizational labor." Härtel and her colleagues provide a long list of specific practices and policies that support the creation of such a culture. Further, they recommend that managers seek to provide a positive workgroup emotional climate that provides social support to emotion workers.

Conclusion: It Is Possible to Manage Emotions in the Workplace

Contrary to much that has been written in the management literature, recognition and management of emotions is a legitimate role for managers. By "management," however, we do not refer to "suppression" or "control." Instead we refer to the considered role of emotion as a part of everyday work and management of work. While there is still much that we have to learn about emotions in organizational settings, the chapters in this volume, and especially the list of twenty-one "tools" that we have identified in this chapter, suggest that there is much that we can utilize from what we know already.

In our preface to the present volume, we described our role in the development of research into emotions in workplace settings. This book is the second in the series of books arising out of the biannual conferences on emotions and organizational life. The third conference will be held following publication of this book, in July 2002, and will result in the next book in this series. The 2004 conference is already in the early planning stages. By our activities, we hope that we can engender a fuller understanding of this fascinating and exciting new field that will ultimately benefit the science and practice of management of tomorrow's organizations.

REFERENCES

Abraham, R. 1998. "Emotional Dissonance in Organizations: Antecedents, Consequences, and Moderators." *Genetic, Social and General Psychological Monographs* 124 (2): 229–246.
———. 1999. "Negative Affectivity: Moderator or Confound in Emotional Dissonance-Outcome Relationships?" *Journal of Psychology* 133 (1): 61–72.
Adams, J. 1965. "Inequity in Social Exchange." In *Advances in Experimental Social Psychology,* ed. L. Berkowitz, 267–299. New York: Academic Press.
Adams, R.M. 1985. "Involuntary Sins." *The Philosophical Review* 94: 3–31.
Adelmann, P.K. 1995. "Emotional Labor as a Potential Source of Job Stress." In *Organizational Risk Factors for Job Stress,* ed. S.L. Sauter and L.R. Murphy, 371–381. Washington, DC: American Psychological Association.
Agor, W.H. 1984. *Intuitive Management: Integrating Left and Right Brain Management Skills.* New York: Prentice Hall Press.
———. 1986. *The Logic of Intuitive Decision-Making: A Research-Based Approach for Top Management.* New York: Quorum Books.
———, ed. 1989. *Intuition in Organizations: Leading and Managing Productively.* Newbury Park, CA: Sage.
Agyris, C. 1962. *Interpersonal Competence and Organisational Effectiveness.* Homewood, IL: Dorsey Press.
Alliger, G.M., and Williams, K.J. 1993. "Using Signal-Contingent Experience Sampling Methodology to Study Work in the Field: A Discussion and Illustration Examining Task Perceptions and Mood." *Personnel Psychology* 46: 252–549.
Allinson, C.W., and Hayes, J. 1996. "The Cognitive Style Index: a Neuropsychological Theory of Positive Affect and its Influence on Cognition." *Psychological Review* 106: 529–550.
Alloy, L.B., and Abramson, L.T. 1979. "Judgment of Contingency in Depressed and Non-Depressed Students: Sadder But Wiser?" *Journal of Experimental Psychology General* 108: 441–485.
———. 1982. "Learned Helplessness, Depression, and the Illusion of Control." *Journal of Personality and Social Psychology* 42: 1114–1126.
Alloy, L.B., Abramson, L.Y., and Viscusi, D. 1981. "Induced Mood and the Illusion of Control." *Journal of Personality and Social Psychology* 41: 1129–1140.
Allport, G.W. 1954. *The Nature of Prejudice.* Cambridge, MA: Addison-Wesley.
Ambady, N., and Rosenthal, R. 1992. "Thin Slices of Expressive Behavior as Predictors of Interpersonal Consequences: A Meta-Analysis." *Psychological Bulletin* 111: 256–274.

Ambrose, M., Harland, L., and Kulik, C. 1991. "Influence of Social Comparisons on Perceptions of Organizational Fairness." *Journal of Applied Psychology* 76: 239–246.

Andersen, J.A. 2000. "Intuition in Managers: Are Intuitive Managers More Effective?" *Journal of Managerial Psychology* 15: 46–67.

Aristotle, 1984. In *The Complete Works of Aristotle: The Revised Oxford Translation,* ed. J. Barnes. Princeton: Princeton University Press, 1984.

Arvey, R.W., Renz, G.L., and Watson, T.W. 1998. "Emotionality and Job Performance: Implications for Personnel Selection." *Research in Personnel and Human Resources Management* 16: 103–147.

Ashby, F.G., Isen, A.M., and Turken, U. 1999. "A Neuropsychological Theory of Positive Affect and its Influence in Cognition." *Psychological Review* 106: 529–550.

Ashford, S. 1988. "Individual Strategies for Coping With Stress During Organizational Transitions." *Journal of Applied Behavioural Science* 24: 19–36.

Ashford, S.J., Lee, C., and Bobko, P. 1989. "Content, Causes and Consequences of Job Insecurity: A Theory-Based Measure and Substantive Test." *Academy of Management Journal* 32: 803–829.

Ashforth, B.E., and Fried, Y. 1988. "The Mindlessness of Organizational Behaviors." *Human Relations* 41: 305–329.

Ashforth, B.E., and Humphrey, R.H. 1993. "Emotional Labor in Service Roles: The Influence of Identity." *Academy of Management Review* 18: 88–115.

———. 1995. "Emotion in the Workplace: A Reappraisal." *Human Relations* 48: 97–125

Ashkanasy, N.M., Fisher, C.D., and Härtel, C.E.J. 1998 (April). "Investigating the Causes and Consequences of Emotional Experience at Work." In *Emotion At Work: New Research Directions,* Symposium Presented at the Annual Meeting of The Society of Australasian Social Psychologists, Christchurch, NZ.

Ashkanasy, N.M., Härtel, C.E.J., and Zerbe, W.J., eds. 2000a. *Emotions in the Workplace: Research, Theory, and Practice.* Westport, CT: Quorum Books.

———. 2000b. "Emotions in the Workplace: Research, Theory, and Practice— Introduction." In *Emotions in the Workplace: Research, Theory, and Practice,* ed. N.M. Ashkanasy, C.E.J. Härtel, and W.J. Zerbe, 3–18. Westport, CT: Quorum Books.

Ashkanasy, N.M., and Tse, B. 2000. Transformational Leadership as Management of Emotion: a Conceptual Review. In *Emotions in the Workplace: Research, Theory, and Practice,* ed. N.M. Ashkanasy, C.E.J. Härtel, and W.J. Zerbe, 221– 236. Westport, CT: Quorum Books.

Averill, J.R., Catlin, G., and Chon, K.K. 1990. *Rules of Hope.* New York: Springer-Verlag.

Axelrod, R.H., and Sashkin, M. 2000. *Outcome Measurement in a Leadership Development Program.* Paper Presented at The Academy of Management, Toronto, Canada, August.

Ayoko, O.B., and Härtel, C.E.J. 2000. "Cultural Differences at Work: How Managers Deepen or Lessen the Cross-Racial Divide in Their Workgroups." *Queensland Review* 7 (1): 77–87.

Babakus, E., Cravens, D., Johnston, M., and Moncrief, W. 1999. "The Role of Emotional Exhaustion in Sales Force Attitude and Behavior Relationships." *Journal of the Academy of Marketing Science* 27 (1): 58–70.

Bagozzi, R.P., Gopinath, M., and Nyer, P.U. 1999. "The Role of Emotions in Marketing." *Journal of the Academy of Marketing Sciences* 27: 184–206.

Bailey, F.G. 1983. *The Tactical Uses of Passion.* Ithaca, NY: Cornell University Press.

Bar-On, R. 1997. *Bar-On Emotional Quotient Inventory: A Measure of Emotional Intelligence.* Toronto: Multi-Health Systems.

Baron, R.A. 1993a. "Affect and Organizational Behavior: When and Why Feeling Good (or Bad) Matters." In *Social Psychology in Organizations,* ed. J.K. Murningham, 63–88. Englewood Cliffs, NJ: Prentice Hall.

———. 1993b. "Interviewers' Moods and Evaluations of Job Applicant: The Role of Applicant Qualifications." *Journal of Applied Social Psychology* 23: 253–271.

Barry, B. 2001. "Influence in Organizations from a Social Expectancy Perspective." In *The Use and Abuse of Pow,* ed. A.Y. Lee-Chai and J.A. Bargh, 19–40. Philadelphia: Psychology Press.

Barry, B., and Oliver, R.L. 1996. "Affect in Dyadic Negotiation: A Model and Propositions." *Organizational Behavior and Human Decision Processes* 67: 127–143.

Barry, B., and Watson, M.R. 1996. "Communication Aspects of Dyadic Social Influence in Organizations: A Review and Integration of Conceptual and Empirical Developments." In *Communication Yearbook,* ed. B.R. Burleson, 269–318. Thousand Oaks, CA: Sage.

Barsade, S.G. In press. "The Ripple Effect: Emotional Contagion in Groups. *Administrative Sciences Quarterly.*

Barsade, S.G., Ward, A.J., Turner, J.D.F., and Sonnenfeld, J.A. 2000. "To Your Heart's Content: A Model of Affective Diversity in Top Management Teams." *Administrative Science Quarterly* 45: 802–836.

Bartel, C.A., and Saavedra, R. 2000. "The Collective Construction of Work Group Moods." *Administrative Science Quarterly* 45: 197–231.

Basch, J., and Fisher, C.D. 2000. "Affective Events-Emotions Matrix: A Classification of Work Events and Associated Emotions." In *Emotions in the Workplace: Research, Theory, and Practice,* ed. N.M. Ashkanasy, C.E.J. Härtel, and W.J. Zerbe, 36–48. Westport, CT: Quorum Books.

Bass, B.M. 1998. *Transformational Leadership: Industrial, Military, and Educational Impact.* Mahwah, NJ: Lawrence Erlbaum.

Bass, B.M., and Avolio, B.J. 1990. "The Implications of Transactional and Transformational Leadership for Individual, Team, and Organizational Development." *Research in Organizational Change and Development* 4: 231–272.

———, eds. 1994. *Improving Organizational Effectiveness: Through Transformational Leadership.* Thousand Oaks, CA: Sage.

Bastick, T. 1982. *Intuition: How We Think and Act.* New York: John Wiley.

Behling, O., and Eckel, N.L. 1991. "Making Sense Out of Intuition." *Academy of Management Executive* 5: 46–54.

Bell, P.A., and Baron, R.A. 1990. "Affect and Aggression." In *Affect and Social Behaviour,* ed. B.S. Moore and A.M. Isen, 64–88. Cambridge, UK: Cambridge University Press.

Bellas, M.L. 1999. "Emotional Labor in Academia: the Case of Professors." *The Annals of the American Academy of Political and Social Science* 561: 8–26.

Bem, S.L. 1974. "The Measurement of Psychological Androgyny." *Journal of Consulting and Clinical Psychology* 42: 155–162.

Ben-Ze'ev, A. 1993. *The Perceptual System: A Philosophical and Psychological Perspective.* New York: Peter Lang.

———. 2000. *The Subtlety of Emotions.* Cambridge, MA: MIT Press.

———. 2002. "The Logic of Emotions." In *Philosophy and The Emotions,* ed. A. Hatzimoysis. Cambridge: Cambridge University Press.

Bergson, H. 1907. *Creative Evolution.* New York: Holt.

Berkowitz, L. 1978. "Whatever Happened to the Frustration-Aggression Hypothesis?" *American Behavioral Scientist* 21: 691–708.

———. 1982. "Aversive Conditions as Stimuli to Aggression." *Advances in Experimental Social Psychology* 15: 249–288.

Berscheid, E. 1983. "Emotion." In *Close Relationships,* ed. H. Kelley, E. Berscheid, A. Christensen, J. Harvey, T. Huston, G. Levinger, E. McClintock, A. Peplau, and D.R. Peterson. New York: W.H. Freeman.

Best, R.G., Downey, R.G., and Jones, R.G. 1997. "Incumbent Perceptions of Emotional Work Requirements." Paper presented at Society for Industrial and Organizational Psychology, St. Louis.

Bies, R., Martin, C., and Brockner, J. 1993. "Just Laid Off But Still a 'Good Citizen'? Only If the Process Is Fair." *Employee Rights and Responsibility Journal* 6: 227–237.

Bies, R., and Moag, J. 1986. "Interactional Justice: Communication Criteria of Fairness." In *Research on Negotiation in Organizations,* ed. R. Lewicki, B. Sheppard, and B. Bazerman, 1: 43–55. Greenwich, CT: JAI Press.

Bion, W.R. 1961. *Experiences in Groups and Other Papers.* New York: Basic Books.

———. 1994. *Experiences in Groups and Other Papers.* New York: Routledge.

Bitran, G.R., and Lojo, M. 1993. "A Framework for Analyzing Service Operations." *European Management Journal* 11 (3): 271–282.

Bless, H., Bohner, G., Schwarz, N., and Strack, F. 1990. "Mood and Persuasion: A Cognitive Response Analysis." *Personality and Social Psychology Bulletin 16:* 331–345.

Bless, H., Mackie, D.M., and Schwarz, N. 1992. "Mood Effects on Attitude Judgments: Independent Effects of Mood Before and After Message Elaboration." *Journal of Personality and Social Psychology* 63: 585–595.

Bless, H., Schwarz, N., Clore, G.L., Golisano, V., and Rabe, C. 1996. "Mood and the Use of Scripts: Does a Happy Mood Really Lead to Mindlessness?" *Journal of Personality and Social Psychology* 71: 665–679.

Bodenhausen, G.V., Kramer, G.P., and Süsser, K. 1994. "Happiness and Stereotypic Thinking in Social Judgment." *Journal of Personality and Social Psychology* 66: 621–632.

Boles, J., Johnston, M., and Hair, J. 1997. "Role Stress, Work-Family Conflict and Emotional Exhaustion: Inter-Relationships and Effects on Some Work-Related Consequences." *Journal of Personal Selling and Sales Management* 17 (1): 17–28.

Booth-Butterfield, M., and Booth-Butterfield, S. 1990. "Conceptualizing Affect as Information in Communication Production." *Human Communication Research* 16: 451–476.

Boucouvalas, M. 1997. "Intuition: The Concept and the Experience." In *Intuition: The Inside Story. Interdisciplinary Perspectives,* ed. R. Davis-Floyd and P.S. Arvidson, 3–18. New York: Routledge.

Bowen, M. 1978. *Family Therapy in Clinical Practice*. New York: Jason Aronson.

Bowers, K.S., Farvolden, B., and Mermigis, L. 1995. "Intuitive Antecedents of Insight." In *The Creative Cognition Approach*, ed. S.M. Smith, T.B. Ward, and R.A. Finke. Cambridge, MA: MIT Press.

Boyle, M.V. 1997. *Love the Work, Hate the System: A Qualitative Study of Emotionality, Organizational Culture and Masculinity Within an Interactive Service Workplace*. Unpublished doctoral dissertation, University of Queensland.

———. 1999. *Factors influencing the Quality of Emotional Process Work: The Influence of Organizational Legitimacy*. Paper Presented At the 3rd Meeting of The Australian International Industrial and Organizational Psychology Conference, Brisbane, June.

Braithwaite, V. 1990. *Bound to Care*. Sydney: Allen and Unwin.

Brehmer, B. 1976. "Social Judgement Theory and the Analysis of Interpersonal Conflict." *Psychological Bulletin* 83: 985–1003.

Brewer, M.B. 1979. "In-Group Bias in Minimal Intergroup Situation: A Cognitive–Emotional Analysis." *Psychological Bulletin* 86: 307–324

Brief, A.P., and Roberson, L. 1989. "Job-Attitude Organization—An Exploratory Study." *Journal of Applied Social Psychology* 19: 717–727.

Brockman, E.N., and Simmonds, P.G. 1997. "Strategic Decision-Making: The Influence of CEO Experience and Use of Tacit Knowledge." *Journal of Managerial Issues* 9: 454–467.

Brockner, J., Dewitt, R., Grover, S., and Reed, T. 1990. "When It Is Especially Important to Explain Why: Factors Affecting Managers Explanations of a Layoff and Survivors' Reactions to the Layoff." *Journal of Experimental and Social Psychology* 26: 389–470.

Brockner, J., and Wiesenfeld, B. 1993. "Living on the Edge: The Effects of Job Layoffs on Those Who Remain." In *Social Psychology in Organizations: Advances in Theory and Research*, ed. J.K. Murnighan, 119–140. Englewood Cliffs, NJ: Prentice Hall.

———. 1996. "An Interactive Framework for Explaining Reactions to Decisions: Interactive Effects of Outcomes and Procedures. *Psychological Bulletin* 120: 189–208.

Bruins, J. 1999. "Social Power and Influence Tactics: A Theoretical Introduction." *Journal of Social Issues* 55: 7–14.

Bryman, A. 1992. *Charisma and Leadership in Organizations*. Newbury Park, CA: Sage.

Bryne, D. 1971. *The Attraction Paradigm*. New York: Academic Press.

Buck, R. 1988. "Nonverbal Communication: Spontaneous and Symbolic Aspects." *American Behavioral Scientist* 31: 341–354.

Burke, L.A., and Miller, M.K. 1999. "Taking the Mystery out of Intuitive Decision-Making." *Academy of Management Executive* 13: 91–99.

Burke, M., Boruski, C., and Hurley, A. 1992. "Reconceptualizing Psychological Climate in a Retail Service Environment: A Multiple-Stakeholder Perspective." *Journal of Applied Psychology* 77 (5): 717–729.

Burke, M.J., Brief, A.P., George, J.M., Roberson, L., and Webster, J. 1989. "Measuring Affect at Work: Confirmatory Analyses of Competing Mood Structures with Conceptual Linkage to Cortical Regulatory Systems." *Journal of Personality and Social Psychology* 57: 1091–1102.

Burneko, G. 1997. "Intuition, Integral Consciousness, and the Pattern That Connects." In *Intuition: The Inside Story,* ed. R. Davies-Floyd and P.S. Arvidson, 81–100. New York: Routledge.

Cacioppo, J.T., and Gardner, W.L. 1999. "Emotion." *Annual Review of Psychology* 50: 191–214.

Cacioppo, J.T., Gardner, W.L., and Berntson, G.G. 1999. "The Affect System Has Parallel and Integrative Processing Components: Form Follows Function." *Journal of Personality and Social Psychology* 76: 839–855.

Caldwell, D.F., and Burger, J.M. 1997. "Personality and Social Influence Strategies in the Workplace." *Personality and Social Psychology Bulletin* 23: 1003–1012.

Callahan, J.L. 2000a. "Emotion Management and Organizational Functions: A Case Study of Patterns in Not-for-Profit Organizations." *Human Resource Development Quarterly* 11 (3): 245–268.

———. 2000b. "Women in a 'Combat, Masculine-Warrior Culture': The Performance of Emotion Work." *Journal of Behavioral and Applied Management* 1 (2): 104–114.

———. In press. "Masking the Need for Organizational Change: Emotion Structuration in a Non-Profit Organization." *Organization Studies.*

Cameron, K. 1998. "Strategic Organizational Downsizing: An Extreme Case." *Research in Organizational Behaviour* 20: 185–229.

Campbell, J. 1988. *The Power of Myth.* New York: Doubleday.

Campbell, K.E., Marsden, P.V., and Hurlbert, J.S. 1986. "Social Resources and Socioeconomic Status." *Social Networks* 8: 97–117.

Caplan, R.D. 1983. "Person-Environment Fit: Past, Present and Future." In *Stress Research: Issues for the Eighties,* ed. C.L. Cooper, 35–77. Ann Arbor, MI: Institute for Social Research.

Cappon, D. 1993. "The Anatomy of Intuition." *Psychology Today* 26 (May–June): 40–91.

———. 1994. *Intuition and Management: Research and Applications.* Westport, CT: Quorum Books.

Carnegie, D. 1936. *How to Win Friends and Influence People.* New York: Simon and Schuster.

Carroll, C., Pandian, J.R.M., and Thomas, H., ed. 1993. *The Role of Analytic Models in Strategic Management.* Vol. 4. Chichester, West Sussex: John Wiley.

Cartwright, S., and Cooper, C.L. 1992. *Mergers and Acquisitions: The Human Factor.* Oxford: Butterworth.

———. 1993. "The Psychological Impact of Merger and Acquisition on the Individual: A Study of Building Society Managers." *Human Relations* 46 (3): 327–347.

Carver, C.S., and Scheier, M.F. 1990. "Origins and Functions of Positive and Negative Affect: A Control-Process View." *Psychological Review* 97: 19–35.

Cascio, W. 1993. "Downsizing: What Do We Know? What Have We Learned?" *Academy of Management Executive* 7: 95–104.

Cascio, W., Young, C., and Morris, J. 1997. "Financial Consequences of Employment-Change Decisions in Major U.S. Corporations." *Academy of Management Journal* 40: 1175–1189.

Chatman, J.A., Polzer, J.T., Barsade, S.G., and Neale, M.A. 1998. "Being Different Yet Feeling Similar: The Influence of Demographic Composition and

Organisational Culture on Work Processes and Outcomes." *Administrative Science Quarterly* 43 (4): 749.

Cialdini, R.B. 1988. *Influence: Science and Practice.* New York: HarperCollins.

Ciarrochi, J.V., Chan, A.Y.C., and Caputi, P. 2000. "A Critical Evaluation of the Emotional Intelligence Construct." *Personality and Individual Differences* 28: 539–561.

Ciarrochi, J., Forgas, J., and Mayer, J., ed. 2001. *Emotional Intelligence in Everyday Life: A Scientific Inquiry.* Philadelphia: Psychology Press.

Clark, C. 1990. "Emotions and Micropolitics in Everyday Life: Some Patterns and Paradoxes of Place." In *Research Agendas in the Sociology of Emotions,* ed. T.D. Kemper, 305–334. Albany: State University of New York Press.

Clark, L.A., and Watson, D. 1988. "Mood and the Mundane: Relations Between Daily Life Events and Self-Reported Mood." *Journal of Personality and Social Psychology* 54: 296–308.

Clark, M.S., and Isen, A.M. 1982. "Toward Understanding the Relationship Between Feeling States and Social Behavior." In *Cognitive Social Psychology,* ed. A. Hastorf and A.M. Isen, 73–108. New York: Elsevier.

Clark, M.S., Pataki, S.P., and Carver, V.H. 1996. "Some Thoughts and Findings on Self-Presentation of Emotions in Relationships." In *Knowledge Structures in Close Relationships: A Social Psychological Approach,* ed. G.J.O. Fletcher and J. Fitness, 247–274. Mahwah, NJ: Lawrence Erlbaum.

Clore, G.L., and Ortony, A. 1999. "Cognition in Emotion: Always, Sometimes, or Never?" In *The Cognitive Neuroscience of Emotion,* ed. L. Nadel and R. Lane. New York: Oxford University Press.

Clore, G.L., Ortony, A., and Foss, M.A. 1987. "The Psychological Foundations of the Affective Lexicon." *Journal of Personality and Social Psychology* 53 (4): 751–766.

Clore, G.L., Schwarz, N., and Conway, M. 1994. "Cognitive Causes and Consequences of Emotion." In *Handbook of Social Cognition,* ed. R.S. Wyer and T. K. Srull, 2d ed., 323–417. Hillsdale, NJ: Lawrence Erlbaum.

Cobb, A., Vest, M., and Hills, F. 1997. "Who Delivers Justice? Source Perceptions of Procedural Fairness." *Journal of Applied Social Psychology* 27: 1021–1040.

Cobb, A., Wooten, K., and Folger, R. 1995. "Justice in the Making: Toward Understanding the Theory and Practice of Justice in Organizational Change and Development." *Research in Organizational Change and Development* 8: 243–295.

Cohen, S., and Rodriguez, M.S. 1995. "Pathways Linking Affective Disturbances and Physical Disorders." *Health Psychology* 14: 374–380.

Colvin, T. 1993. "Managing Workforce Reduction: A Survey of Employee Reactions and Implications for Management Consultants." *Organization Development Journal* 11: 67–76.

Conger, J.A. 1990. "The Dark Side of Leadership." *Organizational Dynamics* 19: 44–55.

Connolly, J.J., and Viswesvaran, C. 2000. "The Role of Affectivity in Job Satisfaction: A Meta-Analysis." *Personality and Individual Differences* 29: 265–281.

Cooper, R. 1998. "Sentimental Value." *People Management* 4 (7): 48–50.

Cooper, R.K., and Sawaf, A. 1997. *Executive EQ: Emotional Intelligence in Business.* London: Orion Business.

Côté, S., and Moskowitz, D.S. 1998. "On the Dynamic Covariation Between Interpersonal Behavior and Affect: Prediction from Neuroticism, Extraversion, and Agreeableness." *Journal of Personality and Social Psychology* 75: 1032–1046.

Cox, J.R.W. 1997. "Manufacturing the Past: Loss and Absence in Organizational Change." *Organization Studies* 18 (4): 623–654.

Coyne, J.C. 1994. "Self Reported Distress: Analog or Ersatz Depression?" *Psychological Bulletin* 116: 29–45.

Cropanzano, R., and Greenberg, J. 1997. "Progress in Tunnelling Through the Maze." *International Review of Industrial and Organizational Psychology* 12: 317–372.

Cropanzano, R., Weiss, H.M., Suckow, K.J., and Grandey, A.A. 2000. "Doing Justice to Workplace Emotion." In *Emotions in the Workplace: Research, Theory, and Practice*, ed. N.M. Ashkanasy, C.E.J. Härtel, and W.J. Zerbe, 49–62. Westport, CT: Quorum Books.

Crossan, M.M., Lane, H.W., and White, R.E. 1999. "An Organizational Learning Framework: From Intuition to Institution." *Academy Management Review* 24: 522–537.

Csikszentmihalyi, M., and Csikszentmihalyi, I.S., eds. 1988. *Optimal Experience: Psychological Studies of Flow in Consciousness*. Cambridge, NY: Cambridge University Press.

Cummings, T., and Worley, C. 1993. *Organization Development and Change*. St. Paul, MN: West Publishing.

Czepiel, J., Solomon, M., and Surprenant, C. 1985. "Service Encounter: An Overview." In *The Service Encounter: Managing Employee/Customer Interaction in Service Business*, ed. J.A. Czepiel, M.R. Solomon, and C.F. Surprenant. Lexington, MA: Lexington Books.

Dailey, R., and Kirk, D. 1992. "Distributive and Procedural Justice as Antecedents of Job Dissatisfaction and Intent to Turnover." *Human Relations* 45: 305–317.

Daly, J., and Geyer, P. 1994. "The Role of Fairness in Implementing Large-Scale Change: Employee Evaluations of Process and Outcome in Seven Facility Relocations." *Journal of Organizational Behaviour* 15: 623–638.

Damasio, A.R. 1994. *Descartes' Error: Emotion, Reason, and the Human Brain*. New York: Avon Books.

———. 1998. "Emotion in the Perspective of an Integrated Nervous System." *Brain Research Reviews* 26: 83–86.

———. 1999. *The Feeling of What Happens: Body and Emotion in the Making of Consciousness*. New York: Harcourt Brace.

Davey, J.A., Kinicki, A., Kilroy, J., and Scheck, C. 1988. "After the Merger: Dealing with People's Uncertainty." *Training and Development Journal* (November): 57–61

Davidson, R.J. 1992. "Emotion and Affective Style: Hemispheric Substrates." *Psychological Science* 3: 39–43.

Davies, M., Stankov, L., and Roberts, R.D. 1998. "Emotional Intelligence: In Search of an Elusive Construct." *Journal of Personality and Social Psychology* 75: 989–1015.

Davis-Blake, A., and Pfeffer, J. 1989. "Just a Mirage: The Search for Dispositional Effects in Organizational Research." *Academy of Management Review* 14: 385–400.

Deery, M., and Shaw, R.J. 1999. "An Investigation of the Relationship Between

Employee Turnover and Organizational Culture. *Journal of Hospitality and Tourism Research* 23: 387–400.

Dekker, S.W.A., and Schaufeli, W.B. 1995. "The Effects of Job Insecurity on Psychological Health and Withdrawal: A Longitudinal Study." *Australian Psychologist* 30: 57–63.

Denes-Raj, V., and Epstein, S. 1994. "Conflict Between Intuitive and Rational Processing: When People Behave Against Their Better Judgment." *Journal of Personality and Social Psychology* 66: 819–829.

Denison, D. 1996. "What Is the Difference Between Organizational Culture and Organizational Climate? A Native's Point of View on a Decade of Paradigm Wars." *Academy of Management Review* 21 (3): 619–654.

Dent, E., and Goldberg, S.G. 1999. "Challenging 'Resistance to Change.'" *Journal of Applied Behavioral Science* 35: 25–41.

DePaulo, B.M. 1992. "Nonverbal Behavior and Self-Presentation." *Psychological Bulletin* 111: 203–243.

De Rivera, J. 1992. "Emotional Climate: Social Structure and Emotional Dynamics." *International Review of Studies of Emotion* 2: 197–218.

Descartes, R. 1984. "The Passions of the Soul." In *The Philosophical Writings of Descartes,* trans. J. Cottingham, R. Stoothoff, and D. Murdoch. Cambridge: Cambridge University Press.

De Sousa, R. 1987. *The Rationality of Emotions*. Cambridge, MA: MIT Press.

Deutsch, M. 1987. "Experimental Studies of the Effects of Different Systems of Distributive Justice." In *Social Comparison, Social Justice and Relative Deprivation,* ed. J. Masters and W. Smith, 151–164. Hillsdale, NJ: Lawrence Erlbaum.

Deutsch, M., and Shichman, S. 1986. "Conflict." In *Political Psychology,* ed. M.G. Hermann, 219–250. San Francisco: Jossey-Bass.

Diener, E., and Emmons, R.A. 1984. "On the Independence of Positive and Negative Affect." *Journal of Personality and Social Psychology* 47: 1105–1117.

Diener, E., and Fujita, F. 1995. "Resources, Personal Strivings, and Subjective Well-Being: A Nomothetic and Idiographic Approach." *Journal of Personality and Social Psychology* 68: 926–935.

Diener, E., and Larsen, R.J. 1993. "The Experience of Emotional Wellbeing." In *Handbook of Emotions,* ed. M.L., and J.M. Haviland, 405–416. New York: Guilford.

Diener, E., Suh, E.M., Lucas, R.E, Smith, H.L. 1999. "Subjective Well-Being: Three Decades of Progress." *Psychological Bulletin* 125 (March): 276–302.

Dollard, J.L., Doob, L.W., Miller, N.E., Mowrer, O.H., and Sears, R.H. 1939. *Frustration and Aggression*. New Haven, CT: Yale University Press.

Doppler, K., and Lauterburg, C. 1994."Change Management." *Den Unternehmenswandel Gestalten*. Frankfurt A.M.: Campus.

Dreher, G.F., Dougherty, T.W., and Whitely, W. 1989. "Influence Tactics and Salary Attainment: A Gender-Specific Analysis." *Sex Roles* 20: 535–550.

Druskat V.U., and Wolff, S.B. 2001. "Building the Emotional Intelligence of Groups." *Harvard Business Review* 79 (3): 80.

DuBrin, A.J. 1991. "Sex and Gender Differences in Tactics of Influence." *Psychological Reports* 68: 635–646.

Dundes, A. 1984. *Sacred Narrative: Readings in the Theory of Myth*. Berkeley: University of California Press.

Eckenrode, J. 1984. "Impact of Chronic and Acute Stressors on Daily Reports of Mood." *Journal of Personality and Social Psychology* 46: 907–918.

Eid, M., and Diener, E. 1999. "Intra-individual Variability in Affect: Reliability, Validity, and Personality Correlates." *Journal of Personality and Social Psychology* 76: 662–676.

Eisenberg, N., and Fabes, R.A. 1992. "Emotion, Regulation, and the Development of Social Competence." *Review of Personality and Social Psychology* 14: 119–150.

Eisenhardt, K.M. 1989. "Making Fast Strategic Decisions in High-Velocity Environments." *Academy of Management Journal* 32: 543–576.

———. 1999. "Strategy as Strategic Decision-Making." *Sloan Management Review* (Spring): 65–72.

Eisenhardt, K.M., and Zbaracki, M.J. 1992. "Strategic Decision-Making." *Strategic Management Journal* 13 (Special Issue): 17–37.

Ekman, P. 1973. "Cross Culture Studies of Facial Expression." In *Darwin and Facial Expression: A Century of Research in Review*, ed. P. Ekman, 169–222. New York: Academic Press.

———. 1992. "An Argument for Basic Emotions." *Cognition and Emotion* 6: 169–200.

———. 1993. "Facial Expression and Emotion." *American Psychologist* 48 (4): 384–392.

———. 1994. "Moods, Emotions, and Traits." In *The Nature of Emotion,* ed. P. Ekman and R.J. Davidson, 56–58. New York: Oxford University Press.

Elangovan, A.R., and Shapiro, D.L. 1998. "Betrayal of Trust in Organizations." *Academy of Management Review* 23 (3): 547–566.

Elsbach, K.D., and Barr, P.S. 1999. "The Effects of Mood on Individual's Use of Structured Decision Protocols." *Organization Science* 10: 181–198.

Elstad, J.I. 1998. "The Psycho-Social Perspective on Social Inequalities in Health." In *The Sociology of Health Inequalities,* ed. M. Bartley, D. Blane, and G. Davey, 39–58. Oxford: Blackwell.

Elster, J. 1999. *Alchemies of the Mind: Rationality and the Emotions*. Cambridge: Cambridge University Press.

Engel, C.E. 1993. "Not Just a Method But a Way of Learning." In *The Challenge of Problem Based Learning,* ed. D. Bond and G. Felletti, 23–33. London: Kogan Page.

England, P. 1992. *Comparable Worth: Theories and Evidence.* New York: Aldine De Gruyter.

England, P., and Farkas, G. 1986. *Households, Employment, and Gender.* New York: Aldine De Gruyter.

England, P., and Folbre, N. 1999. "The Cost of Caring." *The Annals of The American Academy of Political and Social Science* 561: 39–51.

Epstein, S. 1990. "Cognitive-Experiential Self-Theory." In *Handbook of Personality Theory and Research,* ed. L. Pervin, 165–192. New York: Guilford Press.

———. 1998. "Emotions and Psychology from the Perspective of Cognitive-Experiential Self-Theory." In *Emotions in Psychopathology: Theory and Research. Series in Affective Science,* ed. W.F. Flack and J.D. Laird, 57–69. New York: Oxford University Press.

———. 2001. Personal Correspondence. 18 January. Brisbane, Australia.

Epstein, S., Pacini, R., Denes-Raj, V., and Heier, H. 1996. "Individual Differences in Intuitive-Experiential and Analytical-Rational Thinking Styles." *Journal of Personality and Social Psychology* 71: 390–405.

Erickson, R.J., and Wharton, A.S. 1997. "Inauthenticity and Depression: Assessing the Consequences of Interactive Service Work." *Work and Occupations* 24: 188–213.

Estrada, C.A., Isen, A.M., and Young, M.J. 1994. "Positive Affect Improves Creative Problem-Solving and Influences Reported Source of Practice Satisfaction in Physicians." *Motivation and Emotion* 18: 285–299.

———. 1997. "Positive Affect Facilitates Integration of Information and Decreases Anchoring in Reasoning Among Physicians." *Organizational Behavior and Human Decision Processes* 72: 117–135.

Etzion, D., Eden, D., and Lapidot, Y. 1998. "Relief from Job Stressors and Burnout: Reserve Service as a Respite." *Journal of Applied Psychology* 83: 577–585.

Etzioni, A. 1988. *The Moral Dimension: Toward a New Economics*. New York: Free Press.

Evans, D. 2001. *Emotion: The Science of Sentiment*. Oxford: Oxford University Press.

Evans, G.W., Johansson, G., and Rydstedt, L. 1999. "Hassles on the Job: A Study of a Job Intervention with Urban Bus Drivers." *Journal of Organizational Behaviour* 20: 199–208.

Falbe, C.M., and Yukl, G. 1992. "Consequences for Managers of Using Single Influence Tactics and Combinatory Tactics." *Academy of Management Journal* 35: 638–652.

Fechner-Bates, S., Coyne, J.C., and Schwenk, T.L., 1994. "The Relationship of Self-Reported Distress to Depressive Disorders and Other Psychopathology." *Journal of Consulting and Clinical Psychology* 62: 550–559.

Fineman, S., ed. 1993. *Emotion in Organizations*. London: Sage.

———. 1996. "Emotion and Organizing." In *Handbook of Organization Studies*, ed. S. Clegg., C. Hardy, and W. Nord. London: Sage.

———, ed. 2000. *Emotion in Organizations*. 2d ed. London, England: Sage.

Fisher, C.D. 1998. "Emotional Experiences at Work: Do Personality and Demographic Differences Matter." Paper presented at the first conference on Emotions and Organizational Life. San Diego, CA, August.

———. 2000. "Mood and Emotions While Working: Missing Pieces of Job Satisfaction?" *Journal of Organizational Behaviour* 21: 185–202.

Fisher, C.D., and Ashkanasy, N.M. 2000. "The Emerging Role of Emotions in Work Life: An Introduction." *Journal of Organizational Behaviour* 21: 123–129.

Fisher, C.D., and Noble, C.S. 2000. "Affect and Performance: A Within-Person Analysis." In *Academy of Management Best Paper Proceedings (CD-ROM)*, ed. S.J. Havolic. Pleasantville, NY: Academy of Management.

Fiske, S.T. 1993. "Controlling Other People: The Impact of Power on Stereotyping." *American Psychologist* 48: 621–628.

Folkman, S., and Lazarus, R. 1980. "An Analysis of Coping in a Middle-Aged Community Sample." *Journal of Health and Social Behaviour* 21: 219–239.

Forgas, J.P. 1992. "Affect in Social Judgments and Decisions: A Multiprocess Model." In *Advances in Experimental Social Psychology*, ed. M.P. Zanna, 227–276. San Diego, CA: Academic Press.

————. 1994. "The Role of Emotion in Social Judgments: An Introductory Review and an Affect Infusion Model (AIM)." *European Journal of Social Psychology* 24: 1–24.

————. 1995. "Mood and Judgment: The Affect Infusion Model (AIM)." *Psychological Bulletin* 117 (1): 39–66.

Fox, S., and Spector, P.E. 2000. "Relations of Emotional Intelligence, Practical Intelligence, General Intelligence, and Trait Affectivity with Interview Outcomes: It's Not All Just 'G'." *Journal of Organizational Behaviour* 21: 203–220.

Frank, R.H. 1988. *Passions Within Reason: The Strategic Role of the Emotions.* New York: Norton.

Fredrickson, B.L. 1998. "What Good Are Positive Emotions?" *Review of General Psychology* 2 (3): 300–319.

Fredrickson, B.L., and Levenson, R.W. 1998. "Positive Emotions Speed Recovery from the Cardiovascular Sequelae of Negative Emotions." *Cognition and Emotion* 12: 191–220.

French, J.R.P., and Raven, B.H. 1959. "The Bases of Social Power." In *Studies in Social Power,* ed. D. Cartwright. Ann Arbor: University of Michigan Press.

Friedman, E. 1985. *Generation to Generation: Family Process in Church and Synagogue.* New York: Guilford Press.

Frijda, N.H. 1986. *The Emotions.* Cambridge, NY: Cambridge University Press.

————. 1988. "The Laws of Emotion." *American Psychologist* 43 (5): 349–358.

————. 1993. "Moods, Emotion Episodes and Emotions." In *Handbook of Emotions,* ed. M. Lewis and J. Haviland, 381–403. New York: Guilford Press.

Frijda, N.H., and Mesquita, B. 1994. "The Social Roles and Functions of Emotions." In *Emotion and Culture: Empirical Studies of Mutual Influence,* ed. S. Kitayama and H. Markus, 51–87. Washington, DC: American Psychological Association.

Fujimoto, Y., Härtel, C.E.J., Härtel, G.F., and Baker, N.J. 2000. "Openness to Dissimilarity Moderates the Consequences of Diversity in Well-Established Groups." *Asia Pacific Journal of Human Resources* 38 (3): 46–61.

Gabbaro, J.J. 1990. "The Development of Working Relationships." *Intellectual Teamwork,* ed. J. Galegher, R.E. Kraut and C. Egido, 79–110. Hillsdale, NJ: Lawrence Erlbaum.

Gabennesch, H., and Hunt, L. 1971. "The Relative Accuracy of Interpersonal Perception of High and Low Authoritarians." *Journal of Experimental Research in Personality* 5: 43–48.

Gardener, H. 1983. *Frames of Mind.* New York: Basic Books.

Gayle, B., and Preiss, R. 1998. "Assessing Emotionality in Organizational Conflicts." *Management Communication Quarterly* 12: 280–303.

George, J.M. 1989. "Mood and Absence." *Journal of Applied Psychology* 74: 317–324.

————. 1991. "State or Trait: Effects of Positive Mood on Prosocial Behaviors at Work." *Journal of Applied Psychology* 76: 299–307.

————. 1995. "Leader Positive Mood and Group Performance: The Case of Customer Service." *Journal of Applied Social Psychology* 25: 778–794.

————. 1996. "Trait and State Affect." In *Individual Difference and Behavior in Organizations,* ed. K.R. Murphy, 145–171. San Francisco: Jossey-Bass.

————. 2000. "Emotions and Leadership: The Role of Emotional Intelligence." *Human Relations* 53: 1027–1055.

George, J.M., and Bettenhausen, K. 1990. "Understanding Prosocial Behavior, Sales Performance, and Turnover: A Group Level Analysis in a Service Context." *Journal of Applied Psychology* 75: 698–709.

George, J.M., and Brief, A.P. 1992. "Feeling Good-Doing Good: A Conceptual Analysis of the Mood at Work-Organizational Spontaneity Relationship." *Psychological Bulletin* 112: 310–329.

————. 1996a. "Motivational Agendas in the Workplace: The Effects of Feelings on Focus of Attention and Work Motivation." *Research in Organizational Behaviour* 18: 75–109.

————. 1996b. "Negative Affectivity and Coping With Job Loss." *Academy of Management Review* 21: 7–9.

Gerpott, T.J. 1993. *Integrationsgestaltung Und Erfolg Von Unternehmensakquisitionen.* Stuttgart: Schäffer-Poeschel.

Giacobbe-Miller, J., Miller, D., and Victorov, V. 1998. "A Comparison of Russian and U.S. Pay Allocation Decision, Distributive Justice Judgements, and Productivity Under Different Payment Conditions." *Personnel Psychology* 51: 137–163.

Gibson, D.E. 1997. "The Struggle for Reason: The Sociology of Emotions in Organizations." In *Social Perspectives on Emotion,* ed. R.J. Erickson and B. Cuthbertson-Johnson, 211–256. Greenwich, CT: JAI Press.

Goffman, Erving. 1956. "The Nature of Deference and Demeanor." *American Anthropologist* 58: 473–502.

Goffman, E. 1959. *The Presentation of Self in Everyday Life.* New York: Doubleday.

Goldstein, M.D., and Strube, M.J. 1994. "Independence Revisited: The Relation Between Positive and Negative Affect in a Naturalistic Setting." *Personality and Social Psychology Bulletin* 20: 57–64.

Goleman, D. 1995. *Emotional Intelligence.* New York: Bantam.

————. 1996. *Emotional Intelligence.* London: Bloomsbury.

————. 1998a. "What Makes a Leader?" *Harvard Business Review* 76 (6): 92.

————. 1998b. *Working With Emotional Intelligence.* New York: Bantam.

Goodman, S.K. 1993. "Information Needs for Management Decision-Making." *Records Management Quarterly* 27: 12–23.

Gotts, G., and Cox, T. 1988. *Stress and Arousal Checklist: A Manual for Its Administration, Scoring and Interpretation.* Melbourne, Australia: Swinburne University Press.

Graham, S., Hudley, C., and Williams, E. 1992. "Attributional and Emotional Determinants of Aggression Among African-American and Latino Young Adolescents." *Developmental Psychology* 28: 731–740.

Grandey, A.A. 1998. "Emotional Labor: A Concept and Its Correlates." Paper presented at the First Conference on Emotions and Organizational Life, San Diego, CA, August.

————. 2000. "Emotion Regulation in the Workplace: A New Way to Conceptualize Emotional Labor." *Journal of Occupational Health Psychology* 5: 95–110.

Greenberg, J. 1990. "Organizational Justice: Yesterday, Today and Tomorrow." *Journal of Management* 16: 399–432.

Greenhalgh, L. 1982. "Maintaining Organizational Effectiveness During Organizational Retrenchment." *Journal of Applied Behavioral Science* 18: 155–170.

Gross, J.J., and John, O.P. 1995. "Facets of Emotional Expressivity: Three Self-Report Factors and Their Correlates." *Personality and Individual Differences* 19: 555–568.

———. 1998. "Mapping the Domain of Expressivity: Multimethod Evidence for a Hierarchical Model." *Journal of Personality and Social Psychology* 74: 170–191.

Gross, P.R. 1994. "A Pilot Study of the Contribution of Empathy to Burnout in Salvation Army Officers." *Work and Stress* 8: 68–74.

Grzywacz, J.G., and Marks, N.F. 2000. "Reconceptualizing the Work-Family Interface: An Ecological Perspective on the Correlates of Positive and Negative Spill-Over Between Work and Family." *Journal of Occupational Health Psychology* 5: 111–126.

Gutek, B.A. 1995. *The Dynamics of Service.* San Francisco: Jossey-Bass.

———. 1980. *Work Redesign.* Reading, MA: Addison-Wesley.

Hall, E.J. 1993. "Smiling, Deferring and Flirting: Doing Gender By Giving 'Good Service.'" *Work and Occupations* 20 (4): 452–471.

Hambrick, D.C. 1994. "Top Management Groups: A Conceptual Integration and Reconsideration of the 'Team' Label." In *Research in Organizational Behaviour,* ed. B.M. Shaw and L.L Cummings, 171–213. Greenwich, CT: JAI Press.

Hammer, M., and Stanton, S.A. 1994. *The Reengineering Revolution: A Handbook.* New York: Harper Business.

Hammond, K.R., Hamm, R.M., Grassia, J., and Pearson, T. 1987. "Direct Comparison of The Efficacy of Intuitive and Analytical Cognition in Expert Judgment." *IEEE Transactions on Systems, Man, and Cybernetics* 17: 753–770.

Hanisch, K.A., and Hulin, C.L. 1990. "Job Attitudes and Organizational Withdrawal: An Examination of Retirement and Other Voluntary Withdrawal Behaviors." *Journal of Vocational Behaviour* 37: 60–78.

Harbort, B. 1997. "Thought, Action, and Intuition in Practice-oriented Disciplines." In *Intuition: The Inside Story,* ed. R. Davies-Floyd and P. S. Arvidson, 129–144. New York: Routledge.

Härtel, C.E.J., Barker, S., and Baker, N. 1999. "A Model for Predicting the Effects of Employee-Customer Interactions on Consumer Attitudes, Intentions, and Behaviours. The Role of Emotional Intelligence in Service Encounters." *Australian Journal of Communication.* 26 (2): 77–87.

Härtel, C.E.J., Douthitt, S., Härtel, G.F., and Douthitt, S. 1999. "Equally Qualified But Unequally Perceived: General Cultural Openness as a Predictor of Discriminatory Performance Ratings." *Human Resource Development Quarterly* 10 (1): 79–89.

Härtel, C.E.J., and Fujimoto, Y. 1999. "Explaining Why Diversity Sometimes Has Positive Effects in Organizations and Sometimes Has Negative Effects in Organizations: The Perceived Dissimilarity Openness Moderator Model." In *Academy of Management Best Papers Proceedings (CD-ROM),* ed. S.J. Havolic. Chicago: Academy of Management.

———. 2000. "Diversity Is Not a Problem to Be Managed By Organisations but Openness to Perceived Dissimilarity Is." *Journal of Australian and New Zealand Academy of Management* 6 (1): 14–27.

Härtel, C.E.J., Gough, H., and Härtel, G.F. In press. "Work Group Emotional Climate, Emotion Management Skills and Service Attitudes and Performance." *Asia Pacific Journal of Human Resources.*

Härtel, C.E.J., and Härtel, G.F. 1996. "Making Decision-Making Work." *Training Research Journal: The Science and Practice of Training* 2: 69–84.
————. 1997. "SHAPE-Assisted Intuitive Decision Making and Problem Solving: Information-Processing-Based Training for Conditions of Cognitive Busyness." *Group Dynamics: Theory, Research, and Practice* 1 (3): 187–199.
Härtel, C.E.J., McColl-Kennedy, J.R., and McDonald, L. 1998. "Incorporating Attributional Theory and the Theory of Reasoned Action Within an Affective Events Theory Framework to Produce a Contingency Predictive Model of Consumer Reactions to Organizational Mishaps." *Advances in Consumer Research* 25: 428–432.
Hatfield, E., Cacioppo, J., and Rapson, R. 1994. *Emotional Contagion.* New York: Cambridge University Press.
Hay, P., and Härtel, C.E.J. 2000. "Toward Improving the Success of Change Management Efforts: Modelling the Factors Contributing to Employee's Resistance During Change Implementation." *Management Development Forum* 91–119.
Heise, D.R., and O'Brien, J. 1993. "Emotion Expression in Groups." In *Handbook of Emotions,* ed. M. Lewis and J Haviland, 489–497. New York: Guilford Press.
Herrmann, N. 1982. "The Brain and Management Learning." *The Bureaucrat* (Fall): 17–21.
Higgins, E.T., Kuiper, N.A., and Olson, J.M. 1981. "Social Cognition: A Need to Get Personal." In *Social Cognition: The Ontario Symposium.* Vol. 1, ed. E.T. Higgins, C.P. Herman, and M.P. Zanna, Chap. 12. Hillsdale, NJ: Lawrence Erlbaum.
Himmelweit, S. 1999. "Caring Labor." *The Annals of the American Academy of Political and Social Science* 561: 27–38.
Hochschild, A.R. 1979. "Emotion Work, Feeling Rules, and Social Structure." *American Journal of Sociology* 85 (3): 551–575.
————. 1983. *The Managed Heart: Commercialization of Human Feeling.* Berkeley: University of California Press.
Hodges, S.D., and Wilson, T.D. 1993. "Effects of Analyzing Reasons on Attitude-Change: The Moderating Role of Attitude Accessibility." *Social Cognition* 11: 353–366.
Hofmann, D.A., and Gavin, M.B. 1998. "Centering Decisions in Hierarchical Linear Models: Implications for Research in Organizations." *Journal of Management* 24: 623–641.
Hofstede, G. 1984. *Culture's Consequences: International Differences in Work-Related Values.* Abridged version. Beverly Hills: Sage.
Hogan, E.A., and Overmayer-Day, L. 1994. "The Psychology of Mergers and Acquisitions." In *International Review of Industrial and Organizational Psychology,* ed. C.L. Cooper and I.T. Robertson, 247–281. Chichester, England: John Wiley.
Holmes, T.H., and Rahe, R.H. 1967. "The Social Readjustment Rating Scale." *Journal of Psychosomatic Research* 11: 213–216.
Howard, A., and Bray, D.W. 1989. *Managerial Lives in Transition.* New York: Guilford Press.
Hsee, C.K., Hatfield, E., Carlson, J.G., and Chemtob, C. 1990. "The Effect of Power on Susceptibility to Emotional Contagion." *Cognition and Emotion* 4: 327–340.

Hume, D. 1978. *A Treatise of Human Nature.* Oxford: Clarendon.

Humphrey, R.H. Guest ed. Planned for 2002. Special Issue on Emotions and Leadership. *Leadership Quarterly.*

Humphrey, R.H. 2000. "The Importance of Job Characteristics to Emotional Displays." In *Emotions in the Workplace: Theory, Research, and Practice,* ed. N.M. Ashkanasy, C.E.J. Härtel, and W.J. Zerbe, 236–249. Westport, CT: Quorum.

Huy, Q. 1999. "Emotional Capability, Emotional Intelligence, and Radical Change." *Academy of Management Review* 24 (12): 325–345.

Isen, A.M. 1993. "Positive Affect and Decision Making." In *Handbook of Emotions,* ed. M. Lewis and J.M. Haviland, 261–278. New York: Guilford Press.

———. 1999. "Positive Affect." In *Handbook of Cognition and Emotion,* ed. T. Dalgleish and M.J. Power, 521–539. Chichester, England: John Wiley.

Isen, A.M., and Baron, R.A. 1991. "Positive Affect as a Factor in Organizational Behavior." In *Handbook of Emotions,* ed. B.M. Staw and L.L. Cummings, 1–54. Greenwich, CT: JAI Press.

Isen, A.M., Daubman, K.A., and Nowicki, G.P. 1987. "Positive Affect Facilitates Creative Problem Solving: When We Are Glad, We Feel as If the Light Has Increased." *Journal of Personality and Social Psychology* 51: 1122–1131.

Isenberg, D.J. 1984. "How Senior Managers Think." *Harvard Business Review* (November–December): 81–86.

ISR 1999. *International Survey Research Report on Mergers and Acquisitions.* International Survey Research.

Iverson, R. 1996. "Employee Acceptance of Organizational Change: The Role of Organizational Commitment." *International Journal of Human Resource Management* 7: 122–149.

Iverson, R.D., Olekalns, M., and Erwin, P.J. 1998. "Affectivity, Organizational Stressors, and Absenteeism: A Causal Model of Burnout and its Consequences." *Journal of Vocational Behaviour* 52: 1–23.

Izard, C.E. 1985. "Emotion-Cognition Relationships and Human Development." In *Emotions, Cognition, and Behaviour,* ed. C.E. Izard, J. Kagan, and R.B. Zajonc, 17–37. New York: Cambridge University Press.

Jackall, R. 1983. "Moral Mazes: Bureaucracy and Managerial Work." *Harvard Business Review* (September–October): 118–130.

Jackson, S.E., Turner, J.A., and Brief, A.P. 1987. "Correlates of Burnout Among Public Service Lawyers." *Journal of Occupational Behaviour* 8: 339–349.

James, N. 1989. "Emotional Labor: Skill and Work in the Social Regulation of Feelings." *Sociological Review* 37: 15–42.

Jehn, K.A. 1992. *The Impact of Intragroup Conflict on Group Effectiveness: A Multimethod Examination of the Benefits and Detriments of Conflict.* Unpublished doctoral dissertation, Northwestern University, Evanston, IL.

———. 1995. "A Multimethod Examination of the Benefits and Detriments of Intragroup Conflict." *Administrative Science Quarterly* 40 (2): 256–284.

———. 1997. "Qualitative Analysis of Conflict Types and Dimensions in Organizational Groups." *Administrative Science Quarterly* 42: 530–566.

Jehn, K.A., Northcraft, G.B., and Neale, M.A. 1999. "Why Differences Make a Difference: A Study of Diversity, Conflict and Performance in Workgroups." *Administrative Science Quarterly* 44 (4): 741.

Johnson, S.M. 1998. "Introduction Special Issue: The Use of Emotions in Couples and Family Therapy." *Journal of Systemic Therapies* 17 (2): i–iii.

Jones, E.E., and Pittman, T.S. 1982. "Toward a General Theory of Strategic Self-Presentation." In *Psychological Perspectives on the Self*, ed. J. Suls, 231–262. Hillsdale, NJ: Erlbaum.

Jones, R.G. 1997. "A Person Perception Explanation for Validation Evidence from Assessment Centers." *Journal of Social Behavior and Personality* 12: 169–178.

Jordan, P., Ashkanasy, N.M., and Härtel, C.E.J. 2000. "Job Insecurity and Innovation: A Bounded Emotionality Analysis." In *Academy of Management Best Papers Proceedings (CD-ROM)*, ed. S.J. Havolic. Pleasantville, NY: Academy of Management.

Jordan, P.J., Ashkanasy, N.M., Härtel, C.E.J., and Hooper, G.S. In press. "Workgroup Emotional Intelligence: Scale Development and Relationship to Team Process Effectiveness and Goal Focus." *Human Resource Management Review*.

Kahn, B.E., and Isen, A.M. 1993. "Variety Seeking Among Safe, Enjoyable Products." *Journal of Consumer Research* 20: 257–270.

Kahn, R.L., Wolfe, D.M., Quinn, RP., Snoek, J.D., and Rosenthal, R. 1964. *Organizational Stress: Studies in Role Conflict and Ambiguity*. New York: John Wiley.

Kanner, A.D., Coyne, J.C., Schaefer, C., and Lazarus, R.S. 1981. "Comparison of Two Modes of Stress Measurement: Daily Hassles and Uplifts Versus Major Life Events." *Journal of Behavioral Medicine* 4 (1): 1–39.

Kanner, A., Feldman, S.S., Weinberger, D.A., and Ford, M.E. 1987. "Uplifts, Hassles, and Adaptational Outcomes." *Journal of Early Adolescence* 7 (4): 371–394.

Kanter, R.M. 1977. *Men and Women of the Corporation*. New York: Basic Books.

———. 1985. "Managing the Human Side of Change." *Management Review* (April): 52–56.

Karasek, R. 1999. "Labour Participation and Work Quality Policy: Outline of an Alternative Economic Vision." In *Labour Market Changes and Job Insecurity: A Challenge for Social Welfare and Health Promotion*, ed. J.E. Ferrie, M. Marmot, J. Griffiths, and E. Ziglio, 169–239. Copenhagen: World Health Organization.

Keaveney, S.M., and Nelson, J.E. 1993. "Coping with Organizational Role Stress: Intrinsic Motivational Orientation, Perceived Role Benefits, and Psychological Withdrawal." *Journal of the Academy of Marketing Science* 21 (2): 113–124.

Kelley, H.H. 1967. "Attribution in Social Psychology." *Nebraska Symposium on Motivation* 5: 192–238.

Kelman, H.C. 1974. "Social Influence and Linkages Between the Individual and the Social System. Further Thoughts on the Processes of Compliance, Identification, and Internalization." In *Perspectives on Social Power*, ed. J.T. Tedeschi, 125–171. Chicago: Aldine.

Kelman, H.C., and Hamilton, V.L. 1989. *Crimes of Obedience: Toward a Social Psychology of Authority and Responsibility*. New Haven, CT: Yale University Press.

Kemper, T.D. 1978. A *Social Interactional Theory of Emotions*. New York: John Wiley.

———. 1990. "Social Relations and Emotions: A Structural Approach." In *Research Agendas in the Sociology of Emotions*, ed. T.D. Kemper, 207–237. Albany: State University of New York Press.

————. 1991. "Predicting Emotions from Social Relations." *Social Psychology Quarterly* 54: 330–342.

Kemper, T.D., and Collins, R. 1990. "Dimensions of Microinteraction." *American Journal of Sociology* 96: 32–68.

Kenny, D.A., Albright, L., Malloy, T.E., and Kashy, D.A. 1994. "Consensus in Interpersonal Perception: Acquaintance and the Big Five." *Psychological Bulletin* 116: 245–258.

Kiefer, T. 2002. "Understanding the Emotional Experience of Organizational Change: Evidence from a Merger." In *Advances in Developing Human Resources,* 4 (1): 39–61.

Kiefer, T., and Eicken, S. 1999. *Emotions at Work - Bedeutung Von Emotionen Bei Der UBS-Fusion.* Forschungsbericht 1. Universität St. Gallen: Lehrstuhl Für Organisationspsychologie.

Kiefer, T., and Müller, W. 2001. *Befindlichkeit in Der Chemischen industrie.* WWZ-Studie Nr. 59, Basel: WWZ.

Kipnis, D. 1976. *The Powerholders.* Chicago: University of Chicago Press.

————. 1984. "The Use of Power in Organizations and in Interpersonal Settings." In *Applied Social Psychology Annual,* ed. S. Oskamp, 179–210. Beverly Hills, CA: Sage.

Kipnis, D., and Schmidt, S.M. 1985. "The Language of Persuasion." *Psychology Today* 4: 40–46.

Kipnis, D., Schmidt, S.M., and Wilkinson, I. 1980. "Intraorganizational Influence Tactics: Explorations in Getting One's Way." *Journal of Applied Psychology* 65: 440–452.

Kirkman, B., Shapiro, D., Novelli, L., and Brett, J. 1996. "Employee Concerns Regarding Self-Managing Work Teams: A Multidimensional Justice Perspective." *Social Justice Research* 9: 47–67.

Klein, G. 1998. *Sources of Power: How People Make Decisions.* Cambridge, MA: MIT Press.

Kolb, D.A., Osland, J.S., and Rubin, I.M. 1995. *Organizational Behavior.* Englewood Cliffs, NJ: Prentice Hall.

Kolb, D.A., and Putnam, L. 1992. "Introduction: The Dialectics of Disputing." In *Hidden Conflict in Organizations: Uncovering Behind the Scenes Disputes,* ed. D.A. Kolb and J. Bartunek, 1–31. Newbury Park, CA: Sage.

Konovsky, M., and Brockner, J. 1993. "Managing Victim and Survivor Layoff Reactions: A Procedural Justice Perspective." In *Justice in the Workplace,* ed. R. Cropanzano. Hillsdale, NJ: Lawrence Erlbaum.

Konovsky, M., and Cropanzano, R. 1991. "Perceived Fairness of Employee Drug Testing as a Predictor of Employee Attitudes and Job Performance." *Journal of Applied Psychology* 76: 698–707.

Konovsky, M., and Folger, R. 1991. "The Effects of Procedures, Social Accounts, and Benefits Level on Victims' Layoff Reactions." *Journal of Applied Social Psychology* 21: 630–650.

Kopelman, R.E., Brief, A.P., and Guzzo, R.A. 1990. "The Role of Climate and Culture in Productivity." In *Organizational Climate and Culture,* ed. B. Schneider, 282–318. San Francisco: Jossey-Bass.

Koslowsky, M., and Schwarzwald, J. 2001. "The Power Interaction Model: Theory, Methodology, and Empirical Applications." In *The Use and Abuse of Power,* ed. A.Y. Lee-Chai and J.A. Bargh, 195–216. Philadelphia: Psychology Press.

Kotter, J.P. 1985. *Power and Influence: Beyond Formal Authority.* New York: Free Press.

Koys, D., and DeCotiis, T. 1991. "Inductive Measures of Psychological Climate." *Human Relations* 44 (3): 265–285.

Kozlowski, S., Chao, G., Smith, E., and Hedlund, J. 1993. "Organizational Downsizing: Strategies, Interventions and Research Implications." *International Review of Industrial and Organizational Psychology* 8: 263–332.

Kraiger, K., Billings, R.S., and Isen, A.M. 1989. "The Influence of Positive Affective States on Task Perceptions and Satisfaction." *Organizational Behavior and Human Decision Processes* 44: 12–25.

Krantz, J. 1999. "Comment on 'Challenging 'Resistance to Change.'" *Journal of Applied Behavioral Science* 35: 42–44.

Kreft, I., and De Leeuw, J. 1998. *Introducing Multilevel Modeling.* London: Sage.

Kreft, I., De Leeuw, J., and Aiken, L.S. 1995. "The Effects of Different Forms of Centering in Hierarchical Linear Models." *Multivariate Behavioral Research* 30: 1–21.

Kriger, M.P., and Barnes, L.B. 1992. "Organizational Decision-Making as Hierarchical Levels of Drama." *Journal of Management Studies* 29: 439–450.

Kring, A.M., Smith, D.A., and Neale, J.M. 1994. "Individual Differences in Dispositional Expressiveness: Development and Validation of the Emotional Expressivity Scale." *Journal of Personality and Social Psychology* 66: 934–949.

Kruml, S.M., and Geddes, D. 2000. "Catching Fire Without Burning Out: Is There an Ideal Way to Perform Emotional Labor?" In *Emotions in the Workplace: Theory, Research, and Practice,* ed. N.M. Ashkanasy, C.E.J. Härtel, and W.J. Zerbe, 177–188. Westport, CT: Quorum.

Kurstedt, H., McCollum, E.E., White, O., and Wiswell, A.K. 1999. "A Cross-Disciplinary Course in Relationship Competence for Systems Engineers." Paper presented at the 13th International Conference on Systems Engineering, Las Vegas, NV, August.

Lang, P.J. 1995. "The Emotion Probe: Studies of Motivation and Attention." *American Psychologist* 50: 372–385.

Langley, A., Mintzberg, H., Pitcher, P., Posada, E., and Saint-Macary, J. 1995. "Opening Up Decision-Making: The View from the Black Stool." *Organization Science* 6: 260–279.

Larsen, R.J. 1987. "The Stability of Mood Variability: A Spectral Analysis Approach to Daily Mood Assessments." *Journal of Personality and Social Psychology* 52: 1195–1204.

Larsen, R.J., and Diener, E. 1992. "Promises and Problems with the Circumplex Model of Emotion." In *Review of Personality and Social Psychology,* ed. Margaret S. Clark, no. 13: 25–59. Thousand Oaks, CA: Sage.

Larsen, R.J., and Kasimatis, M. 1990. "Individual Differences in Entrainment of Mood to the Weekly Calendar." *Journal of Personality and Social Psychology* 58: 164–171.

Larsen, R.J., and Ketelaar, T. 1991. "Personality and Susceptibility to Positive and Negative Emotional States." *Journal of Personality and Social Psychology* 61: 132–140.

Latack, J.C., Kinicui, A.J., and Prussia, G.E. 1995. "An Integrative Process Model of Coping with Job Loss." *Academy of Management Review* 20: 311–342.

Latack, J.C. 1986. "Coping With Job Stress: Measures and Future Directions for Scale Development." *Journal of Applied Psychology* 71: 377–385.

Lawler, E. 1995. "Organizational Effectiveness: New Realities and Challenges." In *The Performance Imperative,* ed. H. Risher and C. Fay. San Francisco: Jossey-Bass.

Lawler, E.J., and Thye, S.R. 1999. "Bringing Emotions into Social Exchange Theory." *Annual Review of Sociology* 25: 217–244.

Lazarus, R.S. 1966. *Psychological Stress and the Coping Process.* New York: McGraw-Hill.

———. 1982. "Thoughts on the Relations Between Cognition." *American Psychologist* 37: 1019–1024.

———. 1991a. *Emotion and Adaptation.* New York: Oxford University Press.

———. 1991b. "Progression on a Cognitive-Motivational-Relational Theory of Emotion." *American Psychologist* 46 (8): 819–834.

———. 1993. "From Psychological Stress to the Emotions: A History of Changing Outlooks." *Annual Review of Psychology* 44: 1–21.

Lazarus, R.S., and Folkman, S. 1984. *Stress Appraisal and Coping.* New York: Springer.

Leana, C.R., and Feldman, D.C. 1989. "When Mergers Force Layoffs: Some Lessons About Managing the Human Resource Problems." *Human Resource Plan*ning 2: 123–140.

LeDeaux, J.E. 1996. *The Emotional Brain: The Mysterious Underpinnings of Emotional Life.* New York: Simon & Schuster.

Leidner, R. 1991. "Selling Hamburgers and Selling Insurance: Gender, Work, and Identity in Interactive Service Jobs." *Gender and Society* 5 (2): 154–177.

———. 1993. *Fast Food, Fast Talk: Service Work and the Routinization of Everyday Life.* Berkeley: University of California Press.

———. 1999. "Emotional Labor in Service Work." *The Annals of the American Academy of Political and Social Science* 561: 81–95.

Leonard, D., and Sensiper, S. 1998. "The Role of Tacit Knowledge in Group Innovation." *California Management Review* 40: 112–132.

Levenson, R.W., and Ruef, A.M. 1992. "Empathy: A Physiological Substrate." *Journal of Personality and Social Psychology* 63: 234–246.

Leventhal, H., and Patrick-Miller, L. 1993. "Emotion and Illness: The Mind Is in the Body." In *Handbook of Emotions,* ed. M.L. Lewis and J.M. Haviland, 365–380. New York: Guilford Press.

Lewicki, R.J., Mcallister, D.J., and Bies, R.J. 1998. "Trust and Distrust: New Relationships and Realities." *Academy of Management Review* 23 (3): 438–458.

Lind, E.A., Kanfer, R., and Earley, P.C. 1990. "Voice, Control and Procedural Justice: Instrumental and Noninstrumental Concerns in Fairness Judgements." *Journal of Personality and Social Psychology* 59: 952–959.

Lind, E., and Tyler, T. 1988. *The Social Psychology of Procedural Justice.* New York: Plenum Press.

Lively, K.J. 2000. "Reciprocal Emotion Management: Working Together to Maintain Stratification in Private Law Firms." *Work and Occupations* 27 (1): 32–63.

Locke, E.A., and Latham, G.P. 1990. *A Theory of Goal Setting and Task Performance.* Englewood Cliffs, NJ: Prentice Hall.

Locke, K. 1996. "A Funny Thing Happened! The Management of Consumer Emotions in Service Encounters." *Organization Science* 7: 40–59.

Lord, R.G., Klimoski, R.J., and Kanfer, R., eds. In press. *Emotions At Work*. San Francisco: Jossey-Bass.

Lorenzo, R.V. 1984. "Effects of Assessorship on Managers' Proficiency in Acquiring, Evaluating, and Communicating Information About People." *Personnel Psychology* 37: 617–634.

Lovaglia, M.J., and Houser, J.A. 1996. "Emotional Reactions and Status in Groups." *American Sociological Review* 61: 867–883.

Lyons, W. 1980. *Emotion*. Cambridge, NY: Cambridge University Press.

Mackay, C., Cox, T. Burrows, G., and Lazzerini, T. 1978. "An Inventory for the Measurement of Self-Reported Stress and Arousal." *British Journal of Social and Clinical Psychology* 17: 283–284.

Maidique, M.A., and Hayes, R.H. 1984. "The Art of High Technology Management." *Sloan Management Review* (Winter): 18–31.

Mangham, I. 1973. "Faciliating Intraorganizational Dialogue in a Merger Situation." *Journal of Interpersonal Development* 4: 133–147.

Mann, S. 1999. *Hiding What We Feel, Faking What We Don't: Understanding the Role of Your Emotions at Work*. New York: Harper-Collins.

Mano, H., and Oliver, R. 1993. "Assessing the Dimensionality and Structure of the Consumption Experience: Evaluation, Feeling and Satisfaction." *Journal of Consumer Research* 20: 451–466.

Marks, M., and Mirvis, P. 1992. "Rebuilding After the Merger: Dealing With Survivor Sickness." *Organizational Dynamics* 2: 18–32.

Markus, H.R., and Cross, S. 1990. "The Interpersonal Self." In *Handbook of Personality: Theory and Research,* ed. L.A. Pervin, 576–608. New York: Guilford Press.

Martin, J., Knopoff, K., and Beckman, C. 1998. "An Alternative to Bureaucratic Impersonality and Emotional Labor: Bounded Emotionality at the Body Shop." *Administrative Science Quarterly* 43: 429–469.

Martin, L.L. 2000. "Moods Do Not Convey Information: Moods in Context Do." In *Feeling and Thinking: The Role of Affect in Social Cognition,* ed. J.P. Forgas, 153–177. Cambridge, UK: Cambridge University Press.

Marx, K. 1867/1990. *Capital*. Vol. 1, trans. B. Fowkes, New York: Penguin Books.

Maslach, C. 1982. *A Burnout: The Cost of Caring*. New York: Prentice Hall.

Maslach, C., and Jackson, S.E. 1981. "The Measurement of Experienced Burnout." *Journal of Occupational Behaviour* 2: 99–113.

———. 1982b. *Maslach Burnout Inventory*. 2d ed. Palo Alto, CA: Consulting Psychologists Press.

Mayer, J.D., and Salovey, P. 1993. "The Intelligence of Emotional Intelligence." *Intelligence* 17: 433–442.

———. 1995. "Emotional Intelligence and the Construction and Regulation of Feelings." *Applied and Preventive Psychology* 4: 197–208.

———. 1997. "What Is Emotional Intelligence?" In *Emotional Development and Emotional Intelligence: Implications for Educators,* ed. P. Salovey and D. Sluyter, 3–31. New York: Basic Books.

Mayer, J.D., Caruso, D.R., and Salovey, P. 1999. "Emotional Intelligence Meets Traditional Standards for an Intelligence." *Intelligence* 27: 267–298.

McClane, W.E. 1991. "Implications of Member Role Differentiation: Analysis of

Key Concept in The LMX Model of Leadership." *Group and Organization Studies* 16 (1): 102–113.

McConville, C., and Cooper, C. 1992. "Mood Vairability and Personality." *Personality and Individual Differences* 13 (November) : 1213–1221.

McCrae, R.R., and Costa, P.T., Jr. 1985. "Updating Norman's 'Adequate Taxonomy': Intelligence and Personality Dimensions in Natural Language and in Questionnaires." *Journal of Personality and Social Psychology* 49: 710–721.

McDonald, L., and Härtel, C.E.J. December, 1999. "Use of Affective Events Theory to Explain the Impact of Company Mishaps on Consumer Anger and Purchase Intentions." In *Proceedings of the 13th International Conference of the Australia New Zealand Academy of Management (CD-ROM)*. Hobart, Tasmania: Australia New Zealand Academy of Management.

McIntosh, D., Zajonc, R., Vig, P., and Emerick, S. 1997. "Facial Movement, Breathing, Temperature and Affect: Implications of the Vascular Theory of Emotional Efference." *Cognition and Emotion* 11 (2): 171–195.

Messick, S., ed. 1976. *Personality Consistencies in Cognition and Creativity*. San Francisco: Jossey-Bass.

Meyer, J.W., and Rowan, B. 1977. "Institutionalized Organizations: Formal Structure as Myth and Ceremony." *American Journal of Sociology* 83: 340–363.

Meyerson, D.E. 1998. "Feeling Stressed and Burned Out: A Feminist Reading and Re-Visioning of Stress-Based Emotions Within Medicine and Organization Science." *Organization Science* 9 (1): 103–118.

Michener, H.A., and Schwertfeger, M. 1972. "Liking as a Determinant of Power Tactic Preference." *Sociometry* 35: 190–202.

Middleton, D.R. 1989. "Emotional Style: the Cultural Ordering of Emotions." *Ethos* 17 (2): 187–201.

Milgram, S. 1963. "Behavioral Study of Obedience." *Journal of Abnormal and Social Psychology* 67: 371–378.

Miller, K., and Monge, P. 1985. "Social Information and Employee Anxiety About Organizational Change." *Human Communication Research* 11: 365–386.

Miller, V., Johnson, J., and Grau, J. 1994. "Antecedents to Willingness to Participate in Planned Organizational Change." *Journal of Applied Communication Research* 22: 59–80.

Milliken, F.J., and Martins, L.L. 1996. "Searching for Common Threads: Understanding the Multiple Effects of Diversity in Organizational Groups." *Academy of Management Review* 21 (2): 402–433.

Mintzberg, H. 1989. *Mintzberg on Management: Inside Our Strange World of Organizations*. New York: Free Press.

Mintzberg, H., Ahlstrand, B., and Lampel, J. 1998. *Strategy Safari: A Guided Tour Through the Wilds of Strategic Management*. New York: Free Press.

Mintzberg, H., Raisinghani, D., and Theoret, A. 1976. "The Structure of Unstructured Decision Processes." *Administrative Science Quarterly* 21: 246–275.

Mobley, W.H., Griffeth, R.W., Hand, H.H., and Meglino, B.M. 1979. "Review and Conceptual Analysis of Employee Turnover Process." *Psychological Bulletin* 86: 493–522.

Monsay, E.H. 1997. "Intuition in the Development of Scientific Theory and Practice." In *Intuition: The Inside Story*, ed. R. Davis-Floyd and P.S. Arvidson, 103–120. New York: Routledge.

Morris, J.A., and Feldman, D.C. 1996. "The Dimensions, Antecedents, and Conse-
quences of Emotional Labor." *Academy of Management Review* 21: 986–1010.
———. 1997. "Managing Emotions in the Workplace." *Journal of Managerial Is-
sues* 9 (3): 257–274.
Morris, W.N. 1989. *Mood: The Frame of Mind.* New York: Springer-Verlag.
———. 1999. "The Mood System." In *Well-Being: The Foundations of Hedonic
Psychology,* ed. D. Kahneman, E. Diener, and N. Schwarz, 169–189. New York:
Sage.
Moskowitz, D.S. 1994. "Cross-Situational Generality and the Interpersonal
Circumplex." *Journal of Personality and Social Psychology* 66: 921–933.
Moskowitz, D.S., Brown, K., and Côté, S. 1997. "Reconceptualizing Stability: Us-
ing Time as a Psychological Dimension." *Current Directions in Psychological
Science* 6: 127–132.
Moskowitz, D.S., and Côté, S. 1995. "Do Interpersonal Traits Predict Affect? A
Comparison of Three Models." *Journal of Personality and Social Psychology*
69: 915–924.
———. 1999. "Interpersonal Correlates of Affect." Manuscript submitted for
publication.
Motowidlo, S.J., and Van Scotter, J.R. 1994. "Evidence that Task Performance Should
Be Distinguished from Contextual Performance." *Journal of Applied Psychol-
ogy* 79: 475–480.
Muchinsky, P.M. 1993. *Psychology Applied to Work* 4th ed. Belmont, CA: Brooks
Cole.
Mulder, M. 1977. *The Daily Power Game.* Leiden, The Netherlands: Martinus Nihoff.
Müller-Stewens, G. 1991. "Personalwirtschaftliche Und Organisationstheoretische
Problemfelder Bei Mergers and Acquisitions." In *Neue Entwicklungen—Neues
Denken—Neue Strategien,* ed. K.F. Ackermann and H. Scholz, 157–171. Stutt-
gart: Poeschel.
Mumby, D.K., and Putnam, L.A. 1992. "The Politics of Emotion: A Feminist Read-
ing of Bounded Rationality." *Academy of Management Review* 17: 465–486.
Nemeth, C. 1986. "Differential Contributions of Majority and Minority Influence."
Psychological Review 93: 23–32.
Newton, T. 1995. "Becoming 'Stress-Fit.'" In *Managing Stress: Emotion and Power
at Work,* ed. T. Newton, 97–119. Newbury Park, CA: Sage.
Nippa, M. 1996. *Empirische Untersuchung Ausgewählter Erfolgsmerkmale
organisatorischer Veränderungsprozesse* (Freiberger Arbeitspapiere 12, III).
Freiberg.
Nutt, P.C. 1984. "Types of Organizational Decision Processes." *Administrative Sci-
ence Quarterly* 29: 414–450.
———. 1999. "Surprising But True: Half the Decisions in Organizations Fail."
Academy of Management Executive 13: 75–89.
Nygren, T.E., Isen, A.M., Taylor P.J., and Dulin, J. 1996. "The Influence of Positive
Affect on the Decision Rule in Risk Situations: Focus on Outcome (and Espe-
cially Avoidance of Loss) Rather Than Probability." *Organizational Behavior
and Human Decision Processes* 66: 59–72.
Oakley, J. 1991. *Morality and the Emotions.* London: Routledge.
Oatley, K. 1992. *Best Laid Schemes: The Psychology of Emotions.* Cambridge: Cam-
bridge University Press.

———. 1993. "Social Construction in Emotions." In *Handbook of Emotions,* ed. M. Lewis and J. Haviland, 341–351. New York: Guilford Press.

Oatley, K., and Jenkins, J.M. 1996. *Understanding Emotions.* Cambridge, MA: Blackwell.

O'Brien, M. 1994. "The Managed Heart Revisited: Health and Social Control." *Sociological Review* 42 (3): 393–413.

O'Driscoll, M.P., and Cooper, C.L. 1996. "Sources and Management of Excessive Job Stress and Burnout." In *Psychology at Work,* ed. P.B. Warr, 188–223. Harmondsworth, England: Penguin.

Offerman, L.R., and Schrier, P.E. 1985. "Social Influence Strategies: The Impact of Sex, Role, and Attitudes Toward Power." *Personality and Social Psychology Bulletin* 11: 286–300.

Organ, D.W. 1990. "The Motivational Basis of Organizational Citizenship Behavior." *Research in Organizational Behaviour* 12: 43–72.

O'Reilly, C.A., Caldwell, D.F., and Barnett, W.P. 1989. "Workgroup Demography, Social Integration, and Turnover." *Administrative Science Quarterly* 34: 21–37.

Ortony, A., Clore, G.L., and Collins, A. 1988. *The Cognitive Structure of Emotions.* New York: Cambridge University Press.

O'Shea, M., Ashkanasy, N.M., Gallois, C., and Härtel, C.E.J. 1999. "The Relationship Between the Work Environment and Work Attitudes/Behaviours: A Preliminary Test of Affective Events Theory." Paper presented at the Annual Meeting of the Society of Australasian Social Psychologists, Coolum, Australia, May.

———. 2000a. "On the Relationship Between the Work Environment and Work Attitudes and Behaviors: Laboratory Tests of Affective Events Theory." In *Causes and Consequences of Emotions in the Workplace,* chairs Y. Cohen-Charash and R. Cropanzano. Symposium Presented at the 2000 Annual Meeting of the Society for Industrial and Organizational Psychology, New Orleans, April.

———. 2000b. "The Mediating Role of Affective Reactions in Affective Events Theory." In *Recent Advances in the Study of Affective Events Theory,* chair M. O'Shea. Symposium Conducted at the Second Conference on Emotions and Organizational Life, Toronto, ON, August.

Palmer, H. 1998. "Introduction to Inner Knowing." In *Inner Knowing,* ed. H. Palmer, xv–xxi. New York: Jeremy P. Tarcher/Putnam.

Parikh, J., Neubauer, F., and Lank, A.G. 1994. *Intuition: The New Frontier in Management.* Cambridge, MA: Blackwell.

Park, J, and Banaji, M.R. 2000. "Mood and Heuristics: The Influence of Happy and Sad States on Sensitivity and Bias in Stereotyping." *Journal of Personality and Social Psychology* 78 (June): 1005–1023.

Parker, S., and Wall, T.D. 1998. *Job and Work Design: Organizing Work to Promote Well-being and Effectiveness.* Thousand Oaks, CA: Sage.

Parkinson, B. 1991. "Emotional Stylists: Strategies of Expressive Management Among Trainee Hairdressers." *Cognition and Emotion* 5: 419–434.

———. 1995. *Ideas and Realities of Emotion.* London: Routledge.

———. 1997. "Untangling the Appraisal-Emotion Connection." *Personality and Social Psychology Review* 1: 62–79.

Parsons, T. 1951. *The Social System.* New York: Free Press.

Paules, G.F. 1991. *Dishing It Out: Power and Resistance Among Waitresses in a New Jersey Restaurant.* Philadelphia: Temple University Press.

Payne, R., and Cooper, C.L. 2001. *Emotions at Work: Theory, Research and Applications for Management.* Chichester, England: John Wiley.

Pearlman, L.A., and Mac Ian, P.S. 1995. "Vicarious Traumatisation: An Empirical Study of the Effects of Trauma Work on Trauma Therapists." *Professional Psychology: Research and Practice* 26: 558–565.

Pekrun, R., and Frese, M. 1992. "Emotions in Work and Achievement." *International Review of Industrial and Organizational Psychology* 7: 153–200.

Pelled, L.H., Eisenhardt, K.M., and Xin, K.R. 1999. "Exploring the Black Box: An Analysis of Work Group Diversity, Conflict and Performance." *Administrative Science Quarterly* 44 (1): 1–28.

Penner, L.A., Shiffman, S., Paty, J.A., and Fritzsche, B.A. 1994. "Individual Differences in Intraperson Variability in Mood." *Journal of Personality and Social Psychology* 66: 712–721.

Pervin, L.A. 1993. "Affect and Personality." In *Handbook of Emotions,* ed. M. Lewis and J. Haviland, 301–311. New York: Guilford Press.

Petitmengin-Peugeot, C. 1999. "The Intuitive Experience." *Journal of Consciousness* 6: 43–77.

Petty, R.E., and Cacioppo, J.T. 1986. *Communication and Persuasion: Central and Peripheral Routes to Attitude Change.* New York: Springer-Verlag.

Petty, R.E., Gleicher, F., and Baker, S.M. 1991. "Multiple Roles for Affect in Persuasion." In *Emotion and Social Judgments,* ed. J.P. Forgas, 181–200. Oxford: Pergamon Press.

Pfeffer, J. 1981. *Power in Organizations.* Marshfield, MA: Pitman.

———. 1983. "Organisational Demography." In *Research in Organisational Behaviour* 5: 299–357.

———. 1992. *Managing With Power: Politics and Influence in Organizations.* Boston: Harvard Business School Press.

Picard, R.W. 1997. *Affective Computing.* Cambridge, MA: MIT Press.

Piderit, S.K. 2000. "Rethinking Resistance and Recognizing Ambivalence: A Multidimensional View of Attitudes Toward An Organizational Change." *Academy of Management Review* 25 (4): 783–794.

Pierce, J.L. 1995. *Gender Trials: Emotional Lives in Contemporary Law Firms.* Berkeley: University of California Press.

Pitcher, P. 1997. *The Drama of Leadership.* New York: John Wiley.

Plato. 1963. *The Republic IV: 440.* In *The Collected Dialogues of Plato,* ed. E. Hamilton and H. Cairns. Princeton, NJ: Princeton University Press.

Plous, S. 1993. *The Psychology of Judgment and Decision-Making.* New York: McGraw-Hill.

Ployhart, R., and Ryan, A.M. 1998. "Applicants' Reactions to the Fairness of Selection Procedures: The Effects of Positive Rule Violation and Time of Measurement." *Journal of Applied Psychology* 83: 3–16.

Plutchik, R. 1994. *The Psychology and Biology of Emotion.* New York: HarperCollins College Publishers.

Polzer, J.T., Neale, M.A., and Glenn, P.O. 1993. "The Effects of Relationships and Justification in an Interdependent Allocation Task." *Group Decision and Negotiation* 2: 135–148.

Popp, R.D. 2000. "Workshop for Workout Specialists with Delinquent Homeowners." Unpublished master's thesis, Virginia Tech University, Blacksburg, VA.

Porras, J., and Hoffer. S. 1986. "Common Behaviour Changes in Successful Organization Development Efforts." *Journal of Applied Behavioral Science* 22: 477–494.

Pounds, W.F. 1969. "The Process of Problem Finding." *Industrial Management Review* 11: 1–19.

Pratt, M.G., and Dutton, J.E. 2000. "Owning Up or Opting Out: The Role of Emotions and Identities in Issue Ownership." In *Emotions in the Workplace: Research, Theory, and Practice*, ed. N.M. Ashkanasy, C.E.J. Härtel, and W.J. Zerbe, 103–129. Westport, CT: Quorum Books.

Pruitt, D.G., and Rubin, D.B. 1986. *Social Conflict: Escalation, Stalemate and Settlement*. New York: Random House.

Pugh, D. 2001. "Service With a Smile: Emotional Contagion in Service Encounters." *Academy of Management Journal* 44: 1018–1027.

Radloff, L.S. 1977. "The CES-D Scale: A Self Report Depression Scale for Research in the General Population." *Applied Psychological Measurement* 1: 385–401.

Rafaeli, A. 1989a. "When Clerks Meet Customers: A Test of Variables Related to Emotional Expressions on the Job." *Journal of Applied Psychology* 74 (3): 385–393.

———. 1989b. "When Cashiers Meet Customers: An Analysis of the Role of Supermarket Cashiers." *Academy of Management Journal* 32 (2): 245–273.

Rafaeli, A., and Sutton, R.I. 1987. "Expression of Emotion as Part of the Work Role." *Academy of Management Review* 12: 23–37.

———. 1989. "The Expression of Emotion in Organizational Life." *Research in Organizational Behaviour* 11: 1–42.

———. 1991. "Emotional Contrast Strategies as Means of Social Influence: Lessons from Criminal Interrogators and Bill Collectors." *Academy of Management Journal* 34: 749–775.

Rahim, M.A. 1986. "Referent Role and Styles in Handling Interpersonal Conflict." *Journal of Social Psychology* 125 (1): 79–86.

Rahim, M.A., Garrett, J.E., and Buntzman, G.F. 1992. "Ethics of Managing Interpersonal Conflict in Organisations." *Journal of Business Ethics* 11 (5): 423–433.

Ramsey, K.B. 1985. "Counseling Employees." In *Human Resources Management and Development Handbook*, ed. W.R. Tracey, 821–836. New York: AMACOM.

Raven, B.H. 1990. "Political Applications of the Psychology of Interpersonal Influence and Social Power." *Political Psychology* 11: 493–520.

———. 1993. "The Bases of Power: Origins and Recent Developments." *Journal of Social Issues* 49: 227–251.

———. 2001. "Power/interaction and Interpersonal Influence: Experimental Investigations and Case Studies." In *The Use and Abuse of Power*, ed. A.Y. Lee-Chai and J.A. Bargh, 217–240. Philadelphia: Psychology Press.

Raven, B.H., and Rubin, J. 1976. *Social Psychology: People in Groups*. New York: John Wiley.

Reber, A.S. 1989. "Implicit Learning and Tacit Knowledge." *Journal of Experimental Psychology: General* 118: 219–235.

Reddy, M. 1994. "Eaps and Their Future in the UK: History Repeating Itself?" *Personnel Review* 23: 60–78.

Reiss, M. 1995. "Implementierung." In *Handbuch Unternehmensführung*, ed. H. Corsten and M. Reiss, 291–302. Wiesbaden: Gabler.

Richardson, P., and Denton, D.K. 1996. "Communicating Change." *Human Resource Management* 35: 203–216.

Ridgeway, C., and Johnson, C. 1990. "What Is the Relationship Between Socioemotional Behavior and Status in Task Groups?" *American Journal of Sociology* 95: 1189–1212.

Ridgeway, C.L., Boyle, E.H., Kuipers, K.J., and Robinson, D.T. 1998. "How Do Status Beliefs Develop? The Role of Resources and Interactional Experience." *American Sociological Review* 63: 331–350.

Rind, B., and Kipnis, D. 1999. "Changes in Self-Perceptions as a Result of Successfully Persuading Others." *Journal of Social Issues* 55: 141–156.

Robbins, S., Waters-Marsh, T., Cacioppo, J.T., and Millett, B. 1994. *Organizational Behavior: Concepts, Controversies and Applications.* New York: Prentice Hall.

Rook, K.S. 1985. "The Functions of Social Bonds: Perspectives from Research on Social Support, Loneliness and Social Isolation." In *Social Support: Theory, Research and Applications,* ed. I. G. Sarason and B. R. Sarason, 243–267. Dordrecht, The Netherlands: Matinus Nijhoff.

———. 1987. "Social Support Versus Companionship: Effects on Life Stress, Loneliness, and Evaluations by Others." *Journal of Personality and Social Psychology* 52: 1132–1147.

———. 1990. "Social Relationships as a Source of Companionship: Implications for Older Adults' Well-Being." In *Social Support, An Interactional View,* ed. B.R. Sarason, I.G. Sarason, and G.R. Pierce, 219–250. New York: John Wiley.

Roseman, I.J. 1984. "Cognitive Determinants of Emotion: A Structural Theory." *Journal of Personality and Social Psychology* 5: 11–36.

Rosenberg, E.L. 1998. "Levels of Analysis and the Organization of Affect." *Review of General Psychology* 2: 247–270.

Ross, R.S. 1989. "Conflict." In *Small Groups in Organizational Settings,* ed. R. Ross and J. Ross, 139–178. Englewood Cliffs, NJ: Prentice Hall.

Rowan, R. 1986. *The Intuitive Manager.* Boston: Little, Brown.

Ruffin, C.L. 1993. "Stress and Health—Little Hassles Vs. Major Life Events." *Australian Psychologist* 28 (3): 201–208.

Russell, J.A. 1980. "A Circumplex Model of Affect." *Journal of Personality and Social Psychology* 39 (December): 1161–1178.

Russell, J.A. 1994. "Is there Universal Recognition of Emotion from Facial Expression? A Review of the Cross-Cultural Studies." *Psychological Bulletin* 115: 102–141.

Russell, J.A., and Feldman-Barrett, L. 1999. "Core Affect, Prototypical Emotional Episodes, and Other Things Called Emotion: Dissecting the Elephant." *Journal of Personality and Social Psychology* 76: 805–819.

Rusting, C.L., and DeHart, T. 2000. "Retrieving Positive Memories to Regulate Negative Mood: Consequences for Mood-Congruent Memory." *Journal of Personality and Social Psychology* 78: 737–752.

Sagie, A., and Koslowsky, M. 1996. "Decision Type, Organisational Control, and Acceptance of Change: An Integrative Approach to Participative Decision Making." *Applied Psychology: An International Review* 45: 85–92.

Salancik, G.R., and Pfeiffer, J. 1977. "Who Gets Power—and How They Hold Onto It: A Strategic Contingency Model of Power." *Organizational Dynamics* 5: 3–21.

Saleker, J. 1995. *Der Kommunikationsauftrag Bei Merger and Acquisitions.* Bern: Haupt.

Salovey, P., and Mayer, J. 1990. "Emotional Intelligence." *Imagination, Cognition and Personality* 9: 185–211.

Salter, F.K. 1995. *Emotions in Command: A Naturalistic Study of Institutional Dominance.* Oxford, UK: Oxford University Press.

Sandelands, L.E., Glynn, M.A., and Larson, J.R. 1989. "Control Theory and Social Behavior in the Workplace." *Human Relations* 44: 1107–1130.

Sashkin, M., and Rosenbach, W.E. 1993. "A New Leadership Paradigm." In *Contemporary Issues in Leadership,* ed. W.E. Rosenbach and R.L. Taylor, 87–108. Boulder, CO: Westview Press.

Sauter, V.L. 1999. "Intuitive Decision-Making." *Communications of the ACM.* 42: 109–115.

Saxton, M.J., Phillips, J.S., and Blakeney, R.N. 1991. "Antecedents and Consequences of Emotional Exhaustion in the Airline Reservations Service Sector." *Human Relations* 44 (6): 583–595.

Schaubroeck, J., and Jones, J.R. 2000. "Antecedents of Workplace Emotional Labor Dimensions and Moderators of Their Effects on Physical Symptoms." *Journal of Organizational Behaviour* 21: 163–183.

Schein, E.H. 1992. *Organizational Culture and Leadership.* 2d ed. San Francisco: Jossey-Bass.

Schelling, T. 1960. *The Strategy of Conflict.* Cambridge, MA: Harvard University Press.

Scherer, K.R. 1984. "Emotion as a Multicomponent Process. A Model and Some Cross-Cultural Data." In *Review of Personality and Social Psychology,* ed. P. Shaver, 37–63. Beverly Hills, CA: Sage.

Scherer, K.R., Wallbott, H.G., and Summerfield, A.B., eds. 1986. *Experiencing Emotion: A Cross-Cultural Study.* Cambridge, Melbourne: Cambridge University Press.

Schmidt-Atzert, L., and Ströhm, W. 1983. "Ein Beitrag Zur Taxonomie Der Emotionswörter." *Psychologische Beiträge* 25: 123–141.

Schneider, B. 1990. "The Climate for Service: An Application of the Climate Construct." In *Organizational Climate and Culture,* ed. B. Schneider, 383–412. San Francisco: Jossey-Bass.

Schneider, B., and Bowen, D.E. 1985. "Employee and Customer Perceptions of Service in Banks: Replication and Extension." *Journal of Applied Psychology* 70: 423–433

Schneider, B., Parkington, J.J., and Buxton, V.M. 1980. "Employee and Customer Perceptions of Service in Banks." *Administrative Sciences Quarterly* 25: 252–267.

Schoemaker, P.J.H., and Russo, E.J. 1993. "A Pyramid of Decision Approaches." *California Management Review* 36: 9–31.

Schon, D.A. 1983. *The Reflective Practitioners: How Professionals Think in Action.* New York: Basic Books.

Schriesheim, C.A., and Hinkin, T.R. 1990. "Influence Tactics Used By Subordinates: A Theoretical and Empirical Analysis and Refinement of the Kipnis, Schmidt, and Wilkinson Subscales." *Journal of Applied Psychology* 75: 246–257.

Schwarz, N., Bless, H., and Bohner, G. 1991. "Mood and Persuasion: Affective States Influence the Processing of Persuasive Communication." In *Advances in Experimental Social Psychology,* ed. M.P. Zanna, 161–199. New York: Academic Press.

Schwarz, N., and Bohner, G. 1996. "Feelings and Their Motivational Implications. Moods and The Action Sequence." In *The Psychology of Action. Linking Cognition and Motivation to Behaviour,* ed. P.M. Gollwitzer and J.A. Bargh, 119–145. New York: Guilford Press.

Schwarz, N., and Clore, G.L. 1996. "Feelings and Phenomenal Experiences." In *Social Psychology: A Handbook of Basic Principles,* ed. E.T. Higgins and A. Kruglanski, 433–465. New York: Guilford Press.

Schweiger, D., and Denisi, A. 1991. "Communication With Employees Following a Merger: A Longitudinal Field Experiment." *Academy of Management Journal* 35: 110–135.

Scott, W.R. 1994. "Institutions and Organizations: Toward a Theoretical Synthesis." In *Institutional Environments and Organizations,* ed. W.R. Scott and J.W. Meyer, 55–80. Thousand Oaks, CA: Sage.

Seligman, M.E.P., and Schulman, P. 1986. "Explanatory Style as a Predictor of Productivity and Quitting Among Life Insurance Sales Agents." *Journal of Personality and Social Psychology* 50: 832–838.

Shapiro, S., and Spence, M. 1997. "Managerial Intuition: A Conceptual and Operational Framework." *Business Horizons* 40: 63–69.

Shaver, P., Schwartz, J., Kirson, D., and O'Connor, C. 1987. "Emotion Knowledge: Further Exploration of a Prototype Approach." *Journal of Personality and Social Psychology* 52 (6): 1061–1086.

Shaw, J., and Barrett-Power, E. 1997. "A Conceptual Framework for Assessing Organization, Work Group, and Individual Effectiveness During and After Downsizing." *Human Relations* 50: 109–127.

Sheldrake, R. 1987. "Mind, Memory and Archetype: Morphic Resonance and the Collective Unconscious: I." *Psychological Perspectives* 18: 9–25.

Shirley, D.A., and Langan-Fox, J. 1996. "Review of Intuition." *Psychological Reports* 79: 563–584.

Simon, H.A. 1960. *The New Science of Managerial Decision.* New York: Harper and Row.

———. 1976. *Administrative Behavior: A Study of Decision-Making Processes in Administrative Organization.* 3d ed. New York: Free Press.

———. 1987. "Making Management Decisions: The Role of Intuition and Emotion." *Academy of Management Executive* 1: 57–64.

———. 1997. *Administrative Behavior: A Study of Decision-Making in Administrative Organizations.* 4th ed. New York: Free Press.

Simonton, D.K. 1975. "Creativity, Task Complexity, and Intuitive Versus Analytical Problem Solving." *Psychological Reports* 37: 351–354.

Sinclair, R.C., and Mark, M.M. 1992. "The Influence of Mood State on Judgment and Action: Effects on Persuasion, Categorization, Social Justice, Person Perception, and Judgmental Accuracy." In *The Construction of Social Judgments,* ed. L.L. Martin and A. Tesser, 165–193. Hillsdale, NJ: Lawrence Erlbaum.

Singer, D.S. 1998. "Using SAS PROC MIXED to Fit Multilevel Models, Hierarchical Models, and Individual Growth Models." *Journal of Educational and Behavioral Statistics* 24: 323–355.

Singer, M. 1993. "The Application of Organizational Justice Theories to Selection Fairness Research." *New Zealand Journal of Psychology* 22: 32–45.

Sitkin, S.B., and Weingart, L.R. 1995. "Determinants of Risky Decision-Making

Behavior: A Test of the Mediating Role of Risk Perceptions and Propensity." *Academy of Management Journal* 38: 1573–1592.

Skarlicki, D., and Folger, R. 1997. "Retaliation in the Workplace: The Roles of Distributive, Procedural, and Interactional Justice." *Journal of Applied Psychology* 82: 434–443.

Sloman, S.A. 1996. "The Empirical Case for Two Systems of Reasoning." *Psychological Bulletin* 119: 3–22.

Smeltzer, L. 1991. "An Analysis of Strategies for Announcing Organization-Wide Change." *Group and Organization Studies* 16: 5–24.

Smeltzer, L., and Zenner, M. 1992. "Development of a Model for Announcing Major Layoffs." *Group and Organization Management* 17: 446–472.

Smith, A.C. III, and Kleinman, S. 1989. "Managing Emotions in Medical School: Students' Contacts with the Living and the Dead." *Social Psychology Quarterly* 52: 56–69.

Smith, C.A., and Ellsworth, P.C. 1985. "Patterns of Cognitive Appraisal in Emotion." *Journal of Personality and Social Psychology* 48: 813–838.

Smith C.A., Haynes, K.N., Lazarus, R.S., and Pope, L.K. 1993. "In Search of the 'Hot' Cognitions: Attributions, Appraisals, and Their Relationship to Emotion." *Journal of Personality and Social Psychology* 65: 916–929.

Smith, C.A., and Kirby, L.D. 2000. "Consequences Require Antecedents: Toward a Progress Model of Emotion Elicitation." In *Feeling and Thinking: The Role of Affect in Social Cognition,* ed. J.P. Forgas, 83–106. Cambridge, UK: Cambridge University Press.

Smith, C.A., and Lazarus, R.S. 1990. "Emotion and Adaptation." In *Handbook of Personality: Theory and Research,* ed. L.A. Pervin. New York: Guilford Press.

Smith, C.A., and Pope, L.K. 1992. "Appraisal and Emotion: The Interactional Contributions of Dispositional and Situational Factors" In *Emotion and Social Behavior. Review of Personality and Social Psychology,* ed. M.S. Clark, vol. 14, 32–62. Thousand Oaks, CA: Sage.

Snodgrass, S.E. 1985. "Women's Intuition: The Effect of Subordinate Role on Interpersonal Sensitivity." *Journal of Personality and Social Psychology* 49: 146–155.

———. 1992. "Further Effects of Role Versus Gender on Interpersonal Sensitivity." *Journal of Personality and Social Psychology* 62: 154–158.

Snyder, M. 1974. "The Self-Monitoring of Expressive Behavior." *Journal of Personality and Social Psychology* 30: 526–537.

Solomon, R.C. 1990. *A Passion for Justice: Emotions and the Origins of the Social Contract.* Reading, MA: Addison-Wesley.

Sondak, H., and Moore, M.C. 1993. "Relationship Frames and Cooperation." *Group Decision and Negotiation* 2: 103–118.

Spielberger, C.D., and Sarason, I.G. 1975–1986. *Stress and Anxiety.* Vols. 1–10. New York: John Wiley.

Spinoza, B. 1985. "Ethics." In *The Collected Works of Spinoza,* ed. E. Curley. Princeton, NJ: Princeton University Press.

Staw, B.M., and Barsade, S.G. 1993. "Affect and Managerial Performance: A Test of the Sadder-But-Wider Vs. Happier-and-Smarter Hypotheses." *Administrative Science Quarterly* 38: 304–331.

Staw, B.M., Bell, N.E., and Clausen, J.A. 1986. "The Dispositional Approach to Job

Attitudes: A Lifetime Longitudinal Test." *Administrative Science Quarterly* 31: 56–77.

Staw, B.M., Sutton, R.I., and Pelled, L.H. 1994. "Employee Positive Emotion and Favorable Outcomes at the Workplace." *Organization Science* 5: 51–71.

Stearns, C.Z., and Stearns, P.N. 1986. *Anger: The Struggle for Emotional Control in America's History.* Chicago: University of Chicago Press.

Stein, N.L., Trabasso, T., and Liwag, M. 1993. "The Representation and Organization of Emotional Experience: Unfolding the Emotion Episode." In *Handbook of Emotions,* ed. M.L. Lewis and J. Haviland, 279–300. New York: Guilford Press.

Steinberg, R.J. 1999. "Emotional Labor in Job Evaluation: Redesigning Compensation Practices." *The Annals of the American Academy of Political and Social Science* 561: 143–157.

Steinberg, R.J., and Figart, D.M. 1999a. "Emotional Labor Since the Managed Heart." *Annals of the American Academy of Political and Social Science* 561: 8–26.

———. 1999b. "Emotional Demands at Work: A Job Content Analysis." *Annals of the American Academy of Political and Social Science* 561: 177–191.

Steiner, D., and Gilliland, S. 1996. "Fairness Reactions to Personnel Selection Techniques in France and the United States." *Journal of Applied Psychology* 81: 134–141.

Steinross, B., and Kleinman, S. 1989. "The Highs and Lows of Emotional Labor: Detectives' Encounters With Criminals and Victims." *Journal of Contemporary Ethnography* 17: 435–452.

Stepanovich, P.L., Uhrig, J.D., and Armstrong, K.M. 1999. "Decision-Making in High-Velocity Environments: Implications for Healthcare." *Journal of Healthcare Management* 44: 197–205.

Stewart, W., and Barling, J. 1996. "Daily Work Stress, Mood and Interpersonal Job Performance: A Mediational Model." *Work and Stress* 10: 336–351.

Stone, A.A., and Neale, J.M. 1984. "New Measure of Daily Coping: Development and Preliminary Results." *Journal of Personality and Social Psychology* 46: 892–906.

Strazdins, L. 2000. "Integrating Emotions: Multiple Role Measurement of Emotional Work." *Australian Journal of Psychology* 52: 41–50.

Strazdins, L., Galligan, R.F., and Scannell, E.D. 1997. "Gender and Depressive Symptoms: Sharing Instrumental and Expressive Tasks When the Children Are Young." *Journal of Family Psychology* 11: 222–233.

Sullivan, H.S. 1940. *Conceptions of Modern Psychiatry.* New York: W.W. Norton.

Sutton, R.I. 1991. "Maintaining Norms about Expressed Emotions: The Case of Bill Collectors." *Administrative Science Quarterly* 36: 245–268.

Sutton, R.I., and Rafaeli, A. 1988. "Untangling the Relationship Between Displayed Emotions and Organizational Sales: The Case of Convenience Stores." *Academy of Management Journal* 31 (3): 461–487.

Taggart, W.M., Valenzi, E., Zalka, L., and Lowe, K.B. 1997. "Rational and Intuitive Styles: Commensurability Across Respondents' Characteristics." *Psychological Reports* 80: 23–33.

Tagiuri, R., and Litwin, H. 1968. *Organizational Climate: Explorations of a Concept.* Boston: Harvard University Press.

Tajfel, H., and Turner, J.C. 1986. "The Social Identity Theory of Intergroup Behaviour." In *Psychology of Intergroup Relations,* ed. S. Worchel and W.G. Austain, 7–24. Chicago: Nelson-Hall.

Taylor, F.W. 1911. *The Principles of Scientific Management.* New York: W.W. Norton.

Taylor, M.S., Tracy, K., Renard, M.K., and Harrison, J.K. 1995. "Due Process in Performance Appraisal: A Quasi-Experiment in Procedural Justice." *Administrative Science Quarterly* 40: 495–523.

Taylor, S., and Bodgan, R. 1984. *Introduction to Qualitative Research Methods: The Search for Meanings.* New York: John Wiley.

Tellegen, A. 1985. "Structure of Mood and Personality and Their Relevance to Assessing Anxiety, with an Emphasis on Self-Report." In *Anxiety and the Anxiety Disorders,* ed. A. Hussain Tuma and J.D. Maser, 681–786. Hillsdale, NJ: Lawrence Erlbaum.

Terry, D., Callan, V., and Sartori, G. 1996. "Employee Adjustment to an Organizational Merger: Stress, Coping and Intergroup Differences." *Stress Medicine* 12: 105–122.

Teuchmann, K., Totterdell, P., and Parker, S.K. 1999. "Rushed, Unhappy, and Drained: An Experience-Sampling Study of Relations Between Time Pressure, Perceived Control, Mood, and Emotional Exhaustion in a Group of Accountants." *Journal of Occupational Health Psychology* 4: 37–54.

Tews, M.J., and Glomb, T.M. 2000. "The Feelings at Work Scale: Theoretical Basis, Development of the Instrument, and Preliminary Validity Testing." Paper presented at the Second Conference on Emotions and Organizational Life, Toronto, Ontario, August.

Thacker, R.A., and Wayne, S.J. 1995. "An Examination of the Relationship Between Upward Influence Tactics and Assessments of Promotability." *Journal of Management* 21: 739–756.

Thayer, R.E. 1996. *The Origin of Everyday Moods.* New York: Oxford University Press.

Thayer, R.E., Newman, J.R., and McClain, T.M. 1994. "Self-Regulation of Mood: Strategies for Changing a Bad Mood, Raising Energy, and Reducing Tension." *Journal of Personality and Social Psychology* 67: 910–925.

Thibaut, J., and Walker, L. 1975. *Procedural Justice: A Psychological Analysis.* Hillsdale, NJ: Lawrence Erlbaum.

Thoits, P.A. 1985. "Self-Labeling Processes in Mental Illness: The Role of Emotional Deviance." *American Journal of Sociology* 91: 221–247.

———. 1996. "Managing the Emotions of Others." *Symbolic Interaction* 19: 85–109.

Thompson, J.D. 1967. *Organization in Action.* New York: McGraw-Hill.

Thompson, L., Nadler, J., and Kim, P. 1999. "Some Like It Hot: The Case for the Emotional Negotiator." In *Shared Cognition in Organizations: The Management of Knowledge,* ed. L. Thompson, J. Levine, and D. Messick, 139–161. Mahwah, NJ: Lawrence Erlbaum.

Thorndike, E.L. 1920. "Intelligence and Its Uses." *Harper's Magazine* 140: 227–235

Tiedens, L.Z. 2001. "Anger and Advancement Versus Sadness and Subjugation: The Effect of Negative Emotion Expressions on Social Status Conferral." *Journal of Personality and Social Psychology* 80: 86–94.

Tiedens, L.Z., and Ellsworth, P.C. 1998. "Sentimental Stereotypes: Emotional Expectations for High and Low Status Group Members." Manuscript submitted for publication.

Tiedens, L.Z., Ellsworth, P.C., and Moskowitz, D.S. 1998. "Feeling Your Place: Emotional Consequences of Social Status Positions." Manuscript submitted for Publication.

Tolich, M.B. 1993. "Alienating and Liberating Emotions at Work: Supermarket Clerks' Performance of Customer Service." *Journal of Contemporary Ethnography* 22 (3): 361–381.

Totterdell, P. 1999. "Mood Scores: Mood and Performance in Professional Cricketers." *British Journal of Psychology* 90: 317–332.

Tracy, S.J. 2000. "Becoming a Character for Commerce: Emotion Labor, Self Subordination and Discursive Construction of Identity in a Total Institution." *Management Communication Quarterly* 14: 790–827.

Trobst, K.K., Collins, R.L., and Embree, J.M. 1994. "The Role of Emotion in Social Support Provision: Gender, Empathy and Expressions of Distress." *Journal of Social and Personal Relationships* 11: 45–62.

Trzicky, N. 1998. "Stakeholder Einer Fusion Und Deren Feindbilder." In *Fusionen Gestalten Und Kommunizieren,* ed. M.E. Henckel Von Donnersmarck and R. Schatz, 37–56. Bonn: Innovatio.

Tsojvold, D. 1991. "Rights and Responsibilities of Dissent: Cooperative Conflict." *Employee Responsibilities and Rights Journal* 4: 13–23.

Tsui, A.S., Egan, T.D., and O'Reilly, C.A. 1992. "Being Different: Relational Demography and Organisational Attachment." *Administrative Science Quarterly* 37: 549–579.

Turner, J.C. 1985. "Social Categorisation and Self Concept: A Social Cognitive Theory of Group Behaviour." *Advances in Group Processes* 2: 77–121.

Turner, J.C., Hogg, M., Oakes, P.J., and Reicher, S.D. 1987. *Rediscovering the Social Group: A Self Categorization Theory.* New York: Basil Blackwell.

Van Dierendonck, D., Schaufeli, W.B., and Buunk, B.P. 1998. "The Evaluation of an Individual Burnout Intervention Program: The Role of Inequity and Social Support." *Journal of Applied Psychology* 83: 392–407.

Van Maanen, J. 1991. "The Smile Factory: Work in Disneyland." In *Reframing Organizational Culture,* ed. P. Frost, L. Moore, C. Lundberg, C. Louis, and J. Martin, 58–76. Newbury Park, CA: Sage.

Van Maanen, J., and Kunda, G. 1989. "'Real Feelings': Emotional Expression and Organizational Culture." *Research in Organizational Behaviour* 11: 43–103.

Van Reekum, C.M., and Scherer, K.R. 1997. "Levels of Processing in Emotion-Antecedent Appraisal." In *Cognitive Science Perspectives on Personality and Emotion,* ed. G. Matthews, 259–330. Amsterdam: Elsevier.

Van Scotter, J.R., and Motowidlo, S.J. 1996. "Interpersonal Facilitation and Job Dedication as Separate Facets of Contextual Performance." *Journal of Applied Psychology* 81: 525–531.

Vaughan, F.E. 1979. *Awakening Intuition.* New York: Doubleday.

Verbeke, W. 1997. "Individual Differences in Emotional Contagion of Salespersons: Its Effect on Performance and Burnout." *Psychology and Marketing* 14: 617–636.

Vitaliano, P.P., Russo, J., Carr, J.E., Maiuro, R.D., and Becker, J. 1985. "The Ways of Coping Checklist: Revision and Psychometric Properties." *Multivariate Behavioral Research* 20: 3–26.

Vittengl, J.R., and Holt, C.S. 1998. "A Time-Series Diary Study of Mood and Social Interaction." *Motivation and Emotion* 22: 255–275.

Wagner, U., Lampen, L., and Syllwasschy, J. 1986. "In Group Inferiority, Social Identity and Out-Group Devaluation in a Modified Minimal Group Study." *British Journal of Social Psychology* 25: 15–23.

Wagstaff, G. 1994. "Equity, Equality and Need: Three Principles of Justice or One? An Analysis of 'Equity as Desert'." *Current Psychology, Developmental, Learning, Personality, Social* 13: 138–152.

Wally, S., and Baum, R.J. 1994. "Personal and Structural Determinants of the Pace of Strategic Decision-Making." *Academy of Management Journal* 37: 932–956.

Ward, L.G., and Throop, R. 1989. "The Dewey-Mead Analysis of Emotions." *Social Science Journal* 26 (4): 465–479.

Watson, D. 1988. "Intraindividual and Interindividual Analyses of Positive and Negative Affect: Their Relation to Health Complaints, Perceived Stress, and Daily Activities." *Journal of Personality and Social Psychology* 54: 1020–1030.

———. 2000. *Mood and Temperament.* New York: Guilford Press.

Watson, D., and Clark, L.A. 1984. "Negative Affectivity: The Disposition to Experience Aversive Emotional States." *Psychological Bulletin* 96 (3): 465–490.

———. 1994. "Emotions, Moods, Traits, and Temperaments: Conceptual Distinctions and Empirical Findings." In *The Nature of Emotion,* ed. P. Ekman and R.J. Davidson, 89–93. New York: Oxford University Press.

Watson, D., Clark, L.A., McIntyre, C.W., and Hamaker, S. 1992. "Affect, Personality, and Social Activity." *Journal of Personality and Social Psychology* 63: 1011–1025.

Watson, D., Clark, L.A., and Tellegen, A. 1988. "Development and Validation of Brief Measures of Positive and Negative Affect: The PANAS Scales." *Journal of Personality and Social Psychology* 54: 1063–1070.

Watson, D., and Tellegen, S. 1985. "Toward a Consensual Structure of Mood." *Psychological Bulletin* 98: 219–235.

Watson, D., Wiese, D., Vaidya, J., and Tellegen, A. 1999. "The Two General Activation Systems of Affect: Structural Findings, Evolutionary Considerations, and Psychobiological Evidence." *Journal of Personality and Social Psychology* 76: 820–838.

Weber, M. 1946. *From Max Weber: Essays in Sociology,* trans. H.H. Gerth and C.W. Mills. New York: Oxford University Press.

Wegener, B. 1991. "Job Mobility and Social Ties: Social Resources, Prior Job, and Status Attainment." *American Sociological Review* 56: 60–71.

Wegener, D.T., Petty, R.E., and Smith, S.M. 1995. "Positive Mood Can Increase or Decrease Message Scrutiny: The Hedonic Contingency View of Mood and Message Processing." *Journal of Personality and Social Psychology* 69: 5–15.

Weick, K.E. 1999. "That's Moving: Theories That Matter." *Journal of Management Inquiry* 8 (2): 134–142.

Weierter, S.J.M. 1997. "Who Wants to Play 'Follow the Leader?' A Theory of Charismatic Relationships Based on Routinized Charisma and Follower Characteristics." *Leadership Quarterly* 8: 171–193.

Weiner, B. 1986. *An Attributional Theory of Motivation and Emotion.* New York: Springer-Verlag.

Weiss, H.M. Guest ed. 2001. Special Issue on Emotions in the Workplace. *Organizational Behavior and Human Decision Process* 86, no. 1.

Weiss, H.M., and Cropanzano, R. 1996. "Affective Events Theory: A Theoretical Discussion of the Structure, Causes and Consequences of Affective Experiences at Work." *Research in Organizational Behaviour* 18: 1–74.

Weiss, H.M., Nicholas, J.P., and Daus, C.S. 1999. "An Examination of the Joint Effects of Affective Experiences and Job Beliefs on Job Satisfaction and Variations in Affective Experiences over Time." *Organizational Behavior and Human Decision Processes* 78: 1–24.

Westley, F., and Mintzberg, H. 1989. "Visionary Leadership and Strategic Management." *Strategic Management Journal* 10: 17–32.

Wharton, A. 1993. "The Affective Consequences of Service Work: Managing Emotions on the Job." *Work and Occupations* 20 (2): 205–232.

———. 1999. "The Psychosocial Consequences of Emotional Labor." *Annals of the American Academy of Political and Social Science* 561: 159–176.

Wharton, A., and Erickson, R. 1993. "Managing Emotions on the Job and at Home: Understanding the Consequences of Multiple Emotional Roles." *Academy of Management Review* 18 (3): 457–486.

———. 1995. "The Consequences of Caring: Exploring the Links Between Women's Job and Family Emotion Work." *Sociological Quarterly* 36: 273–296.

Wheeler, L., and Reis, H.T. 1991. "Self-Recording of Everyday Life Events: Origins, Types, and Uses." *Journal of Personality* 59: 339–354.

Wichroski, M.A. 1994. "The Secretary: Invisible Labor in the Workworld of Women." *Human Organization* 53: 33–41.

Wiggins, J.S. 1991. "Agency and Communion as Conceptual Coordinates for the Understanding and the Measurement of Interpersonal Behavior." In *Thinking Clearly About Psychology,* ed. W.M. Grove and D. Cicchetti, 89–113. Minneapolis: University of Minnesota Press.

Williams, S., and Shiaw, W.T. 1999. "Mood and Organizational Citizenship Behavior: The Effects of Positive Affect on Employee Organizational Citizenship Behavior Intentions." *Journal of Psychology* 133: 656–668.

Wilson-Evered, E., Härtel, C.E.J., and Neal, M. 2001. "A Longitudinal Study of Work Group Innovation: The Importance of Transformational Leadership and Morale." *Advances in Health Care Management* 2: 315–340.

Wouters, C. 1989. "The Sociology of Emotions and Flight Attendants: Hochschild's Managed Heart." *Theory, Culture and Society* 6: 95–123.

———. 1992. "On Status Competition and Emotion Management: The Study of Emotions as a New Field." *Theory, Culture and Society* 9: 229–252.

Wright, T.A., Bonett, D.G., and Sweeney, D.A. 1993. "Mental-Health and Work Performance: Results of a Longitudinal-Field Study." *Journal of Occupational and Organizational Psychology* 66: 277–284.

Wright, T.A., and Cropanzano, R. 1998. "Emotional Exhaustion As a Predictor of Job Performance and Voluntary Turnover. *Journal of Applied Psychology* 83: 486–493.

Wright, T.A., and Staw, B.M. 1999. "Affect and Favorable Work Outcomes: Two Longitudinal Tests of the Happy-Productive Worker Thesis." *Journal of Organizational Behaviour* 20: 1–13.

Wrzesniewski, A., and Dutton, J.E. 2001. "Crafting a Job: Revisioning Employees as Active Crafters of Their Work." *Academy of Management Review* 26: 179–201.

Young, C.A. 1999. *Checking In and Out at an Urban Hotel: A Contextually Grounded Conceptualization of Service Workers' Coping Responses*. Unpublished dissertation, Cornell University, Ithaca, NY.

Yukl, G., and Falbe, C.M. 1990. "Influence Tactics and Objectives in Upward, Downward, and Lateral Influence Attempts." *Journal of Applied Psychology* 75: 132–140.

———. 1991. "Importance of Different Power Sources in Downward and Lateral Relations." *Journal of Applied Psychology* 76: 416–423.

Zajonc, R.B. 1985. "Emotion and Facial Efference: A Theory Reclaimed." *Science* 228: 15–21.

Zarandona, J., and Camuso, M.A. 1985. "Study of Exit Interviews: Does the Last Word Count?" *Personnel* 3: 47–49.

Zautra, A. 1983. "Social Resources and the Quality of Life." *American Journal of Community Psychology* 11: 275–289.

Zautra, A., and Simons, L.S. 1979. "Some Effects of Positive Life Events on Community Mental Health." *American Journal of Community Psychology* 7: 441–451.

Zeitlin, L. 1995. "Organizational Downsizing and Stress-Related Illness." *International Journal of Stress Management* 2: 207–219.

Zenger, T.R., and Lawrence, B.S. 1989. "Organisational Demography: The Differential Effects of Age and Tenure Distributions on Technical Communication." *Academy of Management Journal* 32: 353.

Zerbe, W.J., Härtel, C., and Ashkanasy, N., 2000. "The Nature of Emotions in Organizations." In *Emotions in the Workplace: Research, Theory, and Practice*, ed. N.M. Ashkanasy, C.E.J. Härtel, and W.J. Zerbe, 63–68. Westport, CT: Quorum Books.

Zohar, D. 1999. "When Things Go Wrong: The Effect of Daily Work Hassles on Effort, Exertion and Negative Mood." *Journal of Occupational and Organizational Psychology* 72: 265–283.

Zonderman, A.B., Herbst, J.H., Schmidt, C., Costa, P.T., McCrae, R.R. 1993. "Depressive Symptoms as a Non-Specific, Graded Risk for Psychiatric Diagnoses." *Journal of Abnormal Psychology* 102: 544–552.

Zuroff, D.C., Moskowitz, D.S., and Côté, S. 1999. "Dependency, Self-Criticism, Interpersonal Behavior, and Affect: Evolutionary Perspectives." *British Journal of Clinical Psychology* 38: 231–250.

ABOUT THE EDITORS AND CONTRIBUTORS

Neal M. Ashkanasy is a professor of management in the School of Management, UQ Business School, The University of Queensland, Brisbane, Australia. He has a PhD in Social and Organizational Psychology from the University of Queensland, and has research interests in leadership, organizational culture, business ethics, and, more recently, in emotions in organizational life. He is on the editorial board of the *Academy of Management Journal* and the *Journal of Management,* and has published in journals such as *Accounting, Organizations and Society,* the *Journal of Management,* the *Journal of Organizational Behavior, the Journal of Personality and Social Psychology,* and *Organizational Behavior and Human Decision Processes.* He is coeditor of two recent books: *The Handbook of Organizational Culture and Climate* and *Emotions in the Workplace; Theory, Research, and Practice.* In addition, he administers two e-mail discussion lists: "Orgcult," the Organizational Culture Caucus list; and "Emonet," the Emotions in the Workplace list. He has organized two "International Conferences on Emotions in Organizational Life," and is now planning the third conference to be held in Australia in 2002. Finally, he is chair of the Managerial and Organizational Cognitions Division of the Academy of Management.

Oluremi B. Ayoko is a lecturer in conflict management and business communication at the Graduate School of Management, The University of Queensland, Brisbane, Australia. Her research interests include managing workplace diversity, conflict management, emotions and leadership, as well as intercultural communication and diversity training. Remi has published on how managers deepen or lessen the cross-racial divide in their workgroups and she is lead author on the paper entitled "Disentangling the Complexity of Productive and Destructive Conflict in Culturally Heterogeneous Workgroups: A Communication Accommodation Theory Approach" that received a Best Paper recognition at the 2001 Academy of Management in Washington, DC.

Aaron Ben-Ze'ev is rector at the University of Haifa, Israel, as well as professor of philosophy and director of the Center for Interdisciplinary Research on Emotions. Among his numerous publications are *The Perceptual System* (1993), *Good Gossip* (1994), and *The Subtlety of Emotions* (2000). He is now completing a book on romantic affairs in cyberspace.

Maree V. Boyle is a lecturer in organizational behavior and theory within the School of Management at the University of Queensland, Australia. Her research interests include emotions in the workplace, emotion, power and organizational change, and gender and organization.

Jamie L. Callahan is an assistant professor in the Educational Human Resource Development Program at Texas A&M University. She is actively involved in the Academy of Human Resource Development and the Managerial and Organizational Cognition Division of the Academy of Management. Her primary research interests focus on emotion management and its relationship to organizational learning, leadership, and culture. Her empirical work has appeared in journals such as *Human Resource Development Quarterly, Journal of Behavioral and Applied Management,* and *Organization Studies.* A former U.S. Air Force officer specializing in human resources and organization development consulting, she continues to actively consult with public, private, and nonprofit institutions.

Prithviraj Chattopadhyay is a senior lecturer in the graduate School of Management at the University of New South Wales, Australia. He received his PhD degree in 1996 in management from the University of Texas at Austin. His research interests include relational demography, organizational citizenship behavior, managerial beliefs and perceptions and their consequences, and employment externalization. He has published in the *Academy of Management Journal,* the *Strategic Management Journal*, and in the *Journal of Applied Psychology.*

Stéphane Côté is an assistant professor of organizational behavior at the Rotman School of Management at the University of Toronto, Canada. He received his PhD in 2001 in Organizational Psychology from the University of Michigan, Ann Arbor. His research interests include the influence of affective experiences and emotional intelligence on work performance, the effects of emotional labor on worker strain, and the prediction of affective experiences at work from personality and context. He has published in the *Journal of Personality and Social Psychology* and *Current Directions in Psychological Science* and has presented his research at meetings of the Academy of Management.

Donald E. Gibson is an associate professor of management at the Dolan School of Business, Fairfield University in Fairfield, Connecticut. Professor Gibson's research examines the management of individual emotional experience and expression in organizations, emotions and power, anger in the workplace, the attributes and impact of organizational role models and mentors, and effective organizational communication. He has written about how men and women differ in their strategies of identifying role models, the meaning and importance of group emotion, and the scripts organizations generate to shape individuals' emotional responses. He received his PhD and MBA from the University of California at Los Angeles, and taught for six years at the Yale School of Management.

Charmine E.J. Härtel is reader in human resource management at the School of Management, Monash University, Melbourne, Victoria, Australia. She received her BA in psychology with distinction from the University of Colorado and completed her Masters and PhD in Industrial and Organizational Psychology at Colorado State University. Her work in the area of emotions to date has examined emotional intelligence and competencies, workgroup emotional climate, and the link between culture and emotion. Her publications in the area of emotions include her coedited book *Emotions in the Workplace: Research, Theory, and Practice,* her coauthored paper in the *Journal of Management,* her coauthored paper in *Human Resource Management Review,* and her coauthored paper in *Advances in Consumer Research.*

Alice C.F. Hsu is a doctoral student at the School of Management, Monash University, Australia. She received her Honours degree in Business Management at the University of Queensland in 1999. Her research interests are in the areas of emotion labor in the workplace and organizational creativity.

Robert G. Jones is associate professor of psychology at Southwest Missouri State University in Springfield, Missouri. He received his BA (History) from Saint Olaf College (1977) and his MA (1989) and PhD (1992) from Ohio State University (Industrial and Organizational Psychology). His research, teaching, and practice deal with issues of performance measurement and management in groups and individuals. In particular, his work deals with accuracy and validity of workplace judgments, sources and consequences of emotional responding at work, and uses of assessment for team and individual development.

Tina Kiefer is lecturer in organizational psychology and taught graduate and MBA students at the University of St. Gallen in Switzerland. She is currently a visiting research fellow at the University of British Columbia in Vancouver, Canada. Her research interests focus on the role of emotions at work, especially in the context of organizational change, well-being, and transitions. She has conducted qualitative and quantitative, cross-sectional, and longitudinal studies researching the emotional experience of change.

Eric E. McCollum is associate professor and clinical director for the Marriage and Family Therapy Program at Virginia Tech's Northern Virginia Center in Falls Church, Virginia. In addition to research interests in family therapy and substance abuse, McCollum is interested in applying family systems theory and interventions to organizations. He is especially interested in the impact of emotions on organizational functioning. His publications have appeared in a number of family therapy and substance abuse journals and he regularly presents at national and international conferences. He regularly consults on both organizational and clinical topics.

D.S. Moskowitz is professor of psychology and director of the Doctoral Training Program in Clinical Psychology at McGill University in Montreal, Canada. Her research is focused on interpersonal behavior and affect, including topics related to measurement, situational influences, and intrapersonal variability. In her most recent work, she has begun to explore the new field of "sociopharmacology" in which she is examining the influence of changes in brain neurochemistry on complex social behavior during everyday life. With Scott Hershberger, she coedited the recent (2001) book, *Modeling Intraindividual Variability with Repeated Measures Data: Applications and Techniques.*

Jan M. Paterson is an organizational psychology consultant with a background in education, organizational development, change management, and human resource management. Jan also teaches and researches in areas related to change management, organizational justice, performance appraisal, staff attitudes and well-being, and client satisfaction. She has conducted and participated in organizational analyses and change programs for an array of organizations, including AirServices Australia, the University of Queensland, and Health Waikato, New Zealand.

Anat Rafaeli is professor of organizational behavior at the Faculty of Industrial Engineering and Management at the Technion, Israel's Institute of Technology. She is interested in emotional and symbolic self-presentation in organizations especially as they occur in service interactions. She received her PhD in Industrial and Organizational Psychology from Ohio State University.

Andrea L. Rittman is a doctoral student in the Industrial/Organizational Psychology Program at George Mason University. She is a graduate of Missouri Western State College (1998) and received her MS degree in Industrial/Organizational Psychology from Southwest Missouri State University (2000). One of her major areas of interest is in emotion perception in the workplace. Currently she is conducting research in the area of team dynamics and leadership, with a special emphasis on training and educational systems.

Scott J. Schroeder is currently an associate professor of management and the director of Business and Graduate Management Programs at Chaminade University of Honolulu. His PhD is from the University of California, Los Angeles, with specializations in organizational behavior and counseling psychology. Dr. Schroeder has an active consulting practice specializing in executive development, personal empowerment, and work team effectiveness.

Marta Sinclair is a doctoral candidate and lecturer in the Management School at the University of Queensland, Australia. She has twenty-five years of management experience in software localization, intercultural training, broadcasting, leisure and hospitality, real estate, and translation services from a number of companies in the United States and Europe. Her educational background is in cross-cultural management and linguistics. She is interested in how people make decisions in fast-paced and stress-prone environments, and what role intuition and emotions play in this process.

Lyndall Strazdins is a clinical psychologist with a research and practice background in emotional health, families, work and social relationships. She has worked in the public and private health care sectors, lectured in social psychology at the University of Canberra, continues to work in private practice, and is currently research fellow at the National Centre for Epidemiology and Population Health, The Australian National University. Her research has examined emotional work in interpersonal interactions at work and in the family; measurement of emotional work; consequences of emotional work, including emotional contagion and the association between gender, emotional work, and psychological well-being. She is currently part of a multidisciplinary research team examining the way work conditions shape parent-child interactions and transmission of emotions.

Wilfred J. Zerbe is associate dean (Executive Education) and professor of human resources and organizational dynamics in the Faculty of Management at the University of Calgary, Canada. His research interests focus on emotions in organizations, organizational research methods, service sector management, and leadership. His publications have appeared in books and journals including *The Academy of Management Review, Industrial and Labour Relations Review, Canadian Journal of Administrative Sciences, Journal of Business Research, Journal of Psychology, Journal of Services Marketing, and Journal of Research in Higher Education.* He is an active consultant and executive educator, and is also on the faculty of the Banff School of Advanced Management.

INDEX

emotional labor
  as an influence process 190
  autonomous 223, 224, 277, 293
  compared to emotion work 21
  compared to emotional work 233
  complexity of the issue 280–281
  defined 4, 7–10, 21, 189, 220, 221,
      255–256, 276–277, 279
  and dissonance tolerance 270–271
  effects 277–278
  and EL-ED-EE sequence/model 22
  and emotional contagion 21
  and emotional dissonance 258
  and emotional state 222
  and employee well-being 21–22
  examples 223
  function in an organization 231
  and hassle tolerance 271
  health impact 234–235
  indirect 223, 224–225, 277
    tool for using indirect methods to
        influence 293–294
  and job crafting 282–284
  and leadership development programs
      227
  and organizational culture change
      228–230
  and organizational interventions
      226
  and perceived hassles 263–264
  as a product of work design 281–283
  in service jobs 256–258, 264 see also
      service
  and stress management and wellness
      programs 227–228
  theoretical underpinnings 220–222
  tool to align organizational goals with
      rules for engaging in 293
  tools for managing 292–295
  and work design interventions 228
emotional labor-emotional dissonance-
    emotional exhaustion (EL-ED-EE)
    sequence/model 22, 252–254,
    260–262, 270, 272–273, 275,
    279
  causal sequence 254–255, 261
emotional neutrality 198, 202
emotional outcomes of conflict 91
emotional propensities 29, 36
emotional role demands 239–240
emotional sensitivity 176–179, 208

emotional signals 98, 100–102, 197
  in service situations 104–110, 198
emotional stability 101
emotional states see also emotion,
    management; emotion, work;
    emotional labor; work, environment
  defined 189
  effect of organizational characteristics
      and managerial policies on 5
  and emotional contagion 21
  generalized feelings 5
  organizational awareness of employees'
      73
  specific 5–6
emotional systems and intellectual
    systems 171–175, 183
emotional work see also emotion, work;
    emotional labor
  case study of health care industry 232,
      238–250
  defined 232–234, 246, 277
  duration of contact with other people's
      emotions 238, 248
  and emotional contagion 235–237, 243,
      246–249
  examples 232
  health impact 234–235
  need for rest breaks 248
  three dimensions 233
emotionality see also decision making,
    styles
  bounded 149
emotion-focused coping strategies 28,
    38–41, 71, 73
Emotions in the Workplace: Theory,
    Research, and Practice 3
empathy 13, 14, 16, 177, 235
employee see also conflict; interpersonal
    interactions, organizational; job;
    manager; superior-subordinate;
    topics of interest; work
  blaming 42, 70, 71
  burnout 9, 17, 109, 211, 260, 267
  cooperation 14
  destructive behavior 71
  effect of constant change on 42
  effectiveness and mood 11, 131–133
  enthusiasm 14 see also joy
  health 234–235, 238, 241–242, 277 see
      also employee, well-being
  relations, norms 8